Dear Reader:

I confess.... I fit Peter Drucker's characterization, "monomaniac with a mission." I've devoted my career to just one thing: figuring out how to create high-performing organizations in which every group operates as an empowered, entrepreneurial business within a business.

I've seen that these kinds of organizations earn the position of *supplier of choice* to their customers, and are an *employer of choice* that attracts, inspires, leverages, and retains top talent.

This is not another book about your leadership skills. It's about engineering the *organizational systems* — structure, teamwork processes, resource-governance processes, culture, and metrics — that constitute the "ecosystem" within which we work. It's about building the legacy of a fundamentally well-designed organization that performs brilliantly, now and long after you've moved on.

Snapshot of the Market Organization

This book offers a vision of how organizations *should* work. I call this vision the "**Market Organization**." Here's an overview:

- The **management hierarchy (reporting structure) fulfills its usual roles** of structuring subordinate domains, communications and coordination, and inspirational leadership (including performance management). **But hierarchy is not the way work gets done.**

- Every box on the organization chart is a **business within a business,** defined by the products and services it provides.

- **Groups "sell" their products and services to customers**, be they external or other groups within the company (with or without chargebacks). Thus, **every group is a "shared service."**

- **Staff think and act like entrepreneurs**. They're customer focused, accountable, prudent about spending, and innovative.

- **Project teams form dynamically** across the entire organization, as groups "subcontract" for help from their peers. Within each team, it's **clear who's accountable for the entire project/service** and what sub-deliverables every other team-member is accountable for.

- Thanks to this excellence in teamwork, there's no need for self-contained silos. And with a culture of customer focus, there's no need for decentralization. **Staff can specialize, which lowers costs and significantly augments performance.**

- **Budgets are based on what groups are expected to deliver** (not past years' spending), so resources match expectations.

- **Priorities are adjusted dynamically** throughout the year, as opportunities and imperatives require. For internal service providers, their internal customers are in control of their priorities.

- **Staff are empowered** with authorities (resources, information, and decision rights) that match their accountabilities.

Warning: It's About Vision and Possibilities

This book is not a compendium of "best practices" (what the so-called "best" companies are already doing). And it's certainly not about common practices (what most of our peers are doing).

This book is about *ideal* practices — the best we can imagine. It's about aspirations and possibilities.

And it *is* possible. All the pieces of this operating model have been successfully implemented many times. This book envisions an organization where all those pieces are working in concert.

But please don't ask who's done all this. For leaders, the right question is, *could I do this?* That's why we call them leaders!

'T is not too late to seek a newer world...
to sail beyond the sunset...
to strive, to seek, to find, and not to yield.

— Lord Alfred Tennyson, *Ulysses*

Applicability

The Market Organization applies to all industries, including government and not-for-profits.

It applies to companies that sell off-the-shelf products and services, as well as custom solutions and professional services. (The imaginary technology company I chose to illustrate the concepts does all of that.)

It applies to organizations of all sizes and stages of growth, starting with ventures where it can build scalable organizations with mature processes while retaining their entrepreneurial spirit, on up to multi-nationals where it breaks the paradox of localization and global synergies.

And this operating model applies to departments (such as IT) as well as entire companies. *Throughout this book, the word "organization" refers to either an entire enterprise, or a department within it.*

This book can help leaders in two situations:

- You might have the opportunity to drive an organizational transformation. If so, this book provides a detailed blueprint of an inspirational end-state, as well as step-by-step guidance on how to plan and implement a transformation.

- Alternatively, you might face pressing problems and need to fix them quickly. The vision in this book will help you design a series of incremental changes that address immediate needs, work well together, and build toward a consistent end-state.

My goal is to help you envision and communicate, clearly and in detail, a compelling goal — one that stretches people's thinking, builds excitement and commitment, and guides the design of each organizational change you make on the way to your vision.

Follow me as far as you can,
and for the rest let us remain good friends.

— Irving Stone, *The Passions of the Mind,* Book 4

Told as a Story

I explain the Market Organization through a story....

A CEO is about to start a new job, and decides to dedicate the next phase of his career to creating a *truly great* organization.

He seeks out another CEO who's done exactly that, and he's introduced to each of that company's senior leaders.

Through a series of conversations, he discovers a high-performing organization where people at every level are empowered, entrepreneurial, customer focused, team oriented, frugal, and innovative.

Imagination is the first step in invention.

He also learns how this operating model was implemented, through a series of step-by-step, principle-based, participative change processes.

NAVIGATION AID: If you become impatient with the prose, there's a Book Summary (akin to Cliff's Notes[R]) at the end.

My Hopes for this Book, and for You

I hope this book provides you with inspiration, vision, and a pragmatic handbook for your transformation initiatives.

And with the help of your team, I hope it helps you engineer, and lead, an organization that performs brilliantly and is a really great place to work.

— Dean Meyer

*What professional leader wouldn't relish a day or two
to reflect on what constitutes an ideal organization!?*

"Dean Meyer has had an immense influence on my life. This book is **yet another masterpiece** that teaches us the framework of a high-performing organization. It's a book every transformational CEO should read."

Sergio Paiz, CEO, PDC

"Following the eras of hierarchical, matrix, and networked organizations, Meyer provides **a welcome new perspective: the Market Organization**. It's a comprehensive, modular business operating model, built on solid organizational principles. This experience-rich book provides a practical blueprint for organizational transformation, necessary to survive in the face of turbulence, complexity, and disruption."

Peter G. W. Keen, Professor (retired), Stanford, MIT, and Harvard

"This is an extraordinary leadership book that every manager in any company can use. It takes you through every imaginable element of a corporate organization — structure, financial governance, incentives, and more — challenges conventional wisdom, and clearly lays out new ways of thinking. It was **a real eye-opening experience** for one who has spent his career in traditional organizations. I kept saying, 'Yeah, that *is* the way organizations should work!'"

Richard Hartnack, Chairman of the Board, Synchrony Financial

"Standing ovation! This book is incredible! Internal entrepreneurship blows away bureaucracy. Teamwork obviates silos. Internal value-chains build alignment so much better than top-down plans and cascading objectives. You don't need to pick your poison — innovation versus efficiency, empowerment versus control — you can have your cake and eat it too. **You won't believe what's possible in organizations** until you read this groundbreaking book."

Fred Dewey, serial startup and turnaround CEO

"This book is fantastic! It's real world (the 'conversations' are so familiar) and yet **incredibly thought provoking**. This is a must for anyone leading transformational change in their organization."

Mark Eustis, President & CEO (retired), Fairview Health Services, and Founding Board Member, VillageMD

"I've never read anything like this. It's **profound!** This book really **stretched my thinking about what's possible** as a leader."

Juan Pablo Zelaya, Professor, Universidad Galileo,
and Founder and General Manager, The Fit Center

"This is inspired work! It's big picture, yet detailed, in a way that **expands and rewires my brain.**"

Huron Low, Co-founder, Virtuoso Card Company (Singapore)

"There are thousands of books about how organizations should work and nearly all of them are inane. This book is a happy exception — predictable given its author. Dean Meyer has a decades-long track record of **deep research, fresh thinking, innovation, big ideas and solid advice**. When you read this book, you're going to learn a lot that will help you build a better organization, and that's something I rarely say."

Don Tapscott, Chancellor Emeritus, Trent University,
and best-selling author

"Over the years and in several roles, Dean's unique organizational genius has been instrumental to me in diagnosing organizational problems and putting in place structures, systems, and ways of thinking that improve everything: engagement, productivity, results. This book is Dean's masterpiece — **not only does he show how it all works together at all levels, not only is every figure indexed and every reference cited, but he tells you how to get there** using a philosophy and approach that brings everyone along with the change."

Remy Evard, (former) CIO, Novartis Institutes for BioMedical Research

"When I first discovered Dean's vision for 'Market Organizations,' I worried that it was overly aspirational, theoretical, and failed to address the practical realities of running a business. As I dug deeper, I realized that our 'practical realities' were largely symptoms of our violating fundamental principles: accountabilities not aligned with authorities; a focus on tasks rather than deliverables; people going too many ways at once; etc. Applying Dean's work was a turning point in my career as an entrepreneur, and in my company. Now, **we're delivering more of what matters; our customers (internal and external) are more engaged and happier; and an entrepreneurial spirit is returning** to the company in a way I never would have conceived possible."

Sam Prochazka, CEO, GoodMorning.com

"In my 30+ years of working at the crossroads of leadership, technology, and human communication, I've never found a more **comprehensive and systematic approach to building a high-performing organization**. Meyer's fundamental organizational design principles are timeless and effective."

Mary Boone, author, *Leadership and the Computer*
and *Managing Interactively*

"The best organizations are a collection of cohesive, agile small teams that are effectively aligned and coordinated. But what is simple in concept is challenging in execution. Dean Meyer provides a **highly readable and eminently practical** roadmap for leaders to get it done."

Gen. Stanley McChrystal, author, *Team of Teams* and *Risk: A User's Guide*

"Dean Meyer has singularly cracked the code on how to organize a company for performance, innovation, and scalability. In a field replete with muddled thinking, his blueprint is **simple, clear, concise, and utterly effective**. Dean's books are genuinely some of the few that I keep within arm's reach in my office."

Kirk Botula, serial tech-venture CEO

"**Having read most of Meyer's other books**, I had a good understanding of his approach to organizational structure, teamwork, governance, and culture. But *How Organizations Should Work* **crystalized everything for me**, clearly showing how all the pieces fit together in a comprehensive description of a truly great organizational design. If you are thinking about working on your organization's performance, this is the book for you!"

Mike Fulton, VP of Product Strategy and Innovation, Expedient

"This book is a **fun read**, a breath of fresh air from preachy tomes. And it offers **creative solutions to so many common organizational issues**."

Wes Clelland, Founder and CEO (retired), Acacia Capital

"This book is **a transformational leader's bible.** From a new and power-ful operating model down to the details of how each function should work, it's a comprehensive blueprint of an amazing organization, and a handbook that tells you exactly how to build it."

Yomi Famurewa, Executive Partner, Gartner

"This book packs **decades of wisdom into just hours of reading**. Every chapter is packed with amazing insights!"

Janma Bardi, General Manager, PDC Red (LatAm tech company)

"In the past, I worked at a large company that had engaged Dean to implement the Market Organization, and it was **the healthiest organization I've ever been in.**"

Mark R. Schultze, COO, PerformanceG2, Inc.

"This book imagines **a company that I'd love to work for, and dream to create.**"

Don Martin, CIO

"Employee expectations have evolved. To attract and retain talent, leaders must create organizations that people want to work for. The Market Organization is exactly that. It's a work environment that respects employees' need for job fulfillment and work-life balance, while delivering business results. This book will help you **create an organization that is both high-performing and humanistic.**"

Gary Rietz, CIO, Blommer Chocolate

"This book is filled with powerful insights. If more organizations foster this kind of leadership and entrepreneurship among their team members, surely that would **contribute to leaving a better planet for future generations.**"

Ramiro Castillo, Transformation and People Director, Corporacion AG;
and Board member, Del Valle University

"*How Organizations Should Work* is insight rich. The Market Organization induces leaders and staff to **evolve from being cogs in factory-like processes to internal entrepreneurs.**"

Ade McCormack, author, thought leader, and keynoter

"Dad raised me to be a problem solver. Until I read Meyer's work, I'd jump in and solve problems as they arose, believing that if I wanted it done right, I'd have to do it myself. I took everything on myself; and despite long hours, there wasn't enough of me to go around. Now, **I solve *organizational* problems, and empower our great people to solve all those business problems**. These principles of organizational design changed my life!"

Dave Shepherd, CEO, New Millennium

"**If endlessly plugging the leaks** springing up all over your business has left you exhausted, uninspired, and doubting yourself or business, you owe it to yourself and those depending on you to read this book. Meyer's principles gave my 25-person company the vision, roadmap, and tools to shatter our growth ceiling, making our business more fun, easy, and profitable than ever before."

Derek Weber, President, goBRANDgo!

"It doesn't matter **whether you're a Fortune-100 company or a startup**, Dean does a fantastic job of providing the tools and roadmap to create your ideal organization."

Maxwell H. Sims, co-founder and COO, MindTrace

"*How Organizations Should Work* **should be on every CEO's reading list**. It's a field guide to running a healthy, effective business wrapped in a compelling fable. A must read for anyone that wants to know how great businesses sound, think, and operate."

Jessica Rovello, CEO, Arkadium

"**Boards of directors and venture investors**, multiple studies show that 65% of venture deals return less than invested capital. If you want to increase your 'winners,' give this book to your operating executives and demand *organizational* leadership. Companies built on these principles maintain the passion and vision of the founders, while maturing their processes as they grow and create value."

Charlie Shalvoy, Executive Chairman, Voxel8, Inc.

"A well-engineered organization promotes capital efficiency, streamlines growth, and provides a sustainable competitive edge. And yet, startup companies are generally designed on the fly without any blueprint, or even expert advice. This extraordinary handbook by Dean Meyer is an easy-to-read reference and guide, and reflects the distilled wisdom of one of the foremost practitioners in organizational design. It **should find a place in the library of every Silicon Valley VC and CEO**."

Faruq Ahmad, Founding Partner, Palo Alto Capital Advisors

"**Even in the smallest companies**, organizational processes matter! In fact, the concepts in this book are best implemented at that early stage of growth. They clarify who's accountable for what, and (perhaps more importantly) whose job it is to think about all the things we're not yet thinking about. And they build an organization that scales while maintaining entrepreneurship at every level. Meyer's book is a great body of work."

August J. Ceradini, Jr., President/Partner (Former), Circle Line & World Yacht; and Chairman Emeritus, Culinary Institute of America

"To handle the rapid growth we see ahead of us, we have to **'grow up' from a venture to a mature company, but without losing our entrepreneurial spirit**. This book brought together all the principles that we needed. It caused us to ask tough questions about how we do business, and have conversations we'd avoided. And it helped our leaders to develop a clear, shared vision of the company we're out to create."

Leo De La Fuente, COO, Berkey

"**Government leaders** who say, 'We are not a business,' just don't get it. Every department exists to deliver services to constituents or other departments. I've implemented these business-within-a-business concepts, and the impacts on performance and employee engagement have been astounding!"

Steve Monaghan, Agency Director, IT and General Services, Nevada County CA

"As the **head of a library system**, I want our branches to be empowered and customer focused, while working as a tight team coordinated by our strategies. This book helped me elucidate a clear vision of where we're going, and chart a pragmatic path forward. I'm a better leader for having read it."

Nick Wilczek, Library Director, Nevada County CA

"After 16 years with the organization, I was appointed to **my first C-level job**. Meyer's book provided the guidance I needed to rise above the day-to-day tasks, and build an organization that delivers on its vision. It showed me how to be an effective executive, a real organizational leader."

Lee Gerney, CIO, Yolo County CA

"**Strategic planners** need to focus on *organizational* strategy right alongside business strategy. Great strategies won't amount to much if the organization doesn't have the capability to execute them. To understand organizational strategy, you need go no further than this book. It not only says it all. It's inspirational!"

Victor Jerez, corporate strategic planning and business development executive

"**Executive coaches** generally focus on interpersonal skills, talent management, and business strategies. But organizational strategy is every bit as important — in many situations, even more so. This book gives executive coaches the tools to help clients see the root causes of many of their concerns, and to become transformational leaders. It's a critical competency for all executive coaches."

Barbara Healy, executive coach and former corporate executive

"**Organizational development and HR** professionals, you need to study Meyer's latest book. I'm amazed that any one person could have amassed this much knowledge about how organizations should operate, and communicate it in such simple, readable terms. From a vision that inspires to systemic change processes, Meyer delivers a practical roadmap to high performance."

Roger Young, Partner, Excel Leadership Group

"**Organizational design experts**, take note. Meyer's book is the core of what high-performance means. It's a practical application of the open systems model across an entire business, and brings to life those often-esoteric concepts in a delightful, jargon-free, compelling read."

Stu Winby, founder and CEO, SPRING Network

"**Systems thinkers** will appreciate the way Meyer channels the theories of Beer, Snowden, and so many others into a practical organizational operating model. He explains how to handle the complexity of today's real world in great detail and clarity, and with lots of patience. If you have questions on how to adopt a systems approach, this book will provide the answers."

Javier Livas, attorney and cybernetician

"I've long believed **CIOs should run IT as a business**. This book explains exactly how to do that — the foundational principles, the details of how it will work, and the implementation process to get there."

Paul Edmisten, CIO

"**IT professionals**, you need to read this book! Not only does it provide practical solutions to just about every management challenge, but you'll also come to understand the organizational dynamics, and that will let you reimagine how you serve your internal customers (maybe even some external customers, too)."

Geoff Routledge, Google engineer

"**Agile experts**, take note! There's a new guy in the scaled Agile community, and things are never going to be the same. Meyer is prominent in the world of organizational effectiveness, but it's high time he became a household name in ours. I don't consider it an exaggeration to say we may look back and see that his work was the missing link that moved scaled Agile to the next stage of its evolutionary journey."

Stuart Ward, Enterprise Agile Coach (SPC5, CSP, CSM, ICP-ACC, PMP)

"**The IT Service Management community** really must read Meyer's book, *How Organizations Should Work*. It not only aligns perfectly with ITIL-4's focus on delivering products and services (outcomes) via end-to-end value chains, enabled by service relationships between provider and consumer groups. It explains how to do exactly that — how to become the preferred supplier and reduce shadow IT by winning new business through value creation and building good relationships with internal customers."

Troy DuMoulin, VP, Research and Development, Pink Elephant

"**Information security leaders (CISOs)**, this book is the key to transforming your group into a service organization that extends accountability for information security to everyone, empowering you to exit the command-and-control style that makes you a scapegoat for others' mistakes and ultimately is unsuccessful."

Jonathan Maurer, CISO

How Organizations *Should* Work

*envisioning a high-performing organization
made of a network of internal entrepreneurs*

by

N. Dean Meyer

How Organizations *Should* Work:
**envisioning a high-performing organization
made of a network of internal entrepreneurs**

Meyer, N. Dean

Keywords: LEADERSHIP, ORGANIZATION, TRANSFORMATION, VISION, market organization, organizational effectiveness, organizational performance, organizational design, high-performing organization, business agility, organizational agility, dynamic organization, organizational structure, organization chart, organizational design, organizational operating model, corporate culture, job design, roles and responsibilities, employee engagement, job satisfaction, motivation, employee retention, empowerment, accountability, business within a business, entrepreneurship, intrapreneurship, teamwork, innovation, digital business, business planning, resource governance, demand management, priority setting, internal economy, cost accounting, shared services, decentralization, outsourcing, customer focus, business relationship managers.

NDMA Publishing, N. Dean Meyer and Associates Inc., Danbury, CT

www.ndma.com
ndma@ndma.com

ISBN   978-1-892606-33-4

Printed in the United States of America.

*To those who lead organizations,
in the hope that this helps you
lead us to the right place.*

CONTENTS

FIGURES

~ FOREWORD ~

Building a High-performing Organization

case study by Preston T. Simons

I don't know of any leaders who have fully achieved the ambitious vision described in this book. But I came close, and it was a thing of beauty.

Beyond that, as a leader, it was quite an adventure. Let me tell you the story....

The Situation

When I took on their CIO role, Aurora Health Care was ready to invest in technologies that would help them lead the industry in clinical outcomes, patients' experiences, digital business, and other metrics of a world-class health care provider.

I knew the organization I'd inherited was not up to the task. So, before I created business and technology strategies, I had to build an organization that could deliver on those promises.

Before I created business and technology strategies,
I had to build an organization that could deliver on those promises.

I engaged Dean Meyer right from the start. With his help, I created a vision, analyzed the gaps, and put together a plan.

Vision and Gaps

My vision of how organizations should work is simple: I like running businesses, even if they're inside a larger business. So, just as Dean advocates, I believe that every manager should run his or her own *business within a business,* and think and act like an entrepreneur.

This vision provided a consistent direction for every change we made. It also provided a benchmark against which we could identify the gaps we needed to work on.

My Organizational Strategy

As to the gaps, I hate rework — solving the same problems again and again. Instead, I like to diagnose *root causes,* and solve problems once and for all.

Root-cause analysis is not about blaming people. It's about finding glitches in the organizational "ecosystem" in which we work. Analysis of our gaps showed that, ultimately, we needed to treat all five of the organizational systems that Dean defines. [1] *More*

But organizations can only absorb a limited amount of change at a time. I believe it's best to do one thing at a time and do it well, rather than do a shallow effort at many things in parallel. Therefore, I sequenced our transformation initiatives into five steps:

1. Structure (tier-one only) and leadership talent
2. Internal economy: investment-based budgeting
3. Internal economy: demand management (governance)
4. Structure (remaining levels)
5. Fine tuning: metrics (benchmarking), culture, processes and tools; and metrics (KPIs and dashboards)

1. Structure (Tier One) and Leadership Talent

Step one was a quick restructuring, just at the level of my direct reports (tier one). Since we needed to get on to step two quickly, I moved existing groups under the new tier-one structure *intact* (no changes below the leadership level for now).

Although I knew this wouldn't be sufficient for the long term, we couldn't afford the time for a comprehensive restructuring (complete with re-thinking accountabilities and workflows) at this stage. But this quick restructuring wasn't a throw-away; we based it on the same principles of structure that we'd later use to do a comprehensive restructuring.
2 More

The major benefit of this step was that it allowed me to recruit top talent into key tier-one positions — functions and leadership competencies that were missing from the prior organization.

2. Investment-based Budgeting

I was eager to get on to step two: investment-based budgeting. Here's why....

When I first arrived, Aurora was nearing the end of its budget planning cycle. The CFO surprised me with a significant budget cut.

"Of course," I said. "As a corporate officer, I'm all for frugality. Just tell me what the impacts will be on patient care and other mission-critical directives."

Neither my staff nor Finance could answer that simple question!

Our budget that year was based on prior years' spending, and wasn't nearly sufficient to satisfy the needs of the business. As in past years, we severely underfunded critical challenges such as strategic projects, infrastructure maintenance, information security, business continuity, reliability, and investments in our people.

So, the top priority for my first year on the job was to implement *investment-based budgeting* — a budget for the *projects and services* we planned to deliver, not just what we planned to spend. [3 More] This allowed me to say, "With that level of funding, here's what we can (and cannot) deliver."

We got four big benefits:

- **Perception of value:** For the first time, executives understood what they were getting for their money.

- **Fact-based budget decisions:** It gave us the numbers so we could decide our budget based on business needs. As a direct result, that year's IT budget was increased by about 30 percent.

- **Managing expectations:** Since everybody understood what was funded and what wasn't, we were no longer blamed for not delivering projects that the company couldn't afford.

- **Progress on culture:** My leaders came to understand their products and services, their customers (both clients and one another), their cost structures (rates), and their individual accountabilities within project teams.

3. Demand Management (Governance)

See if this sounds familiar: For years, our organization had been pressured to deliver far more than its resources permitted. Staff were eager to please, so we had a long history of over-promising and under-delivering. This left us with little time or money to invest in the strategic things I was brought in to do.

I knew that simply increasing my budget wouldn't help. We'd just have the same problems on a larger scale.

We certainly didn't need a committee to "steer" or "govern" us. And we needed more than simply a committee that prioritizes (rank orders) major project requests.

To get this untenable situation under control, we installed a demand-management process that empowered clients to decide our priorities *within the limits of available resources* (as provided by my budget).
4 More

Again, we got the benefits I was looking for:

- **Alignment:** We stopped low-payoff projects and services, and focused on those with the most value to the business.

- **Supply/demand balance:** Clients knew what they could (and couldn't) expect of us. And staff only had to work exceptional hours on exceptional occasions.

- **Trust:** We no longer made promises and then failed to deliver for lack of resources.

- **Relationships:** Business executives appreciated our respecting their priorities, and saw us as a partner, not an obstacle.

- **Client commitment:** Clients involved us earlier in their thinking to ensure that they had a strong case to present to their own executives for funding (prioritization).

- **Benefits realization:** Because they'd promised benefits to their own executives to get the funding, clients became far more committed to making their projects pay off.

- **Progress on culture:** More each day, our staff were thinking like entrepreneurs and respecting internal clients as customers.

4. Structure (Remaining Levels)

The structure I inherited was a mess. We expected staff to be experts at multiple professions. Some professional specialties were scattered all over our organization chart. Groups were defined in vague terms (a few words in a box) and by their "roles and responsibilities" (tasks, not results). Boundaries were unclear.

Also, we had independent "silos" instead of centers of excellence. This reduced our ability to specialize, which reduced performance in every aspect of our work.

I think good executives know that just re-drawing boxes doesn't accomplish much. I wanted our restructuring to be transformational — a step toward our vision.

I engaged my entire leadership team in designing and implementing the new structure, starting with "a clean sheet of paper." Dean's clear principles, meticulous change process, and experienced facilitation ensured fact-based decisions (not battles of opinions). *5 More*

We also planned how cross-boundary teamwork would work. This was crucial in a structure based on specialization. Essentially, we designed a new *organizational operating model,* not just a new organization chart.

We saw many benefits:

- **Internal boundaries:** We clarified accountabilities, eliminated redundancies, and reduced territorial friction.

- **Specialization and teamwork:** We broke down "silos," allowed people to specialize, and developed effective cross-boundary teamwork.

- **Entrepreneurship:** The spirit of entrepreneurship took hold.

- **Results:** Performance improved across the board.

Progress

At this point, two years into our transformation, we'd accomplished a lot. We were reliably delivering projects. We'd stabilized operational services, and addressed business-continuity challenges. We'd greatly enhanced information security and regulatory compliance. And we'd built excellent working relationships with our clients throughout the business.

The transformation was good for our staff as well. With demand under control, we stopped routinely overworking people. We gave people well-focused jobs that they could succeed at, and empowered them to run their internal businesses. In short, we became a great place to work. Turnover dropped from over 10 percent to under 4 percent, and employee engagement scores rose to among the best in the company.

In just two years, we'd put in place an entirely new paradigm — a scalable organization built on principles of empowerment, entrepreneurship, customer focus, and teamwork.

Thinking Back

At that point, Aurora was acquired and my career moved on. Nonetheless, I'm so very pleased with my transformation experience. We delivered a lot of value to the company, its patients, physicians, and employees.

Also, it was a tremendous development opportunity for our staff. We gave them a vision of what's possible — insights that will serve them throughout the rest of their careers.

For me, it was a profoundly rewarding experience. If I get the opportunity, I'll do it again (with Dean's help). [Editor: He did!]

How Organizations *Should* Work

envisioning a high-performing organization
made of a network of internal entrepreneurs

OUTLINE OF TERMS AND CONCEPTS
for reference as you read

Goals
 Supplier of choice to customers *[Chapter 34]*
 Employer of choice to staff *[Chapter 34]*
 Other leadership challenges *[Part 6]*
  Agility (Chapters 8, 14)
  Scalability without loss of synergies (even in multi-nationals) *[Chapter 30]*
  Acquisitions integration (ease of) *[Chapter 31]*
  Innovation (including disruptive) *[Chapter 32]*
  Digital business (value of technology) *[Chapter 33]*

Two Pillars of organizational design
 Business-Within-a-Business Paradigm *[Chapter 5]*
  Group = entrepreneurship = product manager for its products/services
  Network of entrepreneurs: customers may be external and/or internal
  Contract: commitment to deliver a specific result to a specific customer (SLA, project charter)
 Empowerment *[Chapter 6]*
  Accountabilities and authorities match
  Measure by results; accountable for the *what,* don't dictate the *how*

Organizational Systems
 Structure
  Framework: Types of Businesses *[Chapter 7, and Part 4]*
   Sales and Marketing *[Chapter 15]*
    Account
    Function
    Retail
    Customer Success
    Sales Support
    Marketing (marketing communications, market research)
   Engineering *[Chapter 16]*
    Applications (purpose-specific solutions)
    Base
     Components of applications
     Purpose-independent solutions
     Infrastructure

Service Providers

Asset-based (Operations) *[Chapter 17]*

Manufacturing, Logistics

Infrastructure-based services

Off-the-shelf products (product management, not engineering)

People-based

Specific to organization's business: Customer Service, Field Technicians, PMO, etc. *[Chapters 18, 19, 20]*

Generic ("business office"): Finance, Procurement, HR, General Counsel, Facilities, Administration, etc. *[Chapter 24]*

Coordinators

Information Security *[Chapter 21]*

Generic: Organizational Effectiveness (including Diversity, Safety, Quality), Planning, Research and Innovation, Business Continuity, Policies, Regulatory Compliance, Audit Response *[Chapter 22]*

Product-specific: design standards, patterns ("Enterprise Architect") *[Chapter 23]*

Organization Chart *[Chapter 7]*

Boxes = Groups = Jobs for leaders (goal: Groups contain only a single Type of Business (no Rainbows)

└ Domain for each group (boundaries, a business charter)

└ Lines of Business = specialties (Domains include one or more; fewer is better because more specialization)

└ Catalog of products and services (for each Line of Business)

Teamwork: Walk-throughs (team-formation process) *[Chapter 8]*

Prime Contractor for each project or service

Subcontractors = team-members (any number of them)

Each row: specific deliverables (from their respective Catalogs) = potential Contract

Internal Economy

Planning: business/one-year/operating plan, investment-based budget *[Chapter 10]*

Demand-Management: checkbooks, pursers, project intake, priority setting *[Chapter 11]*

Actuals = historic data: accounting, time tracking, reporting, variance tracking *[Chapter 28]*

Culture (best defined by behaviors, not values) *[Chapter 12]*

Processes and Tools: cross-boundary processes, common methods and tools

Metrics and Consequences *[Chapter 13]*

Performance management (appraisals, incentives, managing deficiencies)

Dashboards

CAST OF CHARACTERS
for reference as you read

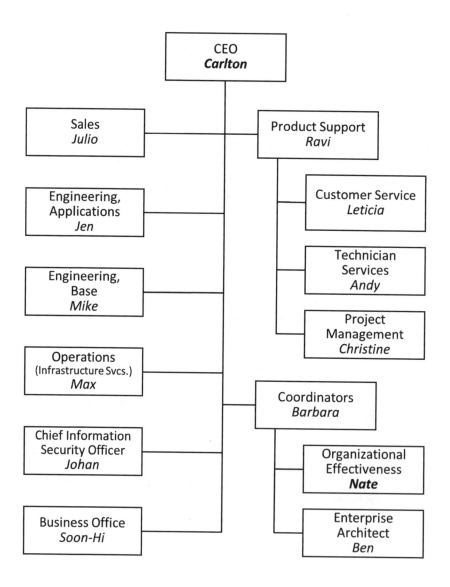

(Characters are inspired by many friends and colleagues, but all are fictitious.)

~ PART 1 ~

My Next Career Adventure

in which I decide to create an amazing organization

As a seasoned corporate executive, I certainly didn't expect that a single day would fundamentally change my world-view.

Yet one extraordinary day did just that.

In that one day, I got more valuable insights than I'd gotten in years of leadership experience and hobnobbing with other C-level leaders — insights on how to make organizations work *significantly* better.

Beyond that, I left that day with a profoundly different understanding of what great leadership is about.

You're skeptical? I was too. With all the leadership advice we get these days, we have to be.

Nonetheless, I pride myself on being a life-long learner and went in with an open mind. That paid off. Let me tell you the story of that day....

Dean's eloquent 'storification' of the protagonist's enlightenment makes it an extremely digestible read.

— Ade McCormack, author, thought leader, and keynoter

Chapter 1:
My Next Adventure: Build a Legacy

Chapter summary (key take-aways): page 465

Why the heck would a seasoned executive like me take a whole day to study a "model" organization?

Before I take you on my journey that day, let me attempt to answer that question....

I Quit!

I'd been a CEO in two prior companies. In my last job, my company was reasonably successful; I enjoyed working with a good leadership team; the Board was happy with me; and I was compensated quite well.

But I was bored and tired.... I was tired of having to settle controversies among my senior leaders. I was tired of getting drawn into doing my leaders' strategic thinking for them. I was tired of solving the same internal problems, under different guises, again and again.

It was a treadmill, each day more of the same.

Sure, launching new strategies and doing acquisitions deals was fun. But then came the tedious work of making sure the organization executed those strategies and integrated those acquisitions. It seemed there were so many obstacles: confused accountabilities, poor teamwork, misaligned resources, a lethargic culture.

With each passing day, I felt more and more worn down. And worse, I became increasingly annoyed — at my colleagues, at my job, at the world, at myself. I'd lost touch with my WHY. *6 Ref*

This was not what I wanted to be doing with my life! And I knew that the burn-out I was feeling could cause serious health issues. So I quit.

For My Next Job, a Worthwhile Adventure

I took some time with my family and my hobbies. After six months, the burn-out faded and I began to feel the itch to take on another challenge. But I wasn't at all clear on what that challenge would be. I certainly didn't want to jump into another situation like the one I'd just left.

I spent time with friends, including other C-level executives. And I spent time alone, contemplating what drove me to quit and what I really wanted out of the next (perhaps the last) phase of my career.

What I eventually came to understand was this: I didn't want to just run a company. It wasn't even enough to turn around a losing company. Been there, done that!

I wanted my next job to be something meaningful, something more than just making money for shareholders — a *worthwhile adventure*.

With that in mind, I committed to really challenging myself as a leader. For my worthwhile adventure, I decided I was going to build a real showcase — a company that's really *great*.

So, that got me thinking about what "great" means.

Is it just making innovative products and services that please customers, beat the competition, and generate shareholder value? Of course we have to do all that. But that alone isn't greatness. Many companies do that.

There must be something more....

I want a <u>worthwhile adventure</u> as a leader.
I want to build a showcase — a company that's really <u>great</u>.
So, that got me thinking about what "great" means.

What Is "Great" Leadership?

For some reason, thinking about what makes for a "great" organization brought Frederick the Great to mind.

I remembered a college history professor saying that Frederick the Great of Prussia lost the battle of Jena in 1806. [7 Ref] This was an interesting observation since he'd died 20 years earlier, in 1786.

Despite his personal skills at battle strategy, Frederick left the legacy of a dysfunctional organization. In the war with Napoleon, the Prussian army consisted of three squabbling chiefs of staff, each with their own armies and battle strategies, and very poor communications among them.

The organization had failed at innovation; tactics and training had not been updated for decades. They were overly dependent on outsourcing (mercenaries). And there was a culture of arrogance.

As a result, Napoleon was able to swiftly destroy the Prussian army before a large Russian contingent could arrive to reinforce it.

Frederick the Great was, ahem, great — *as an individual.* But his organization's success depended on him, personally, being there to direct everything. Once he was gone, things fell apart. He certainly did *not* build a great organization.

With that, it clicked! I realized that "great" isn't a matter of me, personally, making great decisions and leading the charge. That's exactly how I'd signed up for those 60-hour weeks that were killing me. And by the way, that was a losing strategy. Despite my long hours, there was never enough of me to go around.

I used to think my job was to deliver great business results. But I came to believe in a higher purpose. I came to understand that truly great leaders leave the lasting legacy of organizations that perform brilliantly now and long after they've moved on.

Great leaders leave the lasting legacy of organizations that
perform brilliantly now and long after they've moved on.

Engaging Every Bright Mind

With this goal in mind, it was easy to see that "great" isn't just about recruiting a great senior leadership team. Sure, I always try to surround myself with top talent. But people come and go. Frederick the Great had excellent generals under him; but that didn't mean he'd built an organization that worked great.

The truth is, there are smart people at every level of a company, all of whom should be contributing all they can. I don't mean some little suggestion box. I mean an organization that liberates *all* their creative energies.

In a great organization, *everyone* thinks strategically, in concert with one another. *Everyone* leads initiatives that deliver those strategies. *Everyone* runs today's business, and creates tomorrow's. Innovation occurs in every corner of the organization.

Not to innovate is the single largest reason
for the decline of existing organizations.

— Peter F. Drucker [8 Ref]

If I could build that kind of organization, I'd be remembered for all the careers that I helped to develop, and the successes that those people delivered on my watch and long afterwards.

And by the way, I noted, this also gave me a path out of the day-to-day grind that had burned me out in my last job.

A Different Kind of Leadership

At this point, I was excited about my new purpose: to build an organization that fully engages all its talent. On to the practicalities....

All those people would have to be coordinated somehow — and not by me and my top executives, or we'd be a bottleneck (and no better than Frederick). Traditional hierarchical decision-making is not the answer.

This insight led me to understand that I'd have to design a very different kind of company — a different *organizational operating model*. (This is the point where the word "transformation" first came to mind.)

Transform: make a thorough or dramatic change
in the form, appearance, or character.

— Chambers Dictionary, 13th edition

I came to see that the design of the organization is the key to performance, agility, and innovation. That insight made me look at my job in a very different way — not as the biggest cog *in* the machine, but rather as the designer *of* the machine — of that organizational operating model.

I had to admit to myself that I needed a new set of competencies: organizational design. I'd never studied this, at least not formally. But I felt confident that, with my years of experience and a bit of study, I could figure it out. And I liked the idea of learning something new.

The more I thought about this challenge and the adventure that lay ahead, the more enthused I got. I felt reinvigorated, and eager to get back to work. This would be fun!

My new perspective could have enlivened my last job; but of course, it was too late for that. So I started my search for a company where I could build my dream of a truly high-performing organization.

Great leaders are not cogs <u>in</u> the machine.
They're designers <u>of</u> the machine.

My New Company

You know the old adage, "Be careful what you wish for, because you might get it!" Well, my search was successful. In just six weeks, I was to start my new job as CEO of a well-established company that's in desperate need of transformation (whether it knows it yet or not).

My job interview process had included one-on-ones with Board members and key executives. And I did a bit of independent "research" (a.k.a. snooping). What I learned was disturbing (a.k.a. challenging).

Margins were adequate; but they were on a steady downward slide. It wasn't because of a bad economy; startups were prospering all around us. In recent years, competitors had beaten the company to market with innovative new products and lower prices, again and again.

Customers viewed the company's products as safe but boring. We had many loyal customers, but our market share was slipping. The whole situation felt highly vulnerable to disruption.

To make matters worse (more challenging), employee morale was upside-down: Engagement was low, and turnover was high.

I knew I could turn the numbers around with some fresh business strategies and two-way employee communications, as I'd done in past companies. But this time, I wanted to do more. This company will be the platform for my new challenge, for my next leadership adventure.

I just had one little problem....

Chapter 2:
If You Don't Know Where You're Going...

Chapter summary (key take-aways): page 465

Most leaders are familiar with Stephen Covey's second "habit": *begin with the end in mind.* [9 Ref]

Or as the old aphorism says: "If you don't know where you're going, any road will do."

I can build anything. I can drive change. But what the heck was I going to build? Change to *what*?

Need for a Vision of the End-state

My goal was clear. But before I could develop an action plan, I needed a clear definition of the end-state — a blueprint, a detailed *vision* of the future organization.

I needed that vision for at least three reasons:

- To capture hearts and minds, we leaders have to explain to people what we're transforming them into — an inspirational goal. Vision should attract great talent, motivate staff, and convince customers that we're working to delight them.

- Vision provides a benchmark. The gaps between that "stretch assignment" and today's reality tell us what we need to work on. This way, we won't just react to the crises of the day.

- With a well-defined blueprint of the end-state, each step we take will be in a consistent direction. We won't zig-zag, or worse, make changes that take us in the wrong direction.

More fundamentally, a vision *creates the possibility* of it coming to be.

What's a Vision?

So, what's a "vision"? In thinking about that, I came to these conclusions....

A vision is not a business goal (like market share or revenue growth), or a strategy (like acquisitions or digital business). It's a *description of an organization that can invent and deliver a continual stream of strategies to meet ever-evolving goals, year after year.*

And to be visionary, it has to be something big — a breakthrough. It can't be just fine-tuning ("rearranging the deck chairs on the Titanic").

Vision is not about current "best" practices (what others are already doing); or worse, common practices (where the lemmings went yesterday). It's about *ideal* practices — the best we can imagine. My vision may read like science fiction, but I'm not worried about that. I want to look as far into the future as I possibly can see.

In technology we expect bold experiments that... lead to major advances.
But in matters of social organization we usually propose only
timid modifications... and balk at daring experiment and innovation.
But it is time to apply to business organizations the same willingness
to innovate that has set the pace of scientific advance.

— Jay W. Forrester [10 Ref]

Clarity and Detail

I also realized that a vision that can inspire and serve as a blueprint has to be crystal clear.

It has to be much more than a marketing slogan like, "To deliver great stuff that helps our customers succeed."

And it has to be much more than a vague promise like, "We are committed to delighting customers with products and services that are of awesome value to them."

It's certainly not something we want to *get* like, "We will be recognized as wonderful."

To serve as a practical guide, a vision should describe exactly how the end-state organization will work, in as much detail as possible.

And I knew I had to put that vision in writing so that I could consistently communicate it, evolve it, and implement it.

A vision is... a dream created in our waking hours
of how we would like the organization to be.

— Peter Block [11] *Ref*

I Needed a Role Model

Once I was clear on the need for a detailed vision of the end-state, the real work began. I had a rough sense of the direction I wanted to take the organization — a highly engaged staff working in concert. But that wasn't enough. I needed to understand all the details — exactly how a really great organization works.

Despite what my spouse might say, I'm not so arrogant as to believe I have all the answers. If only I could see a high-performing organization in action....

I remembered a book on organizational design that had impressed me. I contacted the author (who coincidentally resembles the author of this book) and we had a great conversation.

He calls himself an "organizational coach" because (as he explained it) he's not only spent his entire career developing a science of organizational design; he helps executives apply that science as they drive transformation processes.

He shared a compelling concept, what he calls the "Market Organization," where every group on the organization chart is a business within a business, serving a market comprised of the rest of the company and beyond. And he explained some of the principles and frameworks involved in transformations.

In a "Market Organization," every group on the organization chart operates as a business within a business, serving a market comprised of the rest of the company and beyond.

I told him of my desire to build a really great organization, and my need for a clearer vision of the end-state. And I asked him if he knew of any examples — perhaps not perfect, but getting there.

"Yes," he said, "one comes to mind."

He told me about a CIO who built an IT organization that transformed the entire company, inspiring technology-enabled strategies that gave it unique competitive advantages. Some say they even "disrupted" their industry thanks to this CIO.

He talked about how successful this organization was at attracting top talent in a very competitive labor market; and at building excellent relationships with IT's peers throughout the business (and not just the CIO's personal relationships with other corporate officers).

"And," the organizational coach concluded, "it was a sustainable success. As far as I know, it's still a great organization, even though he's moved on."

"Did he build the IT organization as part of a company-wide transformation?" I asked.

"No, he was the thought leader. CIOs don't need permission to develop high-performing IT departments. It's their job."

"You say he moved on," I said. "Is he still a CIO?"

"It's interesting," the organizational coach replied. "A smart headhunter viewed IT as a business within a business. Indeed, it is. [12 IT] And she saw that this CIO was, in essence, a highly successful 'CEO' of a large tech business.

"He's now a real CEO of a tech company. And he's doing amazing things there."

"Will you introduce me?" I asked.

"Yes, of course."

The organizational coach emailed the two of us, and Carlton (that CEO) promptly replied and graciously offered me a tour of his company. The following week, I was on an airplane.

How to Use What I Learned

In this book, I'll describe what I saw— the basis for what I've now adapted to be *my* vision of the end-state organization I intend to build.

You may not agree with everything in this vision. You may even strive for the opposite. That's fine, as long as you have your own vision and can describe it clearly to the people you lead.

Once you've defined your own vision, you'll know where you're going. So you'll know which road will do.

"Get on with the story," you're thinking. Okay, let's go....

~ PART 2 ~

Foundations

*in which I learn some fundamental
principles of organizational design*

No doubt as you would, I went into this field trip with a good measure
of skepticism. Could a former CIO now running a mid-sized tech
company be relevant to a CEO like me? Could this particular
organization be all that different from the ones I'd seen over the years?

But I've always said that skepticism is a good thing; it's cynicism that's
unproductive. So, I kept an open mind.

My travels went smoothly. I flew in the night before, and the plane
arrived only 40 minutes late. (Not bad!)

The next morning, I showed up in their lobby on schedule. A few
minutes after presenting myself to the receptionist, a smiling young man
emerged from the elevator to greet me.

"Welcome. My name is Nate. We're so pleased to have you visit us.

"Carlton asked me to be your tour guide," Nate continued warmly. "My
job is to show you around, introduce you to the leadership team, and
explain how things work around here."

"Thanks, Nate," I replied. "I'm in your hands."

As we waited for an empty elevator, I asked, "What's your role here,
Nate?"

Nate explained that he's in charge of Organizational Effectiveness. He was the project leader for the organizational transformation.

I told him that I was looking forward to understanding how he went about it.

"I'm on your schedule," Nate replied with a grin.

Here's the agenda that Nate had arranged for me:

- Carlton: Company background; the two pillars on which the organizational design is based
- Nate: The organizational operating system
- Leaders: How each function works
  - o Julio: Sales
  - o Jen and Mike: Engineering
  - o Max: Operations
  - o Ravi: Product Support, with:
    - └ Leticia: Customer Service
    - └ Andy: Field Technicians
    - └ Christine: Project Management Office
  - o Johan: Information Security
  - o Barbara: Coordinators, with:
    - └ Nate: Organizational Effectiveness
    - └ Ben: Enterprise Architect
  - o Soon-Hi: Business Office
- Nate: Transformation (change management) processes
- Carlton: Leading a transformation

Chapter 3:
The Lay of the Land at this Company

Chapter summary (key take-aways): page 466

My first meeting was with Carlton, the CEO.

"It's great to meet you in person," he said. "Thank you for coming."

"I'm grateful for the opportunity," I replied. "Thank *you*."

Carlton appeared to be a kind and gentle soul, not the larger-than-life personality I'm used to seeing among my peers. Was this the dynamic CEO who led a company to greatness?

Well, first impressions and stereotypes are often misleading. I held off any judgments and focused on the business at hand.

Introduction to Carlton, the Transformational Leader

"To get us started, Carlton, tell me a bit about you and the company."

"Sure," he said. "I'll give you the short form.... I'm not just about making money for shareholders. My goal, in any company I'm with, is to create an organization that's a great place to work, and works great.

"I believe that if we can liberate and channel all the creative energy of all our staff, they'll do amazing things. And when they do amazing things for customers, ultimately, shareholders will be pleased."

---

*Your employees come first. If you treat them well,
then they treat the customers well, and that means
your customers come back and your shareholders are happy.*

— Herb Kelleher, Founder, Southwest Airlines

"Carlton," I said, "that's very insightful for a young guy like you! I have to humbly admit, it's only very recently that I came to the same conclusion. So, tell me about your background."

"Okay. I started out in IT as an engineer. But when I became a manager, obviously the only way I could get anything done was through others; so, I worked on my supervisory skills. Then, as I approached the executive level, I became interested in programming organizations rather than computers.

"Before I came here, I was the CIO in a large, global company. I guess the VCs liked what I did there enough to tap me for the CEO job here."

"I guess so!" I said. "Now, tell me about this company."

Company Overview

"We're a tech company," Carlton said. "Our mission — our *raison d'être* — is to help diverse people work synergistically in service of diverse others.

"We do that by providing tools and services that help companies manage the complexities of serving multiple markets with multiple products and services. Our software pulls in data from many different sources, and with a bit of AI (artificial intelligence) magic, we create a common view of customers, products, and functions or departments.

"But you didn't come here for a sales pitch!" Carlton said with a smile.

I laughed. "Tell me more about your markets," I requested.

"Well, when I started here six years ago, our customers were office-supply retailers. They're complex businesses. They sell both products and services. And they sell to both businesses and consumers. That kind of complexity is where our software really pays off.

"We support everything from mom-and-pop stores to the big chains,"

Carlton said. "That variety gives us the opportunity to sell both products and services — on-premise applications for the big ones; software-as-a-service for the small ones.

"Essentially, we have *two different business models* going: our standard *off-the-shelf* software and services, and a *bespoke* (custom) engineering business that builds customized solutions for the big customers.

"What I mean by 'off-the-shelf,'" Carlton explained, "is that we sell the same things to many different customers. That includes both products (our standard solutions), and services (software-as-a-service, hosting services for the solutions that we've sold, etc.).

"Our other business model — bespoke solutions — is custom solutions which are engineered to customers' specific requirements. In that way, we're like other engineering companies, consulting companies, health care, internal IT departments, etc.

"Our bespoke business necessitates a much larger engineering function than if we were just an off-the-shelf products company. The margins aren't as good as selling software; but it's still a profitable business with a very good return-on-capital.

"We also offer a variety of supporting services," Carlton added. "We even help customers implement solutions other than ours, which we see as a foot in the door. We want our customers to see us as their trusted partner, ultimately their go-to source for everything IT.

"It's complicated to combine both types of businesses. But there are real synergies. I'm sure you'll notice them as you make your rounds today."

"You're not a large company," I observed. "Do you ever worry that you're spreading yourself to thin?"

"Not at all," Carlton replied. "We have distinct groups dedicated to each of those businesses. So, no one is spread too thinly. In the course of the day, I'm sure you'll see how well-focused everyone is."

Multi-product, Multi-market, Multi-geography

Carlton continued to explain his business.... "We're actually more complex than just those two different business models (off-the-shelf and bespoke). We serve multiple market segments, starting with office supply retailers, and now a few other markets.

"And we operate in multiple countries. We're not big enough to call ourselves a 'multi-national.' But we have operations in the US and Europe, and we're planning to enter Asia.

"So," Carlton concluded, "we're a multi-product, multi-market, multi-geography company."

"Are those separate business units?" I asked.

"No, we're a *fully integrated* organization — the opposite of a business unit for each product or geography. Remember our mission: to help diverse people work synergistically. We practice what we preach!

"We have product managers for each product and service," Carlton explained. "They're global.

"Some support functions have groups in each geography. But they're all shared services, and they all work together as one organization. This way, we can maximize synergies and economies of scale, and deploy our best experts wherever they're needed."

"It sounds like you've cut the Gordian knot," I said. "You found a way to focus on products, markets, and geographies, all at the same time."

"I think we have."

"I'm intrigued," I said.

"Eat Your Own Dogfood"

"There's one more thing you should know," Carlton added. "As the saying goes, we 'eat our own dog food' — we're our own customer. We strive to be the IT department for our external customers. So, we'd better be our own company's IT department!"

"How does that work?" I asked.

"Consider the alternative.... Let's say we had two IT groups: one for internal customers, and the other being the rest of the company which is essentially an IT department for external customers. What would you do if, on one side of the house, you had a scarce specialist who was needed for a project on the other side of the house?"

"Loan him over?"

"Of course. You'd assign him to the project.

"Now," Carlton continued, "just extend that concept to every specialty. In a fully integrated organization where *everything* is a shared service, we can assign each specialized resource to whatever project needs it the most, internal or external."

---

*In a fully integrated organization where <u>everything</u> is a shared service,
every specialized resource is available
to whatever project needs it the most, internal or external.*

"I see no reason to split every specialty, or our infrastructure, into one group for external customers and another for internal. That would be expensive.

"And," Carlton explained, "it would reduce our depth of expertise by splitting each profession into two groups of relative generalists (one internal, one external) instead of one bigger group that can specialize to a greater degree.

"Furthermore," he said, "we'd miss out on creative insights, for example market insights that could improve internal services; or internal innovations that might give us a competitive edge. And how would it look if we weren't using our own products and services!?"

"That's interesting," I said. "I understand the synergies. But I don't know of any other tech companies that have pulled this off."

"I've never let 'being first' be an obstacle to doing what's right," he said with a smile.

"I admire you for that, Carlton. I don't think we could eat our own dogfood in my company. We aren't consumers of the products we make. But now that I think of it, a friend of mine runs a marketing services firm; and their HR department uses their marketing services for recruiting." 13 Ref

"There you go," Carlton said. "We're not alone. But even if you don't consume your own products, I think you'll find virtually all of our organizational operating model relevant to you. This is just one added twist.

"And," Carlton concluded, "because you'll essentially see an IT department serving a company (as well as a company serving external customers), what you see in our company could be applied to departments within companies like IT."

At that point I was thinking, the complexity that this little company deals with is impressive. Small but mighty! I was eager to learn how they were able to do so much with so little.

Chapter 4:
The Decision to Invest in Transformation

Chapter summary (key take-aways): page 466

I got to thinking about my upcoming challenge.... Where to start? How to start? If an organization (like the company I was about to lead) is doing okay — not great, perhaps, but getting by — what would motivate you, your staff, and your Board, to take on significant change?

I asked Carlton, "When you first got here, what made you decide to embark on such an ambitious organizational transformation?"

Problems Carlton Inherited

"Well, to be honest," Carlton said, "I inherited a low-performing organization that had done some great things. It had succeeded in spite of itself.

"Like most executives starting a new job, I spent my first couple of months listening to staff, major customers, and some key vendors. And man, I got an earful!"

Carlton summarized some of the problems he'd inherited:

- Customers felt the organization was unresponsive, not meeting commitments, and lacking customer focus. And it wasn't delivering as much strategic value as they'd hoped.

- Margins were under pressure; and many departments were accused of costing too much. But they had no way to defend their spending, and no one really knew if their functions were overly costly.

- Managers complained that they were severely underfunded. The business was growing, so they were supporting an ever-increasing installed base; and they were delivering new services. But their budgets were always their prior year's spending plus a few percent, which wasn't necessarily correlated with expected workloads.

- Despite long hours, staff still couldn't meet customers' expectations. They were overworked, burned out, and discouraged.

- Staff were so busy scrambling to satisfy customers' demands that they didn't have time for training, process improvements, relationship building, innovation — they were "eating their seed corn."

- Individual accountabilities were unclear, and there was in-fighting and finger-pointing.

- Staff had a "silo" mentality, and teamwork was poor.

- Staff weren't engaged or motivated to excel.

- Leaders spent lots of time fire-fighting, and were solving the same problems again and again.

"I could go on. It was pretty obvious why my predecessor, the founder, was asked to step aside," Carlton concluded.

A Comprehensive Approach

"You could have tackled each of these problems, one by one," I noted. "What made you decide to do a major transformation?"

"Well, I guess it was my experience in my prior job," Carlton replied. "Back when I was a CIO, in my first two years, I followed the recommendations of a variety of industry 'experts' and made quite a few changes — I hired some great leaders, and implemented things like the Agile development method, Product Owners, DevOps, and ITIL.

"Looking back, I'm embarrassed to admit that I was looking for a 'silver bullet.' And no surprise, I didn't find one.

"Those initiatives weren't bad things," Carlton observed. "Each of them solved some specific problems. But after a couple of years of that, in the greater scheme of things, they didn't move the needle on the big issues all that much.

"I don't know why I thought I could implement a point-solution to solve one problem, and then another point-solution to solve some other problem, and have any hope that it would add up to a coherent organizational operating model." Carlton smiled in a self-deprecating way.

I nodded, thinking back on how I'd done exactly that in prior jobs. And to be honest, it didn't work out too well for me either.

Implementing a point-solution to solve one problem,
and then another point-solution to solve another problem,
won't add up to a coherent organizational operating model.

Carlton continued, "The organization was functioning... just not at all well. There were so many different problems. So, I went looking for a more comprehensive approach, one that would lead to deeper change.

"I had read some of the work of our mutual friend, the organizational coach. I contacted him, and we arranged a phone call where I shared my challenges and he gave me a quick overview of his thinking.

"His vision of the Market Organization made absolute sense," Carlton said. "And I liked that it was so comprehensive. I was a little concerned that it was *too* leading edge, but it felt like the right answer.

"Also, his approach to transformation was so logical. He doesn't address problems; he addresses the *root causes* of problems — the *organizational systems* that make or break our performance.

"And I liked his pragmatic, participative change-management processes.

"After that phone call," Carlton said, "I spent a day in private with him

— what he called a 'study day.' I came back convinced that this was what we needed, and that despite it being out there on the leading edge, it was practical. I felt sure we could make it work."

"And apparently you did," I said with a smile.

We're at the end of tinkering our way into the future.
In a world that's changing so quickly in such fundamental ways,
incrementalism can't work.

It's time to get past re-engineering
(squeezing more productivity out of current processes)
and start re-thinking how organizations should work.

— Peter G. W. Keen, Professor (retired), Stanford, MIT, and Harvard

---

Structure Follows Strategy, No?

Stepping back a moment, I said, "Carlton, there's an old maxim, 'structure follows strategy.' [14 Ref] Did you start off with strategic planning before you got into organizational transformation?"

"No, we quite deliberately did it the other way around," he said.

"You're bucking a 60-year-old common wisdom. Why is that?" I asked.

"You're right," Carlton replied. "That maxim came from the 1950s and 1960s, the post-WW2 era of steady growth. In those days, strategies were relatively long-term and stable.

"But now, we're in a world of VUCA — volatility, uncertain, complexity, and ambiguity. [15 Ref] So, we have to be agile. We need an organization that can spot opportunities and rapidly reconfigure itself to execute a set of ever-changing strategies. And strategy is not monolithic; we need to be able to pursue multiple strategies at once.

"If we had designed a structure around our current strategies, it might fail to deliver future strategies — or, we'd have to restructure every time a new strategy came along.

"But worse than that, if we designed a structure around today's strategies, it would fail to *discover* tomorrow's strategies. That old maxim just doesn't make sense anymore."

Identifying new opportunities and organizing effectively and efficiently to embrace them are generally more fundamental to private wealth creation than is strategizing.
— David Teece, Gary Pisano, and Amy Shuen *[16 Ref]*

"Also, to be honest," Carlton admitted, "I was concerned that getting our Board excited about a new business strategy might not be wise when the organization wasn't really capable of delivering it.

"So, the first thing I wanted to do was to build a high-performing organization. Then, I could let all the talented people in the firm both deliver today's business and generate tomorrow's growth. To me, *organizational* strategy comes before business strategies."

"By 'organizational strategy,' do you mean the org chart?" I asked.

"Oh, it's much more than that," Carlton exclaimed. "It's the whole organizational ecosystem: structure, teamwork processes, resource-governance processes, culture, metrics, and more."

Health care has been undergoing a transformation of its business model. To deliver that new value proposition, I knew I had to drive an organizational transformation to get people thinking and behaving in a very different way.
— Mark Eustis, President & CEO (retired), Fairview Health Services, and Founding Board Member, VillageMD

Executive Support

"So, in this job, you went right to work on the organization?" I asked.

"Exactly. We began the transformation soon after I arrived."

"No doubt, transformation was a big investment," I said.

"It was. During my first three years, we invested heavily in it, including our leaders' time and attention. So, revenues were flat and profits actually declined for awhile. By my fourth year, things were working reasonably well. That's when we began to see the payoff."

"That took a lot of patience," I noted. "Did you need to get the support of the Board up front? And back when you were a CIO, I take it you did the same thing; did you need your CEO's approval in advance?"

"Nobody has ever given me a blank check!" Carlton replied. "Executive support is something you earn, not something you demand up front.

"The first step we took, our transformation planning process, did more than figure out what changes were needed. As a result of that process, I was able to give the Board a clear description of the end-state — our vision of how the company *should* work. That motivated their support.

"The process also produced our transformation road-map. That plan gave them confidence that we could pull it off, and it bought us time.

"Nate, are you going to explain our transformation planning process?" Carlton asked.

"I sure will, this afternoon (Chapter 25)," Nate promised.

Results So Far

"Before we discuss what you did, tell me about the payoff," I requested.

"Sure. When I started six years ago, we were around $175 million in revenues. In the last three years (after we had completed most of the transformation), both revenue and profit growth have averaged around 40 percent. We're now just short of $500 million, and projecting $650 million next year. The acquisitions we're working on are over-and-above that organic growth."

"Impressive, Carlton," I said. "What drove that growth?"

"Three things: We broadened the services we sell to our existing customers. We better penetrated the markets we're in. And we opened up new markets."

"That's a great strategy," I joked. "If only it were that easy!"

Carlton laughed. "If only! Of course, there were many strategies and initiatives that made that result happen.

"But remember," he cautioned, "this isn't because I came up with smart business strategies. I didn't. What I brought was a transformational *organizational* strategy. Then, my team did the rest."

I didn't bring smart business strategies.
I brought a transformational <u>organizational</u> strategy.
Then, my team did the rest.

"Our staff have been really entrepreneurial. Folks realized that we'd figured out how to serve an industry (office supply retailers) that sells both products and services, to both retail and B2B. So, they looked for similar industries. We expanded into car dealers and agricultural equipment. Now we're looking at other verticals, like restaurant supply."

This was a remarkable success story by any measure. I really wanted to understand how Carlton built an organization that could do this.

This organizational operating model doesn't just scale.
It's been the engine for our growth.

— Sergio Paiz, CEO, PDC *17 Ref*

Chapter 5:
Coherence Coming from an Underlying Paradigm:
Every Group is a Business Within a Business

Chapter summary (key take-aways): page 467

"Carlton, let me tell you what I'm looking for today.... As I said when I emailed you, I'm about to take on a new CEO job. This time, I'd like to build a real showcase of an organization. To do that, I first need to design a blueprint. I'm looking to understand in detail how things *should* work.

"I spoke with the organizational coach," I continued, "and he said that you're one of the most advanced organizations he knows of."

Carlton smiled humbly. "I'm honored. We're certainly not perfect. But we've come a long way, and we've learned a lot along the way."

Paradigm First

Carlton went on to say, "By the way, I really appreciate that your first step is developing your vision of the end-state. That's so powerful. But there's a critical step that comes before vision — your *paradigm*."

"What's that?" I asked.

"It's your world-view," he said, "your well-spring — the common source from which the many insights in your vision are drawn."

Carlton explained that their vision comprises many detailed statements about how things should work. Those statements must not be in conflict. They all have to add up to a coherent operating model.

"To ensure that consistency," he explained, "all the detailed pieces of your organizational operating model should be drawn from the same underlying paradigm."

Interesting! First a foundational paradigm, then a detailed definition of the organizational operating model which will be my blueprint of the end-state organization.

To ensure consistency,
all the detailed pieces of your organizational operating model
should be drawn from the same underlying paradigm.

The Business-Within-a-Business Paradigm: What It's Not

"In my case," Carlton continued, "I believe in the business-within-a-business paradigm." *18 Ref*

"I've heard that phrase," I said, "but tell me what *you* mean by it."

"Sure. But first let me tell you what I *don't* mean by it....

"It's not about outsourcing, or spinning off departments as separate legal entities.

"It doesn't necessarily mean chargebacks (transfer pricing), or operating internal service functions as profit centers. In fact, we do *not* do internal chargebacks.

"It doesn't mean that staff have free reign, with no oversight, like a bunch of free agents.

"And," Carlton concluded, "it certainly doesn't mean that the customer is always right, and staff are just passive order-takers! Sure, customers are always customers, and deserve respect and the authority to choose what they buy. But good entrepreneurs are proactive in so many ways (Appendix 1)."

The Business-Within-a-Business Paradigm: What It Is

"Okay," I said, "if that's what it's *not,* then what *is* this business-within-a-business paradigm?"

Carlton explained that the business-within-a-business paradigm goes beyond running entire departments (like IT) as businesses. "I want *everyone* at every level to think and act like an entrepreneur," he said.

The big change from managers' points of view, Carlton told me, was treating others throughout the company as *customers* (not wards they take care of, or risks they control). Customers may be peers within their departments, other departments, or external customers. No matter, everyone is accountable for delivering products and services to their customers — things those customers choose to buy.

Well, it may be the devil or it may be the Lord
But you're gonna have to serve somebody.

— Bob Dylan [19 Ref]

Basically, he described the organization as a network of entrepreneurs.

"We're not talking about everybody putting their life-savings at risk and taking home only the profits," he said. "We're just talking about customer focus, accountability for results, competitive quality and price, innovative thinking... that sort of thing."

"You're expecting them to be entrepreneurs," I said. "But there aren't profits to motivate people?"

"That's right," Carlton replied. "Everybody is paid salaries and some incentives. But staff are motivated by other things, like knowing they're doing something meaningful for others. And ultimately, bonuses, raises, and promotions depend on their customers' satisfaction."

> ...*the democratic operation of the market*
> *[does] not stop at the doors of a big business concern....*
> *[It] permeate[s] all its departments and branches....*
> *It joins together utmost centralization of the whole concern*
> *with almost complete autonomy of the parts.*
>
> — Ludwig von Mises [20] *Ref*

The Alternative: "Partners in the Business"

I liked the sound of this paradigm. But I had concerns.

"Doesn't this have risks?" I asked. "You're talking about treating support functions as businesses selling services to internal customers. Might that distance people from their peers? I've heard some say that support functions like IT should be *partners in* the business, not suppliers to it."

"Actually," Carlton replied, "in my early days as a CIO, I tried that 'partners' approach. At least in my case, it didn't work."

"Why not?" I asked.

"Well, for one, it created confusion about accountabilities.

"Some teams felt that, as partners, they should decide everything together," Carlton explained. "IT staff meddled in their customers' business decisions. And business staff meddled in IT's decisions. It slowed things down, produced bad decisions, and disempowered both parties.

"In other cases, IT staff said something like, 'We're the technology experts in this partnership. So, *we'll* make all the technology decisions.' They didn't respect that their customers had businesses to run, and needed to be in control of their factors of production (IT included).

"Either way," Carlton said, "this vague notion of 'partners' confused authorities and accountabilities, and that actually led to strained, not closer, relationships."

"Interesting. I see what you're saying," I said.

Good fences make good neighbors.
— Robert Frost, "Mending Wall"

"Beyond that," Carlton added, "when they saw themselves as business partners, my staff didn't think about running their own businesses.

"They didn't know they were responsible for competitive prices, so they didn't manage costs well. They focused on tasks and processes rather than results, since they didn't know their jobs were to deliver products and services. They resisted outsourcing, since they thought it threatened their empires. They were less innovative, since they didn't know they were responsible for the future of their businesses. I could go on....

"On the other hand, successful entrepreneurs *continually strive to earn customers' business through great relationships and performance.*

"In our experience," Carlton said, "the business-within-a-business paradigm has *not* distanced internal support functions from the business. Just the opposite! It's helped everybody understand their distinct and synergistic accountabilities and authorities.

"The bottom-line is, I've found that the business-within-a-business paradigm, with its mutually respectful internal customer-supplier relationships, builds the *best* partnerships," Carlton stated confidently.

The business-within-a-business paradigm,
with its mutually respectful internal customer-supplier relationships,
builds the best partnerships.

External- Versus Internal-facing Functions

"Okay, I'll go with that," I said. "But do you really consider *everybody* in every function an entrepreneur? I think most CEOs would think of externally facing functions differently from internal support groups."

Carlton's answer was brief and to the point. "We have no second-class citizens here," he said emphatically. "I want *everybody* to be entrepreneurial, no matter who their customers are."

In my model, <u>every</u> internal "department" would be transformed into a full-fledged PSF (personal service firm)/business!

— Tom Peters [21 Ref]

"Okay," I said, "but can support staff really be entrepreneurs if internal customers are forced to use them?"

"Our staff behave as if customers have a right to go elsewhere (even if, for some things, they don't). They really strive to earn the business."

"Perfect," I agreed. "The surest way to lose a monopoly is to behave as a monopolist."

"Exactly! I can use that line!" Carlton exclaimed.

Can Everybody Really Be an Entrepreneur?

I had to ask, "Is everybody really capable of being an entrepreneur?"

"You know," Carlton replied, "I've seen employees in fairly low-level jobs go home to run their own little businesses on the side. Now it's true, not everybody is cut out to start their own company. But at least at some level, I think everybody *is* capable of thinking like a business owner.

"Sure, some are better than others at managing businesses. Some just aren't good at thinking out of the box, and struggle to anticipate customers' needs. A few were so steeped in the old bureaucracy and command-and-control culture that they found it hard to let go.

"But," Carlton continued, "it's not like we expected this mind-shift to occur overnight. Our transformation process didn't depend on people being entrepreneurial up front. It was designed to cultivate it.

"Nate can tell you how the transformation process taught this new perspective. Each step was designed to take people up a notch in thinking like an entrepreneur.

"Over time," Carlton reported, "the bell-curve has moved steadily along in the right direction. And as folks learned to think and work in this very different way, their enthusiasm grew.

"Now that we're six years into our transformation process, I think at least three-quarters of our staff really get it. That's more than enough critical mass to make it work.

"Of course," Carlton concluded, "we're continuing to invest in our people, especially our leaders, to grow their business-management skills. But I think you'll find a really engaged, entrepreneurial team here."

This is exactly what I'm looking for, I thought, an organization that engages every bright mind. So I set aside my concerns, and probed some of the implications of internal entrepreneurship.

...the chief reason for our failure in world-class competition is our failure to tap our work force's potential.

— Tom Peters [22] *Ref*

Everybody is a Product Manager

"Carlton, in the past, I always considered product management to be a marketing function. Does considering everybody an entrepreneur change the way you think about product management?"

"It does," Carlton replied. "Product managers are accountable for the P&L (profit and loss) of a line of business — a set of products and services. This is not a marketing function. It's running a business.

"We do have product managers for all our external-facing products and services. They've got the P&L on those businesses.

"But the concept of product management applies more broadly. I see *all* my leaders at every level as product managers for their respective products and services. Everybody is accountable for running a business, whether they're selling to external customers (with a profit objective) or internal customers (where they're supposed to break even)."

"So, if everybody is a product manager," I said, "what do product managers do?"

Carlton replied, "Product managers conceive and invent new products and services, and deliver them to customers. They're responsible for building market share, customer satisfaction, and long-term value.

"To do all that, they subcontract for help from the rest of the organization." Carlton gave me examples of what product managers typically buy from others in the organization:

- Market research to assess market opportunities, and then to determine specific market requirements (from Marketing)
- Solution design (from Engineering)
- Procurement (if vendor products and services are required, from the Business Office)
- Manufacturing, or infrastructure operations (from Operations)

- Inventory warehousing and logistics (if physical goods are involved, from Operations)
- Marketing strategy and communications (from Marketing)
- Selling (from Sales, like a third-party sales force)
- Support (from Customer Service)

"I'm sure this isn't a complete list," Carlton said, "but you get the idea."

"I do," I said. "And that's exactly how I've always thought of product management. Does everybody really do all that?"

"Absolutely! Everything that product managers do applies to every business within a business. The behaviors we're looking for don't vary based on who your customers are, external or internal."

Everyone is a product manager for their own business within a business.

"By the way, I must caution you," he added, "you'll hear people talking about buying and selling products and services. That doesn't mean that money changes hands. As I said, we don't do chargebacks. When they say 'buy' and 'sell,' they're just thinking like entrepreneurs."

Strategic Thinking at Every Level

"So, everybody is an entrepreneur," I said. "But doesn't top management drive strategy? Some say that executives do the strategic thinking; managers translate those strategies into tactics; and the rest of the staff just execute those tactics. [23 Ref] Does that make sense to you?"

Carlton scowled. "That makes executives a bottleneck that constrains the whole organization's ability to think and innovate! These days, that old top-down approach to strategy just isn't agile enough to survive.

"We believe the opposite of that," Carlton continued. "I'm looking for strategic thinking in every corner of the organization. That's always been important, but especially now in this dynamic world.

"Sure, top executives define strategic challenges. And we coordinate the development of strategies so that individual groups' strategies mesh into our enterprise strategies.

"Nonetheless, *everyone* runs their own small business. *Everyone* develops strategies for their business, and drives their strategic initiatives (in concert with one another, of course). And," Carlton added, "in addition to inducing phenomenal engagement and performance, this cultivates the next generation of leaders."

---

*In an increasingly dynamic, interdependent, and unpredictable world,
it is simply no longer possible for anyone to 'figure it all out at the top.'
The old model, 'the top thinks and the local acts,'
must now give way to integrating thinking and acting at all levels.*

— Peter M. Senge [24 Ref]

The Business-Within-a-Business Mind-shift

"That's certainly intriguing," I said. "I'll need to understand how you get all these independent entrepreneurs' strategies to mesh. But for now, let's step back a moment and get a perspective.... What would your staff say if I asked them to list the most important things they've learned from the business-within-a-business paradigm?"

Here's how Carlton answered:

- **Initiative:** "First and foremost, they own their businesses. They'd say, 'I do whatever it takes to manage my business, rather than just doing assigned tasks or keeping current resources busy.' They're always looking for ways to improve their businesses; they seek out feedback; they're open to new ideas; and they're creative about overcoming obstacles."

- **Customer focus:** "They relate to their peers differently now. I think they'd say, 'I understand those are my *customers,* not nuisances or obstacles.' They want to please their customers, and they respect customers' prerogatives."

- **Results orientation:** "They accept accountability for results (not just for managing resources and processes). They'd say, 'It's my reputation at stake. I'd better deliver everything I promise.'"

- **Quality:** "They'd say, 'I'm proud of the quality of my products and services. It's my name on the door.'"

- **Value:** "They continually look for ways to reduce costs, leverage their assets, and improve their efficiency. Oh, and there's no empire building (increasing spending without revenues). They'd say, 'I have to be a good deal to earn customers' business.'"

- **Customization:** "They're willing to tailor solutions to customers' unique needs, where that's justified. They'd say, 'I'll deliver exactly what you want to buy. I'll never say that one size fits all.'"

- **Innovation:** "They proactively keep their products and services up-to-date. They'd say, 'I have to stay ahead of (or at least keep up with) my competition. So, I'd better innovate.'" [25 Ref]

- **Teamwork:** "People team rather than build empires and defend their territories. They'd say, 'To be the best, I have to focus on my own specialty. Rather than dabbling in other domains, I get help from peers when I need their specialties.'"

- **Use of vendors:** "They'd say, 'I manage a business, not just a group of people. If buying from a vendor is more cost-effective than producing it internally, or if I need more capacity, I procure outside help.' And they remain accountable for results, even if they use vendors to do the work." (For more, see Appendix 2.)

- **Safety:** "They take responsibility for the safety of their products and services, and of their people and assets. They'd say, 'If I hurt anyone, I'm accountable for the damages.'"

- **Judicious risk:** "They'd say, 'I have to take some risks to keep up with my competition; but I do so thoughtfully.'"

- **Alignment:** "They'd say, 'Customers have a right to choose what they buy from me, and I trust that (with my input) they'll buy what they most need.' So, customers' priorities become their priorities, and company priorities ripple through the entire organization."

- **Motivation:** "They'd say they appreciate the challenge, the opportunities for creativity, and knowing that they're producing value for customers. Job satisfaction and engagement are way up."

Summing up, Carlton said, "We've found that this entrepreneurial way of thinking and working has really brought out the best in people."

---

*It is a post-entrepreneurial model that marries
the best of the creative, entrepreneurial approach with the
discipline, focus, and teamwork of an agile, innovative corporation.*

— Rosabeth Moss Kanter [26 Ref]

Using the Business-Within-a-Business Paradigm

To come to a conclusion, I asked Carlton why the business-within-a-business paradigm was so central to his transformation.

Carlton thought for a moment, then replied, "In the IT industry especially, we've seen too many potentially good ideas gone awry.... 'Process owners' who disempower others by dictating processes without accountability for the end results of those processes.... 'Product owners' within IT who claim to own the solutions they build for the business, and make customers' decisions for them....

"Even the way people use the word 'owner' nowadays, when they really mean the person accountable for delivering a product or service to the real owner. Those folks would call car dealers 'car owners'!"

You have but to know an object by its proper name
for it to lose its dangerous magic.

— Elias Canetti [27 Ref]

"The business-within-a-business paradigm is my North Star. It tells me which fads are useful, and which may sound plausible but are heading in the wrong direction."

Carlton continued, "I'm focused on cultivating a team of bright, engaged entrepreneurs; and on orchestrating our great talent to handle all the challenges and opportunities that come our way.

"The business-within-a-business paradigm tells us exactly how to do that. It's the foundation of our organizational operating model, the Market Organization; and it's the basis for who we are today."

I smiled. Despite his calm and humble manner, Carlton's commitment and passion were quite evident.

At this point, the business-within-a-business paradigm made sense, but it seemed rather theoretical to me. I needed to see how it worked in real life. But Carlton held me off a bit longer....

Chapter 6:
The Golden Rule:
Empowerment, and What it Really Means

Chapter summary (key take-aways): page 468

"There's one more thing I'd like you to understand before you dive into the details of how our organization works," Carlton said.

"What's that?" I asked.

"It's a principle that's so important that the organizational coach calls it the 'Golden Rule' of organizational design. This one principle guided the design of every dimension of our organization — our structure, governance processes, culture, and metrics."

"That's intriguing," I said. "So tell me, what's the Golden Rule?"

Need for Empowerment

Carlton explained, "We're in a complicated business that requires lots of different specialties — many different engineering disciplines, services, and support functions.

"It's not just complicated. It's *complex* — we have so many things going on, all interconnected, such that the smallest events (the beating of a butterfly's wings) can cause major and unpredictable shifts throughout the organization.

"There's no way top-down command-and-control can deal with that," Carlton asserted. "Leaders can't process enough information fast enough, and so the organization can't be agile enough. 28 *More*

"I don't want to be a bottleneck, and I don't want my senior leaders to be bottlenecks. With all the expertise required, the number of decisions we have to make, and the short windows of opportunity we face, we can't afford to waste *any* of our bright minds. As we were saying earlier, we have to tap everybody's talents to the fullest."

I smiled and nodded. This was the core of what I wanted to do.

"So," Carlton finally came to the punch line, "we see *empowerment* as the key to organizational performance." [29 More]

Most of us who have created a business... don't pretend
that we're smart enough to make every decision by ourselves.
— Michael Bloomberg, Founder & CEO, Bloomberg L.P. [30 Ref]

Definition of Empowerment

Carlton continued, "So, what's the Golden Rule?" He pulled out a pen and pad of paper, and wrote boldly:

AUTHORITIES   =   ACCOUNTABILITIES
- resources
- information
- decision rights

"This is the essence of empowerment," Carlton stated. "If you ever separate authorities and accountabilities, bad things happen.... The person who has authorities without accountabilities becomes an unconstrained tyrant. And those with accountabilities but insufficient authorities can't succeed. They become helpless victims, and scapegoats when the guy with authority makes bad decisions.

"We make sure people have all the authorities they need to do their jobs. No less, or they'll fail. No more, or somebody else will be disempowered. *Authorities and accountabilities match,*" Carlton said emphatically.

I got it. I can't hold a subordinate accountable for results if I don't give them everything they need to do the job. Well, I guess I could (and some leaders do). But that's just setting them up to fail. What's the up-side of that!?

Any law that uplifts the human personality is just.
Any law that degrades human personality is unjust.

               — Martin Luther King, Jr. *31 Ref*

"I'm with you," I said. "But I have to admit, even with a competent team, I'm a little nervous about putting my fate in others' hands."

"It does make you vulnerable," Carlton sympathized. "But without empowerment, you're not scalable."

An invulnerable leader can be only as good as
her own performance — what a terrifying thought!

               — Max DePree *32 Ref*

Do People Want Empowerment?

"I would think most people appreciate those authorities," I said. "But did you find that some staff don't want to be empowered; they just want to be told what to do? Maybe they don't want the stress, or the risks?"

"There were some," Carlton agreed. "They fell into three categories: (1) Some didn't want to be held accountable for anything. (2) Some resisted accountability because they weren't qualified to do their jobs. (3) The rest were just nervous, perhaps doubting their own abilities."

"What did you do about their push-back?"

"The first category left the company voluntarily when they saw they'd be held accountable, or involuntarily if they repeatedly gave us excuses or blamed others rather than taking responsibility for their work.

"The second category either moved to a job they could succeed at; or if we didn't need their skills, we had to let them go.

"But we have lots of patience with those who try. We did all we could to help that third category grow into their empowered jobs."

...by failing to tap the strengths of every individual in our company, we were heading toward a dead end by dumbing people down.
— Jack Stack and Bo Burlingham, authors, The Great Game of Business [33 Ref]

Mechanics of Empowerment

"Okay," I said, "authorities and accountabilities have to match. How do you ensure that people have everything they need to succeed?"

"Well," Carlton replied, "it's partly a matter of structure. Jobs are defined as businesses within the business, so people are empowered to run their businesses. And no group is chartered to tell another group how to do its job.

"It's also in the culture — specifically, how we ask things of others. The key is we ask for specific deliverables — the What — and leave people free to decide for themselves the How."

Never tell people how to do things.
Tell them what to do, and they will surprise you with their ingenuity.
— George S. Patton, Jr. [34 Ref]

Carlton went on to explain that once they've agreed on the deliverables, the person asking for something is responsible for providing the resources, information, and decision rights needed to deliver those results. (Figure 1 summarizes the requestor's responsibilities.)

Figure 1: Empowerment: When You Ask For Something...

When you ask things of others, you must:

- Clearly **define the deliverable** (the end result).
  - ○ Base the magnitude and complexity of the deliverable on the degree of confidence people have earned.
  - ○ Define the results broadly to include not only the intended outcomes but also side effects. Results could include reporting project status, or producing certain artifacts like documentation.
  - ○ Do not specify tasks, processes, or effort, or tell people how, when, or where they work. But do define any constraints that limit how the work is to be done.
- Provide **resources** either by supplying a budget, or by convincing someone who controls a budget to allocate resources.
- Provide **authorities** either by granting rights which are within your power (like a boss delegating authorities), or by convincing those who have the power to grant them any needed rights.
- Share **information** about the context ("big picture"), where this deliverable fits, and anything else that could help them get the job done.

I found it interesting that they put the onus on the requestor to supply needed authorities. In this organization, they don't coerce staff to accept accountabilities without needed authorities, and then blame them if they aren't able to get those authorities on their own.

But I had a concern. "Doesn't this constrain a supervisor's ability to make work assignments?"

"Not at all," Carlton replied. "In fact, assignments are more clearly defined. And supervisors don't inadvertently force subordinates to accept impossible assignments. But if an employee doesn't agree to a perfectly reasonable assignment, that's treated as a performance issue."

"Got it," I said. "Let's go back to your list of authorities: resources, information, and decision rights. What about skills?"

"We don't think it's a manager's job to drive training downward. Everybody should be accountable for their own career success, and hence for developing their own skills. But while we can't force people to learn and grow, leaders have to ensure that the resources (time, money, training, and growth assignments) are available so that people have the opportunity to develop themselves."

Another concern came to mind. "Isn't there a chance that a boss could empower someone in order to pass blame downward, setting up a subordinate to take the rap in an impossible situation?"

Carlton's answer was simple. "Bosses retains accountability for their requests and their decisions to empower people."

When the Boss *Does* Know Best (Coaching)

"So," I said, "you tell people the What, not the How. But what if the boss knows better than the employee how to do something?"

"Coaching is cool," Carlton replied. "But if you micro-manage — if you tell someone how to do their job — then, if they fail, who's to blame? Did *they* perform poorly, or did *you* tell them to do something stupid!? When you tell someone how to do their job, you're partially accountable for results. And they're less accountable."

I asked Carlton to say more about that fine line between coaching and usurping accountabilities.

"We understand that coaching isn't dictating tasks or overriding decisions, which would mean that you share in the accountabilities," Carlton said. "So when we coach (and we do a lot of that), we try to help staff think things through; and we share what we've learned. Meanwhile, we make it absolutely clear that our advice is not a command."

I had another concern. "What if you've got a new person who's still learning to do their job, or who doesn't have the maturity to take on responsibility for an entire project. How can you empower them?"

"In smaller chunks!" Carlton replied. "You can have them report back more frequently, but still make them fully accountable for results. Just break projects into a series of small deliverables. Then, as they build a track record, you can increase the size of the chunks."

Trust is not a gift from others,
it is compensation for work done.

— Russell L. Ackoff [35 Ref]

Work From Home (Or Whenever/Wherever You Want)

"When you manage by the What, not the How," I asked, "does that mean that people are free to work from home any time they want?"

Carlton explained that within the law, labor contracts, and policies ensuring equitable HR practices, people can choose when and where they work. But if getting the job done requires being in the office or working certain hours (to work alongside others or cover a shift), then that's what they choose to do because they're accountable for results.

"Are you worried that work-at-home staff will goof off and not be as productive since they're not being watched?" I laughed, letting Carlton know that I personally wasn't that kind of Neanderthal.

His response was unequivocal. "Well first, I think working from home is often more productive than coming into the office.

"Second, if they're unproductive, we're going to know it, regardless of where they physically sit.

"Third, and perhaps most importantly, that whole notion of managers watching over people to be sure that they're putting in required hours and efforts is completely out of step with our empowered culture. *We manage people by results, not effort.*"

I nodded. This was exactly the answer I expected.

But was it worth the risks? "Has work-from-home paid off for you?"

"I believe so. As I said, people are more productive. Collaboration across offices is better, which has helped us maintain our shared-services approach (no decentralization) even as we expand geographically."

Carlton continued, "It's allowed us to access high-quality people that we might not otherwise have been able to recruit, like stay-at-home parents and people with mobility issues. And it's helped us attract talent from all over the country, even internationally — even a few great people in distressed countries who really needed the work.

"In that same vein," Carlton added, "learning to manage by results helped us make better use of 'gig workers' — the contractors we use, here and off-shore.

"And there was an interesting side benefit.... When Covid-19 hit, we were better prepared than most to manage remotely because we'd already learned to manage by results rather than by tasks and effort."
36 More

People who love going to work are more productive and more creative....
They treat their colleagues and clients and customers better.
Inspired employees make for stronger companies and stronger economies.

— Simon Sinek *37 Ref*

Work on Whatever You Want?

"Let me test how far empowerment goes," I said. "I've heard that some tech companies allow their staff to sign up for any projects that interest them. Is that part of empowerment?"

"No, absolutely not!" Carlton replied. "In that kind of world, how could we ever be sure we have resources aligned with strategies? How could we ensure that projects have all the needed specialists, or even that all the needed specialists exist within the organization? I guess if you have huge margins, you can get away with that. But it's not for us.

"Here, individual accountabilities are clear; we're pretty good at aligning priorities; and people know they serve customers. So, we empower staff to deliver *what their customers choose to buy from them* in the best way they know how. It's no different from the empowerment of any business owner.

"I don't think that letting people sign up for whatever they want is necessary. What people want is respect, an energized and high-performing culture, control over their destiny, and the knowledge that they're making a difference in the world.

"They can have all that," Carlton concluded, "by being empowered to run a business within a business, even if what they produce is determined by (internal) customers' needs, not their personal preferences."

Performance Management and Controls

"All this rests on your ability to hold people accountable," I said. "Performance management is really important, not just to get results, but also because there's nothing quite as demotivating as seeing others around you perform poorly and get all the same rewards. Say more about how you manage performance in an empowered organization."

"We're firm about performance management," Carlton agreed. "We just manage people by the bottom line, not the top line."

"I had a hunch you were going to say that," I said. (More on metrics in Chapter 13.)

Role of Hierarchy in an Empowered Organization

"Does empowerment obviate the need for a management hierarchy?" I asked.

"You know," Carlton said thoughtfully, "a hierarchical organization chart is a great way to ensure that every needed specialty exists somewhere in the organization, and that there are no redundancies."

"And the reporting structure has value, too. There are lots of things that bosses do without micromanaging or disempowering their staff.

"It's just that hierarchy is *not* a good way to get work done," Carlton said. "I'm sure Nate will explain how our entrepreneurs work together laterally, not up and down the hierarchy."

A hierarchical organization chart is a great way to ensure that every needed specialty exists somewhere in the organization. But hierarchy is not a good way to get work done.

Leadership in an Empowered Organization

Going back to Carlton's statement that there are lots of things that bosses do, I said, "In your empowered organization, managers are out of the command-and-control business. So, what's left for them to do?"

"The *important* things," Carlton replied. "Let's think about it.... What would you do if you had more time?"

Together, we brainstormed a good start on a list of management duties in empowered organizations (Figure 2).

Figure 2: What Managers Do in an Empowered Organization

- **Purpose:** Illuminate the value of people's jobs; create a sense of shared purpose.
- **Vision:** Synthesize the big picture; envision the future.
- **Ecosystem:** Nurture the organizational ecosystem; structure subordinate domains; optimize processes; remove hurdles.
- **Talent:** Recruit, coach and mentor, and engage people; negotiate objectives; provide fast feedback; manage performance.
- **Inspiration:** Set a high bar; stretch people's thinking; ask questions that drive innovation; put forward challenges that drive performance; question mental models that get in the way; expect the best (without demanding the unreasonable).
- **Motivation:** Make people feel appreciated; instill self-esteem, confidence, and a desire to win; set a positive, friendly tone; build esprit de corps; engender a sense of fun, excitement, and adventure.
- **Resources:** Negotiate budgets; propose and defend investments in the group; manage commitments; assign work.
- **Coordination:** Coordinate shared decisions within the group (e.g., common methods, tools, standards of practice); make decisions when consensus cannot be reached.
- **Strategies:** Inspire, coordinate, and guide business and product strategies for the group (recognizing that subordinate leaders are empowered to determine their own sub-strategies).
- **Risk:** Approve decisions involving risks above given thresholds (e.g., budget signing authorities, reputational risks, security risks).
- **Connective tissue:** Communicate up, down, and sideways; engender a sense of being part of the larger whole.
- **Representation:** Represent the group in leadership discussions (involving staff in leadership meetings whenever they're needed).
- **Sales:** Represent the group in walk-throughs (Chapter 8); promote the group to peers; assess customer satisfaction.
- **Model behaviors:** Exhibit in one's own behaviors the culture, habits of personal effectiveness, and spirit (attitudes). [38] *More*

All of these are higher-value uses of leaders' time — and things I personally wanted to do more of.

"Oh," Carlton added, "and unlike some CEOs, I don't expect my leaders to have all the answers. I want them to bring their staff forward, and let the people in the best position to know answer my questions. When they do, I get the facts; I get to know more of the staff; and that tells me that my leaders are empowering and cultivating their people."

Carlton concluded, "I think that without micro-management, leaders and staff alike are delivering results now that we would have considered extraordinary in the past. And really, I think leaders working at this more strategic level have *more* control, not less, because their time and efforts are so highly leveraged."

Goodbye For Now

"I certainly can't argue with the Golden Rule!" I quipped. I was sincere. I'd never want my organization to disempower staff. I have too much respect for people to allow that. But I needed to learn more in the course of the day before I'd feel comfortable implementing it.

Carlton smiled. "So, now you know our underlying paradigm (business-within-a-business) and the principle at the core of our organizational operating model (the Golden Rule). I'll leave it to Nate to explain our organizational design, and introduce you to our senior leaders so you can see how each of their internal lines of business works. Then, you and I can get back together at the end of the day."

After an elbow bump and a warm smile, Nate ushered me out the door.

After implementing this vision, I'm in awe of how the organization is doing so many great things without my intervention.

— Sergio Paiz, CEO, PDC

~ PART 3 ~

Organizational Operating Model

*in which I get an overview of the
key components of organizational design*

"What's next?" I asked Nate, as we waited for the machine to make our coffee.

"Actually, I've got you next, to give you an overview of our organizational operating model."

"What do you mean by the term 'operating model'?" I asked.

"Fair question," Nate replied. "By 'organizational operating model,' we mean the 'ecosystem' within which we work. It includes our organization's structure, teamwork processes, resource-governance processes (like budgeting and priority setting), culture, and metrics — the organizational systems that guide us day-by-day, and determine how we get work done.

"When you design all those organizational systems based on the business-within-a-business paradigm and the Golden Rule," Nate said, "you get what the organizational coach calls the Market Organization."

With coffee in hand, we walked to a small meeting room.

Nate continued, "We implemented the Market Organization by reimagining our organizational operating model. We saw it as an engineering challenge. You could say we've 'reprogrammed' the organization.

"I'm going to give you an overview of our operating model before you talk to the individual leaders about their functions."

"Great," I said. "But can you give me a 'table of contents' first?"

Nate described the basic components of an organizational operating model — a checklist of sorts (Figure 3).

Figure 3: Components of an Organizational Operating Model

- **Organization chart:** Jobs defined as businesses, clustered in a hierarchy to optimize specialization and professional synergies.

- **Cross-boundary teamwork:** A team-formation process that gets all the right specialists on each team, regardless of where they report, with clear individual accountabilities and a clear chain of command within each team.

- **Investment-based budgeting:** A budget process that decides funding based on what the enterprise chooses to "buy" from each function.

- **Market-based demand management:** A demand-management (project intake and prioritization) process that's business driven and dynamic throughout the year.

- **Culture:** Actionable behavioral principles that define ethics, integrity, interpersonal relations, productive meetings, cooperation, teamwork, empowerment, customer focus, entrepreneurship, contracts, quality, risk, and feedback.

- **Processes, method, tools:** Cross-boundary processes, and shared methods and tools.

- **Metrics:** Dashboards that help people succeed, and performance metrics that encompass all long- and short-term goals.

- **Consequences:** Consequences of achieving/missing performance metrics, including rewards for exceptional performance and firm, fair performance management.

"That's helpful," I said. "I'm interested in understanding each of these components."

NAVIGATION AID: This Part 3 explains each organizational system. Then, Part 4 demonstrates how they all work in practice. Part 5 explains how to implement them.

Chapter 7:
Organization Chart

Chapter summary (key take-aways): page 469

"Let's start with structure," I said, initiating my exploration of their organizational operating model.

"Okay. But hang on to your hat!" Nate grinned. "The Market Organization completely changed the way we think about jobs, by which I mean the boxes on the organization chart."

"I expect it would. But before we go there, let's 'begin with the end in mind.' What were you trying to accomplish with the restructuring?"

Problems Addressed by Structure

"That's easy.... It was to fix a total mess!" Nate laughed. He gave me examples of problems whose root cause was their old structure:

- Confusion about who does what; redundant efforts; territorial disputes; internal competition; political tensions

- Unclear individual accountabilities for results; staff who are focused on tasks or processes (rather than results)

- Poor performance due to people going too many ways at once; jobs which are too big for most people to master; a need for all "A-players" just to break even

- Difficulties with cross-boundary teamwork; inflexible, bureaucratic processes; an organization of independent "silos"

- Lack of customer focus; weak relationships with internal customers

- Lagging in innovation; little effort planning and creating the future

- Lack of entrepreneurial spirit; staff weren't creative, and didn't take initiatives to improve their businesses

- Low morale and motivation; dead-end jobs; cynicism

"I've seen it all over the years," I said.

"We'd lived that way for years," Nate agreed. "We'd been through a bunch of restructurings that didn't change much. So over time, we just came to assume that this was normal. Without Carlton, we probably never would have done a 'clean sheet of paper' restructuring."

Structure is a Science

"Clean sheet of paper? Okay, so now tell me, what's so different about your organizational structure?" I asked.

"Carlton knows how critical structure is to performance," Nate replied. "And it has to embody the Market Organization, and move us along that path. So, we weren't about to just draw boxes based on our past experiences and intuition."

Nate said that Carlton had asked all the leaders to read a book on structure written by the organizational coach. [39 Ref]

"It was a real eye-opener," Nate said. "I didn't know that organizational structure is a hard *science,* like engineering, until I read that book."

"I didn't know that either," I said. "Tell me about that science...."

Principles of Structure

"Well," Nate said, "like any applied science, there are firm principles and frameworks."

Nate pulled out his copy of the book, sprouting dozens of sticky notes. He turned to a list of seven principles of structure design (Figure 4).

Figure 4: Seven Principles of Structure

Principle 1: Empowerment (the Golden Rule): Authorities and accountabilities must match.

Principle 2: Specialization and Teamwork: You can only be world-class at one thing at a time; but you can't specialize if you can't team.

Principle 3: Precise Domains: Define clear boundaries with no overlaps or gaps.

Principle 4: Basis for Substructure: Divide a function into sub-groups based on what it's supposed to be good at.

Principle 5: Avoid Conflicts of Interests: Don't expect people to go in two opposing directions.

Principle 6: Cluster by Professional Synergies: Cluster groups under a common boss based on similar professions.

Principle 7: Business Within a Business: Every group is defined as a business whose job is to satisfy customers (internal and external) with products and services.

Empowerment: The Golden Rule

"Carlton really emphasized the first principle: empowerment — the Golden Rule," I said. "What exactly does that mean for structure?"

"A number of things," Nate replied. "I'll give you a few examples:

"First, we never create one box that tells another box how to do its job.

"We're even careful about our language," Nate said. "For example, we only use the word 'ensure' to refer to ourselves, never other people. No one is in the business of 'ensuring' other people's behaviors.

"Second," Nate continued, "we never separate learning from doing, like an ivory-tower innovation group that doesn't deliver products day by day. Nobody imposes innovations on you. Every group both delivers current products, and invents its own next-generation products. *40 More*

"And third, when one group develops the tools or infrastructure that another group uses, we make sure that the customer group is empowered to decide what it buys.

"I'm sure the Golden Rule guided lots of other structure design decisions along the way," Nate said. "But those are three that come to mind."

Specialization and Teamwork

"Okay," I said, "tell me about Principle 2, specialization and teamwork."

"Sure," Nate said. "We wanted as much as specialization as possible."

"Why is that?"

"It's simple. Specialists always outperform generalists," Nate stated unequivocally. He showed me a list of some of the reasons (Figure 5).

Figure 5: Why Specialists Outperform Generalists

- They're more **productive** because they know the best way to do things.
- They're **faster** since they don't have to repeatedly climb the learning curve, and because they're up on the latest methods and tools.
- They produce higher **quality** because they're more experienced.
- Their estimates and project delivery are more **reliable** because they've done similar things before.
- **Innovation** improves because they keep up with developments in their fields.
- They're **less stressed** because they're confident of their abilities.
- They're **more motivated**, since they like succeeding at what they do, and career opportunities for specialists are better.

To drive home the point, Nate said, "If you need surgery, you're not going to go to your general practitioner, right!?"

"You're right," I confirmed. "I'd go to a specialist."

"Exactly!" Nate said. "In fact, specialization is the reason organizations exist at all. *41 Ref* An organization of generalists can't perform much better than an equal number of individuals; it may as well be disbanded and the staff scattered among its customers.

"Similarly, a bunch of multi-disciplinary groups dedicated to customer business units would perform no better than decentralization. The whole point of consolidating a function into a shared service is that you can then afford a higher degree of specialization within that profession.

"So," Nate concluded, "we maximized specialization. Each job on the org chart is focused on just one profession."

"Tell me what the word 'specialist' means to you," I requested.

As Nate answered, he sketched Figure 6.

Figure 6: T-shaped Specialists

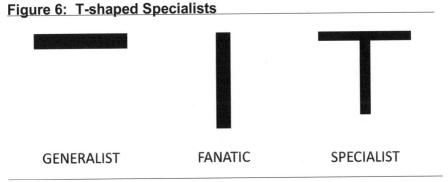

GENERALIST   FANATIC   SPECIALIST

"The generalist is a jack of all trades and master of none," Nate explained. *42 Ref* "They can't compete.

"Then, there are fanatics who know everything about one topic, and virtually nothing about anything else. That doesn't work! You can't team with them.

"What we mean by a specialist," Nate said, "is a T-shaped person.

"The top-of-the-T represents a generalist's knowledge, so they can see the big picture and collaborate with other disciplines. The top-of-the-T also includes basic skills required to do any job, like managing people.

"But everyone in our organization also has a bottom-of-the-T which represents real depth in one field of study, their specialty."

"That makes sense," I said. "Now, why does Principle 2 combine specialization and teamwork?"

"They're intertwined," Nate replied. "People will do what it takes to get the job done. If they can't get help from their peers, they'll have to dabble in other people's specialties to get work out the door. So, if you're not good at cross-boundary teamwork, your organization will naturally devolve into silos of independent generalists, no matter what the organization chart says."

"Got it," I said.

You can't specialize if you can't team.

Nate continued, "We were committed to working on both the organization chart and our processes of teamwork (Chapter 8). Trusting that we'd get good at cross-boundary teamwork, we didn't need to build self-sufficient silos with all the skills needed for each different product or service. We could use the organization chart to gather together everyone in each specialty; and then as projects happen, we combine those different specialists on cross-boundary teams."

So far, Nate had asserted that great cross-boundary teamwork permits consolidation of professions, which allows more specialization, which enhances performance. The logic made perfect sense to me.

Precise Domains

Moving on, I asked, "Doesn't any organization chart satisfy Principle 3, precise domains?"

"No," Nate said. "Just a few words in a box are never enough. People can interpret those vague group-names in so many different ways.

"It takes a paragraph or two to really define a group's boundaries. The key is to define each group's domain so clearly that we can be sure there are no gaps and no overlaps — like a jig-saw puzzle."

He showed me some examples. I found it interesting that their domains read like business charters. They bound what each group *sells,* not what it does (in keeping with managing empowered people by results).

And they go beyond just today's products and services. They define who's accountable for finding tomorrow's opportunities, making everybody accountable for the future of their businesses.

Basis for Substructure

"Tell me about Principle 4, the bases for substructure. By substructure, I assume you mean how you sorted out the boxes at the levels underneath each senior leader?" I asked.

"Yes, exactly," Nate replied. "Structure defines people's specialties. It tells people what they're supposed to be good at. So, we subdivided each department into groups based on the nature of their specialty."

Subdivide departments into groups at the next level based on their specialties — what they're supposed to be good at.

"An example?" I requested.

"Sure. Account representatives specialize in knowing customers, so they were divided by markets, and internally by business units.

"If we did the opposite and aligned Sales with products/services — you know, a sales force for each product line — that tells them they should specialize in products rather than customers.

"Furthermore, we could end up with more than one Account Representative calling on a given customer. If two Reps called on each customer, we'd either need twice the number of Reps (which isn't going to happen!) or we'd cut their face-time in half, which would undermine their very mission — to build close partnerships.

"And beyond that, Sales couldn't really be business driven and recommend whatever would be best for the customer. Instead, they'd always pitch the products they represent. That's no way to maximize the value we deliver, or build a long-term partnership."

"What about a new product line?" I asked. "Sales goes where the commissions are; and it's easier to sell well-understood products. Would you have a dedicated sales force for a new product launch?"

"No," Nate replied. "If we look like product-pushers rather than problem solvers, even in just that one case, it would jeopardize our trusted-advisor relationships and our reputation in the market.

"The problem you raise is a metrics issue, not a structure issue," he explained. "We make sure incentives are aligned with what we want from people. So, product managers may pay higher commissions for things that are more difficult (and hence more costly) to sell."

"Okay. What about the substructure in the rest of the functions?"

Nate replied, "They're *not* aligned with customers! That would create small teams of generalists for each customer, like decentralization.

"Other lines of business are substructured by *their* specialties... Engineers by engineering disciplines, Service Providers by services, etc. Once you define a function's 'bottom of the T,' the right basis for sub-structure is always clear," Nate asserted.

Dedicating groups to what they're supposed to be good at made absolute sense. I said, "Back to specialization, I suppose you can't do this if you mix up multiple specialties within a group."

"That's right," Nate agreed. "Do what's right for one, and the other specialties that are mixed in are then scattered across groups at the next level, and have to be generalists in their fields. So, that's another reason to focus each group on a single profession."

Avoid Conflicts of Interests

"In addition to breaking specialties down through the tiers in the hierarchy," Nate continued, "we also clustered some functions together. That's where Principle 5 comes in. We were careful never to combine lines of business in a way that would create conflicts of interests."

Never combine lines of business in a way that creates conflicts of interests.

"Give me an example," I requested.

"Sure. We separated infrastructure services (who advocate stability to keep services flowing reliably) from the engineers (who advocate innovation which inevitably disrupts smooth operations)."

"I thought Carlton said everybody innovates," I challenged Nate.

"That's true," he said. "I should differentiate *invention* from innovation — quantum leaps versus incremental improvements. Everybody innovates. Even Service Providers who mainly focus on stability continually improve the quality of their services and their processes.

"But when it comes to big changes, like introducing new products and services — we call them 'inventions' — Services Providers only move forward *when it's safe.* It's their job to be cautious about big changes so they won't risk operational stability.

"Engineers, on the other hand, are a hot-bed of invention. They're continually exploring breakthrough ideas."

"So," I summarized, "separating Service Providers and Engineers avoids a conflict of interests. But how do you find the right balance if they're under separate managers?"

Nate explained that Engineers understand that Service Providers are their customers. They sell them the infrastructure that's the basis for new services. So, they put forward innovative proposals.

"Service Providers want to hear about those new opportunities," he said. "But being cautious, they ask if they can operate that new technology reliably. And they evaluate the readiness of the market — will customers buy the service? When the time is right, *then* Service Providers buy the Engineer's invention and put it into production."

Nate listed other conflicts of interests (Figure 7), pointing out that all five can be avoided if groups are dedicated to a single type of business (Figure 9).

Figure 7: Five Conflicts-of-Interests in Every Organization

- Invention (major innovations) -versus- operational stability
- Purpose-specific solutions (applications) -versus- common components that contribute to various purposes
- Enterprisewide thinking -versus- specialization in products/services
- Unbiased, business-driven sales -versus- specialization in products/ services
- Customer-focus -versus- audit

Cluster by Professional Synergies

"After you identified all the lines of business," I said, "you then had to cluster all of them under the management hierarchy."

"Yes, of course," Nate said. "That's where we applied Principle 6.

"We knew we were going to work on our cross-boundary teamwork processes. So, that meant that we didn't have to put people under a common boss just because they frequently work together."

With effective cross-boundary teamwork,
you don't have to put people under a common boss
just because they frequently work together.

"Instead," Nate continued, "we put all the sub-specialties in a given profession together under a single leader. For example, all the applications engineers report to a very experienced applications-engineering executive. And all the operations managers report to an executive who has a passion for the services business.

"Putting people under a boss who's in their profession produced a lot of synergies," Nate asserted. He talked me through a list of professional synergies (Figure 8).

Every Group a Business Within a Business

"Throughout this discussion," I noted, "we've been talking about boxes on the organization chart, or groups, as 'lines of business.' That's a profound change, so different from the typical roles-and-responsibilities approach to job design."

"You're right," Nate said. "Jobs used to be defined by 'roles' in processes and 'responsibilities' for tasks — not by *results*. Now, every box on the org chart is a business within a business, defined by what it sells (not what it does) — by its products and services. We expect every manager to be an entrepreneur."

Figure 8: Types of Professional Synergies

- **Management synergies** occur when people report to someone who understands their profession, and can mentor and inspire them. Also, a manager who knows all the sub-disciplines in a profession can adjust sub-domains as new disciplines and technologies emerge.
- **Competencies synergies** occur when similar specialists exchange experiences and best practices, and share tools and work products (reusable components).
- **Workload synergies** are when a manager handles peak loads in one domain by temporarily borrowing related specialists from another.
- **Negotiating synergies** are gained when buying power is consolidated, e.g., for common tools and methods.
- **Product-design synergies** occur when related professionals collaborate, so products are more consistent and better integrated.
- **Talent synergies** result from improved career paths when a larger group of related professions has supervisory positions.

"In defining all the boxes," he continued, "we used a framework of all the types of businesses that exist in any organization, which we got from the organizational coach (Figure 9).

"Most of these functions existed prior to the restructuring," Nate said. "But we didn't define jobs this way."

Reflecting on the framework, I saw how it countered an old maxim. By dedicating separate groups to each of these types of businesses, organizations can pursue operational efficiency (Service Providers), innovation (Engineers), and customer focus (Sales and Marketing), all at the same time — you don't have to pick just one as your core competency. *43 Ref*

Figure 9: Types of Businesses Within Organizations   *44 Ref*

- Service Providers: sell ongoing services
    - o   Asset-based: operational services, off-the-shelf products
    - o   People-based: support services
- Engineers: sell new solutions
    - o   Applications: purpose-specific solutions
    - o   Base: purpose-independent solutions, components
- Coordinators: facilitate consensus on shared decisions (e.g., plans and policies)
- Sales and Marketing: link the organization to customers
- Audit: inspect, judge, and perhaps veto others

NAVIGATION AID: See Appendix 3 for examples of these types of businesses in various industries and functions.

Value of the Principles of Structure

"All seven principles of structure (Figure 4) make sense," I said. "How did you use them?"

"For one," Nate replied, "they helped us see the flaws in fads like customer-aligned structures, matrix, decentralization, federated models, and organizing around 'value streams' or customers' business processes (as suggested by Lean and SAFe) or our own processes (as suggested by ITIL). All those approaches scatter professions across groups and reduce our degree of specialization and performance.

We rejected simplistic span-of-control formulas (I prefer 'span of super-vision') since we have many distinct lines of business in small groups with working managers. And we're too big and complex for an Accountabilities Matrix. *45 More*

"We knew we wanted nothing to do with Holacracy and Teal, which discard the management hierarchy out of fear of hierarchical decision making. They discourage specialization, and there's no guarantee that the organization will contain all the needed lines of business. Strategic alignment is haphazard, at best. Performance management is loose. And it comes with a heavy bureaucratic load. *46 Ref*

"But the real value," Nate said, "was when we designed our org chart. Whenever we had a debate — and we had many — the principles gave us the basis for a fact-based discussion (rather than opinions, politics, and emotions).

"We didn't design a 'pure' organization chart by the book," Nate concluded. "But we debated each exception based on its pros and cons, in an objective manner, thanks to the principles.

"The end result," he asserted, "is an organization chart that defines jobs as entrepreneurships, all existing within a management hierarchy. This gave us well-focused jobs, crisp accountabilities for results, recognition of who our customers are, and an entrepreneurial spirit."

Why would anybody think a job was more than a job
when that's all the company expects it to be?
— Jack Stack and Bo Burlingham, authors, The Great Game of Business *47 Ref*

Impact of Technologies

"I have one last question (for now) on structure," I said. "I hear people talking about artificial intelligence (AI) and robotic process automation (RPA) replacing people. Does that impact these principles of structure?"

"As I see it," Nate replied, "those technologies are a continuation of a long-standing trend to delegate routine tasks to machines (dating back to the industrial era). Now, with these new digital technologies, even tasks which aren't entirely routine can be done by machines.

"So yes," he continued, "they may reduce headcount in some areas. But if you look over the centuries, individuals have been displaced by technologies but the overall level of employment hasn't been affected. I think technologies release people from mundane jobs to do more interesting work, which creates more high-paying jobs."

"I agree with you on that," I said. "Of course, we'll have to step up to the challenge of educating people to survive in a world that doesn't need as many low-skilled workers. But you haven't answered my question: Will new technologies have any impact on your structure principles?"

"I don't think so," Nate replied. "Technologies aren't going to manage businesses, find creative ways to achieve results, or drive strategies. Tools belong in the hands of people. I believe the structure of the future will have all the same lines of business, and boxes with people in them, even if we get more done with fewer staff thanks to new tools."

"That makes a lot of sense to me," I said.

What machines can't do is figure out how to make money.
— Jack Stack and Bo Burlingham, authors, The Great Game of Business [48 Ref]

"And perhaps more interesting," Nate added, "new technologies may allow us to do things that otherwise would be impossible — technology-enabled business strategies. I think that's much higher potential than just saving money by displacing people.

"Those new opportunities create new functions and new jobs," Nate concluded. "But those new functions should fit neatly into that framework of the types of businesses in organizations (Figure 9), and they'll live by the same principles."

NAVIGATION AID: Chapter 27 describes the restructuring process. Chapter 30 addresses scalability, startups, and multi-product/multi-national companies. Chapter 31 discusses acquisition integration.

Chapter 8:
Cross-boundary Teamwork: Walk-throughs

Chapter summary (key take-aways): page 470

"Nate, I've got to say, I can't see an organization chart like yours work-ing without a *quantum* leap in cross-boundary teamwork," I said. "And that's something that every organization I've led has struggled with."

"You're right on!" Nate exclaimed. "As we said when we discussed Principle 2, if teamwork isn't happening, people will naturally do what it takes to succeed on their own. And since most every project requires a mix of skills, we'd devolve back into silos of generalists. You can't specialize if you can't team!"

"Exactly," I said. "In my experience, teamwork has been the gating factor in most everything."

Poor cross-functional coordination and communications
is the principal element in the delay of everything.

— Tom Peters *49 Ref*

Definition: High-performance Teamwork

"When some executives want to improve teamwork," I continued, "they think of business process engineering. It that how you approached it?"

"Some of our work," Nate replied, "is like an assembly line where we optimize the efficiency of a stable, structured process. That's where business process reengineering is applicable.

"But in most of the company, our world is dynamic and each project is unique. We need to be able to quickly reconfigure our talent to handle any challenge that's thrown at us.

"And we need to do that laterally, not by working our way up and back down the hierarchy (which would be too slow)."

I nodded, appreciating the challenge.

Organizations must rapidly reconfigure themselves
to execute a set of ever-changing strategies.

Nate clarified the goal: "What we mean by high-performance teamwork is to form each project team...

> with just the <u>right specialists</u> (from anywhere in the organization)...

>> at just the <u>right time</u> (as contributions are needed, not fixed teams for the whole project)...

>>> with a common purpose, but also with <u>clear individual accountabilities</u>...

>>>> and a <u>clear chain of command</u> within each team (with one group accountable for the entire project, who leads and coordinates the team)."

"The Holy Grail!" I exclaimed.

Focus on the Team-Formation Process

"So, Nate, what I want to know is, how'd you get that kind of teamwork going? Did you work on interpersonal relationships and team-building?"

"We addressed that in our culture, which I'll come to later. But that was just fine tuning, not the real catalyst to cross-boundary teamwork.

"What we focused on," Nate explained, "is how we bring different groups together to collaborate on projects and services — the way we form teams and define processes that cut across the organization chart."

I was intrigued. I'd spent years trying to get people to team across boundaries, with only limited successes. Traditional team-building never seemed to do much good. Maybe poor interpersonal relationships and lack of trust weren't the real root causes of poor teamwork.

"Okay, Nate," I said, "on to the punch line. How'd you do it?"

Walk-throughs

"The answer is," Nate inserted a pause for effect, then said, "*walk-throughs*. They're just as precise as business process engineering, but a lot more flexible. Whenever a project comes in, the first thing we do is a walk-through."

"Okay, what's a walk-through?" I asked.

Nate explained their team-formation process: "The leaders of groups that might be involved in a project get together and talk until we have a shared understanding of exactly what product or service the customer wants to buy. That tells us who the 'prime contractor' is — the one group that's in the business of selling that. (There's only one thanks to clear domains.)

"That prime contractor is 100 percent accountable for delivery of the project. If that prime needs help, they 'subcontract' to other groups — for products and services, not people. That makes subcontractors accountable for sub-results, like components or support services. And subs may have subs, etc.

"It's just like in the real world," Nate said, "where a general contractor who's building a house subcontracts to an electrician, a plumber, etc."

Interpersonal exchange of goods and services
weaves the bond which unites men into society.

— Ludwig von Mises [50 Ref]

"So, what exactly comes out of a walk-through?" I asked.

"Walk-throughs lay out a tree-structured project team, tailored to the needs of each unique project. They tell us who's accountable for the whole project, who's on the team, and exactly what every team member (each participating group, to be exact) is accountable for producing.

"I think it's what General Stanley McChrystal would call a 'team of teams.' [51 More] We'd call it a team of groups."

Walk-throughs define
who's accountable for the whole project,
who's on the team, and
exactly what every team member
is accountable for producing.

"It's kind of like a skunk-works," Nate continued, "in that it's a small, interdisciplinary team dedicated to a mission. But it's not a separate group. It cuts across the org chart. And members of the team could be working on deliverables for multiples projects simultaneously.

"Walk-throughs allow us to flexibly combine specialists from anywhere in the organization onto teams for each unique project or service," Nate concluded. "They're the key to our organization's agility, without any loss of accountability or clarity in our processes."

Example of a Walk-through

"Can you give me an example of a walk-through?" I requested.

"Sure," Nate said. "A really complex, but interesting, one is launching a new service. How about a high-level fly-by of that?"

"Okay. We don't need to go into all the details," I said.

"I'll simplify it, just to give you a sense of what a walk-through looks like (Figure 10). But the real thing took up three pages."

Figure 10: Snapshot of a Walk-through: A New Service

Product Manager buys market research from Marketing to help define the requirements for the new service.

Product Manager buys a solution (which will produce the service) from Applications Engineering.

> Applications Engineering buys project facilitation from the Project Management Office.

> Applications Engineering buys subcomponents from Base Engineering.

> Applications Engineering buys installation into production from Operations to prepare the infrastructure to receive the solution.

>> Operations buys manufacturing engineering to augment or configure its infrastructure for the new service.

Product Manager buys infrastructure services (manufacturing and logistics) from Operations.

Product Manager buys customer support from Customer Service.

> Customer Service buys domain-specific support from Applications Engineering.

Product Manager buys pricing analysis, advertising, promotions, etc., from Marketing.

Product Manager buys the selling service from Sales.

Facilitation of Walk-throughs

"Do you really take the time to do walk-throughs for every project?"

"Absolutely!" Nate said. "Every project, and every new service, starts with a walk-through. And if the nature of a project changes, we revisit the walk-through.

"We've learned our lesson," Nate asserted. "If we skip the walk-through and dive right in, problems inevitably arise, and we have to take a step back and do a walk-through. Now, we *always* start with a walk-through. It's just the way we work."

"Does the project-management office (PMO) facilitate walk-throughs?"

"No." Nate replied. "My Organizational Effectiveness group does. We're the experts on how our structure is supposed to work.

"Walk-throughs come before project planning," he said. "Once they're done, the PMO translates walk-throughs into detailed project plans."

Both Stable and Dynamic: The Role of Hierarchy in Teamwork

"I hear some people pushing back on hierarchical organizations as rigid and slow," I said. "Maybe you have the answer here."

"I think we do," Nate concurred. "Hierarchical organization charts and walk-throughs go hand in hand. Hierarchy makes sure we have all the right specialists available (with no gaps, and no overlaps).

"But we don't form teams that way. We work laterally (not up and down the org chart) in walk-throughs."

Hierarchy makes sure we have all the right specialists available as needed. Walk-throughs assemble specialists from across the hierarchy onto teams.

"We have an organization that's both stable and dynamic," Nate said proudly. "It's stable in that everybody has a home where they can cultivate their specialized competencies. And we're dynamic in that we can flexibly combine our specialists on teams as needs warrant."

"That's impressive," I said sincerely.

We're both stable and dynamic...
stable in that everybody has a home
where they can cultivate their specialized competencies;
and dynamic in that we flexibly combine our specialists
on teams as needs warrant.

I reflected on past experiences: executives under me struggling with teamwork, pointing fingers at one another, causing delays when one asks another for help at the last minute, wasting time meddling in others' domains without the necessary expertise....

And as Nate said, when teamwork breaks down, organizations inevitably fracture into independent silos that reduce the degree of specialization, and hence performance.

Walk-throughs at the start of every project seemed like something I could use in my company.

The open networked organization ... is a
modular organizational architecture in which business teams operate
as a network of ... client and server functions.

— Don Tapscott and Art Caston [52 *Ref*]

NAVIGATION AID: The restructuring process described in Chapter 27 includes implementing the practice of walk-throughs.

Chapter 9:
Resource Governance: Internal Market Economics

Chapter summary (key take-aways): page 471

NAVIGATION AID: If your company or department isn't big enough to assign budgets to managers at the level below you, please skip to Chapter 12.

After our discussion of walk-throughs, Nate noted, "Of course, cross-boundary teamwork depends on resource-governance processes, too."

"How so?" I asked.

"Well, if I need your help on a project, and my highest priority is your lowest priority, teamwork isn't going to happen."

"Ah, true."

Market Economics Within a Company

Nate continued, "Aligning everybody's priorities is the job of the resource-governance processes that manage our time, money, and assets — what the organizational coach calls our 'internal economy.'" [53 Ref]

"Why does he call it an internal economy?" I asked.

"Each of us is a business within a business, right?" Nate asked rhetorically. "Our customers are our markets, both external and internal. We learned to *apply market economics internally.*"

---

*Economics is the study of how [we choose] to employ
scarce productive resources that could have alternative uses,
to produce various commodities and distribute them
for consumption... among various people and groups.*

— Paul A. Samuelson [54 Ref]

"Free and open competition!?" I asked incredulously.

"No, we're not talking about a *free* market where anybody can compete with anybody. Our structure defines everybody's domains.

"And we're not talking about a profit motive; our internal businesses are all not-for-profit. Oh, they create profits for the firm; but those profits appear at the corporate level."

"So, what does internal market economics mean?" I asked.

"The concept is actually simple," Nate explained. "When you go to the store, you're the customer. You decide what you buy, not the store. Of course, you have to limit your purchases to what you can afford. Meanwhile, the store has to earn your business by offering a variety of great products at a fair price. That's the essence of market economics.

"We do the same thing here," he said. "Internal *suppliers* don't decide their own priorities based on some high-level strategic plan. Internal *customers* decide priorities for internal suppliers — i.e., what they choose to buy — based on their own strategies and objectives.

"Our internal entrepreneurs produce what their customers want to buy. And the job of every internal entrepreneur is to earn customers' business through relationships, performance, and value. That's market economics, in a nutshell."

Market economics is <u>the</u> most powerful mechanism
of social coordination known to mankind.

— Dr. Ed Lindblom, Professor Emeritus of
Economics and Political Science, Yale University

"Now, in the real world," Nate continued, "you have to pay the store. Internally, that would be chargebacks. But we've implemented internal market economics *without chargebacks.*"

Interesting.... As I thought about the concept, I wondered about its applicability. "Does this only work in for-profit businesses?" I asked.

"Market economics has nothing to do with what industry the company is in — private sector, non-profit, or government. It's just about the design of our budgeting and demand-management (prioritization) processes."

Objectives of Internal Market Economics

"Before we drill down," I said, "tell me what you were hoping to accomplish with these resource-governance processes."

"We had a number of goals," Nate replied. He listed a few:

- Budgets are driven by business needs and investment opportunities, not prior year's spending or micro-managing groups' costs. And internal customers defend budgets for the internal support services they consume.

- We all understand the work we can expect from internal support functions for a given level of funding. Customer expectations are within the bounds of available resources. Supply equals demand.

- Customers decide what they buy from suppliers. With internal customers in control of support groups' priorities, enterprise strategies ripple through the whole organization, and resources are focused on the investments with the highest value to the business.

- Priorities are adjusted throughout the year as strategies and business needs evolve.

- Managers are able to reinvest in their businesses — their sustainability. That includes things like planning, training, customer relationships, internal process improvements, and innovation.

- Funding is provided for infrastructure maintenance and new capacity, for innovation initiatives, and for corporate-good services like information security and policy facilitation (which no business unit is willing to pay for).

■ Internal suppliers' rates (unit costs) are benchmarked against vendors' prices, creating incentives for cost control.

■ Project cost-estimates include both direct and indirect costs of the prime contractor and all needed subcontracts and support services.

■ Cost accounting does not require allocations based on high-level formulas.

"All good goals," I said. "Now let's get into the details."

Three Subsystems

Nate named three components of an internal economy (Figure 11).

Figure 11: Three Components of an Internal Economy

- Budgeting: annual business plans, budgets, catalog, rates
- Demand management: project intake, estimation, priority setting
- Accounting: financial reporting, time tracking, invoicing

"The way we see it," Nate explained, "budgeting is where we fill up 'checkbooks' (i.e., create pots of money) based on what we know at that point in time, before the year even begins.

"Then, we 'write checks' — that is, set priorities — dynamically throughout the year. That's the demand-management component.

"And accounting is after-the-fact. It's how we track what happened in the past," Nate concluded.

"Okay," I said, "I'm ready to drill down into those three subsystems."

Chapter 10:
Investment-based Budgeting

Chapter summary (key take-aways): page 471

NAVIGATION AID: If your company or department isn't big enough to assign budgets to managers at the level below you, please skip to Chapter 12.

"Obviously, I don't need a primer on finance," I said. "Let's just focus on how market economics changed the way you manage money and priorities. Where shall we start?"

"How about we 'follow the money,'" Nate suggested. [55 Ref]

Revenues Without Chargebacks

"Money comes from the firm's revenues, I assume," I said.

"Yes, it starts there," Nate said. "Of course, those revenues don't just cover the costs of the groups that sold products and services to external customers. Those revenues have to fund *all* the groups throughout the organization.

"One way to make that happen is chargebacks, where the group that sells externally owns the revenues and pays other groups for their services.

"But chargebacks have a significant administrative cost. And they could send the wrong signals — like the group with the revenues might think it has the right to hire vendors or set up decentralized support groups instead of using shared services. We don't want that. If anyone is going to hire vendors, it's the internal supplier that's in that same line of business and knows how to select and manage those vendors. (More on managing vendors in Appendix 2.)

"So," Nate said, "we learned a way to get virtually all the benefits of chargebacks without actually moving money around."

What Is a Budget?

"So," I speculated, "if you don't do chargebacks, you must channel corporate revenues into budgets that pay groups' costs?"

"Not quite," Nate replied. "True, we channel revenues into everybody's budgets. But as entrepreneurs, we understand that nobody gives us money to pay our *costs*. You don't give the grocery store money to pay for rent, electricity, and checkout clerks!"

"That's obvious," I said. "It seems like you're setting me up for my next insight."

"Yep," Nate said. "Here it comes.... If a group's budget isn't to pay its costs, what is it?"

Nate answered his own question. "It's *prepaid revenues* — money put on deposit with a group at the beginning of the year to buy its products and services in the year ahead.

"I mentioned a moment ago that a budget is like a checkbook. The way we see it, that checkbook belongs to your internal customers. Of course, when an customer writes a check to buy something, those revenues cover your costs."

Budgets are <u>prepaid revenues</u> — money
put on deposit with a group at the beginning of the year
to buy its products and services in the year ahead.

"Woah," I said. "I'm so accustomed to thinking about budgets as the way we cover costs. This is a mind twist!"

"It was for us, too," Nate admitted.

"I'm sure this perspective has profound implications," I said.

Investment-based Budgeting

"It absolutely does," Nate said. "For one, budgets are based on what we want to buy from an internal supplier, not what that group wants to spend. When you think about it, would you give any group a budget because they have costs, and expect nothing back? Would you increase a group's budget and expect nothing more?"

"No, no, I get it," I said. "It's totally logical. So, how do you link a department's budget to what you want to buy from it?"

"As a start," Nate replied, "our budgets look quite different....

"Imagine a spreadsheet where the rows represent the products and services a group proposes to deliver in the year ahead, and the columns are our general-ledger expense and capital accounts (Figure 12)."

Figure 12: Investment-based Budgeting

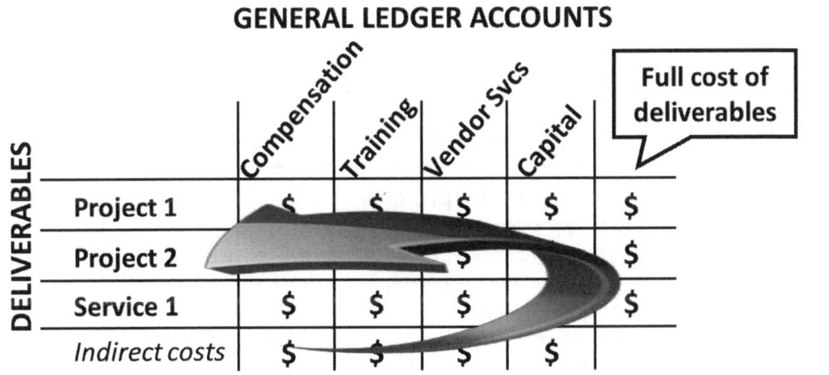

"That's pretty normal," I observed.

"Yes. But what's different here is that we total the rows (the costs of projects and services) as well as the columns. The organizational coach calls it *investment-based budgeting.*"

Nate explained, "We have a 'full cost' model that assigns *all* our costs
— including indirect costs like training, process improvements, even
Carlton and me — to our products and services (just like vendors'
pricing covers their overhead). We never want to ask for funding for
things people don't buy, like a grocery store trying to charge you for its
manager's salary." *56 More*

"And this isn't chargebacks?"

"No, we don't actually move money around. We calculate our rates as
if we did; but then we reflect that in each group's budget."

"Okay, so budgets estimate the costs of proposed products and services.
That's a lot of data," I scowled.

"True," Nate admitted. "But we sort all the rows into 'buckets' like:
keep-the-lights-on services, maintenance of our current assets, catching
up on deferred maintenance, investments necessary for growth, safety
and security, strategic projects, innovation projects, etc. (Figure 13).

Figure 13: "Buckets" of Deliverables in a Budget

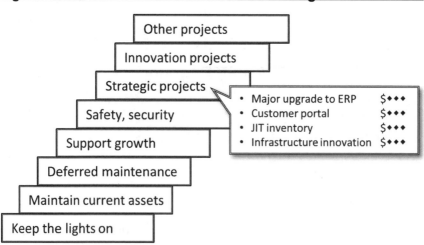

"In each of those buckets, we can drill down to the costs of individual projects and services (or pools of hours for the unknown, like repairs and ongoing product enhancements [57 IT]). That's the level of granularity we need to make informed budget decisions.

"The CFO has a going-in number for each department," Nate continued, "so we see what that would pay for. Then, we take a look at the things which wouldn't be funded if departments are given that initial target, and see if the company is willing to spend more to get more."

"I'm picturing it," I said. "As the CEO, that means that I can decide budgets based on business needs, rather than the old 'last year plus or minus a percentage,' combined with the usual begging and haggling. It seems like a much more rational, data-driven budget process." [58 More]

"It *is*," Nate agreed. "And here's another benefit: Our budgeting process is an alignment mechanism. We fund the total cost of each deliverable, including all the groups in the walk-through. No function is going to be an obstacle to execution of enterprise strategies, because the prime and all the subs are funded to deliver their respective pieces of all the approved strategic initiatives."

"Wow! That's powerful," I said.

Funding for Innovation

"How do you fund innovation?" I asked.

"Well, we don't have a special 'Innovation' group that gets all the budget for innovation initiatives. There are so many reasons why that's a bad idea (Chapter 32). Here, everybody is accountable for innovation within their own line of business. And you're right, they need funding."

Nate described the two ways they fund innovation initiatives:

- "First, in our cost model, every service is priced with direct costs plus its fair share of indirect costs. Those indirect costs include a bit of funding for ongoing innovation. It's like overhead; innovation is just one of things we need to do to sustain our businesses, so it's built into our rates.

"That covers the ongoing types of innovation, like keeping our skills and products up-to-date.

■ "Second," Nate continued, "there are rows in the budget to fund major innovation initiatives. We think of these as loans from the bank (the corporate treasury), like venture capital to our entrepreneurs. In many cases, we assess depreciation, which is how groups pay back the bank.

"One example of an innovation initiative is a new product."

Annual Budgeting and Dynamic Priority Setting

"How can you know, so far in advance, all the rows that should go into the budget?" I asked.

"Really, we don't have to," Nate replied. "Planning is a guess about the future. We have good visibility of ongoing services, and projects that are already underway. And Sales tells us about some potential new projects for external and internal customers.

"Adding to that, everybody lists the projects they anticipate based on enterprise strategies. That includes our own strategic initiatives that each of us would like to propose.

"Beyond that, we just have to make our best guesses. But we don't have to be perfect.

"As I mentioned before," Nate explained, "we fill up checkbooks (budgets) based on the deliverables that we know of during the annual planning cycle. But then we have a monthly demand-management process for writing checks (Chapter 11). That allows us to adjust priorities dynamically throughout the year as things change."

We fill up checkbooks (budgets) based on the
investment opportunities known during the annual planning cycle.
Then we have a monthly governance process for writing checks.

No "Do More With Less"

"Investment-based budgeting sounds like a lot of work. How did folks react?" I asked.

"For our staff, investment-based budgeting was great," Nate said.

"Why is that?"

"Perhaps the biggest benefit to staff," Nate replied, "was that it brought expectations down to the reality of available resources.

"You get what you pay for. There's no fantastical 'do more with less' or 'take it out of hide' demands anymore — as if underfunding us is magically going to make us more productive! It's the opposite; when we're underfunded, we're *less* productive."

"Yes, I know," I sighed. "But I need some way to keep the pressure on leaders for cost efficiencies."

Pressure for Frugality

"Actually," Nate replied, "we look for cost-savings all the time, not just once a year in the budget process."

"That's great," I said. "But how do you get your managers to cut costs if you don't put some pressure on them through the budget?"

"Oh, there are plenty of reasons our leaders are frugal," Nate said.

"For one, we took away any incentive for empire building. For example, we replaced the old job-grading system that associated your title and pay with the size of your budget and headcount. That was dumb; it rewarded people for maximizing spending, not minimizing it.

"But the biggest reason they're frugal is that they benchmark their rates against equivalent vendor services." [59 More]

"What if your rates are higher than the market?" I asked.

"Our entrepreneurs know they have to stay competitive. If they can offer customers a better deal by buying instead of making, they propose that. This way, customers never have to look elsewhere. We're always the best deal in town!" (More on the use of vendors in Appendix 2.)

"But," Nate continued, "if our rates are above market, even after incorporating vendors into our delivery processes, that's a performance problem we'd have to deal with."

I could see how this approach to cost control would be so much more effective than nit-picking budgets and micro-managing leaders once a year.

Cost Cutting

"While we're on the topic of cost control, I've got another question," I said. "As a CEO, I know all too well that we can't forecast everything. Sometimes things turn against us, and we have to do some belt-tightening in the middle of the year. How would you handle that?"

"That actually happened," Nate said, "the year after we implemented investment-based budgeting.

"What we used to do was an across-the-board spending cut. That made all our managers independently decide what not to do, and things failed randomly. Teams fell apart when subcontractors de-prioritized the primes' top priorities. Critical indirect costs like maintenance, training, and process improvements stopped when people tried to continue to deliver more than the company could afford. That negatively impacted everything, even the strategic initiatives. Not good!

"With our internal economy," Nate continued, "what actually happened was the decision-makers had to decide what they were going to *not buy*. Each group pointed out candidates that they thought were low value; but the decision was left to that group's customers.

"Then, when a deliverable was cut, the prime and all subcontractors were able to reduce spending surgically. They knew exactly where they would not need as many resources. So, they were able to cut back without undermining the high-priority projects and services that still had to get done." *60 Ref*

"What about fixed costs?"

"Well, as finance professors say, nothing's fixed in the long term," Nate quipped. "It may take some time to adjust or eliminate indirect costs. In the short term, we had to cut a little deeper on the deliverables to account for that.

"But the key is, we cut demand before cutting supply. That way, we kept expectations in synch with budgets, and the important things fully funded."

"I love it," I said. I'd seen all too often how across-the-board cuts cripple entire companies. But until now, I hadn't seen an alternative.

Rates (With or Without Chargebacks)

Switching to a more optimistic topic, I asked, "How do you estimate the costs of new projects that come up between budget cycles?"

"As I mentioned," Nate replied, "investment-based budgeting produces a cost model that assigns all indirect costs to the appropriate projects and services. That same cost model produces unit-costs, that is, our cost-based rates. There's no need for a separate rate analysis.

"So, when something new comes along, after a walk-through, the prime and subcontractors figure out what's involved and the level of effort. Then, they apply the rates established in the budget process to cost out the project.

"Those rates are useful for other things, too," Nate continued. "They help groups explain why they're costing more, year over year. A group's total budget may be going up due to business growth and new services; but its rates should prove that it's still competitive.

"And remember, another really valuable use of rates is for cost bench-marking." *61 More*

"How often do you update everybody's rates?" I asked.

"Annually. We want a stable environment for decision making through the year. Of course, that means that fluctuations in volumes can create budget variances (which we'd see as a small profit or loss). But those are easily explainable.

"By the way," Nate added, "we take those year-end profits and losses up to the corporate level. We don't try to credit them back to internal customers (like a farmers' cooperative). That would make customers liable for internal supplier's bottom lines, which always creates lots of politics when uncontrollable costs hit customers' budgets."

"So," I summarized, "you do an annual operating plan, and that (rather than past years' spending) is the basis for your investment-based budget and your rates."

"Exactly."

NAVIGATION AID: Chapter 28 describes the internal economy implementation process.

Chapter 11:
Demand Management (Priority Setting)

Chapter summary (key take-aways): page 472

NAVIGATION AID: If your company or department isn't big enough to assign budgets to managers at the level below you, please skip to Chapter 12.

"Nate, you said you fill up checkbooks once a year in the annual planning cycle. But then you have a dynamic governance process for writing checks throughout the year."

"That's right. We adjust priorities monthly as strategies and business needs change. That's our project-intake and demand-management process."

"I want to know how that works," I said. "But let's start with the problems you were trying to solve with this organizational system."

Over-promised, Under-delivered

"Okay," Nate said. "You know, after budgets are set and the new fiscal year begins, things happen. New business needs and opportunities are identified, and strategies change. So, groups are always getting new requests for services.

"In the past, people really wanted to serve the business, so they said yes to everything. They routinely over-promised and under-delivered. That wasn't good for their reputations.

"And it wasn't good for their internal customers, either," Nate continued. "Those customers had businesses to run, and they depended on internal suppliers to deliver the stuff they needed."

"I've seen this sort of problem everywhere I've been," I said. "So, how did you resolve it?"

"Well, the problem was, we had no demand-management process. Let's use IT as an example. In those days, we had a steering committee that prioritized major projects. But they didn't know how much they could spend — how much was in their checkbook — or what things would cost. So, they didn't know where the line would be drawn. They expected it all, in that order!

"And for all the little requests that didn't go through the steering committee, IT had no basis for telling internal customers that they couldn't afford what they were asking for. They were buried under an unending pile of low-payoff requests.

"Basically — and this was true in every internal support function, not just IT — they had no way to say 'no.' No matter how hard staff worked, they were accused of unresponsiveness, of hiding money, of being the obstacle... all kinds of crazy things."

I smiled, having mediated many heated conversations between my business leaders and corporate staff.

Nate summarized the challenge: "We have to respond dynamically to an ever-changing business, while limiting demand to available resources (or else come up with more resources for additional work)."

Using Structure to Solve Internal Economy Problems

"Years ago," Nate continued, "IT tried to solve this by assigning a group of developers to each of our three business units. Essentially, they gave each business unit a checkbook in the form of a dedicated group of people. That worked... at least for the applications groups.

"But it didn't solve the supply-demand problem for the rest of IT. So, other groups (the subcontractors) became the bottlenecks on projects.

"Meanwhile, it was bad structure. Just like decentralization, those silos of developers created redundant systems and fragmented our data. For example, we ended up with three different customer databases!

"And, their specialization in types of applications was reduced. For example, three different groups had to know financial data management. So, they couldn't specialize in sub-disciplines like receivables and tax.

"Now," Nate said, "we've come to understand that IT was trying to solve an internal-economy problem by messing up its structure. That solved one problem, and inadvertently created many others."

"Interesting diagnosis," I said. "So, what's your alternative?"

Market-based Governance

"Okay, think about market economics," Nate said. "You don't need to own your own grocery store to control what you eat. You're the customer. You own the checkbook. You decide what you'll buy."

"Right." I nodded.

"That's market economics. We do the same here." He talked me through a diagram of how money flows (Figure 14).

Figure 14: How Money Flows in Internal Market Economics

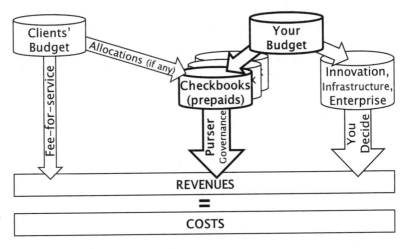

"Each department's budget is that checkbook. The department holds the money in escrow, but the checkbook belongs to its internal customers.

"We established a governance process where internal customers decide what checks to write — not just for major projects, but for all the on-going services and little projects that are essential to business operations. We drafted business-unit leaders onto 'purser' committees which own and manage those checkbooks."

Purser committees representing internal customers decide priorities for all projects/services within a support function's budget.

"Isn't that the steering committee that sets priorities?" I asked.

"It's way beyond that," Nate replied. "They don't just rank-order major projects. They manage the *whole* checkbook. They decide which projects and services to fund. They can turn off low-payoff services in order to fund new, high-payoff projects. It's their checkbook."

"Is that what's meant by project portfolio management (PPM)?" I asked.

"No, it's quite different. In this process, leaders decide priorities among all the possible projects and services they could fund. Once they do, PPM plans each approved project and assigns resources to the portfolio of projects. So, it's more like *investment portfolio management* where they're aligning investments with strategies and operational needs to maximize the return on the whole checkbook.

"Empowering customers to decide suppliers' priorities is really power-ful," Nate continued. "This is what keeps everybody aligned with ever-changing strategies and business needs.

"So," Nate summarized, "by treating budgets as prepaid revenues — and giving internal customers control of that checkbook — we've implement-ed market economics inside the company without chargebacks."

Managing Expectations

"How does this bring expectations in line with resources?" I asked.

"Customers have to live within their means," Nate replied. "They can't write checks if there's nothing left in their checkbooks. In other words, customers can't expect more than they can afford, which equals the internal supplier's resources. Voila! Supply and demand are in balance — what some folks call 'managing expectations.'

"From staff's perspective, this made a huge difference," he said. "We no longer struggle to satisfy unmitigated demand by routinely working ridiculous hours, robbing Peter to pay Paul and coming in late on everything, cutting corners on quality and getting blamed for lousy work, sacrificing our own training and process improvements, etc."

Project Approval (Intake) Process

"Let's say somebody wants something, a project of some sort," I probed. "How do they get it approved?"

"They're not going to get it by just demanding that they need it, and claiming that it's the supplier's job to come up with the resources," Nate joked. "Customers have to pay for what they get. This is business, and everything we deliver has a cost.

"One way they can pay for what they want is to go to that purser and convince them to write a check — that is, make their project a priority within the existing budget, and de-prioritize something else.

"Of course, they have to make their business cases. Customers are responsible for justifying their projects, not suppliers. Which is how it should be. They know the payoff to their businesses the best; and they're the ones who benefit from the investment, not the suppliers."

"What if the purser turns down their request?" I asked. "Is the idea dead?"

"Not necessarily. Another way customers can pay for what they want is to transfer money out of their budgets. (This is where chargebacks occasionally come into play.) Internal suppliers are happy to take the additional money and expand their capacity by bringing in contractors or vendors." [62 More]

If you've got the money, honey, I've got the time.
— Song by James A. Beck and Lefty Frizzell
Originally performed by Lefty Frizzell

"Note that those pursers just manage specific checkbooks," Nate said. "They don't have the power to control other sales. If you don't need their money, you don't have to go through them to spend your own budget on an internal supplier.

"By the way," he added, "those internal customers who pay their own way have to spend less on other things (because they, too, have to break even). So, total enterprise spending is still controlled, just like with traditional variance tracking."

"Hmm, I think I see," I said. "I'm still in control of the budgets given to everybody. So, I can control corporate margins. As long as total spending stays within everybody's revenues and everybody is aligned with our strategies, I shouldn't have to worry about people spending on this versus that, nor should my CFO."

"Of course," Nate noted, "you have the option to supply incremental funding mid-year. That happens when we cook up new strategies during the year that require big new initiatives, or when crises force us to incur additional costs."

Layout of Checkbooks

"Those purser committees," I reflected. "How can executives have time to make all those detailed purchase decisions? Those are senior executives, right?"

"Yes. But the top-level purser just decides the major enterprise initiatives (strategic initiatives and corporate-good services [63 More]), and major departmental infrastructure and innovation investments.

"The rest of their checkbook goes into sub-checbooks which are assigned to lower-level pursers. These include some cross-business-unit committees (like our ERP steering committee), and each of the departments (to pay for what they buy from one another)." (Figure 15 is an overview of checkbooks and pursers.)

"So, how do you decide how much goes into each checkbook?"

"Easy," Nate answered. "We look at the approved budget. We know what those rows cost, and who the customer is. So, we know how much money in total was approved in the budget for each customer (business unit), and that's how much flows into each of their checkbooks.

"Of course, senior executives can move money from checkbook to checkbook at any time, if they want to focus on different strategies."

Sorting Out Committees

"I take it you have lots of committees," I said.

"True," Nate replied. "For each checkbook, we designated a purser committee.

"But I'll tell you, it used to be worse," Nate mused. "We used to have lots and lots of committees. Every committee thought it could set priorities for internal suppliers. And they expected their priority projects to be delivered."

Figure 15: Flow of Budget Through Checkbooks

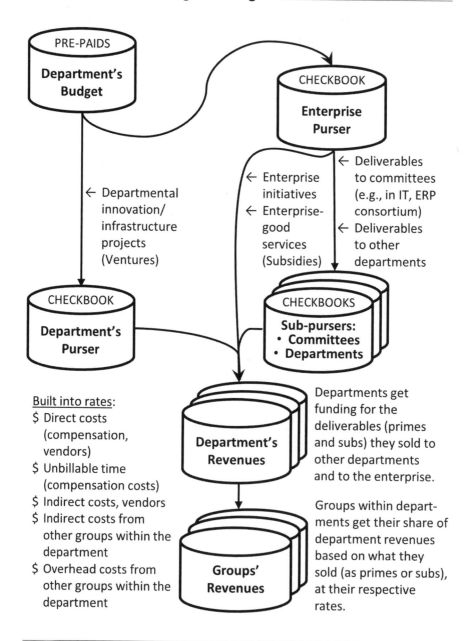

PRE-PAIDS

Department's Budget

CHECKBOOK

Enterprise Purser

← Departmental innovation/ infrastructure projects (Ventures)

← Enterprise initiatives

← Enterprise-good services (Subsidies)

← Deliverables to committees (e.g., in IT, ERP consortium)

← Deliverables to other departments

CHECKBOOK

Department's Purser

CHECKBOOKS

Sub-pursers:
• **Committees**
• **Departments**

Built into rates:
$ Direct costs (compensation, vendors)
$ Unbillable time (compensation costs)
$ Indirect costs, vendors
$ Indirect costs from other groups within the department
$ Overhead costs from other groups within the department

Department's Revenues

Groups' Revenues

Departments get funding for the deliverables (primes and subs) they sold to other departments and to the enterprise.

Groups within departments get their share of department revenues based on what they sold (as primes or subs), at their respective rates.

"The problem was," Nate continued, "they didn't have checkbooks; so they had no way to know whether or not resources were available to satisfy their demands. There was lots of angst when all those committees' top priorities added up to way more than internal suppliers could deliver!

"In reality, those committees could say 'no' and kill a project proposal. But they couldn't say 'yes' because they couldn't pay for anything.

"When we implemented demand management, we gave checkbooks to some of those committees. The rest were informed that, to fund their projects, they'd need to get the approval of one of those selected purser committees, or provide incremental funding from their own budgets.

"So," Nate concluded, "the internal economy actually simplified our committee structure."

Timing of Spending

"What's to stop a purser committee from spending all its checkbook in the first quarter, which would far exceed available staff?" I asked.

"We feed their checkbooks one month at a time," Nate replied. "And the pursers meet monthly to write checks.

"Of course, much of their checkbooks is consumed by ongoing 'keep the lights on' services, and by projects approved in prior months that haven't finished yet (encumbrances). So basically, the pursers are only prioritizing resources that are becoming available in the coming month."

Spending Controls

"Let's talk about controls on spending," I said. "Do you hold managers accountable for budget variances?"

"No, not traditional budget variances (actual spending versus budget)," Nate replied. "We manage by P&Ls (profit-and-loss statements). Our entrepreneurs have to break even; they can't overspend their revenues. Doing that would put them in the hole. So, since revenues are finite, spending is controlled."

I raised a skeptical eyebrow. "Doesn't that amount to the same thing as budget variance tracking?" I asked.

"There's one important difference," Nate said. "Your budget is your planned revenues, so that's your baseline spending limit. But if internal customers want to transfer money to you from their own budgets to buy more from you, or if you get incremental mid-year funding, then you'd spend more — which would appear as a negative variance. But you have the additional revenues to cover it, so you're still at break-even."

"I can see how tracking P&Ls instead of spending-variances supports your entrepreneurial spirit by allowing people to take on additional business," I said.

"And remember," Nate added, "we expect everybody's rates to be competitive; that's one of their performance metrics. So, that's how we control for waste."

Cost of Capital

"Another concern," I said, "one that could lead me to want to control things from the top, is the cost of capital. How do you handle that?"

Nate replied, "We didn't want to set up a battle, where our leaders want to use capital without regard for its cost, and then the CFO or CEO have to step in and control them. We wanted a financial ecosystem where *everybody* is conscious of the cost of capital and uses it wisely."

"Great goal. How did you do it?"

"We have a number of ways," Nate said. "First, on top of depreciation, everybody is assessed an interest charge for capital employed. That cost is baked into their rates. So, they're careful about running up their interest charges because they're accountable for competitive rates.

"Second," Nate continued, "in the budget process, everybody has to defend their requests for funding for their internal investments. That ensures that everybody is thinking through why they need the capital, and what value it'll produce, before going to the bank with a request."

"Just like controls in the real world," I noted.

Contracting

"In addition to balancing supply and demand, and aligning everybody's priorities," Nate added, "there was another important thing that came out of implementing internal market economics."

"What's that?" I asked politely.

"Contracting," Nate said. "Once a project or service is funded by a purser, we have an internal contract. Some companies call it a 'memorandum of understanding' (MOU), or a 'service-level agreement' (SLA). But it's not a general template of service levels or terms of engagement. It's a firm commitment to deliver a specific thing to a specific customer. That's why we call it a contract."

"Isn't that a bit bureaucratic?" I challenged.

"If 'bureaucratic' means administrative work with little added value, then no," Nate replied. "Contracts add a lot of value....

"They specify the customer's and the supplier's respective accountabilities, which ensures that both parties are on the same page *before* we start work, not mid-way through projects when confusions arise.

"They help everybody track their commitments. Of course, we take accountabilities seriously; failing to deliver on a contract has consequences. So, contracts are a big part of performance management.

"And they don't take a lot of time," Nate continued. "Contracts aren't legalistic. Obviously, we're not going to sue each other! They just include the minimum information needed to document internal commitments. *64 More*

"Contracting really improved our reliable delivery and mutual trust," Nate said. "Customers are clear about what's funded and will get done, and what's not funded and won't get done. And suppliers are clear about their commitments."

"Do you track all those contracts?" I asked.

"We do," Nate said. "We set up a very simple contracts database. So, every purser knows what it's bought; and every group knows what it's committed to deliver to its customers, as well as what its internal suppliers will deliver to it."

Impacts on the CFO

"So tell me, how did your CFO react to all this?" I asked.

"Honestly," Nate said, "there was resistance at first. She used to be able to cut our budgets and not worry about the implications for the business. She took credit for saving money, and the rest of us took the blame for not delivering all that was expected of us.

"Now, she has to accept responsibility for the business impacts of budget cuts. So, Finance works with business leaders to decide what deliverables (not costs) to cut. The business can say, 'Yes, we can do without that,' or 'No, you can't cut that; we need it.'

"Now that she's used to it," Nate said, "I think our CFO actually appreciates her ability to manage costs more effectively. She challenges specific project requests, instead of arbitrarily cutting internal suppliers' budgets. And in helping us sort out what's really needed and what's not, she's playing a much more strategic role than a traditional cost controller."

The End of Cost Allocations

"Our internal economy impacted Finance in another positive way," Nate added.

"Tell me," I said.

"Internal service providers used to have to allocate their costs out to business units to help Finance with cost accounting. They did allocations based on high-level formulas, only loosely connected with actual consumption. It wasn't very accurate, to say the least!

"And it caused a lot of political craziness. The business units viewed these allocations as 'taxation without representation'! They hated being hit with costs they couldn't control.

"So, naturally they tried to control their internal suppliers, and get them to cut spending on critical things that suppliers needed but that weren't of direct value to customers — things like training, infrastructure investments, relationship management.... They even challenged some of their internal suppliers' hiring decisions!

"Those allocations led to all kinds of political back-and-forth, none of which was constructive. It was the wrong dialog to have with one's customers and suppliers. We wanted people to focus on making smart purchase decisions, not picking apart other departments' costs.

"Now," Nate concluded, "we don't need allocations to know how much each business unit consumed. We know the full costs of the deliverables they get. So, we saved a lot of administrative work and political stress by eliminating cost allocations. And, the numbers are much more accurate."

Profits

"I want to go back to something Carlton said.... Everybody is a product manager. But you said that everybody is a not-for-profit business within a business."

"That's right. All our managers are tasked with a break-even P&L," Nate replied.

Everybody is a not-for-profit business within a business.

"What about those who sell to external customers?" I asked.

"The way we see it, all external revenues belong to the company (not the one group that made the external sale). That money gets distributed to all the groups that contributed to that sale (those in the walk-through), including the prime contractor who made the external sale.

"Everybody's rates recover their direct costs, and a portion of their departmental indirect costs (including support services they buy from other groups) as well as overhead (the indirect costs that support the whole department). (See Figure 16.) These are fully burdened cost-based rates. So, everybody breaks even."

"So," I summarized, "revenues belong to the firm. Groups get paid at cost. And what's left is profits at the enterprise level."

"Yes, exactly," Nate confirmed. "This way, there's no incentive to ignore internal customers (at break-even rates) while focusing on profit-making external customers. That would be disastrous!

"And also," Nate continued, "this allows Carlton to invest profits where they're needed the most, which may or may not be in the group that generated the profits — like taking from our cash-cows and investing in growth businesses. That's an enterprise decision; it's not up to the individual business units who happen to sell outside."

"Yes, as CEO, I need that ability," I agreed. "But that leads to another question: If everybody is measured on breaking even, what's to motivate people to maximize profits on external sales?"

"The basic metrics are the same for everybody, whether they sell outside or not. But there's one additional performance metric for those who do sell outside: profit targets. It's just one among many. So, we calculate profits as a metric, even though they don't get to keep the money."

"Let's talk more about metrics at some point (Chapter 13)," I said.

Figure 16: Group P&L Accounting

REVENUES	EXPENSES
• Fully burdened costs of deliverables (based on rates)	• Direct costs (labor, vendors) ⎫ • Group-level indirect costs (vendors) ⎬ Traditional budget for planned spending • Indirect costs of other groups' support services • Departmental overhead

PROFIT/LOSS
(target: break-even)

NAVIGATION AID: Chapter 28 describes the internal economy implementation process.

Chapter 12:
Culture

Chapter summary (key take-aways): page 474

It was only mid-morning, and we'd already covered a lot of ground. I said, "A science of structure. Market economics inside a company. Good stuff! But phew, that's a lot to absorb in just a few minutes."

"Then you'll be pleased to hear that our next topic is an easy one: culture," Nate said.

"Culture? Easy? You're joking!"

"No, actually culture isn't all that difficult to change, if you know how."

"Okay, Nate, tell me how," I said skeptically.

Problems Addressed by Culture

Again, we began by discussing their goals, this time for culture change.

"We had two kinds of problems," Nate said, "dysfunctional behaviors, and missing behaviors."

"Dysfunctional behaviors?" I queried.

"Yes," Nate said, "there were many — from some people more than others. But until we defined what's appropriate and what's not, we couldn't effectively manage repeat offenders.

"Meetings are a simple example," he said. "We wasted so much time. But now, our meetings are so much more productive thanks to the practices we've adopted in our culture. *65 Ref*

"Customer focus was another big one. Some staff treated internal customers as either a nuisance, or a risk to be controlled. Or, they went to the other extreme and were passive order takers. Now, we understand what customer focus really means.

"In addition," Nate continued, "we had some problems with interpersonal relations, like handling disagreements. And we had integrity problems, like making promises we couldn't keep."

"I see. Okay, what do you mean by missing behaviors?" I asked.

"We had lots of those, too. There were many things people should have been doing and weren't. But if they didn't know they were supposed to, how could we expect it?"

"Give me an example," I requested.

"A really good example is making commitments for others," Nate said. "We had lots of problems with prime contractors making delivery-date commitments before talking to the subcontractors who would be on their teams. No surprise that we were late on everything.

"So," he said, "the missing behavior was, 'Line up commitments from your subcontractors before you make a promise to your customer.'"

I nodded. "Give me a couple more examples...."

"We weren't entrepreneurial," Nate said, "so we weren't thinking about all the things it takes to run a small business.

"Risk was another. Most of us totally shied away from risks, even when the rewards were high and the odds good."

I'd seen all these problems in past companies. But I'd never seen them effectively fixed through culture initiatives.

...culture constrains strategy...

— Edgar Schein [66 Ref]

Definition of Culture

"Before we go any further," I said, "I'd better ask, what do you mean by the word 'culture'?"

"Excellent question!" Nate replied. "We say that culture is *the way we work around here.* It applies to everybody, and permeates everything we do. In other words, it's not specific to any one function. It's really about how we *all* behave."

"I thought culture was a set of shared values," I postulated.

"Actually, it's both values and behaviors," Nate replied. "On one hand, you have the values, beliefs, attitudes, and feelings inside people. On the other hand, you have habits, rituals, practices, and behaviors."

Figure 17: Culture Cycle: Value and Behaviors

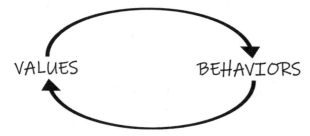

"It's a cycle," Nate continued. "Clearly, values drive behaviors. But the converse is true as well — behaviors drive values. *67 More*

"For example, you could tell people, 'We trust one another.' That's a feeling.

"But you could also say, 'We never make a commitment we can't keep, and we keep every commitment.' That's a behavior. And when we start behaving that way, feelings of trust develop."

"Clearly you can't force people to trust one another," I said. "Give me a better example...."

"Okay," Nate continued. "How about teamwork? We could say, 'We value teamwork.' Are we going to get better at teaming as a result of that shared value? Not likely!

"The alternative is to say, 'We never replicate other groups' skills;' and 'We start every project or new service with a walk-through.' Those are specific behaviors that lead to teamwork.

"Here's another one," Nate added. "'We are customer focused' is an attitude. But does that mean we do anything a customer says? Or the other extreme, do we do what *we* think is best for the customer? In our culture, we say, 'We offer customers alternatives and share all we know about each; and then we respect their choice.' That's a behavior.

"Again, once we started behaving that way, and when people around us responded positively, we learned to feel customer focused."

I nodded. "Okay, I see the cycle, how each drives the other."

Can't we learn to feel what's right and what's wrong?

— From song "A Farewell to Kings" lyrics by Neil Peart
Originally performed by Rush

Behavioral Approach

"The question was," Nate continued, "which side of the cycle should we use to define and change our culture?"

Nate answered his own question. "I've seen a lot of the literature on culture, and most of it points to defining values. But those are the same people who say it takes a generation to change culture. The truth is, the values approach doesn't work all that well."

"Interesting," I said.

"The organizational coach pointed out that so much of learning theory is behavioral," Nate continued. "You know the saying, 'Don't criticize the child; criticize the behavior.'"

"Of course," I said. "I'm a parent."

"Well, look at addiction therapy, cognitive behavioral therapy, and so on.... Many successful approaches to change are based on behaviors.
68 More

"With behaviors, you can teach them; you can model them; and you can measure them. So," Nate concluded, "we decided to move the culture-cycle through behaviors."

What Nate was telling me made a lot of sense. "I see your point. As a boss, I don't really have the right to dictate how people feel, or what they value. But I have every right to say, 'If you want to succeed around here, this is what you have to *do*!'"

We are what we repeatedly do.

— Aristotle

---

13 Themes

"So, how did you define the behaviors?" I asked.

"Basically," Nate replied, "what we did is translate the desired values — we call them 'Themes' — into specific principles of behavior. We worked on 13 Themes (Figure 18)."

"Under each Theme," Nate explained, "we crafted a page or two of behavioral principles along the lines of, 'We do this.' Take a look at some examples, just to illustrate this behavioral approach...."

Figure 18: Culture Themes

- Ethics: knowing right from wrong
- Integrity: earning trust
- Interpersonal Relations: working well with other people
- Meetings: effective scheduled business events
- Cooperation: working as one organization
- Teamwork: collaborating on projects/services
- Empowerment: matching authorities and accountabilities
- Customer Focus: building healthy relationships with customers
- Entrepreneurship: keeping your business-within-a-business competitive
- Contracts: making commitments that you can keep
- Quality: fulfilling commitments well
- Risk: taking appropriate risks
- Feedback: measuring and improving results

Showing me their booklet of cultural principles, Nate pointed out one or two behaviors under each of the Themes (Appendix 4).

"Then," Nate concluded, "we rolled out the behaviors organization-wide."

Results

"What would you say got out of your investment in culture?" I asked.

"Well, let's look down the list of Themes....

"I don't think we had ethics problems. But now, we're really crisp about what is and isn't permissible, so there's no ambiguity and more consistency.

"We work together much better. Trust has improved as we've become diligent about integrity, contracting, and empowerment. We all support one another as one company. And the culture supports the walk-throughs which engender really great teamwork.

"Themes like entrepreneurship, customer focus, and quality taught us how to be good at managing our businesses.

"Innovation has improved as we've learned how to take judicious risks. And thanks to the feedback we give one another, we all are continually learning and improving."

A Recruiting Filter?

"There were some interesting side benefits," Nate added. "I'll tell you a quick story: [69 Ref] Carlton was interviewing an external candidate for an open leadership position. He threw our culture booklet on the table and said, 'If you don't want to work this way, this isn't the place for you.'

"Carlton thought he was using it as a filter, to hire only people compatible with our culture. And that's important. But in fact, it also worked the other way.

"The candidate said, 'I love it! This is exactly how I want to work. And in the past when I started a new job, I'd spend the first few months stumbling around making mistakes until I figured out the culture. Now, you're telling me exactly what I need to do to succeed here.'

"So," Nate concluded, "our culture turned out to be a recruitment *aid,* not just a filter. It's part of how we attract top talent."

I expected I'd need to do something about the culture in my company. It was reassuring to know about a pragmatic way to go about it.

NAVIGATION AID: Chapter 29 describes the behavior-based culture implementation process.

Chapter 13:
Metrics

Chapter summary (key take-aways): page 475

Moving on to the next organizational system, I said, "Nate, you know the saying, 'If you want to fix it, measure it.' Shall we talk about metrics?"

"A great topic!" Nate said. "I think you'll find our metrics are a bit different from most companies."

Problems Addressed by Metrics

"Okay. But first, what problems can metrics solve?" I asked.

Nate replied, "There are two types of metrics that address two different problems:

"(1) If people are failing and don't know it (or don't care), they won't improve. Performance metrics tell people how they did; and when they're tied to promotions and incentives, they give people the incentive to improve.

"And (2), if people don't have dials that tell them how they're doing as they do their work, you can't expect them to perform well. That's what dashboards are for."

Common Pitfalls in Metrics

"Got it," I said. "Let's start with performance metrics. How are yours different?"

"To explain that," Nate replied, "let's talk about some of the pitfalls we believe we've avoided, stupid mistakes that others have made...."

"Sure, that sounds like fun," I said.

"First," Nate said, "while we continually give people feedback, we do performance appraisals annually. We heard of one big tech company that does evaluations every six months. So, people don't willingly take on any projects that'll take longer than six months!" *70 Ref*

I laughed.

"We don't grade on a curve," Nate continued, "where every manager is required to identify low-performers as well as high-performers, and then flush out the low-performers. What does that say to a leader who has successfully attracted a team of all high-performers!?

"Grading on a curve leads to all kinds of unproductive game-playing," Nate added. "Managers keep low-performers until after the ratings period, so that they don't have to grade others down just to make the curve, and so that they can take the low-performers' bonus money and give it to the high-performers.

"And, you know the old story about the two guys out walking, and they encounter an angry bear. They turn to run, and one kicks off his sandals to run faster. The other guy shouts, 'What's the point? You can't out-run a bear.' And the first guy says, 'I don't have to. I only have to outrun you!'"

That's an old joke, but I chuckled.

"When you grade on a curve," Nate said, "people don't want to help one another. In fact, it gives them an incentive to sabotage their peers so that they look better by comparison."

"Couldn't you include an objective related to being helpful?" I asked.

"There's a company that tried that. It just gave people an opportunity to drag their peers down by accusing them of not being helpful!"

"Oops!" I grinned. "I guess I should have anticipated that."

"Here's a really important point," Nate added. "We never evaluate people based on what they *do* (tasks); we only look at *results*. That comes right out of the Golden Rule — people are accountable for results, but how they get there is their business.

"So, we'd never use something like Microsoft's 365 Productivity Score[R] to spy on our staff and gauge how many messages they send or meetings they attend. The last thing we want is people sending lots of spurious messages and maximizing their meeting time to crank up their Score while not getting real work done!"

"I'm with you," I said. "I heard about an insurance company known for its customer service. They put in a metric of the number of outbound calls that agents made. So, one agent set up a bot to repeatedly make calls to phony numbers. You get what you pay for!"

It was Nate's turn to laugh.

Shared and Enterprise Metrics

"Okay, let's talk about what you *do* measure," I said. "Do you use shared metrics, like company financial performance?"

"In a way," Nate replied. "Metrics of enterprise performance give people a sense of shared destiny, so that's a good thing. And that's especially true if there are rewards, like profit sharing and employee-equity growth, associated with those enterprise performance indicators.

"Enterprise metrics can also motivate performance," Nate continued, "but only if people understand how their individual contributions influence enterprise success. And that's a big if! We're still working on training our staff to understand enterprise strategies and financials, and to understand where they fit in the big picture." [71 Ref]

I nodded, appreciating the importance of getting everybody to care about the success of the firm, if for no other reason than their own job security. And I also appreciated their open communications.

Nate added a caution, though. "We use enterprise metrics in conjunction with special incentives, like contests and profit sharing. But as per the Golden Rule, it's inappropriate to measure individuals' performance based on anything that's outside their control. That just leads to a sense of helplessness, cynicism, and disengagement. So here, performance appraisals are based on individual's (or their immediate group's) performance, not enterprise metrics."

"I get that," I said. "But how about measuring people on their contributions to enterprise financials?"

"It's too far away from what they do day-by-day to have an impact on behaviors," Nate replied. "It may even lead to dysfunctional behaviors."

"Like what?" I asked.

"More unintended consequences," Nate replied. "It can undermine internal customer focus. People might say, 'I'm doing this for the good of the company; so I'm going to give you what I think the company needs, not what you want to buy.' When that happens, internal customers are disempowered, teamwork breaks down, and the whole operating model comes unraveled.

"Here's another unintended consequence," Nate added. "There was a tech company that measured people on their contribution to profits and strategic goals. They couldn't get anybody to write documentation, because its bottom-line impact is too obscure! [72 Ref]

"And when people are individually measured on the same metric, there's another risk," he added.

"What's that?"

"Even if we don't grade on a curve," Nate said, "when people are pursuing the same metric, research tells us that human nature creates a pseudo-competition with peers. There's a tendency to want to be first, rather than be the best you can be. That can lead people to sabotage their peers. And when they think they're ahead of peers, they slack off." [73 Ref]

"Really!" I said. "How about instead of corporate financial goals, we measure people on their contributions to the company's strategies?"

"That's really not necessary," Nate replied. "With our internal economy, we're all well aligned. So, if we measure individual performance at serving customers, we're already measuring contribution to our strategies."

"In that same vein," I asked, "how about metrics of team performance, rather than just individual results, to encourage better teamwork?"

"If you have to do that to get people to work well on teams, then something's fundamentally broken. Since we do walk-throughs, if you satisfy your internal customers with your own deliverables, you'll be contributing to the team. We don't need team-level metrics, other than the fact that customer satisfaction is part of everybody's metrics."

OKRs versus Long-term, Comprehensive Metrics

"Do you use objectives and key results (OKRs)?" I asked. [74 Ref]

"No, not for metrics," Nate said. "We're certainly not about agreeing on a few major projects and then checking off the boxes in an annual performance appraisal. There's so much more to running an internal business than just delivering today's projects and services.

"Also, we don't want to encourage myopia. We measure people on long-term value, not just short-term numbers and project results.

"I know that's less tangible," Nate continued. "But we're quite willing to measure people on qualitative metrics as well as quantitative. We believe it's much more important to be comprehensive than to be precise. We don't want people optimizing a subset of their objectives, and ignoring others which are important but more difficult to measure."

With regard to metrics,
it's better to be comprehensive than to be precise.

Examples of Entrepreneurial Metrics

"Would you give me some examples of what you do measure?" I requested. Nate's examples are listed in Figure 19.

Figure 19: Examples of Entrepreneurial Metrics

- Customer satisfaction (internal and external; immediate customer, not your customer's customer)
- Market share (external or internal)
- Your group's profit/loss (break-even, not budget variances)
- Competitive rates (market benchmarks of unit costs)
- Profit targets for those who sell to external customers.
- Product/service quality
- Your reliability, integrity
- Safety and compliance
- Innovation
- The viability and expected value of long-term business strategies
- Compliance with, and contribution to, our organizational operating model
- Subordinate employees' engagement and satisfaction (through engagement scores and surveys), turnover
- Supplier relationships (especially internal suppliers)
- Positive contribution to the community (including the environment)

"Many of these metrics are based on customer input," Nate noted. "That comes through 360-degree surveys, which also give us subordinates' and internal suppliers' feedback."

Metrics of Costs

"What about costs?" I asked.

"We don't look at benchmarks of total spending," Nate said. "If you look at our spending on internal IT, it's well above our peers, according to industry benchmarks. But that's not a bad thing. It's because we're outpacing competitors in using IT as an enabler of business strategies. So, spending more on technology is actually a good thing.

"But as I said earlier," Nate continued, "we benchmark our rates (unit costs). We're always asking, can we buy it cheaper from vendors? If the answer is yes, internal suppliers are expected to buy rather than make. So, with vendors as part of our staff, we should all always be the best deal. If we're not, that's a performance issue."

Dashboards

"You put a lot into performance management," I observed.

"We do. We believe it's very important to give people good feedback, and to incentivize the right behaviors.

"But remember," Nate added, "there's another kind of metric that's arguably even more powerful: dashboards given to the people doing the work, continually updated throughout the year."

"Why do you say that's more powerful than performance metrics?" I asked.

"Imagine this," Nate replied. "A guy is running a machine in a factory. On that machine is a knob and a dial. His job is to adjust the knob so that the machine stays in the green zone on the dial."

I nodded, picturing the hypothetical situation.

"What if you moved that dial up to the supervisor's office, and told him how he did at the end of each year!?" Nate posited.

"I see your point," I said.

"Annual performance appraisals motivate people to try," Nate said. "But dashboards deliver relevant feedback in real time, so that people can optimize their performance and do something about any problems right away."

Performance appraisals can be once a year.
But dashboards must be delivered in time for people
to do something about any problems.

"Oh, and as I said," Nate added, "for performance metrics, we only measure results (the Golden Rule). But for dashboards, it's fine to measure processes and tasks (in advance of results) if that helps people dial in their work before it's too late.

"It's like the dashboard on a race-car," Nate elaborated. "The dials give drivers real-time information that helps them drive the race. But the only performance metric is whether or not they come in first.

"We're still rolling out dashboards," Nate concluded, "tailored to each group's unique businesses and processes."

"Good stuff," I said. They were using metrics to reinforce their whole operating model, not (like OKRs) as a poor substitute for its alignment processes.

Chapter 14:
Reflections on Systemic Governance

Chapter summary (key take-aways): page 475

"So," I summarized, "if I'm tracking you, Nate, you've described four components of your organizational operating system: structure and team-work, the internal economy, culture, and metrics. But you haven't mentioned governance. Empowerment can't mean anarchy!"

Definition of "Governance"

"No," Nate replied, "like every organization, we need controls. But we think about it a little differently. To us, 'governance' means *all* the processes by which we coordinate and control our resources and actions."

I nodded as I absorbed this definition.

"Governance" means all the processes by which we coordinate and control our resources and actions.

Systemic Governance versus Altruism

Nate continued, "As much as possible, we've tried to build governance into our organizational operating model, rather than using people or committees for oversight.

"For example, resource governance is handled by our internal economy. Behaviors are defined in our culture. And we have good metrics.

"What we've tried to do," Nate explained, "is set up the signals so that everybody wants to do the right things, rather than to spend resources catching them when they make a mistake. People do the right things because that's what they have to do to succeed.

"It's the opposite of altruism," Nate observed. "Altruism means expecting people to act against their own best interests for the good of the whole. We don't believe that's right.

"Instead, we've aligned individuals' best interests with the best interests of the enterprise. Here, the way to get what you desire — compensation, relevance, recognition, etc. — is to do what's best for your business-within-a-business and for your customers, which in turn aligns you with enterprise goals."

Set up the signals so that everybody wants to do the right things, rather than spend resources catching them when they make a mistake.

Oversight

"We do have some oversight," Nate noted. "Of course, performance management is handled by one's supervisor. And there's Corporate Internal Audit. But other than that, we don't have groups or committees that 'oversee' and disempower others.

"We think of oversight as the governance mechanism of last resort — the most expensive and least effective form of governance."

"I see why you'd say it's expensive," I said, "because it takes people's time. But I'm curious, why do you say that oversight is less effective?"

"Because," Nate replied, "with oversight, you don't have time to review every decision, so you can't catch every mistake. If you try to, governance becomes a bureaucratic nightmare. But when governance is *systemic,* it's virtually free; it's in real time; and it's ubiquitous."

Wow, I thought, I've really got to get over the knee-jerk reaction that anything that requires controls, requires human oversight. I never really liked all those committees, or support functions, trying to control my business-unit leaders. This systemic approach gives me a better alternative.

We know that in healthy living systems, ...control is distributed.
But we are so habituated to the "someone must be in control" mindset...
that we fail to imagine real alternatives.

— Peter M. Senge [75 Ref]

Role of Committees

"Hey, Nate, this leads me to a question related to governance. I've been in organizations that were buried in committees, all ostensibly for the purpose of governance. To get anything done, I had to get past so many hurdles, and everybody had to agree on everything. That really slowed things down. Does the Market Organization have anything to say about committees?"

"It sure does," Nate replied. "I think we're after the same goals: We don't want unnecessary bureaucracy (steps with little added value); that's costly and reduces our agility. We don't want committees to relieve individuals of their accountabilities, because when everyone is accountable, no one is accountable. And we can't let committees disempower those who *are* accountable for results."

"Agreed," I said.

"Ensuring all that," Nate continued, "depends on establishing a very clear charter for each committee. As it turns out, in a Market Organization, there are a limited number of legitimate roles for committees."

He listed those appropriate roles for committees, and oversight was not on the list. I asked Nate to say a bit more about each (in Appendix 5).

Alignment through Objectives and Key Results (OKRs)?

"Nate, let's look at a specific challenge — strategic alignment — and see how systemic governance addresses it. Carlton told me that everybody develops their own strategies for their internal businesses. So, if you don't roll strategies down through the management hierarchy, how do you coordinate all those independent entrepreneurs?"

"You know," Nate replied, "in some companies, department leaders decide their own strategies (based on their understanding of enterprise strategies, of course); and they set their own priorities (which is where the rubber meets the road on alignment). But then there's some sort of coordination process, like strategic planning, or just executives talking to one another. It's like a high-level alignment overlay on top of anarchy. We think that's not a very effective approach."

"I agree," I said. "But how about something more explicit, like objectives and key results (OKRs)? In some companies, senior leaders set their OKRs, and then they cascade them down through successive levels of management. We talked about why OKRs are a poor metric (Chapter 13). But what's wrong with using them to align priorities?"

"They're too crude," Nate stated. "Either they're written at too high a level and don't drive project priorities. Or when they're granular enough to list projects, they're cumbersome. As we said, strategies are continually changing. And they're reflected in hundreds of projects, many of which pop up mid-year. So, you'd have to revise a very long list of cascaded OKRs every month to keep up. In our Market Organization, that's essentially just keeping up with your contracts."

Goals are good for setting a direction,
but systems are best for making progress.

— James Clear [76 Ref]

Alignment through Internal Market Economics

"So, what's the alternative?" I asked. "How do you align everybody's priorities?"

"Market economics!" Nate exclaimed. "Pursers buy operational services and projects that are aligned with business strategies. When those prime contractors subcontract to others (walk-throughs), alignment ripples through the whole organization.

"Then," Nate explained, "when priorities shift during the year, pursers buy different things and the whole system adjusts dynamically."

"What about innovation initiatives?" I asked.

"They're no different. They're explicitly funded by the enterprise purser. We do walk-throughs on them. Everybody is aligned!"

"And how about just the day-to-day innovation work within groups?"

"That part we leave to the individual entrepreneurs. But of course, their strategies for their businesses are based on what they believe their customers will need in the future. So even there, we have a systemic force for alignment without top-down controls."

If you create an environment where the
people truly participate, you don't need control.
They know what needs to be done and they do it.

— Herb Kelleher, Founder, Southwest Airlines

Nate glanced at his watch and said, "Oops, it's time to get moving. Now you're going to see how things really work around here."

We tossed out our coffee cups, and off we went.

~ PART 4 ~

Internal Lines of Business, and How They Work

*in which I meet with each department leader
and learn how their functions work*

NAVIGATION AID: Busy executives may wish to skip to Part 6 (leadership perspectives), and then, if you find yourself interested in the possibility of implementing a Market Organization, return to Parts 4 (detailed operating model) and 5 (implementation processes) or review those chapters in the Book Summary at the back of this book.

As we walked down the hall, Nate said, "You know, we're a relatively small company. But we have all the same challenges, and all the same functions, as a Fortune 500 company. So, next, you're going to see how each of those functions works in a Market Organization. I've set up a series of meetings with each of our senior leaders."

"Great! Who's first up?"

"Julio. He's our VP of Sales.

"By the way," Nate added, "Carlton mentioned that we 'eat our own dogfood' — we're our own IT department. So, our company is just another sales territory for Julio. Internal service providers like IT need a sales function just as much as whole companies do."

I was taken aback. "Wait a minute! Why the heck would an IT department need *Sales*?"

"Ask Julio! If he can't sell you on the value of a Sales function for internal service providers, no one can!"

Chapter 15:
Sales and Marketing:
Both External and Internal

Chapter summary (key take-aways): page 476

Some typical names for this type of business: sales, commercial, Chief Revenue Officer, client relationship management, marketing, branding, customer success, client liaisons, Business Relationship Managers, HR generalists, public relations, corporate communications, investor relations, government relations (lobbying), community relations.

For examples of this line of business in various industries and internal shared-services functions, see Appendix 3.

This chapter may be particularly relevant to internal service providers (like IT) that are interested in expanding the impact of their Business Relationship Management functions. It may also be useful to those trying to set a higher bar for sales and marketing functions.

As we entered Julio's office, he was placing his laptop on his docking station. "I'm sorry to be out of breath! With our staggered work hours, I come in late; and I just walked in. Please, have a seat. How are you?"

Julio seemed warm and gracious. But the question was, did he have anything to teach me about the Sales function that I didn't already know? I wasn't looking for a primer on selling. I just wanted to learn how the transformation impacted the way the function works.

Eating Your Own Dogfood: Internal Sales of IT

I had to start with my burning question. "Julio, I'd like to get past something right up front.... I understand that the company is its own IT department. Nate mentioned that you treat the company as just another sales territory. So, that's like an internal IT department with a sales force. Help me understand why internal IT needs Sales."

"It sounds odd, I know," Julio replied. "Let me tell you how that came to be....

"As you know, we're a tech company. And, of course, we also need IT internally. So, we committed to using all the same IT resources for both — what Carlton calls 'eating our own dog food.'

"Then, we figured out that everything Sales does for external customers, internal service providers (like IT, HR, etc.) need to do for their internal customers. In other words, an IT department needs what some people call 'Business Relationship Managers' (BRMs) — essentially the Sales function for an IT business within a business.

"And when we got around to talking about where to put the BRMs, well, the leadership team figured that I knew how to manage salespeople. So, they gave the function to me.

"Of course, if you're not an IT company, that wouldn't make sense. You'd leave the BRMs in your IT department," he concluded.

Value of Sales

"Julio, that explains why it's under you," I said, "but I'm still struggling with why an IT department needs a Sales function at all."

"Ah, yes. Please understand, we don't just push deals; we add real value to our customers. And that value is just as relevant to IT's internal customers as it is to the company's external customers."

"Then I need to better understand the value of Sales to customers."

"Certainly," Julio replied. He thought for a moment, then said, "We're not looking to maximize our revenues by pressuring people into buying things they don't need. Maximizing revenues from *internal* customers would be a cost to the company."

I nodded emphatically.

"But that's true of external customers as well," he said. "Whether it's internal or external customers, we're here to deliver two things:"

1.   Highly effective relationships with all our customers

> "Especially at the senior executive level," Julio said, "customers want one person dedicated to them who gets to know them; who can discuss our company's entire relationship with them; who they can call if they have questions or concerns; and who invests in great partnerships and resolves any relationship problems. That's true of internal decision-makers as well as external."

2.   Strategic value to customers

> "Beyond that," Julio continued, "selling starts with customers' needs, and then matches those needs with the capabilities of the company. Our job is to help customers (external and internal) solve real problems and achieve their goals by utilizing the company's products and services. We're laser focused on maximizing the value that the company delivers to all its customers.

> "So, we're the ones who help customers translate their business strategies into high-payoff IT projects."

"Alright," I admitted, "I do see the value in an IT department having a function that does those two things. But that's not what comes to my mind when I hear the word 'sales.'"

"Fair enough," Julio smiled. "If you think selling is about maximizing near-term revenues, I can see how our role internally might be misinterpreted. I know that IT departments in other companies don't call their Business Relationship Managers (BRMs) 'Sales' in public!" He laughed. "But the fact is, they're still a customer-facing function whose purpose is to deliver relationships and strategic value from the use of IT products and services."

Proactive, Not a Part-time Job

I challenged Julio further. "There are IT departments that assign the client-liaison function to their senior leaders, or their applications teams. Obviously, that wouldn't work with external customers. But why not with internal customers?"

"First off," he replied, "our senior leaders don't have the time to maintain contacts with their internal customers, invest in partnerships, study the methods of sales, and proactively discover opportunities.

"You see," Julio continued, "we don't want to be passive order-takers. Even in a tech-savvy company like ours, if we leave customers alone to figure out what they want, they'll just ask us for what they know we can deliver. And that's based on what IT has delivered in the past, which was, until recently, mostly operational and administrative solutions.

"We need to break through that preconception, and help customers discover opportunities for technology to deliver value directly to their business strategies."

I nodded. "Yes, I want my IT department to be very proactive about finding strategic opportunities. You don't think senior technology leaders can do that?"

Unbiased, Not a Job for Leaders of Other Functions

"It's not just that our senior leaders don't have time to learn the methods and study the business. Consider this," Julio said. "What if we asked our engineers to talk to customers about their needs? You know the old saying, 'If you give a child a hammer, everything looks like a nail!'"

I smiled and nodded.

"If customers spoke directly with our applications engineers, everything would look like an application. If they spoke with our end-user computing leader, the answer to every problem would be collaboration or thinking tools. And if they spoke with the head of data analytics, everything would look like a data problem.

"But to deliver strategic value, we have to be business driven and unbiased. Our Account Reps talk to customers (internal and external) about their strategies and explore *all* the ways that IT can contribute."

"I see value in that," I admitted. "It's pretty obvious that external customers need an unbiased sales rep. I don't know why I'm resisting that same concept internally. But let's move on."

No "Solution in Search of a Problem"

"I understand you want to be business driven," I said. "But what if you have a product that you know a customer needs? Like, let's say you did a project for one customer and it saved them a lot of money. Wouldn't you present that solution to other customers?"

"I know this is going to sound odd," Julio replied, "but no, we wouldn't go in with *our* agenda — a 'solution in search of a problem' — and risk the whole relationship. What if that next customer doesn't care all that much about saving money, because they're focused on other things like innovation? If I present that cost-saving solution, they won't have the time of day for me.

"Worse," Julio continued, "if I led with that cost-savings idea, they're going to brand me as someone who doesn't understand their business and isn't relevant to their strategies. I'll have a hard time getting in the door next time."

"I get it," I said. And I really did. Companies have different strategies. And the business units within them are different, too. Some are focused on margins, so costs are critical. But others focus on innovation, or customer intimacy, or analytics and insights, or influence and negotiations. For them, cost savings are good but not strategic.

"So," Julio said, "you can see why we *never* solicit business in a product-driven way. We're all about maximizing our value to customers. To do that, we have to start by understanding *their needs*. Everything we do has to be rooted in that."

"That's exactly what I want from my salesforce," I agreed. "We pay a lot to acquire customers. I don't want to squeeze out a bit more short-term revenues and sacrifice long-term relationships. If we do what's right for the customer, we'll make plenty of money over time."

Product managers build capabilities to satisfy the needs of markets. Sales scans markets for needs that call for those capabilities.

Who Are Account Representatives?

"Internally, you're called Business Relationship Managers (BRMs)," I said. "Are these what others call 'business analysts' (BAs)?"

"No," Julio explained. "Our Account Reps are very senior people. They have business experience on the customer side, and a 'smart buyer' knowledge of all our products and services, and how they add value.

"These are the kind of people that customer executives would love to have in their own organizations in senior leadership positions. And that's true of both our internal and our external Account Reps."

Unique Expertise of Sales

"Aside from having the time to spend with customers and being unbiased," I asked, "what skills do your Account Representatives have?"

"We bring a unique expertise to the table," Julio replied. "Our full-time job is knowing customers — their business strategies, their personalities, even their internal politics. So, we know what's going on with customers far better than any of the other departments.

"But, of course, we'll never know customers' businesses as well as they know their own businesses. The unique thing that we bring to the table is our study of the *linkage* between our products and services and customers' businesses.

"We study how our entire range of products and services can create value for customers. We use that expertise to help customers discover those really high-payoff opportunities. Then, we help them drill down and define exactly what they want to buy — their requirements.

"After that, we help them do business with the rest of the organization."

---

*Sales studies the <u>linkage</u> between
the organization's products and services and customers' businesses.*

Not Project Managers

"At that point," I asked, "are you accountable for delivery of the sales you make?"

"No, no, we're not," Julio replied. "Project management isn't our forte. More fundamentally, we have a competent engineering function. We wouldn't add any value by being in charge of their projects.

"If we did lead delivery projects, we'd be selling Engineering's products. That would create confusion and competition — like when do you buy from us versus them? Or, it might relegate Engineering to just being a body shop (pool of people) for us which, for them, would be disempowering and not at all entrepreneurial.

"Meanwhile, delivering other groups' products and services would take us away from our Sales jobs. We'd have far less time to maintain all the existing customer relationships and find new ones as well.

"It's interesting," Julio reflected. "In the English language, the word 'sell' has two meanings: (A) to provide; and (B) to help a customer to buy.

"We don't *provide* other groups' products and services, as if we buy from them and then re-sell it to customers.

"We do (B). We help customers figure out what they want buy, and then *broker* a clear agreement between the customer and the internal supplier. Then, that supplier is 100 percent accountable for the delivery of its product or service.

"We stay involved," Julio concluded, "to facilitate the relationships between customers and everybody else. But we're not accountable for project management or solution delivery."

Matrix Versus Market Organization

"Let's go back to your internal IT sales function for a moment.... How is that part of your group structured?" I asked.

"Just like the external sales force," Julio said. "We clustered internal business units and corporate functions into territories, and assigned an Account Rep to each."

"Is that a 'matrix' structure?" I asked.

"No, we wouldn't call it that. Nate, help me here.... As I understand it, in a real matrix structure, people have two bosses: one for their profession, and the other being their customer." [77 Ref]

"That's right," Nate said, "although people use the term pretty loosely these days. But the original concept was that profession-bosses just created pools of talent, and a multi-disciplinary team drawn from various pools is assigned to a customer-boss who directs day-to-day activities.

"Basically," Nate observed, "matrix confuses the word 'customer' with the word 'boss.'"

"I want my staff to be very customer focused," Julio asserted. "They're dedicated to external customers and internal business units, and measured on customer satisfaction. But I don't want any confusion as to who their boss is!"

"Furthermore," Nate added, "we're much more dynamic in the way we assemble teams for each project. We don't assign a long-lived team to a customer for any and all projects, the way a matrix does.

"The coach calls it a Market Organization, not a matrix," Nate said. "Customers can buy products and services from any entrepreneur in the organization. And they, in turn, buy help from the right talent anywhere in the organization, via our walk-throughs. So, we're all aligned with customers' needs, without having to report to a customer boss."

Relationship Selling versus Counselor Selling

"Okay, let's get into the methods you use," I requested.

"Perfect," Julio said. "Our methods differ in our two markets: off-the-shelf versus bespoke.

"Sales of off-the-shelf products is relatively straightforward. We compete on two bases: (1) value; our functionality is better, and our price is comparable. (2) We do our best to establish great relationships.

"In industries that sell off-the-shelf products and services," Julio continued, "relationship selling is pretty standard. Even a no-touch business like Amazon invests heavily in relationships, like Amazon Prime [R] and the way they track your preferences."

"Yes. I'm familiar with relationship selling," I said.

Sales are the by-product of great relationships.

— Geoff Routledge

"But for custom solutions," Julio said, "or for selling just the right mix of off-the-shelf solutions from a diverse catalog of products and services, it's more than just relationships. We have to be really good at *helping customers discover strategic opportunities* for just the right subset of our products and services.

"So, we focus on understanding customers' business strategies, and helping them find creative solutions without pushing any one product. In these situations, we're more like consultants than just sales. That's why it's called 'consultative selling' or 'counselor selling.'"

I nodded. "I'm familiar with the concept. How do you decide which approach to use?"

Figure 20: Relationship Selling versus Counselor Selling

Off-the-shelf and single product, or limited interactions	→	Relationship selling
Custom, or multi-product solutions	→	Counselor selling

"We know pretty quickly whether the customer is open to a counselor-selling conversation, or has already pretty much decided what they want.

"We always prefer counselor-selling mode (even though once we get into the analysis, the answer might be an off-the-shelf product or service). This way, we can ensure that every project is directly based on business needs."

"Julio, I'm intrigued with your concept of customer strategy analysis as the basis for a sale."

"Is counselor selling relevant to your company?" Julio asked.

"I think so," I said. "The truth is, my company currently generates most of its revenues from our off-the-shelf product line. But I'm really attracted to the notion of delivering more value, and building more customer loyalty, through added-value services. And that could take us into the world of custom solutions that combine a mix of our off-the-shelf products with added-value services. So, I'm hoping to hear something applicable to that strategy.

"But," I added, "whether it's immediately applicable or not, I'm here to learn as much as possible. I'll see if I can apply it later."

Targeting Key Customers

"So," I continued, "let's focus on counselor selling. Where do you start? Do your Account Reps analyze the needs of your customers?"

"Not of entire companies or business units," Julio said. "We talk to specific individuals.

"Consider this," he posed. "What does everybody in your company have in common? Not their strategies, right? They each have unique roles in enterprise strategies."

I agreed.

"So, if we want to deliver strategic value, we have to focus on specific individuals and what's *unique* about them, not challenges that everybody has in common which are likely to be more administrative in nature.

"And furthermore, *we* don't deliver our customers' strategies. We help *them* deliver. So, we have to know who we're helping."

"Interesting," I said. "You pick key people within a company, and diagnose their specific needs. How do you target those people?"

"Our Account Reps spend time talking with customers, keeping up with their constantly changing business strategies and who's in the hot-seat to deliver what. They're looking for the leverage points — individuals who are in a position to make or break business strategies."

"Are those typically top executives?" I asked.

"Often," Julio said. "But not always. Sometimes it might be, for example, an engineer who's leading the development of a new product, or a manager responsible for launching a new service. We're continually surveying our territories to target the best prospects."

"So, what do you do with these targeted individuals?" I asked.

"Basically, we call them up and say, 'Hey, can I spend one or two hours with you brainstorming how we could help you achieve your goals?'"

I looked at Julio skeptically. "If I understand who you're talking about, these are very busy people. Are they willing to take that much time with you?"

"Excellent question!" he replied. "At first, we didn't have the greatest reputation. So, only a few were.

"But then, when we delivered real value to those few, the word spread. Of course, we helped it spread with case studies and testimonials highlighting our successes. Over time, others caught on; and then others after them, and so on." [78 Ref]

"Nothing succeeds like success!" I observed. [79 Ref]

"Correct!"

Well-focused Opportunities

"So, you've talked your way in the door. Now what?" I asked.

Julio smiled and replied, "First, let's be clear about what we're there to do: Our goal is not to sell our products. We're there to help customers address their business challenges.

"Also, we're not out to sell them everything they might possibly need — 'document all their requirements,' as they say in the IT business — even in a business-driven way.

"We're looking for one really well-focused opportunity to do the most with the least, to address a specific business challenge with just the right solution. *We're trying to maximize customers' ROI, not our scope.*"

Approach each customer with the idea of
helping him or her solve a problem or achieve a goal,
not of selling a product or service.

— Brian Tracy, sales trainer and best-selling author

Opportunity Discovery Method

"I agree," I said. "So, how do you find that one opportunity?"

Julio explained that their opportunity-discovery method takes the form of a semi-structured interview:

First, they ask customers to identify their key <u>deliverables</u>....
> Then, drilling down on just one, they help customers identify their key hurdles — their <u>critical success factors</u> (CSFs)....
>> Focusing on one of those, they identify <u>critical capabilities</u> that customers need (related to their products and services)....
>> Focusing on one at a time, they brainstorm <u>solutions</u>.

As Julio described it, the result is a logical path from a business challenge, to a CSF, to a needed capability, to a specific product or service.

"Brilliant!" I exclaimed. "At that point, what customer wouldn't sign the deal!? Any sales force could benefit from that approach."

"It works!" Julio said enthusiastically. (Julio describes this method in more detail in Appendix 6.)

Role of Function Sales (Evangelists)

"I should note," Julio continued, "our Account Rep might bring a 'Function Sales' consultant into that opportunity-discovery process. Some people call them 'evangelists.'

"They specialize in a *type of value* created by our products and services. By 'type of value,' I mean the applicability of our products and services to specific business strategies, professions, or business processes. You see, this is a linkage function, which is what Sales is all about."

"Give me an example, please," I requested.

"Certainly. We have two Function Sales consultants right now. One is our Chief Digital Officer, who specializes in how businesses use technologies to enhance customer engagement and loyalty (Chapter 33).

"And the other is our Chief Data Officer, a data scientist who specializes in how businesses use data for research and decision making. *80 More*

"Someday," Julio added, "we might have experts in operational excellence, supply chains, mergers and acquisitions, work-force globalization (and work from home), technology in the physical space, etc."

"That'll be a lot of 'Chiefs'!" I joked. "So now you have the Account Rep *and* one of these Function Sales consultants in the room?"

"If the Account Rep finds an opportunity in one of those two areas, then yes," Julio replied. "But for any opportunities where we don't have a Function Sales expert, the Account Rep continues the process alone."

"Do the Function Sales consultants just wait to be called in to help with opportunity discovery?" I asked.

"That's one role," Julio replied. "But they also evangelize — they build awareness of the possibilities, and help all of us, including external customers, develop strategies for tapping opportunities in those areas."

Role of Business Analysts

"So now, tell me," I continued, "where do IT business analysts (BAs) come in? In my last company, they did the IT requirements."

"Yes, perfect. It's *after* the opportunity is defined," Julio replied. "If we're building custom solutions, BAs work with customers, and others who report to or work with them, to document business requirements to the level of detail that our engineers need to bid the project."

"They're kind of like a proposal-writing group?" I speculated.

"Actually, what they're writing is more like requests-for-proposals (RFPs)," Julio replied. "Our engineers then write the proposals."

Agile Iterative Development

"Julio, I'm a little out of my league here, but I've heard about the Agile approach in IT where you build something, learn more about the requirements from that, and then build the next cycle. Isn't getting detailed requirements up front in conflict with that?"

"Not at all," he replied. "Our opportunity-discovery process includes what Agile calls 'problem framing.' But our approach is more strategy driven and detailed than what you'll find in Agile. Problem framing, and defining the solution, are Sales jobs. It requires our knowledge of the clients, their business, and their strategies, and an unbiased, generalist's understanding of all our products and services.

"Once we've defined the opportunity, the next step is business requirements. They include what Agile calls 'user stories' and 'use cases.' This too is a job for Sales, not Engineering — to ensure that every requirement is driven by the business opportunity we're to address.

"Now sometimes," Julio continued, "for a given opportunity, requirements can't be defined in full detail in advance, because it's a new situation and the customer isn't clear about exactly what's needed or how it should look until they see a draft. So, we just define the basic functionality needed. Then, Agile 'way-finding' refines the detailed requirements through that iterative process. *81 More*

"But all the while, every Agile team, and every sprint they do, has to stay focused on the broad requirements we've defined (and the customer has funded). If a new opportunity is discovered along the way, that's a separate project that has to be justified and funded on its own merits."

I was pleased to hear that Agile isn't an excuse to keep developing a product forever, without regard for the returns on those investments.

Synergies Across Customers

"Julio, I'm curious about something.... At least internally, I've seen situations where a number of business units share IT applications, like ERP. It would be expensive if each business unit acquired a separate solution. Plus, there are business synergies when they share a common product. And we need consolidated data. How do you handle that?"

"Another great question," Julio said. "Internal to the company, we provide a service called 'consortium facilitation.' Whenever one business unit wants something that others might also want, especially when they might get business synergies by sharing that solution, we try to pull the relevant business units together into a consortium.

"If they agree, we facilitate a consortium agreement which defines how they'll work together to share a solution." *82 More*

"What if they don't agree?" I asked.

"Then we have no choice but to sell them each individual solutions. Of course, that's going to be more expensive for them.

"But," Julio noted, "since our Engineering group is divided up by type of solution rather than by customer, at least the same engineers will produce those similar-but-separate solutions. So, they can work behind the scenes to deliver some of the economies and synergies." [83 IT]

"What if everybody in the company needs something?"

"Then," Julio explained, "Operations would acquire the solution, and use it to provide a service to the rest of us. Software-as-a-service is one of their businesses. I think you will be talking to Max later?"

"Yes, we will," Nate answered.

Figure 21: Levels of Cross-Business-Unit Sharing

1. Business units buy separate solutions for their unique needs, but they're built by the same shared-services group (shared talent) with the maximum in reusable intellectual property and components.
2. Business units form a consortium to share a single solution.
3. A single solution is owned by shared services, which offers use of it to everybody as a service.

Boundary with Engineering

I was curious about where Sales stops and Engineering picks up a project. I asked Julio, "Does your group also do high-level designs, like business analysts did in my last company?"

"No, no!" he exclaimed. "That's engineering work. We're very clear on the boundary: Sales defines the *What*. Engineering designs the *How*.

"If we were to tell engineers *how* to build that What," Julio explained, "we'd be disempowering them, and then they couldn't be held account-able for the quality of their solutions.

"Furthermore, design at any level requires engineering skills, and that's not our expertise. We're totally focused on studying customers, and the linkage between their businesses and our solutions."

"So, on to Engineering next?" I asked.

"They're your next appointment," Nate said.

Business Cases

"Wait," Julio said, "there's more we need to do before passing the baton to Engineering.

"You see," he continued, "projects require funding. Internally, the next step (which is engineering work) has to compete for funding alongside all the rest of the IT requests. I think Nate will tell you about our resource-governance processes."

"I already did (Chapters 9 through 11)," Nate confirmed.

"Good," Julio continued. "So, to go on to the next step, the customer has to justify spending resources on this opportunity."

"So, you develop a business case?" I speculated.

"Yes. But remember, *customers* have to come up with the funding to pay for what they want to buy, not suppliers. It's their job, not ours, to justify their projects. And by the way, they know the value to their businesses far better than we do.

"Plus," Julio continued, "for internal projects, you want to hold your business units accountable for delivering those business benefits once IT has delivered the solutions, right?"

"I do," I agreed.

"Therefore," he said, "it's the customer's job to make the business case. But we help. We're trained in another method to help them define and quantify the expected business benefits." *84 Ref*

"Cost savings?" I asked.

"If that's what the project is about. But more often, it's about strategic benefits. We help them put numbers on those so-called 'intangibles.'"

"Really? How do you do that?" I asked.

"Again, it's a semi-structured interview technique. We work that logical path back upward, from the proposed solution, to how it will change the way they work, to why those changes are good.

"Once we've helped them define the 'good,' we use decision-science techniques help them quantify that good, and a little bit of finance to convert that to present-value dollars."

"Excellent," I said sincerely. "That's exactly the data I need to make informed decisions about internal projects. And if our company's sales-force could do that, our external customers would be far more likely to get the funding to buy from us."

"Yes," Julio agreed, "it's a strong case when your customer can explain exactly how your product or service will impact their bottom line."

Benefits Realization

"There is one more thing we do on some projects," Julio added. "Do you have a few more minutes?"

Nate nodded his approval. "Sure," I said.

"Thank you," Julio said graciously. "You see, our products and services only have value if customers use them. Often, that means changing the way they do business — their practices or processes."

I nodded grimly. I'd spent too much money on "shelfware" in the past.

"It's certainly not our job to change our customers," Julio continued. "Only they can change themselves.

"And we're not trained in change management or socio-technical systems analysis [85] [Ref] (or derivatives like Lean and business process engineering)."

"So, what value do you add?" I asked.

"Remember, we're the ones who understand how a specific solution is supposed to deliver business value — the linkage. So, we can help customers define exactly what changes they need to make in their business practices to realize that value — a 'business impacts analysis.'

"Once the changes are defined, we can link them up with Nate's Organizational Effectiveness (OE) group to optimize their processes, and with Organizational Development (OD) experts in HR to help them develop adoption plans and facilitate the change process."

Ongoing Services (Beyond the Sale)

"Good stuff," I said. "Is that the end of your project involvement?"

"Pretty much," Julio replied. "We're back in the loop at key decision points to facilitate dialog. But the next step is up to the engineers.

"Now, beyond any one project," Julio continued, "we do stay engaged and add value at a higher level."

"How so?" I asked.

"We're always involved as relationship managers. Yes," Julio laughed, "I'm afraid it's true; sometimes customers get upset with us. We facilitate sensitive communications and resolve relationship issues.

"Also, we offer periodic 'account reviews' to keep customer executives informed about everything we're doing for their business units.

"And internally, we facilitate the business-driven demand management process, where executives (pursers) decide our internal IT priorities."

"Yes, Nate told me about that (Chapter 11)."

Retail Sales

"You've convinced me," I said, "that Sales adds a lot of value. But this is a big investment in each sale. Julio, do you have time to do all this for everybody who might buy something from the company?"

"Honestly, no, we don't have time to work with every customer in such depth. So, within my group, we also have a Retail Sales function that's available, on demand, to help customers buy from us. They're the default point of contact for everybody other than the top execs and the key customers who we target — basically, an inside sales group."

"How does what they do differ from Account Reps?" I asked.

"They do a little for the many, while Account Reps do a lot for the few. And," Julio added, "the Retail Sales group also runs our demo center (our form of storefront) and our e-commerce store."

Customer Success: Hunters and Farmers

"Julio, let's talk about 'Customer Success.' Is that part of Retail Sales?"

"They're both Sales," he said. "But Customer Success is not a store-front (physical or e-commerce) or default point of contact. They're junior Account Reps who work with existing customers.

"They ensure that customers get what they've bought," Julio explained. "They help customers get solutions implemented successfully, at times leading or facilitating teams of our experts to help customers with their projects. They chase down renewals, and look to expand our presence in existing accounts."

"Some people divide sales into 'hunters' and 'farmers,'" I said. "Are these the farmers?"

"Yes, precisely."

"Does this function include pre-sales engineering?" I asked.

"No," Julio replied. "Engineers do engineering, not sales people. And engineers are best managed by engineers, not by me."

"A lot of companies have struggled with the relationship between the hunters and the farmers," I said. "How do you divide accountabilities, and who gets credit for renewals and follow-on sales?"

"Account Reps are completely accountable for their accounts," Julio explained. "They *subcontract* to Customer Success for help. But even if they utilize Customer Success coordinators, Account Reps are still responsible (and get credit) for follow-on sales. By positioning Customer Success as a service to Account Reps, they work great as a team."

"I like it," I said.

Sales as a Business

"You've described a variety of very specific services that your Sales group provides," I noted.

"Yes," Julio said, "we see Sales itself as a business. So, we'd better be clear about our own product line (Figure 22)."

"If you're a business, who are your customers?" I asked.

"Think of us as you would a third-party sales force. We sell our services to all the entrepreneurs in the company. They get to decide how much of our effort to buy, and defend that line-item in my budget."

"How does that work?" I asked.

"We give them options — what we think we can produce for various levels of funding in various market segments. They determine their strategies, revenue goals, and budgets, and decide what to buy from us."

Figure 22: Services of Sales

- Relationship management, including account reviews, status updates, issue mediation
- Participation in customers' strategic planning (if invited; a hallmark of success)
- Opportunity discovery (the key to strategic value; see Appendix 6) [in custom/multi-product organizations]
- Detailed business requirements planning [for custom solutions]
- Benefits estimation facilitation (to help customers justify the purchase)
- Business impacts analysis (to help customers adopt solutions)
- Contract brokerage (clear agreements with others in the organization)
- Consortium facilitation [for internal customers]
- Client-to-client agreement facilitation (when one customer needs something from another to proceed) [for internal customers]
- Program facilitation (single customer, multiple related initiatives) [in multi-product organizations]
- Budget planning assistance (helping customers plan their budgets to include funding for us; another hallmark of success when invited)
- Priority setting facilitation [for internal customers]

Marketing

"Do you also have Marketing under you?" I asked.

"I do," Julio replied. "We have all the traditional marketing functions: marketing strategy (including branding); and marketing communications (including websites, social media involvement, brochures and collateral, advertising, promotions, trade shows, VIP tours, customer events, newsletters, and an annual report). We also do market research (answering questions about what customers think, value, and do).

"Plus, we have public relations (PR), investor relations, government relations (lobbying), and community relations."

"I'm not used to seeing PR, investor relations, and government relations within a marketing department," I said.

"As we see it," Julio replied, "they're all about communicating with audiences. That's a marketing competency. Content comes from others; for example, Finance and Business Planning have a lot of information that investors need. But we manage the communications channels."

"Is there anything unique about your approach to marketing?" I asked.

"Our Marketing group delivers what every Marketing function does: It creates attention, interest, perception, desire, and action. But perhaps we think of their mission a little differently from other companies...."

"Here, just like Sales," Julio explained, "Marketing delivers value to customers. Instead of pushing products directly, we use our communications channels to build awareness of the strategic value of our products and services — to create an emotional connection to our brand by showing how we help people achieve their goals.

"Marketing works both inside the company and, of course, outside. Internally, a key goal of marketing is to get *everybody* thinking creatively about how to use our products and services to create value.

"Actually," Julio mused, "that's really not different from our goals for external marketing."

Sales Support

"Is there anything else under you?" I asked.

"We also have a Sales Support group. They're experts in the profession of selling — our own methods and tools. Also," Julio concluded, "our business analysts (BAs) report to that group."

Julio listed some of the services that Sales Support provides (Figure 23).

Figure 23: Services of Sales Support

- Sales methods development and training
- Informational and motivational sales-force events
- Selling-strategy consulting; account planning facilitation
- Sales staff (and candidates) skills evaluations; developmental planning
- Sales-support instruments like selling guides
- Use of tools (which are owned by this group) such as the customer relationship management (CRM) and scheduling/routing systems
- Data entry, cleansing, and reporting (e.g., in the CRM)
- Data analyses, e.g., funnel analyses and account segmentation to set goals, select target accounts, and determine the best approaches
- Lead generation research, often based on external data
- Territory planning; route planning
- Sales compensation plan design; metrics; contests and rewards
- Proposal writers (primarily for external sales, a service to engineers who are accountable for proposals)
- Requirements analysis for customer solutions (business analysts)

Sales Metrics and Compensation

"I have a question that I think applies to both relationship selling and counselor selling," I said. "In my experience, Sales professionals are intensely focused on their commissions, which are based on this month's (or this quarter's) sales. How do you get them to invest in long-term relationships with customers?"

"You're right," Julio nodded. "If commissions are a big part of their compensation plans, you're telling them to think short-term.

"But we don't want our Reps to unnaturally force deals forward in time to get a commission. That would put long-term relationships at risk. So," Julio said, "we reinforce our longer view with a compensation plan that takes into account more than this month's deals.

"We measure Reps' progress building relationships by assessing things like our access, when they talk to us (early in their thinking, or after they've decided what they want to buy), our value to them (strategic, or just a commodity vendor), and loyalty (how big a price differential it would take for them to go elsewhere).

"Those relationship metrics drive bonuses, which are a significant part of the compensation plan.

"It works," Julio concluded. "As much as sales-people love the 'hunt and kill,' they're also motivated by other things, like knowing they're adding real value to issues customers care about."

Acceptance of Sales

"Counselor selling requires a trusted-advisor relationship with your customers," I observed. "Are internal and external customers accepting your sales function in that role?"

"More so all the time," Julio enthused. "One way to tell is that it's easier to get in doors.

"But the real sign of success is when we get invited to participate in customers' business-strategy discussions. Of course, this helps us understand their strategies so that we can support them better. Beyond that, the big benefit is that we can help customers brainstorm business strategies that are *enabled* by our products and services, such as digital-business strategies that differentiate them in their markets.

"Again," Julio concluded, "as word spread that we deliver real value, we got invited to talk to customers earlier in their thinking."

Nate interjected, "Now, I'm afraid we're going to have to get going."

"Julio, this has been very thought-provoking. Thank you very much."

"No, no," Julio said graciously, "the pleasure was all mine!"

Chapter 16:
Engineering: How Projects Are Delivered

Chapter summary (key take-aways): page 478

Some typical names for this type of business: engineering, product design, subject-matter experts.

For examples of this line of business in various industries and internal shared-services functions, see Appendix 3.

As we hurried down the hall, Nate gave me a quick introduction to the two people I was about to meet.

"Jennifer (she goes by Jen) heads up our Applications Engineering group.

"Mike will be there, too. He leads our Technology Engineering group.

"These are the folks who create our products, as well as engineering all our internal IT systems. I'll let them explain the details."

By the time we got to the meeting room, Mike had already arrived. As we took our chairs, Jen popped up on the screen.

Engineering's Business

After a few courtesies, I started the conversation. "Carlton explained that the company sells both off-the-shelf products and services, and custom solutions. Do you do both?"

"We engineer both. But all we sell is custom solutions," Jen replied.

"Huh?" I was justifiably confused.

Jen explained, "We design custom solutions for specific customer requirements. We have three types of customers:

1. "Internal customers, like with any internal IT department, want custom solutions that address their specific requirements.

2. "Sometimes, external customers ask us to produce custom solutions that address their unique requirements. Generally, these are built on top of our off-the-shelf solutions; but to the customers, they're still custom.

3. "We also design custom solutions for Max in Operations. He takes our designs and stamps them out as off-the-shelf products. Or he owns and operates those solutions and sells software-as-a-service."

"Wait a minute," I said. "Did you just say that Max (Operations) sells your standard off-the-shelf products, not you?"

"That's right," Jen replied. "I'll leave it to Max to explain our reasons. But frankly, we're quite happy to focus on engineering new solutions to meet new requirements, rather than managing what's essentially a manufacturing business."

"I will indeed ask Max about that."

Engineering Specialties

"Anyhow," I said, "you both sell custom solutions. What's the difference between your groups?"

Jen led off. "I sell applications — solutions designed for specific purposes. [86] *IT* Internally, that includes our off-the-shelf products which I sell to Max for re-sale, as well as all the traditional internal applications like finance, HR, order processing, and CRM applications, as well as websites, smart-phone apps, etc."

"You do applications development?"

"We do," Jen replied. "And we also sell commercial off-the-shelf (COTS) products, software-as-a-service (SaaS) solutions, and every combination thereof. It doesn't matter whether we make or buy them. We're accountable for the delivery of purpose-specific solutions."

"In the case of commercial-off-the-shelf (COTS) packages or software-as-a-service (SaaS), why do you need to be involved?" I asked.

Jen replied, "We specify all the technical deliverables in the vendor contract. And we typically get involved in configuring, integrating, and installing the product or service."

"I see. Okay, Mike, what do you do?"

"I do everything else," Mike laughed. "My group is the equivalent of manufacturing engineering, plus components that go into Jen's applications, plus tools that aren't purpose specific." [87 IT]

Jen clarified. "Think of it this way: I sell cars and trucks. Mike sells engines, wheels, and components that go into my cars and trucks, as well as engineering the manufacturing plant."

The split between purpose-specific (or perhaps market-segment-specific) products and more generic multi-product components made sense to me. I want our market-specific product engineers to get a really deep understanding of the needs of specific market segments; and I want other engineers thinking about global, reusable components.

Ethos of Engineering

"Mike," I said, "I'm accustomed to manufacturing engineers reporting to the head of Operations. Why did you separate it out?"

"My engineers have customers other than just Operations," he replied. "For example, we're subcontractors on most of Jen's projects. So, it wouldn't make sense to have us reporting to just one of our customers, and risk neglecting the others. We're best put on neutral ground.

"Beyond that, we didn't want to create a conflict of interests by combining engineering and operations — invention and stability."

I nodded, remembering that discussion with Nate (Chapter 7).

"Plus," Jen added, "we're both engineers. Mike and I together have to make sure all the existing and emerging technologies are covered in one group or the other, with no gaps and no overlaps."

"And professionally, we have a lot in common," Mike said. "We're both creating a culture of curiosity and innovation, to keep up with emerging technologies. And we're continually exploring new methods and tools to make ourselves more efficient."

"We both have to be excellent at project delivery," Jen noted.

"We both focus on engineering quality, architecture, and standards compliance," Mike added. "And we're both committed to supporting and repairing what we sell, so we try to 'do it right the first time.'"

"So," Mike concluded, "my team has more professional synergies with Jen's team than Max's. But we decided that engineering is too big for one senior leader. And here the two of us are, side by side!"

Walk-throughs

"Tell me how your two groups work together," I requested.

"That's really important," Mike said. "There's no such thing as an engineering generalist that can do it all. It takes a team.

"Let's say a customer is buying an application," he continued. "Jen's group is 100 percent accountable for that. But she's going to need help from my group, and others, to implement the solution." [88 IT]

"Let me guess," I said, "you have a development process that lays out everybody's roles."

"We have development methods," Mike replied. "But that's not how we define roles on teams. Each project is a little different, and requires its own unique mix of skills and deliverables. So, we do walk-throughs to figure out who's on the team, and to define each team-member's individual accountabilities."

"Ah, yes," I said. "Nate told me about walk-throughs (Chapter 8). When do you do a walk-through on a new project?"

"We form teams this way right from the start," Mike said, "before we even give the first estimate of the project. That's really important to me. Jen had better not go quoting *my* costs and timeframes!"

Nate nodded emphatically and said, "In our culture, nobody is allowed to make commitments for others."

Here was another implication of the Golden Rule. And it reinforced the value of walk-throughs.

"I have to admit," Jen said sincerely, "at first, walk-throughs took us forever and seemed like a nuisance. But now, we're pretty quick; and I swear by walk-throughs. They're the key to great teamwork and on-time delivery. They've become automatic for us; it's just the way we kick off projects."

Engineering Processes

Moving the discussion on, I said, "Julio told me that he has two different sales processes: relationship selling for off-the-shelf products and services, and counselor selling for custom solutions. But all you do is custom solutions. So, do you have just a single engineering process?"

"Actually," Jen replied, "we have two different processes, both for custom solutions: a sequential process (Waterfall), and an iterative development process where customers refine the requirements after seeing a minimum viable product (Agile)."

"I like a prototyping approach to product development," I said, "checking in with focus groups with each iteration. Isn't that what Agile is?"

"I guess there's nothing new under the sun!" Jen said with a laugh. "Yes, that's the essence of it. Agile has lots of detailed guidelines for methods, roles, timeframes, and so on. And it has a funny language."

"Like a cult?" I quipped.

Jen laughed. "Very much so. But at its essence, it's a prototyping approach."

"How do you know which method to use?" I asked.

"If the requirements are clear," Jen replied, "the Waterfall method is more efficient and can produce higher quality in large complex systems. And there are business situations where we just have to get it right the first time. I know NASA and SpaceX use Agile for software development, to be sure it's usable. But that doesn't work for the spacecraft. You can't get a man on Mars by going part of the way there, and then stopping and refining your equipment!"

I chuckled at that metaphor.

"But," Jen continued, "we're happy to use the Agile method whenever it makes sense and is needed. To us, Agile is not a religion, as some would have it. It's just an arrow in our quiver." [89] *IT*

Phase-gating

"Good," I said. "Julio was talking me through a project. He got me as far as business requirements and a business case, and then tossed the ball to you. What happens next?"

"Julio's right," Jen responded. "By the time a customer is ready for us, they know exactly what they want to buy — that is, they have clear business requirements, at least to some level of detail."

"And," Mike added, "if customers come to us without business requirements, we refer them back to Sales."

Jen continued, "Of course, customers are interested in knowing how much their projects are going to cost. But how can we answer that question just based on the requirements!? We haven't even studied what it will take to build it, and the customer hasn't decided whether they want a silver, gold, or platinum solution.

"We used to try to guess the costs up front. But then we always got in trouble for our estimates being way off.

"So," Jen said, "we established the practice of *phase-gating* (Figure 24)."

Figure 24: Phase-gating

1. Opportunity discovery (Sales)
2. Business requirements (Sales)
3. Solutions alternatives study (Engineering)
4. Solution implementation (Engineering)

"The first phase is definition of a business opportunity. Based on that, business requirements are defined. Those first two steps are done by Sales," Jen reiterated.

"Then, we take over. The third phase is what we call a 'solutions alternatives study,' where we study one or more ways to satisfy those requirements. The fourth phase is the implementation of the chosen alternative — the solution itself."

"And, in our internal economy," Mike continued, "we only approve one phase at a time. You can't give blanket approval to a project up front, when all you have is a business opportunity, or even after requirements when you don't yet have an analysis of the costs and risks."

"Hmm, on the surface, phase-gating seems to be in conflict with the Agile method," I postulated.

"Not at all," Mike said. "Custom development may be one of the alternatives we put forward in a solution alternatives study, perhaps alongside software-as-a-service (SaaS) or commercial off-the-shelf (COTS) products. Then, if custom development is the chosen alternative, the Agile method might be used in Phase 4, solution implementation."

Project Estimation

"How does phase-gating help with project estimation?" I asked.

"The key is that we only give an estimate for the next phase," Jen replied. "Once we see the requirements, we can give a 'T-shirt sizing' (small/medium/large), or a really rough guess, maybe plus or minus 50 percent, of the whole project. But we also provide a reasonably accurate estimate of just the next phase, the solutions alternatives study.

"Then," she continued, "within that solution alternatives study, for each alternative, we do high-level designs (which scopes the project), and provide accurate estimates of the implementation costs and time."

This sounded like common sense to me. And yet, as I reflected on my past experiences — not just with IT but with corporate product development — I realized that this simple insight wasn't common practice. Too often, we'd made promises about cost and time before we'd analyzed how we'd go about delivering a project.

"And this works with Agile?" I asked. (I don't know why I was so fixated on this method. But I know Agile has value beyond just IT.)

"Sure," Jen answered. "In a solutions alternatives study, we make a professional guess about what it'll take to address the requirements as best we know them at that point in time. Then, if the project needs more, the customer goes back through the funding process to get approval for more iterations (sprints)."

Jen concluded, "We use Agile as a development method within the context of a project that has a customer, a defined opportunity, some degree of requirements, and allocated funding."

Solutions Alternatives Study

"If I'm tracking you," I said, "a solutions alternatives study gives the customer a high-level design and a good estimate of implementation costs and time. Is there anything else you provide with it?"

"Yes," Mike responded. "We provide customers with enough information on each alternative so that they can make informed choices. So, we also analyze life-cycle costs of ownership, risks, pros and cons, policy and standards variances, the customer's accountabilities and their level of effort required, etc."

"That's right," Jen added. "We have a philosophy of sharing all we know, then respecting customers' right to choose what they buy. Obviously, we're not going to propose a solution that we can't live with. But even so, we can usually come up with multiple good alternatives."

"What if there's only one alternative?" I asked.

"We still do a solution alternatives study," Mike said. "Customers have to get funding for the implementation phase. So, they still need an accurate estimate of implementation costs and an understanding of the life-cycle costs and risks. Plus, the high-level design that we do in a solution alternatives study is input to the implementation phase. So, we can't skip this phase, even if we're looking at only one alternative."

Jen added, "Sometimes an internal customer comes to us with a solution in mind. But they'll usually let us propose other alternatives as well. They may want custom code, but a vendor package might give them 80 percent of what they want for 20 percent of the cost. Or maybe a quick-and-dirty solution will suffice, especially if it's for short-term use.

"We recently had a great example of that," she continued. "A customer wanted a specific vendor package. They were adamant about it. But we convinced them to allow us to look at one other alternative: adding the same functionality to our existing ERP. The solution alternatives study showed them that the ERP alternative could save quite a bit of money and deliver much better functionality. They changed their minds, and became strong supporters of the ERP approach!" [90 Ref]

"Is this solution alternatives study a product in itself," I asked, "or just the estimation step in the process, like a milestone review?"

"No, it has value in its own right," Mike asserted. "Customers need it to make a decision (or kill the project if it's too expensive or risky)."

"And," Jen added, "it's a serious piece of engineering work. It takes a bunch of people significant time to do the analysis. So, it needs funding in its own right."

Customers in a Rush to Start

I put another challenge to them. "What if you have an impatient customer who doesn't want to take the time for all these steps, and just wants you to get started programming."

"No way!" Jen exclaimed. "Program what!? We can't do anything until we have requirements. 'Just start programming and I'll know it when I see it' never did work. And Agile is not an excuse for doing that. We never skip the requirements phase.

"The same goes for the solutions alternatives study," she continued. "If you skip that and just start programming, you'll never know if a commercial product or a SaaS solution would have been a better choice. And, before we start development, we need to think through all the ramifications of the project, like its impacts on infrastructure and linkages to other systems. That's all part of the solution alternatives study.

"All those so-called shortcuts actually wasted lots of time," Jen asserted.

"So, we had to re-focus customers on the time to *completion* of the project, not the time to when we start programming."

"This sounds like a 'hare and tortoise' situation," I commented. "Slow and steady wins the race." [91 Ref]

"Well, I hope we're not considered slow!" Jen laughed. "But that's exactly right. We deliver results faster when we work through the phases methodically."

Infrastructure Compatibility

"I'd like to go back a bit," I said. "When you're coming up with alternatives, do they all have to run on your existing infrastructure? In my experience, product designs have to work with manufacturing capabilities."

"In our case, not necessarily," Jen replied. "We could look at software-as-a-service (SaaS) in the cloud."

"Oh, of course," I nodded. "That's like outsourcing manufacturing."

"Beyond that," Jen continued, "we *could* put forward an alternative that requires a new type of infrastructure."

"If you do that," I said, "aren't you forcing a decision on Operations, which would disempower them?"

Mike looked at me, raised an eyebrow, and smiled. I'd like to think that he appreciated my understanding of the Golden Rule.

"We wouldn't do that unless Max (Operations) agrees," he explained. "What we do is go to Max and present the idea. If he thinks that this is the first of many customers for a new infrastructure service, he'll agree to gear up for it. He'll go get funding for the new infrastructure in parallel to Jen building the solution for its first customer.

"But if he doesn't see a broader market for it, he won't invest capital in building infrastructure for just one customer."

"What happens then?" I asked.

"Well, I guess we could still propose it," Mike said reluctantly. "Customers would have to pay for the non-standard infrastructure themselves, and pay us for its operations and maintenance. But we don't want to encourage that."

"What's to stop customers from doing that?" I asked.

"It's kind of self-policing," Mike said, "because paying the full life-cycle costs of that dedicated infrastructure is going to be a lot more expensive for them than using our standard, shared infrastructure.

"I suppose there could be cases where specific business needs would justify the costs. But we haven't run across that. Usually, if Max doesn't want to go that direction, customers back off and select an alternative that works on our existing infrastructure."

"Interesting," I said. "You let the numbers guide the decision, rather than rules and oversight which force everybody to get permission for non-standard things."

"Right," Mike agreed. "That way, we never have to be the bad guy saying no. After all, it's a business decision, not a religious matter!"

This was a good example of the systemic governance that Nate and I had discussed (Chapter 14).

Standardization is a business decision, not a religious matter.
Let the numbers guide the decision.

Selecting an Alternative: Not the Usual Recommendations

"Okay, moving on.... What happens next?" I asked.

Jen said, "Once we're done with a solution alternative study, Julio's Account Reps help us present it to the customer. Then, assuming the customer wants to go ahead after seeing the costs, their Account Rep helps them choose an alternative."

"Do you also help by making a recommendation?" I asked.

Jen laughed. "No, not in the usual sense. We'd always point them to the Rolls-Royce; that's what we engineers love building!

"Instead, we say, 'If you're in a rush and don't want to spend much, this is the best alternative. However, if you'd like something that you can depend on for many years to come and want to optimize *life-cycle* costs, then this other alternative is the best.'

"In other words," Jen concluded, "we help them choose based on *their* values, not ours."

This struck me as a very nuanced, and excellent, understanding of customer focus.

We present alternatives, but we don't make recommendations.
We help customers choose based on their values, not ours.

Implementation

"Okay," I said, "let's say I've selected an alternative and have the priority or the funding. The next step is, you'll deliver the solution?"

"We will!" Jen said with a smile.

"Without getting technical, what goes on in the implementation phase?"

Jen replied, "Of course, we start with another walk-through. It's pretty much the same players as the solutions alternatives study. But there may be some minor differences in the make-up of the team, and of course their specific deliverables are different at this phase.

"Then," she said, "the PMO (project management office) converts that into a detailed project plan. [92] *IT*

"We try to optimize development costs by using the right mix of employees, contractors, and vendor services. [93] *IT* We use the best resources, wherever they are (including off-shore). And," Jen emphasized, "we deliver quality products, on time and on budget."

Quality and "Ripple Chasing"

"I'd like to hear more about engineering quality," I said.

Jen responded, "Sure. Let's define quality.... We would never add requirements that the customer didn't specify (if that would add to costs) — you know, over-engineering things. 'Quality' doesn't mean price-point. What we mean by 'quality' is the professionalism that goes into design and delivery *within* customers' requirements, at any price point." [94] *More*

Mike pulled out a list of design goals (Figure 25). As I looked down the list, I noted that these were all things I'd like my engineers (and IT department) to take care of, without my having to ask.

I understood most of the concepts, since they apply to any product-design effort. There was just one that I didn't recognize. "What's this last one about ripples?" I asked.

Jen answered, "Ripples are when changes in one system cause problems in other existing systems, like when data feeds to other applications stop working. Fixing downstream problems that a project causes is not a separate project. Every project comes with ripple-chasing."

Figure 25: What Quality in Engineering Means

At any price point, design for...

- Safety (users are unlikely to be hurt)
- Compliance with all applicable laws and regulations
- Performance in the intended environment
- For off-the-shelf products, manufacturability (ease of reproduction)
- Ease of installation (deployment into intended environments) and decommissioning (removal and disposal at its end of life)
- Reliability (products don't break, and produce predictable outcomes)
- Maintainability (ease of removing defects, restoring operations)
- Resilience to externalities (e.g., disasters), and ease of recovery
- Usability: the right balance between ease of learning (acquiring operational competence) and ease of use (operating at high performance levels) [95] *More*
- Ease of support (incident diagnosis)
- Scalability (changing capacity), adaptability (adjusting functionality), and extensibility (adding functionality)
- Portability to future platforms or operating environments
- Reusability (apply all or part of the design again elsewhere, e.g., global applicability)
- Future integratability (through compliance with standards)
- Ripple-chasing; and minimize future ripples (through design patterns)

"That's absolutely right," I agreed. "I think I have an example...." I related an experience when my past company released a product that required all our dealers to acquire new tooling. There was quite an uproar! To maintain relationships, we ended up providing the tools at below our cost — an expense we didn't anticipate. And we could just as well have designed the new product to use existing tooling.

"That's a great example," Mike said.

"It's important because I don't like surprises," I said. "When I make investment decisions, I've got to know the total cost, including any necessary ripple chasing."

Quality Assurance and TQM

"Continuing the quality theme," I pressed on, "how do you ensure that you deliver the quality you promised?"

"We do peer reviews," Jen said. "And, of course, we do thorough testing. But we really try to build quality in from the start, since any rework we have to do at the testing stage is expensive and causes delays."

Mike added, "And when we have quality problems, we diagnose the root causes — the real reasons defects occurred, not irrelevant excuses. Then, we implement permanent fixes (like improved processes)."

Everybody's accountable for their own quality. Do it right the first time. Root cause and permanent fix. It seems these time-tested principles of Total Quality Management (TQM) apply to every industry. [96 Ref]

Transition Into Operations

"So," I asked, "once the solution is developed, are you done?"

"No, we're not done until the solution is up and running," Jen said. "We have to install it. That involves taking it through change control, where all the stakeholders check off that it's ready and safe.

"Then, we subcontract with Max to install it into his production environment. You know, he's not going to let us march into his data center (his manufacturing plant) and change the configurations of his assets!"

"The Golden Rule again!" I noted. "Okay, *then* are you done?"

"Almost," Jen replied. "Solutions come with brokerage of any ongoing services that customers will need. Since we know what it takes to run our solutions, we help set up SLAs (service-level agreements) with Max for running the solution, with Leticia (our help desk) for support, etc."

"We don't wait until we're done to start brokering those contracts," Mike added. "We do that early in the project so that others have time to gear up to take on this new business."

"That makes sense in any industry," I observed.

Internal Customers Want to Buy Directly from a Vendor

"Let me try out another situation on you," I said. "Do your internal customers ever want to buy a product directly from a vendor? Then, if it turns out to be a poor choice, it's your problem to fix it."

Jen and Mike both laughed. "That used to happen all the time!" Jen replied. "But now, they usually buy *through* us, not around us."

"How did you get them to do that?" I asked.

"Well, for one, we got our act together. We include the vendor product they picked in our solution alternatives study. This shows them that, even if they go with that vendor, there's a lot more to a project than just buying a product. As we said, we have to configure, install, and integrate it.

"And with their permission, we compare the vendor product they picked to other alternatives. We give realistic estimates of cost and time. And we make sure those vendors deliver on their promises.

"But I think something else turned the tide," Jen continued. "Some time back, our HR department wanted to do their own thing developing the HRIS (employee database). They even hired a few IT people in HR.

"They selected a package, and spent an awful lot of time implementing it. When they finally went live, it was a disaster! It almost shut down the business. It took them months to get that system running right. And it never delivered all they promised.

"HR tried to pin the blame on us. But we'd been careful to document each subcontract they asked us for. So, we went down the list.... Development environment: delivered on time. Data integrations: delivered on time. Everything we committed to, we delivered on schedule.

"So," Jen concluded, "HR had to take full responsibility for the mess. I think business-unit executives learned from that fiasco that it's probably better to work with us rather than go directly to vendors." [97 Ref]

"Nice job," I said. They didn't force themselves on customers. They *earned* the business.

Beyond Projects

"Okay, once a solution is up and running, what's your role?" I asked, knowing there had to be more.

"There are a number of after-the-sale services we offer," Jen said. "We help Max with production problems. Leticia's service desk subcontracts to us for escalations. And, of course, we repair the solutions we sold."

Mike jumped in, "Our motto is, 'Those who build, repair their own messes.' That reinforces our accountability for quality. And repairs get done more quickly when the expert who made the mess fixes it." [98 More]

Those who build, repair their own messes.

"Do you do all the routine repairs, even PCs out in the field?" I asked.

"We're responsible for all repairs," Mike asserted. "But we subcontract to Andy's technicians to help with routine or remote-location jobs."

Nate pointed out, "We'll meet with Andy this afternoon (Chapter 19)."

"Good," Mike said. "We're really grateful for his services."

"Is there anything else that you sell?" I asked.

Jen replied, "Customers may come back to us later for enhancements, configuration changes, capacity studies, and product road-maps (a list of potential investments to get more value or life from existing solutions)."

"Yep," Mike confirmed, "we do it all. We support what we built in the past; we build new things; and we continually keep our product line up-to-date through innovation."

Onward

"I'm afraid we're going to have to run," Nate interjected.

"Okay. Thanks for your time, Jen and Mike. It was very insightful."

"Our pleasure."

"Honored to meet you."

At that point, Nate and I were off to see Max.

Chapter 17:
Operations: Ongoing Services
and Off-the-Shelf Products

Chapter summary (key take-aways): page 480

Some typical names for this type of business: operations, manufacturing, logistics, warehousing, facilities management, product management (for off-the-shelf products and services), infrastructure services, hosting services, data center, service administration.

For examples of this line of business in various industries and internal shared-services functions, see Appendix 3.

Having talked about project inception and delivery, it was now time to look into "running the railroad."

As we walked to my next meeting, Nate explained that we'd be talking to three types of operational functions. We were about to meet Max, head of Operations (infrastructure services). The organizational coach calls them "Asset-based Service Providers," where the services they sell are based on ownership of assets (infrastructure). They're akin to Manu-facturing and Logistics in other companies.

Later, I'd meet the "People-based Service Providers" where services are produced by people rather than assets. There are two types of those, Nate explained: product-related like Customer Service, and general-business services like Finance and HR.

"Aren't Jen and Mike in the services business as well?" I asked.

"Yes and no," Nate replied. "Engineers do provide services. But mostly they're there to sell solutions; they do projects which have a beginning and an end. By services, I mean ongoing operations, like water from the tap and electricity from the outlet."

And with that orientation, we arrived at Max's office.

The Golden Rule: Empowering Operations

"Max, tell me how the transformation has affected Operations."

"Well, sir, one of the things we do is run the solutions that our engineers sell. That may not be the case in your business."

"I'm not sure it is," I said. "But your insights could still be relevant to the operational functions in my company."

"I hope so," Max said. "To answer your question, before the transformation, things went like this: Applications engineers would work with infrastructure engineers to acquire and configure the equipment needed to run a new solution — the IT equivalent of manufacturing plants and equipment. Operations wasn't really involved very much. Once the engineers had it all figured out, they would dump all that equipment on us. Our job was to keep whatever they threw at us running.

"That didn't work too well for a couple of reasons....

"For one, how can you expect us to keep things running reliably when we had no control over what went into our operational environment!?"

"The Golden Rule," I noted. I was becoming a sentinel for empowerment issues!

"Yes, sir! New technologies went into the data center which really weren't ready for prime time.

"The second problem was even worse," Max continued. "At least for internal applications, the way we used to think of it was that the infrastructure engineers sold equipment (like servers) to the applications engineers, who sold the whole package to the business customer. Then, Operations would just run what were essentially customer-owned assets.

"We ended up with a mess of servers, each dedicated to specific applications, with tons of excess capacity. We did a server consolidation (virtualization) study, and proved that we could save millions of dollars per year. But customers said, 'That's my server. Don't touch it!' [99 Ref]

"Ironically, although users claimed to own the servers, they expected us to pay for repairs, upgrades, more capacity, etc. It was like they wanted to make all the decisions without any accountabilities."

"Another violation of the Golden Rule," I said.

"Yes, exactly! That whole organizational model wasn't working. We were struggling on every metric: reliability, performance, and costs. And there was nothing that we in Operations could do about it. We were totally disempowered. As you said, we were the victims of a broken Golden Rule.

"Nowadays," Max continued, "we use cloud computing instead of buying our own servers, for the most part. But the principle remains the same: You can't have engineers forcing solutions on us, and then hold us accountable for reliable operations."

"You know," I said, "I saw the same thing in my last company. I kept coming down on Manufacturing for poor reliability, throughput, and costs. No matter how much I pushed, things didn't improve. I hired a new VP of Manufacturing, and she demanded that Manufacturing Engineering report to her. And she made Product Engineering work through her to get their new products into production. And sure enough, she fixed the problems."

"Perfect," Max said. "Now here, I don't need Technology Engineering (Mike) reporting to me, because they do other things than just work on my infrastructure. But the transformation made it clear that we're their *customer,* not their dumping ground. As the customer, *we* get to decide how much capacity, and what types, we need.

"I'll tell you," Max concluded, "performance has really improved because these are *our* services. We're accountable for them, and we're in control, so we can get the job done!"

The Business of Operations

"Max, before you tell me more about how things work, give me an overview of what you do."

"Sure. We offer a range of services to the company and to external markets — not custom solutions, but *off-the-shelf* products and services that we sell to many different customers.

"We're the product managers for three things." Max opened a document labeled "Domains" and showed me his (Figure 26).

Figure 26: Three Sub-domains Within Operations

- Products and services which require the ability to replicate many copies of products (manufacturing services).

- Services which are based on owning and operating assets whose primary intent is for use by others (infrastructure), and services which require expertise in operating those assets (operator services) or in managing the resulting services (service management).

- Standard (off-the-shelf) products (or assemblies of standard components) where the same design is sold to multiple customers.

"Okay," I said. "I understand manufacturing. Talk to me about the second one."

"We look for opportunities for shared-use assets," Max replied. "By that, I mean situations where it makes sense for us to own the asset and sell the use of it as a service to multiple customers."

"Give me an example."

"Okay. A classic example is our telecommunications network. It makes no sense for each business unit to have their own. So, we own the network and sell connectivity as a service."

"That's a pretty obvious case. Give me a few more examples."

"Sure." Max said. "As for IT, we own servers, storage devices, database management systems, our telephone system, widely-used end-user computing software, and business intelligence data. Beyond IT, we own a warehouse and transportation assets (logistics).

"Of course, we sell our services internally," he noted. "But in addition, we sell some of these services to external customers."

Stewardship: Hosting

"All that sounds too technical for business people to deal with," I said.

"We've got you covered," Max said with a smile. "We also offer a service called 'hosting.' That's where we are *stewards of customer-owned solutions* for all the operational issues.

"Customers give us the solutions they bought from Engineering, and we hold them in trust. We arrange the needed infrastructure services (all that technical stuff) and keep their applications running.

"This gives customers a single point of contact for all infrastructure services related to their solutions, and insulates them from all those technical services. We also help them with some of their duties as asset owners. *100 IT* It's been really well received."

"Hmm, you just triggered an idea," I said. "I wonder how well my company assists customers with managing the products we sold them — ordering supplies, repairs, monitoring performance and capacity issues, routine operational tasks.... Maybe we can sell a stewardship service."

Innovation in Service Offerings

"Anyhow," I continued, "you're the IT equivalent of manufacturing, and you own all the plants and equipment. But isn't what you buy for your infrastructure driven by the solutions that Engineering designs? My Manufacturing VP would only buy equipment if it was needed to produce our products."

"Remember," Max replied, "we're more than just manufacturing. Our second sub-domain is services. And we can be proactive about offering new services.

"For example, take business intelligence. Years ago, the Business Relationship Managers told us that there's a need in the company. We hired the Chief Data Officer to hone in on the initial requirements.

"We hired Technology Engineering to write us a solution alternatives study for the needed software and data feeds; I guess they subcontracted to Jen's Applications Engineering group to scope out those data feeds.

"Then, we put together a proposal for venture funding," Max continued. "We were able to sell it as part of the following year's budget.

"Once we got the funding, Technology Engineering built us the solution. Meanwhile, we defined the service offering, developed our operating procedures, and worked with Marketing to build awareness of the new service. So, we were proactive in launching a new service."

"You really are entrepreneurs," I observed.

"Yes, sir, we are! We're a far cry from those passive operators of the past who just ran whatever was thrown at them."

"Do all your ideas for new services come from customers and Julio's relationship managers?" I asked.

"Not all. The engineers are continually tracking emerging technologies.

It's their job to stay up-to-date. So, they bring us all kinds of wild ideas. They're always saying, 'Hey, look at this cool new technology. You ought to buy it!'

"We love being made aware of opportunities," Max said. "But we don't pursue all their ideas. We ask two questions:

1.   "Is there a market for it? (Marketing helps us assess that with market research, external and internal.)

2.   "Has it matured to the point where we can operate it reliably?

"So," Max observed, "in a sense, we're a *damper* on innovation. We're not going to jump at every flashy new technology that comes along.

"But we're also the *spearhead* of innovation. We sell services to markets, not individual customers. So, we don't wait for a customer to tell us they want a service. It's our job to anticipate market needs, get the funding to buy the assets, stand up new services, and market them to all the potential customers."

"Interesting. You're not bleeding edge, but not lagging either," I said.

"That's right," Max said with a smile.

Quality in Services

"How do you know a good service from a bad one?" I asked. "In other words, how do you define *quality* in services?"

"We think about service quality every day. Our services have to be provided with pristine safety, availability, and reliability. That's a must.

"We schedule planned outages to minimize business impacts, and we keep customers informed of the status of problems.

"And we're always looking for ways to improve service quality," Max said. "For example, using data from Customer Service, we identify recurring problems and come up with investments we'd like to make to avoid future incidents ("problem management").

Max continued his definition of service quality: "We deliver required levels of performance. But this doesn't always mean the best perform-ance, since that may cost more than customers are willing to pay. Where we can, we offer choices in levels of service and let customers decide what they're willing to pay for."

Standard (Off-the-Shelf) Products

Pressing on, I said, "Your third sub-domain is off-the-shelf products. I initially thought the engineers were the ones who sell products and you sell services. But Jen and Mike said you sell standard products (which they've designed for you)."

"Yes," Max said. "Engineering sells custom products, including to us. But we're the product managers for off-the-shelf products. That includes the standard products that we sell externally, and internally off-the-shelf products like standard PCs and phones."

"What's the logic in splitting the product business this way?" I asked.

"Well, off-the-shelf products are a lot like services — a continual flow of identical things. One of our core competencies is understanding the needs of markets as a whole, and then keeping services running reliably, day after day. We're all set up for this repeat business.

"Just like with our services, we buy market research from Marketing to define the products. We buy the solution designs and documentation from Engineering. Then, if it's a physical thing, we'd manufacture it. But with software, engineers build it and we just deploy it.

"Julio sells us his sales and marketing services. Leticia sells us order processing and customer service. And there we are; we're in business!"

"Interesting," I said. "Your whole mentality is spotting opportunities in the marketplace, arranging the team to put it together, and then keeping the services or the off-the-shelf products flowing."

"That's us!" Max agreed. "It doesn't take an engineer to manage those businesses. And you see how that leaves the engineers free to focus on emerging technologies and new projects, without getting dragged into the market analysis and day-to-day, ongoing delivery that we're good at.

"By the way," Max added, "during the restructuring, we debated having the product managers for our external product lines under a separate senior leader. But to get the professional synergies in service management, we decided to put them all together here."

From Development to Operations

"Max, I'd like to go back to how solutions get into production. Let's say the engineers are building a solution that will be run on your infrastructure. How does that transition work now?"

"That flow from development into operations works *so* much better than it used to," Max said. "And it's not because of DevOps tools (which we use). It's because of our organizational operating model. [101] IT

"We get involved early in a project, because when they're doing a solutions alternatives study, they have to get the life-cycle cost estimates from us. Obviously, the engineers aren't allowed to decide our prices. Nobody makes commitments for others."

We said in unison, "The Golden Rule!" And we both chuckled.

"So, that gives us a heads-up as to what new business might be coming our way. And it gives us a chance to talk to Engineering about new infrastructure services that some of those alternatives might require."

"Jen and Mike did tell me a bit about that," I said.

"Good." Max continued, "There's another reason they involve us right up front.... Sometimes it takes us longer to get the infrastructure in place than it takes the engineers to build the solution. In the past, we'd get blamed for not being ready in time, even if that was impossible.

"Now, solutions come complete with installation; and we're the ones who prepare our infrastructure to run a new solution ('installation into production'). So, we're a subcontractor in their walk-throughs; and they're not done until we're done. That way, they have to talk to us before making any delivery commitments."

Enterprise Capacity Planning

"A little later," Max continued, "once customers decide which alternative they're going with, we kick into gear and do our best to have the operational services ready to go when the solution is deployed."

"Is that when you procure new infrastructure?" I asked.

"It might be. We don't add capacity for any specific project. But we certainly look at our capacity to be sure we can accommodate new demands.

"We may already have sufficient capacity, or we may need additional capacity. If we do need more, we don't buy a server for an application. We look at an *enterprise* capacity plan.

"We consider volume from new demands, growth in existing services, as well as applications and services that we're retiring. We also decide how much we want to buy ahead of demand, because sometimes it's cheaper to buy in big chunks rather than lots of little chunks.

"Then, based on our enterprise capacity plan, *we* get the funding for the infrastructure. That makes it clear that we own it, not customers.

"Of course," Max noted, "we cover the depreciation, interest charges, and all our operating expenses through our rates for the services. So ultimately, customers do pay for our infrastructure."

We don't add infrastructure for any specific project.
New capacity is based on an <u>enterprise</u> capacity plan.

Service Management: Competencies and Responsibilities

"Let me turn the conversation in a different direction," I said. "I'm learning that everybody here is a specialist in something. Clearly, you're not technology specialists. So, what exactly are you good at?"

I was expecting him to say something like operating the infrastructure, but I was intrigued to hear the broader scope of their skills.

"Thanks for asking," Max said. "In the old days, the engineers didn't have a lot of respect for our profession. They thought they could do our jobs in their spare time. But this *is* a profession.

"Take a look at this," Max said. He pulled up a document titled 'The Profession of Operations Management' (Figure 27). "These are the competencies required in my leaders."

As I looked down the list, I came to appreciate the profession of service management. These are exactly the things I want from all my operations functions.

Take-aways

"Max, you've convinced me that we should treat Operations functions as empowered entrepreneurs. Some of what you've said is IT-specific. But most of it I can translate to my company's Operations functions. Thanks very much."

"Thank *you,* sir!"

Figure 27: The Profession of Operations Management

- Forecast demand and capacity requirements (capacity management).

- Spot market opportunities for new off-the-shelf products/services, and improvements in existing services.

- Define services, including functionality, quality, safety, and terms of use.

- Evaluate alternative delivery models (e.g., outsourcing/cloud); manage vendors who provide all/components of the services.

- Decide requirements for assets needed to deliver services, and acquire those infrastructure assets from Engineering.

- Acquire funding for the development of new or enhanced services and additional capacity.

- Decide pricing; and manage costs to ensure competitive rates.

- Document operating processes.

- Launch new services, with subcontracts for needed operational, support, marketing, and sales services.

- Promote service offerings through Marketing.

- Manage contracts with customers (account administration), including providing access to services by administering passwords and access rights, with help from Access Administration.

- Operate assets reliably and securely, and remedy any service interruptions, buying incident management from Customer Service.

- Manage contracts with other Service Providers, e.g., supporting infrastructure, Customer Service, Finance for billing.

- Manage contracts with Engineering to maintain the assets (e.g., repairs, enhancements, capacity studies, major configuration changes).

- Adjust configurations (configuration management), e.g., to accept new customers or tune performance, with help from Engineering.

- Monitor service quality (performance management) and ensure that all service-level agreements are met.

- Reduce future incidents by analyzing patterns and addressing root causes (problem management).

- Plan for disasters to reduce risks, mitigate damages, and speed recovery (business continuity).

Chapter 18:
Customer Service: How Incidents are Managed

Chapter summary (key take-aways): page 481

Some typical names for this type of business: customer service, customer support, support desk, help desk.

On our way to the next meeting, we stopped by to pick up Ravi, the head of Product Support.

"It's an honor to meet you, sir," he said with grace. "Thank you for your interest in my area of work."

We walked to a meeting room near Ravi's office. Three people were there waiting for us. I was introduced to: Leticia (Customer Service), Andy (Technician Services), and Christine (Project Management Office).

After we settled into our chairs and made our way through a few niceties, Ravi got down to business, "We are the Product Support group," he said. "We differ from Max's Operations group in that our services are produced by our staff (people), not assets. And our services are specific to the organization's products and services, as distinct from the more generic Business Office.

"In addition to these three people," Ravi said, "I also manage Access Administration. We administer access rights to applications and Max's infrastructure services. It's like the front desk at a hotel that hands out keys to rooms owned and managed by others. *102 IT*

"And I have a data administration group that does ad hoc reporting, algorithmic data cleansing, and administrating others' databases (repository administration)."

Ravi continued, "The team was not only excited to meet you, but also they're interested in hearing your dialog with the others. So if you don't mind, we'd like to all stay together while you talk to each of us."

"That's fine with me," I said. "Where shall we begin?"

"May we start with Leticia?" Ravi suggested. "She manages Customer Service — what we used to call the help desk."

I turned to her and smiled. "Leticia, I'm eager to hear how your function works."

"I've never spent much time talking to a CEO," she said quietly. "I hope I can be a little bit useful to you, sir."

Leticia seemed shy, nervous, perhaps intimidated by me. I tried to put her at ease. "Leticia, I'm very interested in your function. I've always believed that it's one of the biggest influencers of customer satisfaction and loyalty. We pay a lot in our sales and marketing budgets to acquire customers. We can't afford to lose them over sloppy customer service!

"And," I added, "understanding what goes wrong is a great way to learn how we can improve customers' journeys and our products."

Leticia smiled broadly. "It's so nice to hear you say that, sir!"

"I mean it," I said. "So, let's start by talking about how you define customer service. What does your group do?"

Defining "Customer Support"

Leticia took a deep breath and dove in. "What motivates us is helping people. Our *main* service is 'customer support.' By that, we mean:

> *"Answers to customers' business and product usage questions. And for operational problems, diagnosis of the root-cause of the issue, resolution (by operating the asset, but no design changes), and if repairs (design changes) are needed, brokerage of repair (but not the repair itself, which is sold by engineers)."*

"What are operational problems?" I asked.

"I guess the technical term is 'incidents,'" she said. "Something went wrong with one of our services, or with a solution we sold. It's not working as expected. So, they call us."

"But you don't sell repairs?" I asked. Jen and Mike had been clear about repairs being Engineering's job.

"We don't," Leticia replied. "We diagnose incidents to find the root cause — exactly what is broken. Then, either we can resolve it without any design changes, like rebooting a system or resetting a password. Or if that doesn't work, we broker a repair contract with the appropriate Engineering group.

"At that point, there's no more value we can add. It's out of our hands. So, we close the ticket."

"Even though the repair isn't done yet?" I asked. I was a bit surprised.

"That's right," Leticia said. "And I know this is different from what you'll hear from most service-management experts. Let me explain....

"First, not all repair orders come from the incidents we manage. It doesn't make sense for us to track just a subset of them.

"Second, not all repair requests are funded; customers may have more important things to do with their money. Of course, customers and Max (Operations) preauthorize any repairs that threaten critical production systems. But we don't leave support tickets open indefinitely while discretionary repairs are waiting for prioritization.

"Third, it's not our job to track requests for repairs. We have another tool for that — our request-tracking system. I don't own that; the PMO does. And we're certainly not in the business of overseeing Engineering to make sure they complete their repair contracts!

"So," Leticia concluded, "we broker the repair contract. And once it's in the request-tracking system, we're done and we close the ticket."

"I can see you've put some thought into that boundary," I said.

Channels of Communications

"So," I said, pressing on, "how do these incidents come in to you?"

"We accept contacts from any channel. Phone is traditionally how we worked — you know, the old help desk. But now, we also accept contacts by email, text messages, and recently web chat (and soon, we'll have chat-bots that gather some initial information about a ticket).

"Also, we're just starting to monitor social media platforms to see what users are complaining about. We're focusing on services that external customers use, like the company's website, our software-as-a-service services offerings, and our smart-phone applications.

"By the way, these other channels did require a new position in my group — the dispatcher, who creates and assigns tickets to our agents."

"I like those other channels," I said. "Nobody likes sitting on the phone on hold for an hour waiting for the next operator."

"Oh, people don't wait on the phone for us!" Leticia exclaimed. "At least, not for long. We try to answer every call within three minutes. But if we're slammed and can't do that, our automated system tells callers how long the wait might be and gives them the option to have us call them back when the next agent is available (without losing their place in line, of course)."

As we got down to business, Leticia clearly became more comfortable talking to me, and her confidence in her group (and herself) emerged. I guess all it took for her to open up was an eager listener and a modicum of respect.

Levels of Service

"By the way," Leticia added, "you especially would never wait long. We can identify VIP callers based on caller IDs. And we give some people a special number to call. That allows us to automatically move them to the head of the queue and get to them more quickly."

"Is that for your top executives?" I asked.

"Certainly they get VIP service. But beyond that, we've got people in the field working with external customers. Some of them get VIP service too. Think of it like in a hospital.... A doctor is in the operating room and a critical system goes down. That doctor isn't a corporate executive, but that call gets answered right away, ahead of the queue.

"Now for our top executives," she said, "we provide 'concierge' service. We have one of our staff stationed in the executive offices, available to come by and help on a moment's notice. This is expensive. But we priced it out and gave them the option; and our executives are willing to pay for it. If they're in a meeting, think of all the high-priced talent that could be wasting time if a PC or teleconferencing system goes down!"

I guess I'd become used to that concierge service. But I wondered what kind of service everybody else was getting. "For the normal, non-VIP callers, how responsive can you be?"

"We can't solve every problem quickly," she said. "Sometimes, they're really complicated and require a lot of investigation. But we always immediately acknowledge receipt of the ticket, and we keep customers informed about what we're doing as we work on it. We do that no matter what level of service we're providing.

"Oh, and in addition to those different levels of service, we also offer multilingual services," she added.

"How do you do that? Doesn't that take a lot of headcount?"

"We use a vendor that offers a translation service. We just bridge them onto the call. And we use software to translate emails and texts.

"So, all in all," Leticia concluded, "we can give our customers choices as to our level of service. It's whatever they're willing to pay for."

Customers of Customer Service

"Who are your customers? The callers?" I asked.

"No, sir; they don't get to decide the level of service, and they don't pay for it," Leticia explained.

"Our services are sold to the *asset owners*. They either use the asset themselves, like their phones. Or they use the asset to provide a service to *their* customers, in which case their service comes with our support.

"For example, Max's services, like email, come with the right to call us for support. So, he buys our support for his infrastructure assets, and builds our costs into his rate for email (and everything else).

"Other business units and external customers who buy solutions are asset owners too. So, they're also my customers for support of their assets."

Customer Service sells support to asset owners,
not callers (who may be the asset owners' customers).

Incident Management Process

"Okay, so I call in with a problem. What happens next?" I asked.

"First," Leticia said, "our contact-center phone system puts the call in a queue, and an agent picks it up. They pull up your profile, which tells us what products and services you're using, and perhaps some history. That helps us provide a more personalized experience.

"The agent opens a ticket in our service-management system (which is up on another screen). That ticket provides a common record for anyone involved in that incident, and ultimately captures the root causes and how it was resolved.

"While we're entering the ticket," Leticia continued, "we talk to the caller until we fully understand the problem. Our service-management system includes a knowledge-base that tells the agents to ask such-and-such; and if the answer is yes, try this; or if no, ask this. A lot of times, that lets us resolve the problem right on the spot."

"And what if that knowledge-base doesn't get you there?" I asked.

"Then, we engage the appropriate engineers and service providers. We're specialists in customer service, but we're generalists in technologies; so we don't try to guess."

Support Knowledge-base

"Tell me more about this knowledge-base that guides you through questioning a caller, and hopefully resolving the problem," I requested.

"Yes, that's really important," Leticia said. "That knowledge-base is what they call a rules-based expert system. The content (the rules) comes from the engineers, the technology experts.

"We've worked with them to define the minimum required support documentation for each new solution. They didn't used to; but now, they build time for that into their project estimates. And then we work with them during the deployment of every new solution to integrate the support documentation into our knowledge-base."

"Who works with them?" I asked.

"We have a full-time person who owns the knowledge-base. She helps engineers translate their knowledge into our format. And sometimes she gets the budget to commission them to fill in gaps for older systems.

"She also adds into the knowledge-base anything we learn through experience, you know, when we engage the engineers and see how they diagnose a problem. That way, over time, we can resolve more and more incidents without needing Engineering's help."

"How did you convince the engineers to write documentation for you?" I asked. "I suspect they'd rather be developing something new."

Leticia laughed. "They don't want to be woken up in the middle of the night! I think they finally realized that the better they do at getting us this documentation, the less often we'll have to bother them.

"By the way," she added, "we also use the knowledge-base to offer self-help services to customers via a phone menu (IVR) and our support website. It's like a bunch of FAQs (frequently asked questions), but structured so you can drill down to the right answer.

"For our off-the-shelf products and services, we're hoping to integrate that with the smart-phone app we give to customers.

"And here's a really cool innovation-initiative that we just started," she added. "We're using predictive analytics with our ticket data to try to identify areas of the knowledge-base which most need improvement. I'm buying help on this project from Mike's AI group."

Subcontracting, Not Hand-offs

"Okay," I said, "if you can't resolve it, even with your knowledge-base, you hand it off to Engineering?"

"I'm sorry, sir, but 'hand off' isn't quite the right term," Leticia replied. "We own the ticket cradle-to-grave — that is, until the issue is either resolved or we broker a repair request with Engineering (where the ticket moves over into the request-tracking system).

"So, we don't 'hand it off' to others. What we do is *subcontract* to others for help. We retain full accountability for the ticket."

Incident Managers

"Do your agents manage those subcontractors?" I asked.

"We have a separate group of incident managers," Leticia replied. "Our level-one agents transfer calls to them once they decipher what the problem is and realize that they can't resolve it quickly.

"The incident managers are more senior, and have the time to focus on difficult incidents. Splitting them out also helps us manage front-line resource-levels to keep our response times down.

"So, they coordinate the subcontractors. If we start out with one Engineering group and they rule out their stuff as the cause of the problem, we subcontract to other groups. Sometimes we get a team of different engineers to work together on a ticket. Meanwhile, we insulate customers from any finger pointing.

"And while the engineers are investigating the incident, we keep the customer informed of the status of their ticket, and if possible, give them an estimate of when they can expect resolution (or at least when they can expect to hear from us next).

"Then," Leticia concluded, "when the incident is resolved or put in the queue for a repair, we make sure the customer understands where things stand and maybe what they need to do next."

Cooperation from Engineers

It sounded too good to be true. I had to ask, "What if the engineers aren't responsive to you? I suspect that helping you chase down glitches isn't their favorite activity."

Leticia smiled. "First, let me tell you what we *don't* do. I am *not* going to start up a group of junior engineers here in my group to do 'second-level' support. I know a lot of companies do that, especially for common technologies like PCs and end-user computing tools.

"But as we see it, us building expertise in areas that our engineers already know would be an expensive waste of resources. Ultimately, the company would have to hire two of every engineering domain — one in Engineering, and one here. If we were to use headcount that way, we'd reduce the degree of specialization in the Engineering community."

I must have looked puzzled, so Leticia elaborated, "Consider this.... If you could only afford two PC experts, would you have one do the serious engineering tasks like tracking new product offerings and designing configurations, while the other works on tickets? Both would have to know all the different platforms — Windows, IOS, etc.

"We think it would be better to have one engineer doing Windows and the other doing Apple, and both helping us out with incidents from time to time. That way, we'll have more technical depth."

"I understand," I said.

"Also, if we had junior engineers here in Customer Service, there's a risk of us going in directions that the real engineers don't agree with. It would just lead to stress between my group and Engineering."

The Golden Rule again. One can't compromise engineers' control over technical decisions, and then hold them accountable for the quality of their products.

"Oh," Leticia continued, "and we'd still need help from Engineering when we get in over our heads. So, if we haven't solved the problem of them being unresponsive, some tickets would still suffer. This level-two support group that some other companies do is a patch for a teamwork problem; and it just isn't scalable.

"The truth is," she said, "there's no way we can be experts in every technology. So, we don't try to be experts in any. It's enough to be experts in customer service! No, we follow the knowledge-base, then get help."

---

*Customer Service does not include
a group of junior engineers for level-two support.
Instead, it buys help from Engineering.*

Returning to my original question, I asked, "So, how did you get the engineers to be responsive to you?"

"We're into addressing root causes," Leticia replied. "So just like we do when we have an incident, we had to understand the root causes of why the engineers weren't responsive to us, and we had to fix that."

"Okay, I'll bite. Why weren't they responsive?" I asked.

"I'm sorry, sir, am I getting preachy?" she asked apologetically.

"Not at all, Leticia. I'm very interested in how you've made this work. I've had all the same issues in past companies between my customer service functions and my product engineers."

"Okay then," Leticia said, "root causes.... Sometimes, it was an attitude problem. Some engineers didn't understand how important we are to customer satisfaction. We addressed that through education (and a little support from Carlton).

"Sometimes, it was a resources problem. They were too busy working on projects to help us. But we're a paying customer. The cost of engineers' time to help us is built into our prices and their budgets. So now, lack of time is no excuse for not helping us.

"In other cases, it was a time-management problem. They'd booked themselves on projects every minute of every day, and didn't leave any time for helping us with incidents or for emergencies like repairs. They've worked on better scheduling, using Christine's PPM (project and portfolio management) system, I think."

Christine nodded in agreement.

"And, Leticia continued, "a few engineers just felt they were too important to work on this little stuff. It's true that the support tasks seem to fall to the younger engineers. But if we need a more senior person, we make them look like heroes for pitching in and saving the day."

I enjoyed the way she played human nature.

"It's working pretty well, now," Leticia said. "Of course, sometimes we have to do some prodding or escalate up a level in Engineering management. But at least accountability for helping us is in the right group."

Second-level Support

"Let's go back to your group of incident managers," I said. "How is that different from a group of junior engineers?"

"Oh, it's very different," Leticia said. "They're trained in customer service, not engineering. They still follow the knowledge base, and subcontract to Engineering and Operations as needed. What they specialize in is a *class of problems,* not technologies like the engineers do."

Level-two Customer Service groups specialize in
classes of problems, not domains of technologies.

"What's the difference?" I asked.

"Here's an example," Leticia replied. "We have a level-two group that handles problems with our solutions, and another one for business issues like invoices and access rights. Both groups work on all the different the solutions and the infrastructure they run on — the same technologies. But the questions we ask during the diagnosis process are different."

Weening Customers from Calling Engineers

I remembered, with a small dose of guilt, that early in my career (before I got VIP service), I used to call an applications developer I knew, by-passing the help desk. So I asked, "When you first got started on this transformation, did you have trouble getting internal customers to call you instead of their favorite engineer?"

"That took a little time," Leticia admitted.

"How did you go about that?"

"First, we had to get our processes in place. Then, we had to convince the engineers to let go. That wasn't too hard. They liked being heroes; but they'd really rather be engineering something than managing tickets. And they used to get calls that weren't even in their domains. Like an application seemed to be down, but really it was a server or the network.

"So, with just a little arm-twisting, they agreed to encourage customers to call us first.

"At first," Leticia explained, "we asked them to say, 'Thanks for calling us. Let me bridge Customer Service into this call, and we'll get your problem registered. And then I'll start work on it right away.'

"Then, after awhile, we asked the engineers to explain why customers are better off calling the Service Desk, and then just transfer the call to us. We gave them a list of reasons why it's best to call us directly, so they could sell the idea to callers (Figure 28)."

"Did that work?" I asked.

"It took time," she admitted. "Some customers kept calling the engineers. But when they found that person to be unavailable — in a meeting, or out of the office — then they'd reluctantly call us. The more we were able to resolve their issues, the more we added value by keeping them informed, the better we got, the more they called us first."

Figure 28: Why Call Customer Service Instead of Your Favorite Engineer

- Customer Service is always available, whereas engineers might be in a meeting, busy on a project, or at home after hours.

- You can call the same number for everything, avoiding confusion about whom to call.

- If a problem crosses domains, Customer Service provides a single point of contact rather than passing you from one Engineering group to another; and it protects you from finger-pointing.

- Customer Service may answer questions more quickly since:

  o They may already be aware of the problem.

  o With their knowledge-base of past problems and solutions, they may already have the answer.

- Customer Service stays in touch with you, while engineers may not have time to keep you informed of their progress.

- Involving Customer Service builds their knowledge-base of problems and solutions; so over time, resolution becomes faster and your cost of support goes down.

- Customer Service accumulates data on problems, to spot trends and prevent future problems ("problem management").

- Engineers are interrupted less often, so they can finish customers' projects sooner.

- You'll find Customer Service staff pleasant, since they're trained to handle upsetting situations ("bedside manner").

Problem Management

I wanted to be sure I understood the full scope of Leticia's Customer Service group. "At the start, you said customer support is your *main* service. Are there other things you do?"

"Oh, my, yes! And while they take less time, they're just as important."

"I'd like to hear about them," I said.

"Well, for one, we provide data about past tickets. This is part of *problem management.* The data tells us what typically breaks, or what confuses users. For example, if we're getting a lot of 'How do I make it do this?' questions, we can tell the engineers they need to improve their user interfaces, online help, or documentation."

"So if I'm following you," I said, "Engineering is your subcontractor for support; but they're your customer for these problem analyses?"

"That's right; they're customers as well as suppliers to us. But we also provide the data to solution owners, like internal business people who own applications and Max's managers who own the solutions that become off-the-shelf products and the infrastructure that produces their services."

Service Requests

"Another thing we sell to Engineering and Operations," Leticia continued, "is 'order processing' — we call them service requests."

"Is this for anything people want to buy from the company?" I asked.

"No, sir; only off-the-shelf products and services — things that customers can pick straight out of our catalog."

"Do you help customers figure out what they should buy?" I asked.

"We can ask if they want a red one or a green one; but if customers aren't clear about what they want, or if they're going to need custom solutions, we transfer them to Julio's Retail Sales group."

Customer Service brokers requests only for off-the-shelf products/services.
Sales analyzes requirements and brokers requests
whenever customers need help deciding what to buy.

"Can you tell customers the price, and when to expect delivery?"

"Generally, yes," Leticia replied. "But that's only because the supplier group has informed us in advance of their prices and delivery lead-times. We'd never make a commitment for others."

"Ah, yes," I nodded. "The Golden Rule. So once you've taken the order, do you work out the service-delivery processes and make sure the other groups deliver?" (I should have known better than to ask this.)

"Absolutely not! We're not the prime contractor for other people's products. Take PCs, for example.... We don't buy PCs and then re-sell them. Max's group sells (well, rents) PCs directly to customers.

"We just take orders on their behalf — a brokerage service. We pass requests along via our request-tracking system. Then, we leave it to the appropriate group to deliver, just like we do with repairs.

"And," Leticia added, "if they need help with their service-delivery processes, that's not us. Nate's Organizational Effectiveness group is in the business of facilitating internal process improvements."

"I see." I must have looked uninterested.

Leticia elaborated, "The cool thing about this service is that customers can order a whole bunch of stuff from different groups with just one call. Like let's say you hire a new employee. They're going to need a PC, phone, network account, email account, and so on. Call us, and we'll run you through the standard checklist — one-stop shopping!"

I could see the value in that.

"If I want something and I don't know whom to call," I asked, "are you the default point of contact?"

"No, that would be Julio's Retail Sales group," she said. "Of course, if we get that kind of call, we'll pass it along to them."

Other Services of Customer Service

"Okay, is there anything else that you do?" I asked.

"We do routine password resets, and update information in customers' accounts," Leticia replied. "Of course, we have to be absolutely sure we know who we're talking to. I won't bore you with the details. But it takes more than a name and a birthday to validate that you're really *you* before we talk about your password or account data."

"That's good to know." I remembered a news item about a German internet provider that paid a $10 million fine for exactly this — lax customer services practices. *103 Ref*

"So, is that it for you?" I asked.

"Well, that's it for now," Leticia said. "But we're always thinking about new ways to add value.

"One potential new service that's been kind of controversial is to have us give callers marketing messages during or at the end of a support call, like other products and services they might want to consider.

"Marketing is pushing for this. And I get that it's their job to think this way. But from my point of view, using customers' time for this without their permission isn't very customer-focused. So, at least for now, we're only willing to do this if another product or service would be directly relevant to the problem they're having. We're working with Marketing now to build those links into our knowledge-base."

Evaluating Customer Service Staff

"Leticia, I want to ask you something.... I presume you've got a lot of people under you. How do you manage their performance?"

"Oh, I love that topic!" she exclaimed. "I love my people!

"So first, we do focus on efficiency. But that doesn't mean we hold a whip over our staff. We don't evaluate them based on how many calls they take in a day, or how quickly they get customers off the phone. Those kinds of metrics would cause the wrong behaviors — they'd just try to get rid of callers as fast as they can.

"And of course, we can't evaluate staff based on how quickly they resolve problems; that's out of their control. (Hmm, maybe we should be evaluating Engineering on that!?)

"My main focus is customer satisfaction," Leticia said. "At the end of every call, we ask customers to rate us from 1 to 5; it's automated and real quick, so most do it. We're concerned about the 1s, 2s, and 3s.

"Later, when we close a ticket, we send out a brief survey. We look for patterns in the data — are they related to specific agents or specific types of problems? Then, I follow up to learn more."

Productivity in Customer Service

"Say more about your no-whip efficiency," I requested.

Leticia laughed at my reference to the whip.

"One important factor," she said, "is we're crisp about scheduling. We deploy staff based on forecasted workloads. When sufficient resources are available, everybody is calmer and more productive.

"We rotate staff so that they're not on the phones for eight straight hours. They might spend some of their day on the phone, some on web-chat, and some time in that incident-management group working on more complex tickets that require subcontracts. But of course, when a call-storm happens, it's 'all hands on deck!'"

"Since we have offices in Europe now and we'll be in East Asia soon, we're working on a follow-the-sun strategy to be available 24x7 while minimizing higher-cost swing shifts and overtime.

"We spend time and money on training," Leticia continued, "including diagnostic capabilities and general technology awareness.

"And I don't know if this counts as efficiency, but we also invest in training and coaching in 'bedside manner' — things like listening skills, empathy, and courtesy. We set up peer and expert reviews where we listen to calls and provide pointers to the agents."

Customer Service Career Paths

I had one last question for Leticia. "Is there a career path for your customer-service staff?"

"Yes, of course!" she exclaimed. "Some of them decide they're interested in selling, and go over to Julio's Retail Sales group. Some get interested in service management, and end up in Max's Operations group. Some get intrigued with technology, and go after training and jobs in Engineering. And we have a few supervisory positions they can grow into here in the Customer Service group.

"Customer Service is a great way for entry-level people to get a big-picture view of the entire organization — all our products and services, and our various internal lines of business. And when they move up and out, I'm proud of them and of what we've done for their careers."

Whew! Strong close. I was really impressed by Leticia's clarity of purpose, competence, and passion.

Chapter 19:
Field Technicians: How to Cover Remote Locations

Chapter summary (key take-aways): page 482

Some typical names for this type of business: field technicians, technician services, field support, local offices.

"Okay," Ravi said, "now it's Andy's turn. Andy, you'll recall, leads our Technician Services group."

I privately questioned what I could possibly learn from a manager of field technicians. But out of courtesy, I said, "Hi, Andy. Tell me about the role of technicians."

"I bet you're expecting the next few minutes to be pretty boring," Andy said with a smile. What was he, a mind reader!?

"But," he continued, "this is an area that many IT departments, as well as whole companies, get wrong. I know before the transformation, we did. And that led to lots of problems. So, I thought you might be interested in seeing how a conventional view of a relatively simple function can be trouble, and how we fixed it."

Andy had caught my attention. How much trouble could field technicians cause? And how different could the role be here?

Problems in Remote Locations

"We've got offices all over the place," Andy explained, "some relatively big, and others might be just one or two people covering an entire region."

"I can picture it," I said. "What was the problem with that?"

"Well, before the transformation, we were part of the internal IT department. We used to think of our staff as full-service IT functions for those remote locations. People came to us for everything. We used to install and repair PCs, printers, networks, everything! We even developed some local applications for internal customers.

"What happened was...." Andy inserted a dramatic pause, then exclaimed, "chaos, utter chaos! I was trying to think of a more diplomatic term; but there's no way to sugarcoat it!

"They all decided their own directions, so we ended up with quite a mess of diverse products to integrate and support. That was expensive, and it also caused trouble at the enterprise level. For example, at times, we thought we were having problems with an application, but the real problem was that local PC configurations couldn't support that application."

Andy continued, "We weren't doing bulk buys, since each location was pretty much doing its own thing. That also drove costs up.

"They all developed their own methods, and they figured things out on the fly. So, they really weren't very good at what they were doing. And we were paying for lots and lots of redundant learning curves.

"And since field staff couldn't be experts in everything, we just focused on the basics — PCs, end-user computing software, and local networks. That meant that if there was a problem out there with a remote server, custom application, or anything else, we'd have to put someone from headquarters on an airplane to go look at it."

Andy was on a roll, so I let him continue uninterrupted.

"We were also the primary point of contact for internal customers in those locations. We were out there making promises that the rest of the organization couldn't live up to. And we were recommending things that weren't in line with where the organization was going.

"Another problem was, we felt more affinity with the customers, who lived in the same town as us, than with folks back here in headquarters.

So, instead of improving relationships between remote customers and the whole organization, we'd point fingers and make the staff back in headquarters look bad. It was 'us versus them.'

"And our folks had no career path. What are you going to do with a renegade generalist in a high-tech field, especially one who has pissed off leaders throughout the organization!?

"It was total chaos!" Andy concluded with a flourish.

"I can see that," I said, smiling at his dramatics. The value of this conversation was dawning on me. In many of the companies I'd worked for, we'd had similar strains between our field support organizations and headquarters. And that had an impact on customer satisfaction.

"And remember," Andy concluded, "at that time, we only supported internal customers. Our product engineers were flying all over to install and support the company's products. The model wasn't scalable."

The Proper Role of Remote Staff

"So, how did you solve this chaos?" I dutifully asked.

"I'll tell you," Andy replied, "when IT was integrated with the rest of the company in the restructuring, we *had* to solve it.

"Start with that basic principle of structure: specialization (Chapter 7)," he said. "That pointed out the obvious. There's no way that one or two people in a remote location could be competent at all the diverse technologies they were supporting. They had to be generalists.

"Meanwhile, back here in headquarters, we had specialists in every one of those domains. So, we realized that, to make this work, we had to be a whole lot better at teamwork.

"Now, there are only two ways that teamwork could be defined. Option One, those guys in remote locations could be full-service technology suppliers, and subcontract to experts in headquarters when they felt they needed help. Or, Option Two, the real experts back here could sell to remote customers, and subcontract to field staff for on-site assistance.

"We'd been operating in Option One," Andy said. "The field staff could have asked for help from headquarters; but they rarely did. And even if they did, that didn't fix the rest of the chaos."

I nodded.

"So," Andy continued, "we flipped it around. Now, I'm in the business of selling 'eyes and hands in the field' to the experts here in headquarters. Sure, we talk to external customers all the time. But our direct customers are within the organization."

Technicians sell 'eyes and hands in the field'
to the experts in headquarters.

"Hang on a minute," I said. "Aren't your technicians like the trained mechanics at a car dealership?"

"That's a fair analogy," Andy said.

"But I buy repairs directly from the dealership, i.e., from technicians."

Andy replied, "And what happens when they get in over their heads?"

"I get frustrated."

Andy smiled. Point taken.

"Okay," I said. "I understand. But how exactly does this work?"

Andy explained, "Let's say, for example, that someone out there needs a PC. The central PC group is the one that sells it to them. They subcontract to me for on-site installation.

"The same thing goes for repairs. The PC Engineering group here in headquarters sold the PC, so they have to repair it. Those engineers subcontract to us for help. They give us documentation and procedures, and maybe guidance over the phone or via remote-control if we have a problem. But if the documentation and guidance they provide isn't good enough for us to fix the problem, then that PC engineer has to take over and finish the job.

"That model applies to everything," Andy said. "If there's a problem in a high-tech remote device, you can't expect my generalists to know what to do. But now, they don't need to. Engineers here in headquarters are accountable for the repair, and use my staff as eyes and hands in the field to help.

"And," Andy said, "that includes working with external customers on company products. That's been a lot of fun for us."

Depending on Teamwork

"Option Two requires a lot more communications with headquarters," I observed.

"It does," Andy agreed. "And that has a cost, I know. But it's worth it.

"You see, by flipping the teamwork model around, we get the best of everything. We still have local responsiveness. But we get in-depth engineering expertise applied to every situation, without those expensive engineers having to travel all the time. We buy centrally to consolidate our suppliers and negotiating power. And we've got consistent technical directions globally.

"Oh, and once we got all this working, the engineers started subcontracting to us for work back here in headquarters, too. We assemble and configure PCs, and install phones, for example.

"And beyond that," Andy continued, "it's not just Engineering that uses us. We help Operations run their equipment in remote locations. And

Leticia uses us to help diagnose problems when customers can't explain things too well over the phone.

"On the sales side," Andy added, "we aren't in the business of discovering opportunities or diagnosing requirements — we're not trained to do that. We do help by passing leads and news to Sales. And sometimes we work for the business analysts gathering requirements.

"So, to make a long story short," he concluded, "we stopped trying to be a full-service IT function in remote locations. Now we just sell technician time, and act as agents of all the experts here in headquarters."

"Brilliant!" I said. "You've got the same people doing essentially the same things. But just by sorting out your services, and who's the prime contractor versus the subcontractor — the walk-throughs — you're getting the advantages of local presence *and* centralization."

Career Paths for Technicians

"But I have a question for you," I said. "Are these jobs satisfying? Are you able to recruit people into jobs where they just do as they're told?"

"Sure," Andy replied. "My staff still get all the same satisfaction from helping customers. But they're much less stressed now. They don't have to pretend to be experts at things that they're not. They don't have to struggle and fail at technical problems that are over their heads. And they're enjoying the teamwork with the rest of the organization, instead of the old adversarial relationships.

"And as relationships improved," he continued, "their career options opened up. Not all of them want to move their families back here to headquarters. But for those who do, or who are willing to work remotely, it's great. They're getting exposure to lots of different domains of technology and services, so they can hone in on what they enjoy. Meanwhile, they're building their network with all the different managers back here."

Site Coordinators

"In the restructuring," I asked, "did *all* the remote staff get assigned to your group?"

"Most, but not all," Andy replied. "In some of the larger locations, we have specialists in specific domains, like a product engineer, or a PC or a network specialist, or a business analyst. Those people mapped to the appropriate other groups. They still live out in the remote locations, but they report to other managers here. Of course, even in those bigger locations, I have one or more field technicians."

"So, the staff in those locations may report to different bosses?"

"Exactly." Andy smiled. "We know how to manage people remotely. But to help the managers here in headquarters (or wherever they live) manage their remote staff, we appoint the most senior person at a location to be what we call a 'Site Coordinator.'"

"What's their role?" I asked.

"Site Coordinators take on some supervisory duties on behalf of the real managers back here. Those are typically things that aren't specific to the domain, you know, not business or technical decisions. They're administrative issues like official business, work scheduling, hours of operations, dress codes, and occasionally some performance-management conversations.

"We think of Site Coordinators as subcontractors to the boss," Andy explained, "selling eyes and hands in the field for supervisory duties. Other than in really large locations (like our European office), this isn't a full-time job. It's over and above their normal duties, and not related to whatever their specialty may be."

The Proof is In the Pudding

"May I just add one more thing?" Andy asked.

"Of course," I said.

"I have to admit that I was originally resistant to this transformation. I thought that I had more power and glory as the full-service provider to the field. I *owned* the field!

"But now," he said, "I'm totally on-board. We're providing better service to remote customers. We're saving money. We're treating my staff better, so morale is up and stress is down. And I think my peers value us.

"As my husband told me, it's better to win at something small than lose at something big. So, if you hear anybody saying that I'm not really a believer in the transformation, well, I sure am now," Andy said in an uncharacteristically serious tone.

"Thanks, Andy," I said. "You've given me some really interesting ideas on how to handle remote offices and global customers better. And I appreciate *your* transformation."

Chapter 20:
Project Management Office:
Roles Within Project Teams

Chapter summary (key take-aways): page 483

Some typical names for this type of business: PMO, project and portfolio management.

"Okay," Ravi said, "we're short on time, so let's move on to our Project Management Office."

Now this could be interesting. I've seen so much controversy over the role of project managers versus engineers.

The Business of a PMO

Before I could even say hello, Christine began. Clearly she was high-energy and enthusiastic about her function.

"My PMO is a group of people trained in project-management methods and tools. They know PMBOK (the project management book of knowledge). Many of them have PMP certifications from the Project Management Institute. [104 Ref]

"In the past, the engineers managed simple projects. But for large projects, my project managers were brought in. The confusion, back then, was about who was really managing those big projects — the engineers or us? In other words, who's accountable for results?"

She'd hit the nail on the head! That was always the root of the tensions.

"In the transformation," Christine continued, "as soon as we stopped talking about who *does* what and started talking about our services, we figured out that we're not in the business of selling solutions (like engineers do). We sell PERT charts, and so on. Engineers are the prime contractors and are accountable for delivery of big and small projects alike. They subcontract to us for services like project planning, project-estimate facilitation, and project data administration (like costs and milestones) when they think we can add value to their projects.

"In other words, despite our name, our job is not to 'manage' projects. It's to help others succeed at managing *their* projects. So really, we sell project *facilitation,* not project management."

A project-management office (PMO) sells project <u>facilitation,</u> not the management of other groups' projects.

"Once we figured out who's the prime contractor and who's the sub-contractor, all the confusion went away," Christine concluded.

She's right. It is indeed as simple as that!

"By the way," she added, "when we got our service catalog sorted out, we realized that we don't just sell to the engineers. For example, Nate wanted our help with the culture roll-out. We helped Max change a major outsourcing vendor. We're available to support anyone who's got a project to manage."

"I like that entrepreneurial spirit," I said. "By clarifying what business you're in and what services you sell, you saw opportunities to add value in new ways."

"We did," Christine said, smiling with pride. And before I could ask, she continued, "There are other things that the PMO sells. We offer training in project-management and project-estimation methods.

"We own the project-management software that everybody uses, and we sell everybody access to it. (Of course, we use Max's group to host it, Leticia for support, and Jen for repairs and upgrades.)

"And we help managers track their resources against projects (project portfolio management). That's where they reserve time for emergencies and for unbillable sustenance activities. And that's how they know when their staff will be available for the next project.

"Also, as Leticia mentioned, we own the request-management system and facilitate project intake.

"Related to that, we sell facilitation services to purser committees," Christine noted.

"The bottom line is, we get our kicks helping people get their projects and resources organized. We know we're helping the whole organization perform better."

Projects Dashboard

"Are there any other services you sell?" I asked, just to be sure I had a complete picture of the PMO.

"There is one more thing," Christine said. "We facilitate the project dashboard that Carlton likes to see."

"I'd like that for my entire company," I said. "How does that work?"

"Well, notice that I said 'facilitate.' We do *not* gather project data and aggregate it to present to Carlton. That's how it looks and how we used to think of it, but that led to problems. Engineers viewed us as spying on them, and they were reluctant to give us truthful data.

"Meanwhile," Christine continued, "we were held accountable for the data that we weren't being given. We looked bad, and Carlton was surprised at the last minute by project delays.

"Thanks to the transformation," she said, "we made it clear that we're not spying on project leaders. Everybody is required — by Carlton, not us — to report project status — to Carlton, not to us.

"We're just here to help them do that. We run the dashboard, but the data in it totally belongs to the people who are accountable for projects. That clarification of the walk-through is what made the dashboard work.

"Of course," Christine concluded, "we hope they buy our 'project data administration' service, which includes helping them update their data in the dashboard."

Where a PMO Might Report

"Perfect," I said. "Just one more question, Christine. You focus on how people get their jobs done. Isn't that similar to what Nate's Organizational Effectiveness group does? Why are you located here in Ravi's product support group, rather than with Nate?"

"Actually, we debated that in the restructuring," she said, "and it could have gone either way. Since walk-throughs flow right into project plans, there are clearly synergies with Nate's OE function.

"But we're really not a Coordinator function," she explained, "although we do help primes coordinate their subs. But that's not like coordinating big shared decisions like plans, policies, and organizational design.

"So, we decided to emphasize the *service* aspects of the PMO over the coordination. But again, it could have gone either way."

Nate interjected, "We'll talk about Coordinator functions next. But now, it's time for us to get going."

"Ravi, Leticia, Andy, and Christine, thank you all," I said. "I'm very impressed with how you've laid out your accountabilities and teamwork relationships — such precise definitions. And I've taken a bunch of notes on concepts I'll be able to use in my company."

Ravi gently bowed his head, while the others beamed.

Chapter 21:
Compliance: The Example of Information Security

Chapter summary (key take-aways): page 483

Some typical names for this type of business: information security, cyber-security; and related to regulatory compliance, quality control, and other compliance functions.

My next meeting was with Johan, their Chief Information Security Officer (CISO). He was a clean-cut young man, erect in his posture, serious, and intense — almost military. (I later learned that he came from a Defense background, in cyber-warfare.)

His countenance was stern, verging on discomforting. And he was rather abrupt. "How can I help you?" he asked as we took our chairs in his office.

This was *not* a warm, hospitable opening. But I suspect that if I ever were under attack, he's a guy I'd want alongside me.

To break the ice, I said, "Johan, as a CEO, I understand the importance of information security. I've seen enough examples where a breach brought down a CEO, even a whole company. And in past jobs, I've spent plenty of time with my CISO explaining to the Board our security strategies and the need for investments."

Johan seemed to relax a bit; he even allowed himself a slight smile. By the way, I wasn't just flattering him. I meant it. This is a critical function for every CEO and Board.

Defining Information Security

"First," I said, "I'd like to understand what you mean by 'information security' to see if we're on the same page."

"Okay," Johan said. "Information security prevents and mitigates the damages of threats of digital espionage (e.g., data theft) and sabotage (e.g., denial of service, data corruption, ransomware)."

I nodded in agreement.

"There's a lot that goes on within that scope," Johan said. "We maintain our security strategy, in alignment with the Board. We identify and track vulnerabilities. We detect and respond to attacks. And we analyze access-rights requests and identify risks.

"By the way," he added, "we go beyond just technologies. We also work with HR, since the wrong employees can be a dangerous source of risk. We work with Physical Security, since we're only as good as our weakest link. We collaborate with our Business Continuity Coordinator on integrated plans to reduce risks and recover quickly from incursions. We coordinate across the enterprise."

Is Security Accountable for Security?

I knew a bit about security, so I didn't want to get into the various initiatives they were implementing. What I wanted to learn was whether the CISO functioned any differently here in a Market Organization.

In that vein, I asked a leading question. "Johan, are you the guy who's accountable for all aspects of information security?"

"Well, sir, I used to think that way — before the transformation. But that was problematic."

"How so?" I asked.

"You've heard about the Golden Rule, right?"

"Of course," I said.

"I wasn't aware of the Golden Rule back then," Johan said, "but it's natural to act that way. When I was accountable for security, I insisted on the authority to make sure we were operating in a safe manner. I used to issue edicts, check up on people, approve or block vendors and software packages — I exercised a lot of power."

"And that didn't work?" I asked.

Why the Traditional Approach Didn't Work

"It did work, to a degree," Johan said. "But there were problems...."

Not their job: "For example, with me taking on all that accountability, the rest of the staff didn't feel accountable at all. They didn't put much effort into something that was my job, not theirs. So, I didn't get the cooperation I needed."

Obstacle to their objectives: "Even worse," Johan continued, "the rest of the staff had incentives to thwart me. They were measured on their delivery of results, and security takes time and slows them down."

To clarify, I asked, "'Results' being the delivery of their projects and services *minus* the security of those products and services?"

"Exactly the problem, sir. The incentives were working against me. Everybody was looking for ways to get around my controls, in order to get their jobs done."

Free to misbehave: "The third factor was the killer," Johan said. "If others messed up and bad things happened, I got the blame, not them. Let me tell you, it's not fun being in the scapegoat business!"

"And," I added, "it's not productive to hold you accountable for others' mistakes."

"That's right!" Johan affirmed with a grim, battle-scarred smile. "Not only was security not their job. There weren't serious consequences if they completely ignored my mandates.

"And you know," he continued, "a lot of security risks come from our own forces — like falling for phishing, or not securing passwords, or copying data to unsecured media. There's only so much my team can do, on our own."

Turning the Dynamics Around

"So, what did you do?" I asked.

"At first, I didn't get it," Johan replied. "I just pushed harder. My staff and I worked even longer hours, but there still was never enough time in my team to catch everybody else's mistakes.

"I demanded even more control," he continued. "Nobody would challenge me, because security is paramount. But I knew things weren't right. And it wasn't pleasant being at odds with my peers all the time. Ultimately, adversarial relations made me less effective."

I'd seen these problems everywhere I'd been. But nobody had ever presented me with a good solution. "Is there a better way?" I asked.

"Yes, absolutely," Johan asserted. "It all became very clear to me during the transformation process. I came to an epiphany. I realized we had to turn the dynamics around 180 degrees."

Everybody is Accountable for their Own Behaviors

"180 degrees?" I was puzzled.

"Yes," Johan said. "We had to make it clear that *everybody* is accountable for their own behaviors. And that includes security.

"Then," he continued, "I redefined my mission to be *helping* everybody fulfill *their* security accountabilities."

This was indeed different. I saw the potential. But I couldn't quite see the path forward. "How did you make everybody accountable?" I asked.

"Carlton did. He made it clear that he holds them all accountable for security, and my function is a service to them to help them get there.

"Essentially," Johan concluded, "Carlton got the company's senior executives to accept accountability for their own staff's behaviors."

"I can do that." I said. And I will.

Everybody is accountable for their own behaviors, including security.
An Information Security function helps them fulfill that accountability.

Security as a Service

"This 180-degree change must have been quite a mind-shift for your staff as well as your peers," I noted.

"It was," Johan concurred. "I had to teach my team to look at others as *customers,* not sources of risk that we had to control.

"When we did our service catalogs, we had to think about what we could offer to help everybody succeed. That exercise really helped with the mind-shift. Oh, and in that process, we came up with some new services that are improving our security profile even more.

"We also got rid of some things," Johan added. "I used to own the network firewalls. That's really an operational function, although the purpose is security. So, we moved that to Network Operations under Max (Operations). They're accountable for selling safe connectivity. And they know how to manage operations better than we do.

"We moved firewall engineering to Mike (Technology Engineering). They know how to engineer devices better than us.

"We help both Max and Mike with product assessments, design reviews, configuration policies, and incursion monitoring.

"We also transferred access administration to Ravi (Product Support). We evaluate the risks of access requests (as a subcontractor to Access

Administration). Using our assessments, asset owners decide what risks they're willing to take, and they own the consequences. But Ravi's team coordinates the whole process and administers the data."

"That all makes sense," I said.

Assessments versus Audits

"One key change," Johan added, "was that we got out of the 'audit' business. We don't check up on people. And we're not a control point where you need our approval for things. We don't need that kind of power anymore."

"What's wrong with giving you that authority?" I asked.

"Here's what happened," Johan replied. "When we were auditors, people saw us as an adversary. So, it undermined our relationships. I can't go to them and say, 'I'm from the Internal Revenue Service (tax collector) and I'm here to help!'"

I laughed. Too true! And Johan looked so serious when he said it.

"Putting them in a defensive posture made us *less* effective in securing the company," he said.

"Now, instead of audits, we offer *assessments* — studies that tell people where their weaknesses are."

"How is an assessment different from an audit?" I asked.

"It's similar in content, but there's one critical difference: In an audit, the people you're evaluating are not your customers; someone else has hired you to judge those people. When the Internal Revenue Service audits your taxes, they're working for the government, not for you.

"In an assessment," Johan explained, "we're working for the people we're assessing. The purpose is to help them prepare for the real audit, which might be done by Corporate Internal Audit, by external regulators, or by the reality of an attack. To continue the analogy, we're like your accountant as distinct from the IRS."

Audit: Sell to <u>A</u> your judgments about <u>B</u>. ("Are they complying?")
Assessment: Help <u>B</u> prepare for <u>A's</u> audit. ("Am I complying?")

"That subtle shift made a huge difference," Johan continued. "For example, they used to resent vulnerability assessments. They saw them as a form of control, something that took time away from their jobs, and potentially a source of embarrassment. With minimal cooperation from the rest of the staff, our assessments couldn't be as thorough, and remediation of the issues we found didn't always happen.

"Once others understood their own responsibility for security, they were eager to buy our assessments and follow our advice. They were more honest and engaged, and results improved. They acted on the findings. And the whole company became more secure."

"And relationships improved?" I asked.

"They sure did," Johan affirmed. "And as they did, I actually ended up with *more influence over them, not less.* Counter-intuitive, isn't it!?"

"It is," I said. "But I get it. Isn't there still some need for audits, though?"

"There is," Johan replied hesitantly. "But we moved that over to the Corporate Internal Audit group. It would be a conflict of interests for us to do audits — to both give advice, and then judge how well that advice worked."

It all made sense. But still, just walking away from controls sounded risky. "Beyond periodic audits, isn't there a need for oversight?" I asked.

"We have oversight.... It's called your boss! But I don't need any oversight power over my peers. Our leaders accept accountability for their groups, take our findings seriously, and look to us for help coordinating security initiatives."

Services of the Security Coordinator

"So, as I understand it," I said, "you've redefined your role to be a service to others, who are accountable for their own security. And to reflect that, you've defined a new service catalog. What's in it?"

"Here, have a look...." Johan showed me his catalog of services (Appendix 7).

"Basically," he summarized, "I've got three lines of business under me. One group focuses on vulnerabilities and preventative measures, and another on threats (detecting them, responding to them, and recovering from them). Using a sports analogy, that's like our offensive team and our defensive team.

"The third group, sometimes called 'governance, risk, and compliance' (GRC), coordinates security strategies, policies, and plans. They maintain the security vulnerabilities in the enterprise risk registry. They also coordinate the security initiatives in the strategy. Of course, I'm deeply engaged in that."

Looking through Johan's catalog, I saw that every item was defined as a service to others who are accountable for their own security.

The Results

"Is this 180-degrees approach working?" I asked. "I heard you say that relationships are better. But would you say the company is more, or less, secure now?"

"There's no question about it, we're more secure," Johan said assuredly. "Let's go back over those services we just discussed...."

Johan took me back through his services one by one, and explained why they're more effective now (Appendix 7). In every case, he insisted, holding everybody accountable for security, and providing the services they need to succeed at it, produced better results than command-and-control.

Universal accountability and a service-oriented approach to compliance produces better results than command-and-control.

The Security / Business Operations Trade-off

"Let me ask you a more nuanced question," I said. "I know there's a trade-off between security and business operations — security can slow things down. How are others doing at balancing that trade-off? Are they tending to favor business operations over security, perhaps because the rewards are more immediate and security threats are less tangible and more distant?"

"Interesting question," Johan said. "I had that concern at first. And maybe at first, there was some of that.

"But you know, we get multiple attacks every day. And some of them are bound to get through our defenses. We had one incident, and it came down to one of Max's Operations staff not following procedures. Carlton came down hard on Max (not me). An operator got fired. And since then, people have been paying a lot more attention to security!

"To be perfectly honest," he said, "I'd have to admit that they're making better decisions than I did. I grant that absolute security would shut down the business, and we can't do that. But since I was not accountable for product delivery, I used to balance that trade-off way over on the side of safety, and I probably did a little damage to business results to avoid some relatively minor risks.

"Now," Johan concluded, "the same people who are accountable for results are also accountable for the security of those results. They're in the best position to understand all the trade-offs and decide the right balance, with our input, of course."

Broader Applicability

"Johan, I see the merits of your approach. And I think it applies not just to information security, but to all a company's risk-management and compliance functions."

"You know," Johan said, "this is hard for a former DoD cyber-warfare guy like me to admit. But I think this is a case where the soft approach is really the strong approach.

"Once Carlton got accountabilities in the right place, I was able to partner with people — on their side of the table, not as their enemy — and we got a lot more done. And by the way, it was a lot less stressful for me and my team.

"It took me awhile to get on board with this transformation," Johan admitted. "But now, I'm one of its greatest advocates."

Chapter 22:
Coordinators: Organization, Plans, and Policies

Chapter summary (key take-aways): page 484

Some typical names for this type of business: planning, policies, business development, organizational effectiveness, diversity, office of transformation, business continuity, risk management, regulatory compliance.

For examples of this line of business in various industries and internal shared-services functions, see Appendix 3.

As we walked down the hall and through their hoteling atrium, Nate said, "Okay, now it's time to meet with my boss."

"No problem. Where shall I park myself while you're doing that?" I asked, looking at the simple but functional work cubicles we were passing.

"No, I meant to say that *you're* going to meet my boss!" Nate explained that as the Organizational Effectiveness leader, he reports to Barbara who heads up all the policy, planning, compliance, and standards functions. They're called 'Coordinators' in the framework of types of businesses (Figure 9).

We met up with Barbara just outside her office. "I guess I'm back just in time," she said with a smile. "Please come in."

There was something about Barbara that immediately made me feel comfortable. She seemed warm, pleasant, self-assured, and present.

As we settled in, Barbara asked, "Has Nate been treating you well today?"

"Very well, indeed! Thank you."

"Good. So, what do you think of our organization so far?" she asked.

"Actually, I'm impressed. I learned something useful in every meeting."

"So far," Barbara joked. "Let's see if I can live up to the expectations set by my esteemed colleagues!"

Role of Coordinators

I smiled, enjoying her breezy style. "So," I said, "tell me what your group does."

"We're called 'Coordinators' for a reason," Barbara said. "Decisions that impact many functions should be made by a consensus of stakeholders (rather than by any one group) — things like plans and policies. We're in the business of pulling together the right stakeholders, and facilitating them to consensus on those shared decisions."

"Isn't that similar to the PMO?" I asked, revisiting a question I'd put to Christine.

"We don't get involved in coordinating projects. That's the job of the prime contractor, with help from the PMO. We work at a higher level, across all projects. What motivates us is seeing the organization come together on *shared decisions* that affect us all."

Coordinators facilitate stakeholders' consensus
on shared decisions (e.g., policies, plans, and standards).

Organizational Effectiveness

"For example," Barbara continued, "Nate's Organizational Effectiveness (OE) group is one of our functions. He's led this entire transformation process, and continues to do so. And all the decisions along the way were made by a consensus of the leadership team.

"Nate," she said, "would you like to describe your function?"

"I'd love to," Nate replied.

"Now that we're getting past the major transformation initiatives," he said, "we're pursuing ongoing improvements, for example, service-management processes like ITIL."

"Also, on an ongoing basis, we coordinate the micro-agreements that make this organizational operating model work. For example, we facilitate walk-throughs for every new project and service, and change control before new solutions go into production.

"My group is also responsible for staff communications and new-employee orientations, because we need everyone to understand the whole organizational operating model (not just HR issues).

"And the company is doing some acquisitions," Nate continued. "So, once the deal is done, we lead our acquisition-integration process (Chapter 31).

"Where's the line between your domain, Nate, and the HR function?"

"HR looks after the employment relationship between our company and our staff," he explained. "OE looks at how we work — the design of the organization, and the collaborative processes within it. These are really different specialties."

"I can see the difference," I said.

"There's more," Barbara added. "Nate leads our Diversity program. Just like information security, Diversity is everybody's responsibility. That's why it's here under the Coordinators.

"Diversity could have reported to Carlton or me," she noted. "But reporting-level doesn't say anything about gravitas. And there are real synergies with Organizational Effectiveness. You know, Diversity is not simply a matter of training or hiring practices (HR issues). It's built into every dimension of our organizational operating model."

Nate added, "I also manage our Safety and Quality programs. They also involve cross-boundary processes and the organizational ecosystem."

"Makes sense," I said. "Clearly, if I'm going to drive a transformation, I'll need an OE function. Thanks, Nate. So, Barbara, what else does your Coordinator group do?"

Planning

"Another Coordinator function is planning," Barbara said, "both strategic and operating plans. Shall we start with the operating plan?"

I smiled as she continued.

"Annually, every department forecasts what it might sell in the year to come. They plan how they'll fulfill those sales, including what resources they'll need. And that's the basis for our budget submissions. That's our operating plan."

"Yes, Nate explained investment-based budgeting (Chapter 10)."

"Great," Barbara continued. "Here's a key question: Who do you think is accountable for coming up with the operating plan?"

"Well," I said, "the obvious answer would be you. But I'll bet you're going to tell me it's everybody."

"You're right!" Barbara smiled. "If Carlton is going to hold our leaders accountable for their businesses, they have to have the authority to plan those businesses. So as entrepreneurs, *everybody* is accountable for their own respective operating plans.

"But," Barbara continued, "investment-based budgeting is a fairly detailed method. So, part of our job is to teach and coach everybody through that process.

"Beyond that, there's the coordinating aspect of it. All the individual groups' operating plans have to come together into a single, integrated companywide plan."

I nodded. This was one of my concerns about empowerment.

"Our Planning group lays out the planning process (complete with leadership-team workshops and dates). They provide common frameworks, assumptions, and tools. They coach leaders in developing their respective plans. And they coordinate all the dialog that's needed to produce an integrated plan.

"This is a good example of what we Coordinators do," Barbara noted. "We help others individually, while also coordinating them to make shared decisions and come up with integrated plans."

"I see." I appreciated the way they kept total accountability for businesses within the business where it belongs, and yet still pursued cohesive plans. I will never again hold my planning group accountable for the company's plans.

"Strategic planning follows the same model," Barbara continued. "It just answers different questions: What lines of business do we want to pursue in the future, and how do we plan to get from here to there? (It's no different for internal service providers like IT. [105 More])

"Carlton and we senior leaders decide strategic goals, often based on ideas that bubble up. Then, everybody proposes strategic initiatives within their domains, with walk-throughs that align all participating groups. And we come together on which ones we'll pursue.

"Of course," Barbara continued, "strategic planning is a specialty in its own right. And everybody's individual plans have to add up to the enterprise strategic plan. Hence, the need for our services as Coordinators."

Barbara concluded the Planning domain with, "This group also provides the Business Development function, since acquisitions are driven by our strategies. And since acquisitions fold into the organization and impact many domains, we can't just dump them on people, That's why this is a Coordinator function."

Research and Innovation

"I assume the strategic plan also drives innovation initiatives, such as new product development," I said. "Do you have a role there?"

"We do," Barbara replied. "Of course, we're not an R&D function. Everybody does innovation within their own lines of business (Chapter 32). We coordinate the innovation funding-request process, and we help Carlton manage the portfolio of innovation investments."

"What value do you add?" I asked.

"Our Research and Innovation Coordinator helps entrepreneurs throughout the company prepare their funding-requests for innovation initiatives. We've adopted Amazon's PR-FAQ process. We help them prepare a future press release that describes the problem — the pain point — and the proposed solution. And we help them create the FAQs — questions they'd expect customers to ask, and questions they'd expect the company to ask.

"Then, we coach them through the process of socializing their idea, refining it, engaging OE for the walk-through, and ultimately presenting the proposal to Carlton for funding. And every once in a while, we're able to bring in external innovation grants.

"We also help them do any necessary research. We can provide external sources of data, and advice on research and innovation methods."

"Is there any stakeholder coordination involved?" I asked.

"We think of these innovation initiatives as an investment portfolio. So, we help Carlton manage that portfolio. We orchestrate presentations, and then help him analyze what we have going and what new initiatives we need in the context of our business strategies."

"He's the 'shark tank' and you're the emcee for the show?" I posited.

Barbara laughed. "Exactly. But Carlton's too nice to call him a shark!"

Business Continuity

"Moving on," I said, "do you coordinate any other types of planning?"

"Yes," Barbara said, "we facilitate business continuity planning (BCP)."

"Is that the disaster recovery plan for the data center?" I asked.

"It's that and much more. If ever there's a disaster, *every* group needs to make sure its people are safe, know its priorities in helping the organization as a whole return to operational, and get its own business going again at the appropriate time.

"So again," she said, "we have a situation where everybody is accountable for their own respective plans. But all those individual plans have to be integrated into a single, coordinated organizationwide plan."

I nodded. This seemed like common sense. But then I recalled what a poor job we'd done of BCP in most of my prior companies.

That realization deepened as Barbara went on. "Business continuity planning goes beyond just disaster recovery planning. We help our leaders think about all the awful things that might happen, and prepare ourselves in advance to limit the risks and damages.

"For example, we think about cyber-attacks, physical attacks, natural disasters (including pandemics), and other risks like key vendors being acquired by a competitor. It's a grim business," she smiled.

"And all this applies to our supply chain as well. We're careful to select vendors that have good business continuity plans; and each group engages its contractors and vendors in our planning process.

"We also coordinate periodic tests of our business continuity plans, and

God forbid, execution of those plans if needed," Barbara added. "And we keep stakeholders (including the Board) informed of the company's readiness and risks." *106 IT*

I nodded. At least we'd done some of that. But not enough. My whole company needs to be disciplined about BCP, I noted.

Policies

"Beyond plans, what else requires your coordination?" I asked.

"Policies, of course," Barbara replied. "We believe that all stakeholders who are materially affected by a policy, or who have something to contribute, should be represented in the policy-making decision."

"That could be cumbersome," I worried.

"It can be, a bit," Barbara admitted. "But the alternative — a policy 'czar' with the power to dictate policies and then force others to comply — would certainly not be compatible with our culture. We couldn't disempower others in this way, and then still hold them accountable for the performance of their businesses.

"Furthermore, we need input from all the stakeholders to make the right policy decisions.

"And you know," she added, "compliance is much less of an issue when everybody was part of the decision."

"But," I objected, "you can't have everybody who's affected by a policy in the room."

"True enough. Our job is to identify the stakeholders and get them to put forward the right representatives. In many cases, those representatives check back with their constituents during the process. But with or without that, it's important to get all the stakeholders represented."

"How many people are typically involved in a policy decision?" I asked.

"It depends on the policy," Barbara replied. "For some, there are only a few stakeholders, like data retention where we involved Operations, Legal, Tax, and HR. [107 IT] Sometimes there are lots of stakeholders, like our work-from-home policy where we engaged the entire leadership team as well as staff representatives.

"But we've gotten pretty good at facilitating discussions and getting large teams to consensus on precisely worded policy statements. The big decision-teams take a little longer, but we get them there."

As I thought about it, I appreciated the value of a consensus-based approach. I'd seen too many policies go awry because they didn't account for some critical realities, or because they were difficult to understand, or because people just didn't believe in them.

Regulatory Compliance

"So far, if I'm tracking, you facilitate consensus on organizational plans and policies. Is there more here?" I asked.

"Just a second," Barbara said. She appeared to be texting someone. "I just asked another member of my team if he could join us."

Returning to my question, Barbara said, "More here? Yes, there is. One other domain is Regulatory Compliance. We're experts on how regulations impinge on the work of this organization. You've spoken to Johan (our CISO), I believe?"

"Yes, just before you."

"Okay, then he probably explained that *everybody* is accountable for security."

Nate and I both nodded.

"Well, we follow the exact same model for regulatory compliance," Barbara said. "We aren't accountable for compliance — *everybody* is.

And we're not the police, either. We help everybody comply by keeping them informed, interpreting regulations in our context, evaluating potential vendor offerings, and doing internal assessments. [108 More]

"Also," Barbara added, "Regulatory Compliance works with our corporate lobbyist to influence regulations, and we bring subject-matter experts from anywhere in the company along with us to offer input. We try to get ahead of the game."

"Why does this report to you rather than to Johan?" I asked.

"It could go either way," Barbara said. "We discussed this during the restructuring. While there are some regulations that relate to security, many do not. And we didn't want to risk neglecting those which don't by putting this function in a group that lives and breathes security. But of course, we work closely with Johan's group."

Risk

"Another Coordinator function is Risk," Barbara said. "We help people anticipate and analyze risks, and develop their risk-mitigation strategies.

"This domain also maintains the enterprise risk registry." [109 More]

Audit Response

"Barbara, is there anything else that counts as a Coordinator?" I asked.

"We have the Audit Response function. There are various people who might audit our organization — not just our own Corporate Internal Audit, but also external regulators, certification companies, and so on.

"We're their point of contact; and we coordinate the response of all the relevant groups to audit questions, so that the organization speaks with one voice. Then, we go on to coordinate the remediation of any audit findings."

"And you take the rap if there are audit findings?" I joked.

Barbara laughed. "We're responsible for coordinating the process. But everybody is accountable for their own answers."

"No 'one throat to choke'?" I asked.

"Well, I suppose from an external auditor's point of view, that would be Carlton. But internally, Carlton knows who's accountable for what, I assure you!

"To be clear," Barbara concluded, "we're not auditors. We do assessments to help folks prepare for an audit, because we study what the auditors are likely to ask. And we help them prepare for and respond to auditors. But we don't audit our peers."

The People Who Coordinate

At this point, Barbara's video-conferencing system beeped. "Ben, good timing," Barbara said. "We're almost ready for you. Ben is our director of Enterprise Architecture."

"Hi, Ben. Barbara, you've got a lot going on here," I said. "How many people are in your group?"

"Not many. We're just coordinating, and everybody else is doing most of the work. Our job is to pull all the right people together and guide them through a process to consensus.

"So," Barbara concluded, "we're a small group of very senior professionals who, I hope, command the respect of all our leaders, and have the ability to delve into the details of the subject matter while staying neutral on outcomes and facilitating a real consensus of the stakeholders."

"Perfect," I said. No doubt this small, but senior, group is a good investment, I thought.

Chapter 23:
Architecture: Integrating Multiple Product Lines

Chapter summary (key take-aways): page 485

Some typical names for this type of business: enterprise architect, product design standards, product line integration.

For examples of this line of business in various industries and internal shared-services functions, see Appendix 3.

"I asked Ben to join us," Barbara said, "to explain our Enterprise Architecture function."

"Is this a function that's specific to IT?" I asked.

"No," Barbara replied. "I think it has applicability to any company's product line, especially where multiple products have to plug together, or where they could use common components. Let's see what you think.... Ben, would you like to explain your business?"

What Enterprise Architecture is *Not*

"Okay," Ben said, "I lead what we call Enterprise Architecture (EA). We call it that, but with some trepidation because that title has been used and abused in so many ways.

"This is *not,* as some would have it, a group of really smart people who do all the future thinking for the whole organization. That would deprive everyone else of the innovative part of their jobs. It would violate the Golden Rule, and undermine everybody's entrepreneurship.

"Plus," Ben added, "there's no way one little group could keep up with every possible domain of technology. So, there's no way to win at that definition of the function."

"In other words," I said, "you're not an innovation group. You don't do the 'R' in 'R&D' and relegate engineers to just the 'D.'"

"That's right. Also, let me be clear that we don't design anything, even at a high level. Engineers do all the designs. And with walk-throughs, we always have the right team of engineers designing every solution."

"Okay, so that's what you're *not*. Tell me what you *are,* Ben."

"Our job is to facilitate consensus on standards and design patterns."

"Explain, please."

Standards

"Sure," Ben said. "Let's start with standards.... The challenge is integrating the solutions we build. In the early days, they used to come up with big, multi-year master plans. Then, they developed these huge multi-product systems, sometimes taking years to finish them. Once they were done, all the products were well integrated because it was all designed from the top down as one thing. *110 IT*

"There's no way that can work today," he asserted. "We have to be agile, addressing constantly changing business needs with solutions that deliver value quickly. We solve a problem for one customer today, and help another customer grab another opportunity tomorrow."

"Most companies have to be agile these days," I agreed. "We continually dream up new products."

"So," Ben continued, "in this kind of world, how can we have any hope of building integrated solutions? Integrating with what exists is easy; that's just part of the requirements. *The real challenge is designing solutions today that will be easy to integrate to in the future, without knowing what we'll be building in the future.*"

Ben paused as I reflected on that challenge. Then, he continued. "That's where standards come in. Standards are deliberate constraints on design for the purpose of eventual integration."

---

*Standards are deliberate constraints on design
for the purpose of eventual integration.*

"Standards are like that electrical outlet over there," Ben explained. "The shape of that outlet is a standard. That standard doesn't tell you that you have to install any outlets or convert all the old outlets to three-prong. But if you do install outlets, that's what they have to look like so that people can plug anything into those outlets in the future." *111 IT*

"I think I get it," I said. "I have a number of power tools at home, all from the same brand. I can swap batteries among them."

"That's exactly the idea," Ben concurred.

"I'm thinking this might apply to product engineering functions in many industries," I said.

Ben thought for a moment, stroking his long gray beard, then said, "I remember a story years ago... maybe I heard it at a conference. This company manufactures heavy equipment, like tractors and construction equipment.

"Well, they surveyed all the different nuts and bolts they used in their various products globally, and found over 40,000 different parts! Think of the costs: loss of purchasing power, inventory carrying costs, speed of repairs, on and on.

"What they did was set some standards for each size and situation, and brought the number of fasteners down to a few thousand, I think."

"Say no more," I said. "I get it. And I need it."

Ben seemed pleased.

How Standards Are Decided

"But as to your role," I asked, "aren't there experts on those standards — engineers, perhaps — who can make these decisions?"

"Yes," Ben replied. "Engineering has experts on all the different standards. But we can't let them make the decisions alone. Other engineers have to incorporate those standards in their designs. Our service providers have to support those standards. As per the Golden Rule, standards are decided by all the stakeholders.

"So, our job is to know when the right time to standardize comes along — not too soon or we could end up going down a dead-end street (who remembers Betamax or HD-DVD!?); and not too late or we'll end up with a mess of disparate technologies.

"When the time is right, we identify the stakeholders and pull them together on a decision team for a specific standard. Then, we facilitate them to consensus. And we keep them focused on integration protocols, not brands and models of products (which each group can decide on its own, hopefully within our standards).

"Once a standard is agreed," Ben continued, "we post it in our architecture framework; and we help people understand the standard and access the documentation that goes along with it."

"What's the role of that one Engineering group that's the real expert in a given standard?" I asked.

Ben explained, "Their role is to put options on the table for the decision team; help the team analyze pros and cons; and eventually, develop the documentation and maybe even some utilities that will help people convert, utilize, or test designs that instantiate the standard."

Standards Compliance (Variances)

"What if someone — an engineer, I guess — wants to build or buy something that doesn't comply with your agreed standards?" I asked. "Do you allow variances?"

"We're not talking about religion, here." Ben smiled. "Standards are there to bring down future life-cycle costs, especially the costs of integrating unknown things in the future. But they never should get in the way of solving today's business problems. If we required absolute adherence to standards, we'd never buy another vendor package, which is often the best way to go.

"It's really a business decision," he continued. "If it would cost more to comply with standards, then we should ask: Should we spend the money now, or risk higher costs in the future?"

"Who makes that decision?" I asked. "Is it you, or a governance committee?"

"Neither, actually," Ben replied. "My job is to help people see the implications. But it's the *buyer of the solution* who has to spend the money now, or in the future. They're the ones who bear the consequences, so they get to make the decision on variances. The Golden Rule, you know."

There it was again. I smiled.

Ben elaborated, "In their solution alternatives studies, engineers identify the variances and the risks. Then, we let customers decide. Or if there are multiple customers who might have to spend more in the future as a result of one customer's decision, then together they decide. We have an interoperability (stakeholder) committee for that (Appendix 5)."

Design Patterns

"Okay," I said, "I think I understand what you mean by standards. You also mentioned design patterns...."

"Hmm, let's see if you can apply this concept to your business," Ben said. "You see, we produce a complex system of systems. They're all interlinked. A change in one system can mess up other systems. It's like tossing a stone into a pond — the ripples spread every which way."

"Yes," I said. "Jen and Mike were clear that they're accountable for 'ripple chasing.'" I remembered telling Jen and Mike my example of a product change that required all our dealers to get new tooling.

"They are," Ben said. "I maintain a map of the interconnections to help them identify those ripples at the start of every project.

"More proactively," Ben continued, "we try to minimize future ripples. We use standard APIs and interface middleware rather than custom linkages. Are you familiar with the concept of a 'microservices architecture'? *112 IT* These are design patterns."

"Okay, now you're getting too technical, Ben."

"Sorry. Anyhow, I work with Engineering to come up with design patterns that minimize ripples. That reduces the costs of future ripple-chasing."

"Interesting," I said. "I collect a certain brand of vintage pens: élysée. Throughout their product line, you can use any pen body for either a fountain pen or a rollerball, and other bodies for either a ballpoint pen or a mechanical pencil. It's a really cool design."

Ben was enthused. "That *is* really cool! They decided what functionality goes in the body, and what goes in the insides. Then, over the years as they came up with new body designs, they didn't have to redesign the insides. No ripples. That's exactly the concept of design patterns."

"There's one more thing we do with our map of the ripples," Ben added. "We look for complexity that we can get rid of, like redundant applications and data stores. That suggests some near-term investments that will save money in the future — in IT, an example is what's called applications rationalization."

"And do those investments to reduce ripples or eliminate redundancies get funded?" I asked.

"Some do; some don't. Again, asset owners have to decide if they want to spend money now to save money in the future. And applications rationalization projects compete for funding with new things that may have more value. As the saying goes, may the best man win!"

"I think this *is* a concept that I can apply," I said. I was thinking about taking a look at all my company's products and services, and the parts that go into them, to see where commonization, simplification, and consolidation could be worthwhile.

"Excellent!" Ben exclaimed.

Legacy Solutions

"I have one more question, Ben. What about all those legacy solutions and external products that aren't compatible with your standards and design patterns?"

"What about them?" Ben smiled flippantly. "Sorry, sir. What I mean to say is, nobody's going to give us money to convert them just for the sake of being compliant with standards.

"Standards and design patterns apply to new solutions," he explained. "Sometimes, while we're doing business-driven enhancements to older solutions, engineers have the opportunity to make them more compliant. And sometimes, there's a need for interoperability that justifies an investment in bringing an old solution in line with standards.

"But," Ben concluded, "those investments are always driven by business needs, not by just the existence of standards."

I nodded. Right answer, as far as I'm concerned — a sensible, ROI-driven approach.

Time's Up

Our time was up, so I thanked Barbara and Ben for their insights.

Barbara gave me a big, warm smile and said, "If you build a company that works as well as ours, it'll be an amazing place. I'd sure be pleased if we've made a small contribution to that. Good luck!"

Chapter 24:
Business Office: Support Services
and Consolidation of Shared Services

Chapter summary (key take-aways): page 486

Some typical names for this type of business: business office, business support services, finance, procurement, human resources, general counsel, facilities, administration.

For examples of this line of business in various industries and internal shared-services functions, see Appendix 3.

The last of my meetings with Carlton's direct reports was with Soon-Hi, the head of their shared-services Business Office.

I wasn't particularly interested in this purely administrative function. But at least this was scheduled to be a short meeting.

Soon-Hi was a petite woman. Her elbow bump was precise, and she made strong eye contact.

She offered me a chair. Or did she order me to sit down? I wasn't sure! But there was no reason to take offense. She was just direct and, as I was soon to learn, no-nonsense.

What Is a Business Office?

Before I could even thank her for spending time with me, Soon-Hi dove right in. "I will tell you about the Business Office. It is a very important function."

I smiled. "Yes, it is," I politely concurred.

"Thank you." Soon-Hi nodded her head in acknowledgement, and continued. "We're here to help the organization run in a businesslike fashion.

"Under me, we have Finance, Procurement, Human Resources, General

Counsel, Facilities, and Administration. I have all the generic services that you'll find in any business — they're not unique to our industry or products. I do not need to tell a CEO like you about what we do."

I nodded in agreement. In the past, I'd had some of these functions (like the CFO) reporting directly to me, and others reporting to my Chief Administrative Officer (or, in another company, the Chief Operating Officer). Here, Carlton had put them all under Soon-Hi.

A Business Office provides generic services
that exist in any business — services which are
not unique to an industry or an organization's products.

"One thing that might be a little different here," Soon-Hi continued, "is that we see all these as services to the business. We're not here to control the business — not even Finance or General Counsel."

"Yes," I interrupted, "I had a good talk with Johan about that approach."

"Then I don't need to explain that. But I do have a story to tell you...."

Shared Services Policy

"When I first took this job," Soon-Hi continued, "which was before the transformation, some departments had their own business-office staff."

"If those services were available from your corporate shared-services group," I asked, "why did departments need their own business support staff?"

"You are correct," she said. "It was wasteful to replicate services which are available from Corporate. Are you interested in how we consolidated these shared services?"

"I'm not a fan of decentralization. So yes, I'm very interested!"

"Okay. I will tell you....

"Even before the transformation," she said, "I worked with the business-unit leaders to establish a shared-services policy."

"Once you had that, did you move all those decentralized groups into your department?" I asked.

"After we agreed on the policy," she said, "over time, we moved some staff. But not all. Even so, there was no redundancy."

"Even though some staff remained decentralized?" I asked.

"Yes. The policy said that business units buy services from shared services whenever possible, and only use decentralized business-support staff for services which my department doesn't provide."

Example of a shared-services policy:
Business units buy services from Shared Services whenever possible,
and only use local business-support staff
for services which Shared Services doesn't provide.

"Would you please give me an example?" I requested.

"Yes. Remember, this was before the transformation, when we had a separate IT group for internal systems.

"IT had its own business office. They used to do everything for the IT department. After the policy, they outsourced to Shared Services anything we could provide. But they continued to do things which are specific to the IT function."

"What's unique about IT's business support services?" I asked.

"I will give you some examples," Soon-Hi said. "Corporate Finance does all the usual accounting and reporting. But the IT business office continued to review cloud vendor invoices, analyze telephone bills for potential savings, and do reports and special analyses for IT leaders.

"Here is another example: All vendor purchases go through Corporate Procurement. That's required. But there are many contractual terms which are unique to IT, especially in software licenses.

"The IT business office was the expert in those technical terms and conditions. They also managed IT license compliance, helped IT managers prepare forms for Corporate Procurement, and facilitated suppliers' integration with their processes."

Soon-Hi didn't need my prompting to continue.

"Corporate HR expected hiring managers to prepare job descriptions. The IT business office helped IT managers do that. They represented IT in college recruiting. And they worked with Corporate HR on compensation studies because the technology labor market has unique job categories, and it is very competitive.

"In Facilities, the IT business office got space from Corporate Facilities, and then sublet offices, meeting rooms, storage, and unfinished space (like for the data center). They coordinated the overall IT space plan. They were the landlord to IT.

"This is not a complete list. But you see from these examples, in all the Corporate Services areas, the IT business office just added value where needed for the IT department only. No overlaps. No competition."

"Elegant!" I acknowledged. "I see that this is not really decentralization of corporate services. It sounds like there was plenty for the IT business office to do over and above your shared services."

"That is correct," Soon-Hi confirmed.

Role of Decentralized Support Staff

I wanted to explore the relationship between decentralized support staff and Soon-Hi's shared-services department, so I asked, "Did IT managers come to you for some things and their local support staff for others?"

"IT leaders liked working with their local IT business office, and left it to them to manage our shared services on their behalf. And we liked having them as a point of contact, especially on issues that required coordinating multiple IT groups."

"So," I asked, "are you saying that IT's business office was a broker, or facilitator, for Corporate business services?"

"No. You are correct that IT managers went to them, and then they came to us. But they were the prime contractor — the full-service provider to IT for everything. They were accountable whether or not they outsourced all or part of the work to shared services, or to any vendor, for that matter."

Soon-Hi summarized, "One-stop shopping. No confusion about where to go. And a single point of accountability for all business services."

Soon-Hi had given me a much more nuanced way to think about the classic decentralization debate — shared services as an outsourcing service to decentralized functional counterparts.

"Now there is no separate IT group," Soon-Hi concluded. "Shared-services provides all of that, even those function-specific services."

Consolidation Process: Earn Market Share

"I believe in consolidation," I said. "But I've never really been success-ful at pushing it. If I just mandate it, I'd be giving my business-unit leaders the opportunity to blame their poor results on my consolidation decision; so I don't want to do that.

"And," I continued, "when my shared-services leaders pushed the issue, they just angered my business-unit leaders and it got political quickly. Inevitably, it ended up in my lap, with shared-services promising cost savings, and business units digging their heels in."

Soon-Hi grinned and said, "I heard about a Fortune-100 CIO who was like those pushy shared-services leaders. [113 Ref] That man hired a big-name consulting company, which developed a compelling financial case for consolidation. Then that CIO invested his time and credibility in selling consolidation to the corporate CFO, CEO, and ultimately the Board of Directors.

"After months of effort," she continued, "his plan was approved. IT infrastructure was consolidated — over the objections of the business units. Two months later, that CIO resigned 'for personal reasons.'"

"Yeah, right!" I said facetiously. We both chuckled.

"So, tell me, Soon-Hi, how did your consolidation go? Was there a lot of resistance?"

"No, because of the way we did it," Soon-Hi replied. "After we agreed on the policy, we could have analyzed what decentralized staff did, and transferred headcount to shared services wherever their work was generic rather than function specific.

"But even though everybody agreed on the policy in principle, grabbing business units' staff would have created a lot of animosity. And we did not want business-unit leaders resenting and criticizing us at a time when we'd be distracted by absorbing the additional headcount and accountabilities. That would have set us up for failure.

"Instead of forcing transfers, we took an entrepreneurial approach. We faced the fact that we have competition — decentralization and outsourcing. Even where we have monopolies, we could lose it all to outsourcing if we're not good. So, we focused on building an organization that *earns* customers' business. We worked on our own transformation first.

"Then," Soon-Hi explained, "I raised opportunities for consolidation to business-unit executives, but not in a pushy way. I would say, 'I have plenty to do as it is. But if you would like to save money and improve the quality of services, we would be happy to bid on your business.' (It was just like what a vendor would do.)

"Some business leaders trusted us and took us up on our offers right away. For them, we did the analysis and transferred the staff.

"But in other cases," Soon-Hi said, "we had to prove ourselves before those business leaders were willing to trust us. We were patient, and we worked hard to earn their business."

I'd rather have a customer than a hostage!

— Preston Simons, CIO, Abbott Laboratories

I liked it. This "earn market share" approach took all that controversy off my back. I could see how this approach would keep shared-services sharp and customer focused. And ultimately, this should lead to the right balance between decentralization and shared services.

"By the time Carlton arrived and began the transformation," Soon-Hi concluded, "most business units had come into alignment with the policy. For generic business services, we had gotten close to 90 percent market share, all through voluntary consolidations.

"Then, in the restructuring, business units transferred not only all generic staff, but also their function-specific staff to us. We know how to manage these business professionals. And we are happy to provide function-specific services, as long as we're funded for that."

The Consolidation "Deal"

"When you moved people into shared-services," I asked, "did you make any promises to your customer business units?"

"We did. The basis of a consolidation was a service-level agreement (SLA). We agreed to provide them with the same or better services, and they paid us by transferring the budget and the staff to us."

"So, you documented what services those people were producing before they were moved?"

"Absolutely. That is a result of the work analysis I mentioned."

Consolidation deal: Shared Services agrees to provide the same or better services (a service-level agreement), paid for by the transfer of budget and staff.

"And were you able to improve the services?"

"Yes. In many cases, we have done so," Soon-Hi asserted. "We can deliver better services at lower costs because, with consolidation, we have a higher degree of specialization and economies of scale. Consolidation has been good for the business.

"It's also good for staff because they're working with their professional peers; and as part of a bigger group, they have better career paths."

Prerequisites to Consolidation

I said, "I love this voluntary-consolidation approach. Tell me, Soon-Hi, what did you have to do to earn market share?"

"We had to be customer focused and build great relationships with our internal customers. We had to deliver on every commitment. And we had to be a good value. Basically, we had to be good entrepreneurs.

"Also, we established our own sales functions to give every business unit a point of contact, and align our work with their needs. I know that we consume our dog food, and Julio handles technology sales internally as well as externally. But he's not equipped to sell business services; his expertise is the linkage between business and technologies."

Performance, competitive prices, and relationships add up to market share. That's the bottom line, I thought, even for support functions.

"You did all this prior to the transformation?" I asked.

"Yes. That is why we were thought-leaders in the transformation."

External Sales of Support Functions

"There is something else I will tell you," Soon-Hi added, "and I warn you, you may find this disturbing...."

"You might think of us as just internal support functions. But my team has become so entrepreneurial that they also sell to external customers."

"Really?" I was indeed surprised to hear this. "Doesn't that take focus away from serving internal customers?"

"Not at all. We have two rules (Figure 29)."

"Number one, we calculate cost-based rates (including staff, depreciation on assets, supporting functions, management, etc.). Then, we mark them up. So, we know that selling externally doesn't dilute internal support resources. External sales pay their own way, plus a margin.

"Number two is that it cannot be *counter*-strategic, like helping a direct competitor or giving away the company jewels.

"Given those two constraints, it has worked well," Soon-Hi asserted.

Figure 29: Two Rules of Selling Internal Services Externally

Any **function can sell externally, as long as:**

- It does not dilute support of internal customers; i.e., revenues cover all fully burdened costs, so that external sales never take resources away from internal customers.

- It is not counter-strategic; i.e., no sales to direct competitors, or sales of anything that's proprietary and critical to competitive advantage.

"This can't be a significant profit contributor," I commented.

"It is not," Soon-Hi agreed. "But we have seen many benefits:

"It does bring in some minor profits. *114 More* And it spreads fixed costs over a bigger base and produces economies of scale, which reduces costs for internal customers.

"We grow, permitting a higher degree of specialization, which also benefits internal customers.

"But the real benefit," Soon-Hi concluded, "is that it teaches my staff what it is like to compete in the real world, to learn from the marketplace what it takes to earn business. That has improved internal service levels, customer focus, and innovation."

"Fascinating!" I said. "It's not really about the money. It's about that entrepreneurial spirit, external and internal."

Onward

"Are there any other questions I can answer for you?" Soon-Hi asked.

"No, Soon-Hi, you've done a great job of answering all of my questions, and even some questions I didn't know I had. Thank you very much."

~ PART 5 ~

Feet on the Ground: Implementing the Vision

in which I learn how to implement an
organizational transformation

That was the end of my tour of the departments. But I had many more questions to discuss with Nate and Carlton — like how they made such a dramatic change happen.

Nate and I stopped to pick up a cold drink on the way to a small meeting room.

"So," Nate said, "what are you thinking at this point?"

"The organizational coach was absolutely right. This really is a show-case. I'm very impressed with the high degree of specialization and professionalism, your clarity on boundaries and accountabilities, the great cross-boundary teamwork, your resource-alignment processes, and of course your empowerment and everybody's entrepreneurial spirit.

"Now, I'm eager to learn how you got here," I said.

"Okay," Nate said, "I'll tell you the story...."

NAVIGATION AID: If you aren't interested in implementation processes, scan the Book Summary at the back of the book; or skip to Part 6 for perspectives on transformational leadership.

Chapter 25:
Planning the Transformation Road-map:
The Foundation for Change

Chapter summary (key take-aways): page 487

Nate began the story of how this organization came to be with a caveat. "Carlton began planning the transformation when he first arrived. This was his job-entry strategy — his first-90-days plan."

"Great!" I said with a smile. I've always begun a new job by doing a lot of listening. But a structured approach to my first 90 days, resulting in a transformation strategy, could be really powerful.

To be most effective Day 1, executives starting a new job should leverage this transformation planning process as their job-entry strategy — "the first 90 days" on steroids. I believe it will produce a practical path forward, motivate support, and position them as visionary and strategic.

— Paul Edmisten, CIO

"I was on the leadership team," Nate said. "But that was before I moved into my Organizational Effectiveness job. In fact, it was his transformation strategy that justified the creation of my job. But I'll tell you the story from the beginning, as best I know it."

Foundation for Change

Nate began, "Carlton knew he had to establish a foundation for change before embarking on a transformation process. The organizational coach said that a foundation for change is made of three things (Figure 30): dissatisfaction with the status quo, a compelling vision of the end-state, and a clear path from here to there."

Figure 30: Three Elements of a Foundation for Change

- **Dissatisfaction with the status quo**: If things are okay (but could be better), people won't want to change much. Documentation of current problems is the "burning platform" that motivates people to change.

- **Vision of the end-state**: People are not going to jump "from the pan into the fire." Vision provides the safe, inspiring place to jump to.

- **Path from here to there**: People need to know they're joining a winning team before they're willing to sign on. A step-by-step plan builds faith that we're going to succeed at this transformation.

"You'll see how Carlton's transformation planning process (Figure 31) not only came up with the road-map, but also satisfied those three components of a foundation for change," Nate promised.

"Okay, walk me through it," I requested.

Figure 31: Transformation Planning Process

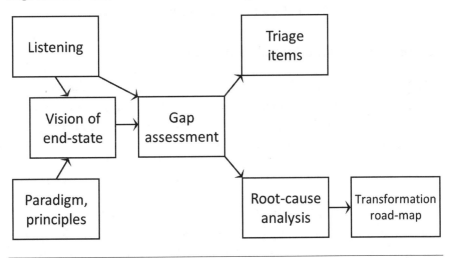

Listening (Data Collection)

"First," Nate said, "Carlton did a lot of listening."

"As would I. What specifically was he looking for?" I asked.

"I know he asked everybody to talk about what was frustrating them about the organization. But he also got them talking about what they'd consider success — what they wanted in an ideal world."

"And whom did he talk to?"

"I think the list included his peers in key customer and vendor companies; all the Board members; all his direct reports and the next level of leadership; and a sampling of the rest of our staff."

"That must have taken some time," I said.

"I think he spent two or three months just meeting people. He wanted to absorb a diversity of perspectives, and to make sure everybody felt heard. And, of course, since he was new, he was building relationships."

"Okay, then what did he do with all that feedback?" I asked.

Vision: Aspirations for the End-state

"Actually, he didn't wait to get started on other steps," Nate said. "In parallel with his listening tour, he went to visit the organizational coach. I think they spent three days together that time. Carlton said it was pretty intense — and really mind-expanding."

"Wow, that's a lot of time for a CEO! What did they do?" I asked.

"In those three days, Carlton crafted his vision. It wasn't just some little phrase. It was a very detailed set of statements that described the organization of the future. It was about our aspirations, about possibilities."

"How was his vision worded?" I asked. "I can't picture it."

"The way the organizational coach framed it," Nate replied, "was, *'What should be expected of this organization if it's the best it can be?'* That prompted Carlton to describe what the end-state organization will do."

Nate explained that their Vision document included eight sections:

1. Customers' view: What it's like to do business with us.
2. View from the top: What value we deliver.
3. Employee's view: What it's like to work in our organization.
4. Vendors' view: What it's like to serve us.
5. Product challenges: How we engineer our products.
6. Services challenges: How we deliver ongoing services.
7. Money challenges: How we get and manage our budget.
8. Governance challenges: How we maintain controls without disempowering anyone.

"In each section," Nate said, "Carlton wrote a page or two of statements about what it's like to work with the organization and how it'll operate.

"And in each of these sections," Nate added, "he sprinkled in quotes from his listening interviews that described people's hopes and desires."

"Can you give me an example?"

"I'll do better than that. I'll show you." Nate handed me their Vision document. I didn't have time to read all 20 pages, but I got a feel for it by skimming just the high-level paragraphs (each of which had more detailed sub-paragraphs) in just the first section, 'Customers' view':

As a consumer of their products and services, I really like doing business with them — for many reasons....

First and foremost, they treat me as a customer (not a victim, or someone that needs to be controlled). It seems they're always striving to earn my business (even though internally, they have a monopoly on some things like enterprisewide services).

But their business-within-a-business approach goes far beyond just good communications. They don't pretend to know what's best for me, or best for the company. They respect that I have a business to run, so I have to be in control of what I buy from them.

It's good that they offer a diverse, relevant, and competitive product line. That way, they can be business driven, and supply whatever it is that I need (no "solution in search of a problem").

They work with me to understand my challenges, and help me discover high-payoff opportunities to apply their products and services. And then they offer me alternative solutions, and give me all the information I need to choose.

I feel I'm getting a fair deal. They've made a real effort to bench-mark their rates (unit costs) against vendors who provide equivalent services; and they share those results openly (even where they're not quite competitive yet, but working on it).

Over time, I've come to trust them. They're professional, and the way they behave inspires belief in their competence. In all, I'd say this is a "supplier of choice" to me and most of my peers.

Leadership requires two things:
a vision of the world that does not yet exist
and the ability to communicate it.

— Simon Sinek *115 Ref*

"So, what did Carlton do with this Vision document?"

"He distributed that document, marked as a draft, to the leadership team. We had some time (a week or two) to read and absorb it, and to take notes on our reactions, concerns, and our own ideas.

"Then," Nate continued, "we got together for a three-day leadership workshop (six half-day sessions). We went over every statement to make sure we all understood them the same way. And we edited them based on everybody's notes and discussions during the workshop."

"Was the organizational coach there?" I asked.

"He was," Nate replied. "He stretched our thinking. He anticipated unintended consequences, like statements that sounded good but, in practice, could lead us in the wrong direction. He facilitated the discussions. And he helped us word things clearly.

"I remember some intense debates," Nate continued. "But we all learned a lot, and we got to consensus on every statement in our vision. So, at that point, we had a shared vision of the end-state."

"That, in itself, is powerful," I noted. Three days is a lot of time for an entire leadership team. But I could see the value of getting everybody on the same page right up front, and everybody bought in to the goal.

"Yes, it *was* powerful," Nate confirmed. "I was really excited, as were a few others on the leadership team. Many were okay with it, but played a 'wait and see' game. And I could tell that some of my peers were uncomfortable with change. But they couldn't dispute the logic; and honestly, they probably didn't want to buck the will of the team."

Few, if any, forces in human affairs are so powerful as shared vision.

— Peter M. Senge *116 Ref*

Gaps

"Okay, what next?" I asked.

"Next, Carlton gave us all a homework assignment. We had to grade the current organization on each of the statements in our vision.

"It was a simple scale: 3 meant we're great; 2 meant we're part way down the right path, so keep doing what we're doing and give it time; 1 meant we'd barely begun; and 0 meant we were seriously deficient.

"Note that we weren't looking at just current problems," Nate said, "even in the context of our current strategies. That would have been totally reactive. We were looking at all the gaps against our *vision*."

May your choices reflect your hopes, not your fears.

— Nelson Mandela

"Then, a week or so later, we had another leadership workshop. We actually went off-site for four days.

"On the first day, we went through all the detailed vision statements and agreed on a grade, 0 to 3. Carlton's listening data helped us decide."

"How were the grades?" I asked.

"We had a few 3s, a few more 2s, but mostly 1s and 0s. Not good!

"So, at that point," Nate continued, "we'd agreed on the vision, and understood that change was needed — and not just a few more little tweaks like we'd been doing for years before Carlton arrived."

"Good," I said. "So, then you decided how to address those 0s and 1s?"

"In a way," Nate said, "but with a twist...."

It's fine to celebrate success, but
it is more important to heed the lessons of failure.

— Bill Gates [117 Ref]

Triage List

Nate continued to describe the process: "We did go through and pick a few 0s and 1s — just the most painful and urgent ones — to work on directly. That was our 'triage' list.

"But we didn't want to make that list too long, because working directly on gaps was just working on symptoms. And the longer the triage list, the more we'd be delaying the *systemic* phase of the transformation."

---

*Beware of paying too much attention to what is coming at you
and not enough attention to your machine...
a solid organization that works well in all cases.*

— Ray Dalio [118] *More*

Organizational Ecosystem

"Systemic phase?" I queried.

"Yes," Nate said. "You see, the 0s and 1s were really just symptoms of deeper problems. Until we addressed those root causes, we'd be fixing one symptom and another would pop out somewhere else. Kind of like the 'Whac-A-Mole'[R] game. We were all getting tired of that."

---

*[For years, we] tried to put band-aids on every issue that comes up.
It sounds good, but when they are layered one on top of the other
they start to choke the organization.* [119] *Ref*

"Interesting," I said. "How did you define root causes? The challenge is always how to know when you're at the root."

"Well, the organizational coach explained that an organization is an 'ecosystem' that we all live in, and it sends *signals that guide people day by day* — 'feedback loops,' in cybernetics. *120 Ref*

"Here's an example that I briefly mentioned this morning," Nate said. "Imagine that your boss tells you to be frugal, cut costs, and conserve headcount. But what if your status, political clout, ability to get things done, your title, and your paycheck all depend on how big an empire you own!?"

"Ah, yes, the old Hay-point job-grading system," I noted.

"Exactly," Nate said. "What would a rational person do? You'd talk about cost cutting, while building an empire! That's an example of a perverse signal built into the ecosystem."

"I'm with you," I said.

"The organizational coach says that the most important job of a leader is to align all those signals, so that you can empower people and they'll naturally do the right things. That's systemic governance (Chapter 14)."

Nate paused as I looked out the window thinking about that statement.

The most important job of a leader is to align all the organizational signals, so that empowered people will naturally do the right things.

"That link between empowerment and getting the organizational ecosystem right is intriguing," I said. "I'll have to reflect on that a bit. But for now, I'm guessing that you're going to tell me that you traced all those gaps to inappropriate signals. Is that right?"

"That's exactly right," Nate replied.

"So, how did you do that?" I asked.

Root-cause Analysis: Five Organizational Systems

"First," Nate replied, "Carlton made it clear that we weren't there to blame people. We were looking for problems in the organizational ecosystem that were getting in our people's way.

"Then, the organizational coach trained us in the five organizational systems (Figure 32). We talked about them this morning (Part 3)."

Figure 32: Five Organizational Systems   *121 Ref*

1. Structure
    o   Organization chart
    o   Teamwork
        (walk-throughs)
2. Internal Economy
    o   Planning (operating
        plan, investment-
        based budget,
        catalog and rates)
    o   Demand
        management
        (governance,
        priority-setting)
    o   Accounting
3. Culture
4. Processes and Tools
5. Metrics and Consequences

Nate continued, "The organizational coach stressed how critical it is to get to the right root causes. For example, this morning (Chapter 11), we talked about how IT once structured their developers into groups dedicated to internal business units.

"That way, each business unit understood the size of its checkbook. But we'd built silos of generalists instead of teams of specialists. This had most of the same problems as decentralization, like lower performance, product dis-integration, redundancies, and missed business synergies.

"These are the costs of trying to solve an internal-economy problem using structure — the wrong root cause," Nate said.

An aid to root-cause analysis summarizing the five organizational systems and common symptoms from each is available to qualified executives; contact <ndma@ndma.com>.

Root-cause Analysis: Findings

"Alright," I said, "the concept of root-cause analysis is not new to me. But the organizational systems are very helpful. That's how you knew when you'd gotten to the root. So, how did you go about this step?"

"We split into sub-teams, and each took a section of the Vision document and analyzed root causes of the gaps. The organizational coach told us to keep asking, 'Why would our good people create that gap?' until we saw how one or more of the five systems (Figure 32) was getting in our way.

"Each sub-team presented its findings. But we didn't spend a lot of time on consensus on the root causes. It quickly became obvious that all those gaps were the result of the same handful of root causes."

You can only truly solve your problems by removing their root causes, and to do that, you must distinguish the symptoms from the disease.

— Ray Dalio *122 More*

"What were the common root causes," I asked.

"Most of them came down to Structure and the Internal Economy. There were also quite a few that pointed at Culture. The last two organizational systems (Processes and Tools, and Metrics and Consequences) were not as much an issue for us."

"Is that normal?" I asked.

"According to the organizational coach, it is. He says that the first three systems are transformational. The last two are for institutionalizing the new way of doing business, and then fine-tuning it over time."

"If I'm hearing you correctly," I said, "at that point you had consensus on the need to address the first three?"

"That's right. On addressing all five, actually," Nate replied.

"And equally important," he added, "everybody on the leadership team could explain to customers and staff why fixing those organizational systems would pay off by closing the gaps and addressing everybody's concerns, thanks to the experience we'd had with root-cause analysis."

When you solve problems at the results level,
you only solve them temporarily.
In order to improve them for good,
you need to solve problems at the systems level.

— James Clear [123 Ref]

Organizational Strategy (Transformation Road-map)

"Okay, what happened next?"

"Well," Nate replied, "at that point, we were in day-four of the workshop. Our last task was to decide the order in which we'd treat the five organizational systems."

I asked, "You didn't want to move forward on multiple fronts in parallel?" (I had hopes of shortening the transformation time-line.)

"No," Nate replied. "The organizational coach advised us to do one thing at a time, and do it well. Honestly, we have businesses to run; we don't have time to be involved in multiple transformation initiatives at the same time. Also, it's a learning process — a different way of thinking — and we all needed time to really absorb each component of the transformation. The coach was right; one change at a time was the only practical thing to do."

"So, you planned the sequence of transformation initiatives?" I asked.

"Exactly," Nate replied. "The organizational coach explained the technical interdependencies among the five organizational systems. And he explained what was involved in reengineering each of them — a quick overview of the change processes, and how long each would take.

"Then, we talked about our sense of urgency. A lot of people wanted to do internal economy first, since everybody was feeling the pain of demands that were so far beyond our resources. Others made a case for structure first, since our confused accountabilities and poor teamwork were getting in the way of delivering results to customers.

"After a good debate," he said, "we agreed to start with structure. Then came internal economy, followed by culture. After that, we'd work on the last two organizational systems."

Coming to the punch line, Nate said, "That sequence of systemic initiatives became our *organizational strategy* — our transformation road-map." (A somewhat different sequence for a different situation is described in the Foreword.)

"How were you all feeling at that point?" I asked. "Were people really on-board?"

"Oh, there was some moaning," Nate recalled, "like, 'We don't have time to do this.' But I think we all knew that if we don't somehow make the time, we'd be solving the same problems again and again, wasting a lot of time and never really achieving our vision. And some of us were really excited about the prospect of being part of a real transformation!"

Organizational Strategy Versus Business Strategy

I found this notion of organizational strategy very compelling.

Please understand, I'm entirely confident of my abilities when it comes to *business* strategies. But this concept of *organizational* strategy was new to me. Sure, I'd designed plenty of organization charts. But I had to admit they were tactical, without the context of principles. And, of course, there's more to an organizational strategy than just structure.

In reflecting on it, I had to admit that *organizational strategy is foundational.* An organizational strategy is a plan for developing a high-performing organization (which should be stable) — an organization that continually develops business strategies (which, by their nature, must be dynamic) and is capable of delivering them.

An organizational strategy is a plan for developing
a high-performing organization (which should be stable),
one that continually develops business strategies (which must be dynamic)
and is capable of delivering them.

Executive Patience

"Nate, how long did the whole transformation take?" I asked.

"Well, it's still ongoing. But we got the major changes in place — the road-map, structure and walk-throughs, the internal economy, and culture — in about four years."

"That's a long time," I remarked. "Most executives are action oriented. We want quick results. So, we tend to rush things."

"Well," Nate said, "there were results all along the way. In the first year, the restructuring had a huge impact on performance.

"But wait a minute," Nate exclaimed. "You think four years is a long time for such a significant transformation!? I think that's pretty quick."

"Fair," I said. "But still, this took real patience and persistence on Carlton's part. I'm not sure many executives are willing to make this kind of investment, or are even capable of doing so."

"That's one of the things that makes Carlton special," Nate said, smiling. "The organizational coach told us an interesting story...."

As Nate relayed it, the coach knew a Canadian steel executive who took a trip to Japan to discover why those competitors were beating his firm in both price and quality. [124 Ref] He expected to find innovative technologies and processes. But the steel mills in Japan looked just like those in North America.

So, he extended his visit until he discovered the difference. As he put it, figuratively speaking, in Japan they spend three months planning a new steel mill, two months building it, and one month commissioning it. In North America, we spend one month planning, two months building, and then *years* trying to get it to run right!

Clearly, Carlton had taken the Japanese approach — a lot of planning, and a lot of time and effort up front engaging his leadership team.

I understood that it was more than just a new org chart and some new financial processes. It was an entirely new operating model — a fundamentally different way of thinking and working. In retrospect, Nate was right. Four years is not a long time.

We don't have the time to do it quickly!
— Dave Anderson, then CIO, later President, American Family Insurance

---

Communications Plan

"So, that was transformation planning," I said.

"Wait, we had one more thing to do that final day," Nate said.

"What was that?"

Nate explained, "The organizational coach insisted that at every significant milestone, including this one, we craft a communications plan. He said that the more we communicate, the more we capture hearts and minds, and the better the transformation would go.

"He encouraged us to openly communicate all we know and could explain consistently, and cautioned us never to engage in rumors or speculation about what we don't know yet."

"Good advice," I said.

"It was. And we stuck to it," Nate asserted. "At each milestone, we listed bullets of what we knew. Then, we looked at the audiences — customers and staff — and decided how we'd get the messages out.

"In this case, we felt it was an important message, so we put a lot into communicating it.

"Carlton presented our vision and strategy to the Board, and he met with his peers in key customer and vendor companies.

"The tier-one leaders met with lots of other customers and vendors.

"And we did an all-staff meeting. That was fun. It wasn't just Carlton presenting. It was a real *team* effort. That sent a strong message that we on the leadership team were all in.

"Then," Nate concluded, "after the all-staff, everyone on the leadership team held staff meetings to answer questions and discuss staff's concerns. And Carlton has been hosting weekly 'lunch and learns' ever since, so staff can talk to him directly."

"What kind of reactions did you get?" I asked.

"With our vision, people said, 'Wow, that's all we hoped for, and more!' It built a lot of support for the transformation.

"Being transparent about the gaps brought us a lot of credibility," Nate continued. "People said, 'Good, you're not defensive. In fact, you're harder on yourselves than we are. We can trust you.' And they understood even better the need for change.

"Sharing the step-by-step strategy bought us time. People said, 'I get it; you're doing it right once and for all, and that will take time. I see that you won't get to my #1 grievance until later. But I'll be patient and support your methodical approach.'"

I was impressed. This wasn't just a logical, explainable process. It was change management at its best. Carlton had satisfied the three essential prerequisites to change — a burning platform, a vision of the end-state, and a clear path from here to there.

"Hmm," I said, "this really *would* be a great way to start my new job."

"Carlton once told me that, in his prior job, he'd wished he'd done this from the start," Nate confirmed. "In this job, he did."

For a template project plan for transformation planning, qualified executives may contact <ndma@ndma.com>.

Chapter 26:
The Power of Participation

Chapter summary (key take-aways): page 488

"That transformation plan is a great start," I said. "But, of course, you then had to implement it."

"And that's when the hard work began," Nate said. "I'll tell you how we implemented each of the organizational systems. But before we get into the details, I'd like to share a philosophy that applied to all the steps in the transformation road-map."

"Let's hear it," I said.

Benefits of Participation

"In every case," Nate said, "we involved our leadership team in a *participative* change process (just like we did in the transformation planning process)."

"That feels right to me," I said. "But tell me why you considered that so important."

"It was a big investment," Nate replied, "bigger than we initially appreciated. But it really paid off.

"First, as you know, we weren't just after a new org chart or budgeting process. We were after a real transformation — a change in our way of thinking and acting. Carlton jokingly calls it 'twisting minds.'"

I grinned, noting the truth in that humorous phrase.

"You can't get that mind-shift by just announcing a change one day," Nate said. "It takes sweat-equity."

I nodded. "That's the investment. What's the payoff?"

---

*Transformation is not just a new structure or new processes.
It's a change in the way people think and act.*

Nate described six benefits of leaders' participation in the implementation processes:

- **Knowledge:** "There's no way Carlton could ever know as much as the combined wisdom of the whole leadership team. We understand our challenges in more detail than he ever will. By being part of the process, we had all that institutional knowledge in the room."

- **Understanding:** "We're talking about a very different way of working. By participating in the process, leaders understood the principles and intent behind the design. That equipped us all to make it work. Also, we're able to apply the concepts to new situations as they arise, and stay true to the design as we evolve."

- **Buy-in:** "You know, people don't resist change; they resist *being* changed. Participation led to real ownership of the change, because we authored it. So, we were committed to making it work."

- **Good for staff:** "Leaders wouldn't design an organization that's bad for their own people."

- **Ability to teach others:** "The depth of understanding we had, combined with our commitment to making it work, prepared the whole leadership team to teach the rest of the staff. In other words, the 'teaching team' was all of us, not just Carlton. So, staff learned more quickly and thoroughly how the new paradigm was to work.

  "And beyond that, our understanding of the new operating model positioned us to inspire our staff. It allowed us to be real leaders."

- **Time to success:** "Put all that together — understanding, buy-in, and the ability to lead others — and the whole transformation went more smoothly. There was less resistance.

  "And by the time we got to rolling out each change," Nate said, "we knew how to accomplish real-life work in the new way. So, there was much less disruption of the business.

  "We spent a lot of time up front on the participative process, designing and planning everything. But I think we got to the end-point — up and running in the new paradigm — much sooner."

People don't resist change; they resist being changed.
Participation is key to change management.

Change Management and Turnover

"I appreciate the value of participation," I said. "But I know change is difficult. Was there much turnover as a result of the transformation?"

"No, not really," Nate replied. "At the staff level, it was under five percent, well below the norm for major changes."

"That *is* quite low. Why do you think that was?"

"Well," Nate said, "as I mentioned, participation ensured that everything we did was good for the staff. And we put a lot of effort into open communications throughout the process.

"But even more salient, because this was a participative process, all our leaders were able to answer people's questions, and were out there advocating for the changes. That calmed fears, and inspired people to stay and ride out the stresses of change."

Decisions by Consensus

"Nate, I'm worried that with all those people participating, every decision will take forever. And there must have been cases where you just couldn't get everybody to agree."

"Ah, this is really critical," Nate said. "If we tried to make every decision by a unanimous vote, you're right, we might never get there.

"We look for *consensus,* not unanimity. And we have a very specific definition of consensus: All stakeholders understand the decision well enough to teach it, and (whether or not it's their first choice) are willing to support the decision.

"Our short-hand for consensus is 'teach and support.'"

Consensus:
All stakeholders understand the decision well enough to teach it, and
(whether or not it's their first choice) are willing to support the decision.

"I like that definition," I said. "It's practical. How did you go about getting the whole team there?"

"The coach taught us the consensus decision process (Figure 33)," Nate said. "It's quite simple; and if you stick to it, it really speeds things up."

"When we had a debate, we'd ask the minority if they could teach and support the majority's preference. If they said yes, the decision was made. But if any participant just couldn't live with the decision, they were obligated to speak up and say, 'Wait, I'm not there. This needs further discussion.'"

Figure 33: Consensus Decision Process

1. Trial vote. Ask minority if they can teach and support, or if they'd like to talk more.
2. Listen respectfully to one side at a time (no debate). People on each side only add new information (no reiterating).
3. Back to step 1.

"If an individual is totally outnumbered," I asked, "why not just go with the majority? Or let Carlton decide? It would be a lot quicker."

"It would be," Nate replied. "But that would come back to haunt us in the future. Consider the Golden Rule.... If a participant is going to be materially affected by the decision, like it could impact their ability to do their job, then we can't let others impose a decision on them. If that were to happen, we couldn't ethically hold them accountable for their own results.

"We use consensus when we need more than everybody's input. We use it to be sure we're not disempowering any of the stakeholders who are affected by the decision.

"And sometimes, the minority is right," Nate added. "You remember the classic movie, *Twelve Angry Men*? We've had many cases where, after respectful listening on both sides, the team came around to the minority's view.

"Some decisions were quick; some took more time. But we always got there. In retrospect," Nate concluded, "I think we all feel that the participative approach was absolutely essential to the success of the transformation."

I'd always engaged my key leaders in major decisions. Nate had just put the rationale behind my intuition.

Chapter 27:
Implementing Change:
Structure

Chapter summary (key take-aways): page 489

"So now," Nate said, "shall we talk about how we implemented each of the organizational systems?"

"Yes, please," I said. "Let's start with structure. That seems really key to the transformation. And you said that was your first step."

Many executives just hire a consulting firm to study them and recommend an organization chart. But remembering our discussion of the science of structure (which few consultants understand) and the importance of leadership team participation, I knew they wouldn't have taken that cheap way out.

"Drawing a new organization chart doesn't seem all that difficult," I said provocatively. "I'm picturing the leadership team using the principles and the framework of types of businesses that we discussed this morning (Chapter 7) to draw boxes. Was there more to it than that?"

Nate laughed. "There sure was!" he said. "The organizational coach had decades of experience doing this. So, we took advantage of his implementation process (Figure 34)."

"Give me an overview," I requested.

Rainbow Analysis

"First," Nate said, "we formed what we called the 'structure design team' consisting of everybody who was a candidate for a leadership position. We wanted everybody who might end up in a leadership position to be a part of designing the structure."

Figure 34: Structure Implementation Process   *125 Ref*

1. **Education (Rainbow Analysis):** principles and framework of types of businesses; and applying them to the current structure to assess the need for change

2. **Design:** identification of all the detailed lines of business needed now and in the future; and clustering them into an organization chart

3. **Selection:** assignment of leaders to each box on the new organization chart, with respect for their preferences

4. **Domains:** crafting precise domains (boundaries); and learning to view your job as a business within a business

5. **Catalogs:** crafting product/service catalogs for each domain; and further understanding boundaries and entrepreneurship

6. **Walk-throughs:** rehearsing cross-boundary teamwork (who's the prime contractor, and what subcontracts are needed) for many different real-life projects and services

7. **Roster:** assigning staff, vendors, and assets to domains

8. **Go-live:** all-staff event; and the official change in reporting

9. **Group training:** management-group training sessions to teach staff the new operating model, and begin the bonding of the new groups

10. **Migration:** meticulous 1:1 transfers of accountabilities for each extant commitment that no longer fits your domain

Nate continued to describe the first workshop: "The organizational coach trained us in the principles (Figure 4) and the framework of the types of businesses in organizations (Figure 9).

"We applied that framework to our old organization chart, color coding each box by the types of businesses it was doing. That experience really helped us internalize the types of businesses in the framework, as they apply to our company."

"That color-coded chart would be an interesting graphic," I commented.

"It was quite colorful!" Nate said with a smile. "That's why the organizational coach calls it the 'Rainbow Analysis.'"

Nate explained that they analyzed the color-coded organization chart to see if there were any of four problems (and noted the dysfunctions each revealed):

1. **Gaps (missing lines of business)**: unreliable processes, poor quality for lack of specialists

2. **Rainbows (groups supporting multiple types of businesses)**: reduced specialization, conflicts of interests

3. **Scattered campuses (lines of business scattered across the chart)**: less professional exchange, less coordination, lost synergies

4. **Inappropriate substructure (by other than core expertise)**: reduced specialization, domain overlaps, inappropriate biases

"It was a colorful mess!" Nate admitted with a laugh. "This confirmed in our minds the need for a clean-sheet-of-paper restructuring."

Organization Chart

"Good start," I said. "What was next?"

"Next," Nate said, "we brain-stormed all the lines of business that we thought we'd need some-where in the organization, now and in the foreseeable future. We stacked them under the types of businesses in the framework — Sales, Engineering, Asset-based Service Providers, People-based Service Providers, Coordinators, and Audit.

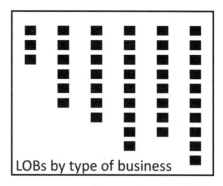

LOBs by type of business

"Those types — with all the detailed lines of business in each — could be tier-one jobs in a 'pure' organization chart," he explained. "With that in mind, we moved a few lines of business from one cluster to

another if we believed that the
synergies would be better there.
That is, we deliberately created a
few rainbows.

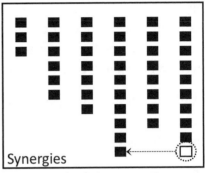

"We didn't do so lightly," Nate
noted. "We weren't allowed to
say 'because I want it' or 'that's
we way we did it in the past.' We
discussed each move proposal, and used the principles to analyze pros
and cons. And we came to consensus on each move.

"At that point, we had clusters of
lines of business that we agreed fit
together. We looked at those
clusters as if they were tier-one
jobs, and divided some that looked
too big for one leader (like
Engineering).

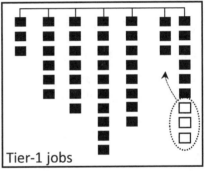

"Now, by looking at the clusters,
we could envision tier-one jobs — boxes on the org chart — where each
box was defined by the list of businesses within it.

"Then," Nate continued, "we broke the tier-one clusters into tier-two

clusters of lines of business. In
some areas, we went down to tier
three. Those clusters became
groups (boxes) and leadership
jobs. Some had another tier of
leaders under them [white boxes];
some just had lines of business
(and typically some staff) to
manage. That was how we decided our org chart.

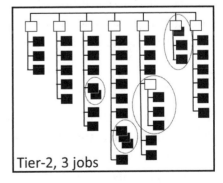

"By the way," he noted, "the organizational coach gave us the option of designing lower levels of the chart later, with a broader design team. But we were small enough to get all the leadership candidates at all levels in the room together. So, we did all levels of leadership at once.

"Anyhow," Nate concluded, "at that point, each cluster became a box on the organization chart. And we had absolutely clarity about each box's lines of business."

"That's a great process," I said sincerely.

Leadership Selection

"Then, Carlton assigned leaders' names to those boxes?" I speculated.

"That's right," Nate affirmed. "We each got to chat with Carlton about our career aspirations and which boxes we'd like — first choice, second choice, and third choice. Then, Carlton picked his tier-one leaders. Then they got together and picked the rest of the leadership team.

"Not everyone on the design team got a leadership position," Nate reported. "(They weren't all leaders beforehand.) But for the most part, those who were chosen got their first or second choices. That ability to have a say in where we ended up meant a lot to us.

"Most of the boxes, however small, were covered (even if that meant putting the same name in two boxes). There were just a few we left open, where we needed to search externally for missing talent."

Domains

Nate continued, "After congratulating one another on our future leadership positions, we crafted 'domains' — a paragraph or two that precisely defines what each group sells, now and into the future. The organizational coach trained us in how to write them, and then coached us on our drafts before we presented our domains to one another.

"We reviewed all the domains as a team, and made sure there were no gaps. A gap would mean that nobody is looking after a line of business. When we identified a gap, we expanded a domain to cover it.

"And we made sure there were no overlaps. We have plenty of competition from outside; we certainly can't afford the costs and stress of competing with one another! We crafted the wording of our domains carefully to ensure there was no ambiguity about our boundaries.

"Crafting domains," Nate said, "helped us see our jobs as running businesses. It was a key step in learning to think like entrepreneurs."

Domains precisely define the boundaries of each line of business.
They bound what each group _sells_, not what it does.

Catalogs

"At that point, you had the organization chart very well defined," I said.

"We did," Nate replied. "But we went on to take our domains to the next level of detail — catalogs. Within each domain, leaders defined their specific products and services."

"You did catalogs as part of your restructuring process?" I asked.

"Yes. We could have waited and done them later. But we thought it worthwhile to get them defined early, to further clarify our boundaries, and to help with the next step in the structure process: walk-throughs."

"From what I've seen," I observed, "people really struggle with service catalogs, sometimes for months."

"We were aware that many catalog efforts go awry," Nate concurred. "In one that I looked at, it was like going to a grocery store and seeing the price of a dozen large eggs (good), the produce aisle (way too high a level), the wrapper on the hamburger (too low a level, not even something people buy), and the check-out clerk (tasks, not deliverables)!

"Fortunately, the organizational coach trained us, and he gave us really clear guidelines. That made a huge difference! We spent our time focusing on the content, rather than struggling with different understandings of what's supposed to go into a catalog.

"After that training," Nate said, "we all brainstormed our catalogs, and had a couple of coaching sessions before presenting to one another."

"How big was your catalog?" I asked.

"It was detailed, but quite manageable — in total, under 2000 items; each department had between a couple dozen and a few hundred. We had to get that granular to get down to the level of discrete purchase decisions."

"How long did it take to develop your catalogs?" I asked.

"It was around three months," Nate replied.

"Not bad," I said. "What value did you get out of doing catalogs?"

"Lots!" Nate exclaimed. "The experience of developing catalogs definitely took us to the next level of understanding of our businesses and boundaries. And it drove home accountabilities for results. Catalogs were definitely transformational.

"And we use our catalogs every day. They give us a crisp language for internal commitments. We're really clear about what we're asking one another for (our accountabilities), and who has what authorities.

"For example, we know the difference between selling 'expert time' where the customer directs the supplier's staff, and a 'solution' where the supplier is accountable for the final results and empowered to run the project."

Walk-throughs

"You put a lot of effort into making sure everybody understood their businesses," I said. "At that point, was the restructuring done?"

"Not yet," Nate replied. "Remember, you can't specialize if you can't team. As you said this morning, this new organization chart couldn't possibly work without really great cross-boundary teamwork. So, the structure implementation process had to include walk-throughs."

You can't specialize if you can't team.
The structure implementation process has to deal with both
the organization chart that lays out everybody's specialties, and
walk-throughs which combine those specialists on cross-boundary teams.

"The organizational coach guided us through a whole series of walk-throughs — a variety of real-life projects and services, from a new-product launch down to a simple customer-service incident.

"I should tell you," Nate admitted, "walk-throughs were harder than designing the org chart. But the time we spent was totally worthwhile. All those walk-throughs got us to a point where we all had a common understanding of exactly how work will get done in the new organization. It was amazing teambuilding!"

"Was the new structure in effect while you were doing walk-throughs?" I asked.

"No, at that point, we were still in planning mode. We wanted to get to this level of shared understanding before we threw the switch. We didn't want to find ourselves announcing a new structure, and then muddling around in public trying to figure out how to make it work!"

Final Steps

"So, after the walk-throughs," I asked, "were you finally ready to go live with the new structure?"

"Almost," Nate replied. "We had a bunch of administrative tasks to take care of. And we put a lot of effort into planning the go-live event.

"Just before go-live, we assigned (rostered) all our staff (employees and contractors), our assets, and vendor contracts. We did that together, as the leadership team."

"Was that controversial?" I asked.

"Surprisingly, no," Nate said. "We assigned people based on what they'd been doing in the past. This way, every group had the talent it needed to meet the commitments it inherited.

"Another thing we did," Nate added, "was training in *transitions* — the feelings people experience as change happens to them. [126 Ref] We leaders were trained early in the process to help us deal with our own transitions; then just before go-live, we were trained to help our staff with their transitions. That also contributed to the low turnover."

Go-live

"And then the big day at last?" I asked.

"Yes." Nate said. "The go-live all-staff meeting was an amazing event!

"We explained to staff the need for change, the science behind the design, the new organization chart, domains, and catalogs. We play-acted a simplified walk-through on stage. And we prepared them for the next steps.

"But the purpose of the day wasn't just education," Nate noted. "We wanted to build everybody's enthusiasm for the new structure. It was a celebration of the birth of our new organization!

"Of course," he continued, "you can only remember so much from a one-day event. So, in the three weeks following go-live, each manager met with their new team for a series of education sessions. They reviewed the principles and the framework of types of businesses; their group's specific domain and catalog; walk-throughs; and personal transitions.

"Those team meetings were also about more than just education," Nate concluded. "That's where we started to bond our new groups."

Migration

"You mentioned you prepared staff for the next steps," I said. "At this point, wasn't the new organization up and running?"

"The new reporting structure was in effect," Nate explained. "But we wanted to be very careful about migrating accountabilities from the old structure to the new. We couldn't afford to drop any balls, and we had to be sure the new groups were ready to pick up commitments that fell into their domains.

"So, we insisted that everybody go on doing what they'd been doing (perhaps under a new boss) until they documented all their commitments. Because of the way we assigned people based on what they'd been doing in the past, most commitments were in the right place. But for the ones that no longer fit their new domains, individuals worked out migration plans with the correct domain leader."

"What went into a migration plan?" I asked.

Nate replied, "Migration plans included documentation, training, and sometimes even one group loaning a person to another group, part-time for a limited time. It was whatever the receiving group needed to take on the commitment. No dump and run!"

A Meticulous Process, Start to Finish

"How long did the process take?" I asked.

"It was around a year and a quarter to go-live. Then, migration took around five months. So, in just over a year and a half, we were fully operating in the new structure, complete with clear domains, catalogs walk-throughs, a careful migration process, and, I'd have to say, a very different way of thinking about our jobs.

"I know that seems like a long time," Nate admitted. "But if we'd done it the usual way — draw the boxes, appoint leaders, announce it, and then try to get it working right — I believe it would've taken a lot longer to get to where we're fully performing in the new paradigm (if ever). And meanwhile, all the confusion would have created a lot of cynicism about the restructuring."

I remembered the story of the steel executive who discovered Japan's secret, and nodded. This process was so different from the restructurings I'd seen throughout my career, which typically fixed some problems while creating others, caused lots of chaos, and led to little in the way of transformation.

I had to admit that this was the best-planned restructuring process I'd ever heard of.

A principle-based structure has been
one of the best investments I've made.

— Sergio Paiz, CEO, PDC *127 Ref*

Chapter 28:
Implementing Change:
Internal Economy

Chapter summary (key take-aways): page 490

"Okay, Nate," I said. "Resource-governance processes came next?"

"Yep. Our internal economy."

"I'm looking forward to shaking up my CFO with this one!"

"Oh, believe me, you will!"

We both laughed.

Budgeting versus Demand Management: Which Comes First?

"I remember this morning you told me about investment-based budgeting (Chapter 10) and your demand-management processes (Chapter 11). So," I asked, "which came first? Or did you do both at once?"

"We were eager to get to demand management," Nate replied, "since we all felt buried under expectations that far exceeded our resources.

"But demand-management processes depend on knowing our products and services and what they cost, as well as how much is in each checkbook. So, we had to start with investment-based budgeting."

Business and Budget Planning (Investment-based Budgeting)

"So, your first step was the budget process?"

"Yes," Nate said, "business and budget planning. They're both parts of the same process. Budgets are based on our operating plan."

"Did you have to develop the method or any tools?" I asked.

"No, we acquired the business planning method, the tool, and the implementation process. They all came as a package. *128 Ref* It would have taken us years if we'd tried to reinvent that wheel! And based on what I know now, I'm not convinced we'd ever have gotten it right."

Nate described the steps in their annual business and budget planning process (Figure 35).

Figure 35: Investment-based Budgeting Process

1. Define (or refine) each group's product/service catalog.
2. Forecast sales (deliverables); link prime and subcontracts; place into "buckets"; estimate volumes.
3. Plan compensation costs, billable-time ratios, and billable hours per deliverable.
4. Plan external costs, and link them to specific products and services.
5. Agree on internal support services, and link those costs to specific products and services on the receiving end.
6. Approve overhead deliverables, the costs of which go into all rates.
7. Identify sources of revenues for each group (external sales, internal budgets, internal chargebacks); decide mark-ups.
8. Review and finalize all the data.
9. Present the plan and negotiate the budget.
10. Upload the agreed budget for tracking; finalize rates.

"The first step is service catalogs," Nate explained. "We'd already developed ours as part of the structure process. (Otherwise, we'd have had to develop catalogs here.) Now, as part of our annual business planning process, we just update our service catalogs as needed.

"Then, we forecast sales of those products and services in the coming year. Those are the rows in the budget (Figure 12) — the *deliverables*. That gets everybody to figure out who their customers are (both within the company and externally).

"We work together to link primes and subs (as in walk-throughs) so that we can add up the rows in all the involved groups to get the total costs of deliverables (each prime with all its subcontracts).

"Next, we sort the deliverables into 'buckets' such as keep-the-lights-on and strategic projects (Figure 13). And we estimate volumes on each deliverable.

"After that," Nate continued, "we plan what it will take to produce those deliverables. That's where resources and costs come into the picture.

"In the staffing analysis part of that, we set aside the right amount of 'unbillable' time for critical sustenance activities (like administration, training, process improvements, planning, and innovation). Then, we assign billable hours to each deliverable."

"Don't you need time-tracking data to do that?" I asked.

"Not really," Nate said. "We have a pretty good sense of what it'll take to deliver the services that we'd done in the prior year. We estimate projects and new services based on our experience. Even without historic time-tracking data, it comes out in the ballpark.

"After that, we forecast all the vendor costs, which is more like traditional budgeting. But we link every cost to our products and services.

"Finally," Nate concluded, "we run the data through a state-of-the-art cost model (that's built into the tool we'd acquired), and out comes our investment-based budget, as well as fully burdened cost-based rates for all the products and services in our catalogs."

"You do all that annually?" I asked.

"Yes."

"How long does it take?"

"The first time through," Nate recalled, "it was a learning experience.

It took us 11 months to learn the new process and set up the model for the first time. But now, it takes us a few months each year — pretty much the same as the time we used to spend doing budgets the old way."

"11 months is a lot of time for budgeting," I said.

"Yes," Nate replied, "but remember, that was a one-time cost. And we saw benefits each step of the way. In the end, the impacts were huge! It not only aligned all our resources with our strategies. It also furthered the transformation in so many ways. It was totally worth it."

NAVIGATION AID: Benefits of investment-based budgeting are described in Chapter 10.

Demand Management

"Okay, after that, you implemented demand management?" I asked.

"Yes," Nate said. "This morning (Chapter 11), we talked about treating budgets as pre-paid revenues (checkbooks owned by each department's customers), and purser committees that decide what checks to write. We use the data coming out of the investment-based budget to load those checkbooks and tell the pursers what things cost.

"There were lots of details in the processes we designed." Nate talked me through Figure 36.

"How long did it take to set all that up?" I asked.

"We designed it in just a couple of months," Nate replied. "This was mostly done by my Organizational Effectiveness group, the PMO, and Finance. We only needed the leaders' time when it came to starting up the new processes."

"As for the start-up," Nate continued, "we had to communicate the processes, get a consolidated request-list together, and appoint and train the pursers. That took another few months.

Figure 36: Demand Management Processes

- **Intake:** Creating the master list of requests
  - o Differentiated channels for maintenance/support, emergency projects, normal projects
  - o Sponsorship to filter requests
  - o Phase-gating (Chapter 16)
  - o Rough cost and time estimates (entire project and next phase)
- **Priority-setting:** Business-driven purchase decisions
  - o Checkbooks (filled by budget) and pursers (committees and subcommittees)
  - o Decision process, purser facilitation
- **Communications:** Keeping requestors informed
  - o Pursers' decisions
  - o Project status
- **Execution:** How suppliers respect pursers' decisions
  - o Execution sequencing (waiting for availability of prime and all subcontractors)
  - o Closing the "back door" (no work without funding)
- **Reporting:** Accounting systems
  - o Invoicing (consumption times published rates)
  - o Checkbook maintenance

"In the end, it all came together nicely," Nate said. "Senior leaders really love being in control of the priorities of internal service providers. And staff love that expectations are in line with their resources, and that they aren't getting jerked around with confused and shifting priorities.

"Ultimately," he concluded, "the big payoff is that all our resources — time and money — are reliably aligned with our business needs and strategies — not just at the start of the year due to investment-based budgeting, but dynamically throughout the year through this demand-management process."

NAVIGATION AID: Benefits of market-based demand management are described in Chapter 11.

Accounting Systems

"That leads to another question," I said. "Did you need new accounting systems? I've heard the term 'TBM' (technology business management), and that seems to require some pretty expensive software."

"We're just in the process of looking at that now," Nate replied. "And you're right; those systems can be really expensive.

"The truth is, we didn't need accounting data to do investment-based budgeting, or to set up these demand-management processes. Historic data is just there to *season* management judgment, not replace it.

"True," Nate continued, "we need accounting data to decrement check-books, so that pursers know how much is left for the rest of the year. But at least temporarily, it's almost as good to invoice (decrement check-books) based on plan (estimates) versus actuals.

"That's especially true since we're filling checkbooks month by month to even out demand for staff time. So, pursers have a good sense of the resources available to them in the coming month.

"In general," Nate noted, "we're not in a rush to do accounting systems. The benefit of better tracking is just a bit of a reduction in the risk in decisions.

"Given that," he said, "we considered accounting to be fine-tuning for later in the transformation road-map. Frankly, accounting just isn't all that transformational."

I smiled. I had to admit Nate was right about that.

"As to software," Nate said, "we aligned cost centers with the new structure when that went live. But we didn't start calculating P&Ls (profit and loss statements) for managers until recently. And we didn't need new software for that; we were able to do that in our ERP.

"We're tracking pursers' checkbooks in spreadsheets for now. There's not much to that.

"So," Nate concluded, "the only software we've acquired so far is the investment-based budgeting tool. Now, we're just about ready to work on invoicing and decrementing checkbooks based on actual consumption. So, we'll see what's needed for that."

Their approach was very different from what those TBM vendors had been trying to sell me. But Nate's logic made a lot of sense.

Time Tracking

"How about time tracking?" I asked. "I guess that's another form of accounting."

"It is," Nate replied. "We don't ask everybody to fill out timecards, at least not yet. The exception is when we're doing hourly work for external clients."

"I see. And I like it," I said. "I know it can be tough to get people to fill out timecards."

"It sure can!" Nate agreed. "If people just view timecards as helping management look over their shoulders, with nothing in it for them, you'll never get good data.

"On the other hand," he said, "have you ever heard of a lawyer who doesn't want to fill out timecards!? They know that's how they get paid. Now that people understand that they're running businesses (and many of them sell by the hour), we think they'll cooperate.

"Mechanically, we had to wait anyhow. We need data coming out of the investment-based budget to set up the categories to assign time to — the projects, services, and definitions of unbillable time. So, it's best done after that step.

"So," Nate concluded, "that's why we waited until now to introduce timecards."

Sequence

"In summary," I said, "investment-based budgeting, then demand management, then the accounting systems and time tracking."

"That's how we did it," Nate said.

Figure 37: Internal Economy Implementation Phases

1. Business plan, investment-based budget, catalog, rates
2. Demand management (resource governance)
3. Accounting systems and time tracking

Chapter 29:
Implementing Change:
Culture

Chapter summary (key take-aways): page 490

"As I recall, your next step was culture, right?" I asked.

"Right," Nate replied. "Since the demand-management processes didn't require much participation from the leadership team, we were able to get started on culture in parallel to that phase."

"Okay, so what's the trick to driving culture change?" As you might imagine, I was skeptical. I'd seen numerous attempts to define organizational culture, none of which generated much in the way of real results.

Behavioral Principles

"Remember, we discussed the behavioral approach (Chapter 12)?" Nate said. "That's the trick. That's what delivers quick, tangible changes in what people actually do, which adds up to a change in culture."

"Ah, yes. So, tell me how you implemented it."

"Well," Nate replied, "the first step was crafting clear, actionable behavioral principles."

"How did you go about doing that?" I asked.

"First," Nate said, "the organizational coach explained the behavioral approach, and gave us guidelines on how to word behavioral principles.

"Then, we selected which of the 13 Themes (Figure 18) we wanted to address. As it turned out, we decided to address all of them.

"Next," Nate continued, "we split into break-out teams and divided up the 13 Themes. Each team brainstormed principles within their assigned Themes that addressed our concerns.

"After the break-outs, the organizational coach distributed his database of 'best practices.' This was a really comprehensive set of behavioral principles that came from all the leadership teams that he'd worked with in the past. (Examples are in Appendix 4.)

"We didn't use his database as 'the answer,'" Nate explained. "We weren't about to take our culture out of a book! But it was super valuable to us in two ways:

"As the break-out teams presented each principle they'd drafted, we discussed the meaning, then the wording. We used the best-practices database to help us word things in clear, actionable language.

"Then, when we were done talking through a break-out team's ideas, we looked at the best-practices database for behaviors that others had thought of and we'd missed, and discussed adding them to our culture.

"We came to consensus on each and every behavioral principle," Nate emphasized. "That way, we were confident that we all supported each one, and we could teach them consistently."

"How long did that take?" I asked.

"We spent seven days over the course of two months crafting our culture principles," Nate replied.

Roll-out

"At that point," I said, "you leaders had defined the desired behaviors. So, I assume you were committed to practicing them. But then what about the rest of the staff? Some say that culture is passed along in the DNA of organizations, and reinforced through the behaviors of an inner-circle of people whom others emulate. They say that's why it takes so long to change culture."

"We didn't buy into that," Nate replied. "We needed culture change to happen quickly. And we certainly weren't going to leave our culture to the mercy of some sort of 'in-crowd'!"

"Okay, so how did you speed the adoption process?" I asked.

"First, we had an all-staff meeting to explain why we were working on culture and what was about to happen. But that was just a heads-up.

"Then came the real work," Nate explained. "We rolled out the behaviors over the course of nine months, a Theme or two per month.

"Each month, every manager met with their team to discuss all the principles in that month's Theme. We gave them an outline in advance, including some discussion questions and role-play exercises that had been prepared by a subcommittee.

"Oh," Nate noted, "and while the managers were teaching the behaviors, they were also listening to staff's feedback.

"After all the Themes were rolled out," he continued, "the leadership team got back together to examine the feedback. We made some revisions to the principles, and added a couple of new principles, thanks to the input we'd gotten from the staff. That way, *everybody* had an opportunity to contribute to our culture."

Figure 38: Culture Implementation Process

1. Leadership team crafts behavioral principles
2. Subcommittee prepares roll-out materials
3. All-staff meeting explains the why and the process to come
4. Team meetings, Theme by Theme, teach and listen
5. Leadership team studies feedback, communicates revised principles
6. Assess and reinforce after 9-12 months

Time Required

"Wow," I remarked. "That was a big investment."

"It was. But again, it paid off," Nate asserted. "Thanks to all those team meetings, *everybody* at every level had the opportunity to understand our culture in detail. And the chance to contribute increased buy-in. So, we really got traction."

"And it was a success?" I asked.

"I'd call it a huge success," Nate said proudly. "By that I mean, *in just one year, 80 percent of our staff were practicing 80 percent of the behaviors 80 percent of the time.*" [129 More]

"That's amazing," I exclaimed. "That *is* a success!"

NAVIGATION AID: The benefits of this culture initiative are described in Chapter 12.

Roles in the Culture Change Process

"What was Carlton's role in this process?" I asked.

"Of course, he sponsored the initiative. He brought in the organizational coach to teach and facilitate us. And he participated right alongside us (and he never pulled rank on us)."

"And what was the role of the organizational coach?" I asked.

"He laid out the project plan and facilitated the process," Nate said. "Also, he coached us as we defined the behaviors. He helped us word things to be clear and actionable. Beyond that, he really stretched our thinking, and made us strive to define the best we could be."

Reinforcement

"So, one year and you were done with culture?"

"Not quite," Nate admitted.

"We have to be sure that new hires understand what's expected of them. So, we installed a culture module in our new-employee orientation process. That's ongoing, of course.

"And as you'd expect, we have to continually reinforce it," Nate added.

"Say more about reinforcement," I requested.

"At the start, Carlton put 'walking the talk,' and helping their staff adopt the new culture, in all leaders' performance metrics. After the roll-out was done, our performance metric expanded to measure leaders by their staff's walking the talk.

"A year after the roll-out, we did an assessment to see which principles stuck and which didn't. We decided which ones needed reinforcement, and pushed out more communications and education on those.

"And," Nate said, "Carlton reinforced it through his own behaviors."

"That's interesting. What did he do?"

"I'll give you an example," Nate said. "We printed all the behaviors in this little booklet. One day, one of our leaders went to Carlton with a sticky situation — a problem with an irate customer. Carlton pulled this booklet out and said, 'Let's see what our culture tells us to do in a situation like this....' [130 Ref]

"Carlton was saying two things: One, I believe in the culture. And two, culture is a practical tool, not shelfware."

"That's great," I said. "I can do that." And I believe I will.

~ PART 6 ~

Leadership Perspectives

in which I get some invaluable insights
on transformational leadership

Having reviewed the transformation planning and implementation processes with Nate, I was impressed with the well-planned change management. The time required and the investment in participation were a bit daunting. But as the old aphorism goes, if you're going to do it, you may as well do it right!

I now understood what it would take to drive a real transformation, and to leave that legacy of a truly great organization which I aspired to.

In all, I was convinced that the investment was more than justified by the remarkable results I'd seen.

Next on the agenda, my final meeting of the day was with Carlton, the CEO who had led this transformation.

I was tired, and feeling the effects of information overload. Nonetheless, this guy was clearly an exceptional executive, and I really wanted to explore a number of "view from the top" questions, including his perspective on transformational leadership.

"It's interesting," I said, as Nate and I walked down the hall. "Carlton doesn't strike me as a particularly charismatic leader. He's more thoughtful and deliberate."

"It doesn't take charisma to inspire us," Nate said. "We trust him, and we believe in his vision — *our* vision. And that's true all the way down the ranks. Carlton is a big part of what inspired people to go along with the transformation."

With that, Nate dropped me off at Carlton's door. "I think my job is done," he said.

"Nate, you arranged a fantastic tour. I got so many valuable insights today. It was really great. *You* were really great. Thank you!"

Nate smiled widely as we said goodbye. Then, Carlton's assistant ushered me into his office.

Chapter 30:
Scalability, Startups, and Multi-nationals

Chapter summary (key take-aways): page 491

"Carlton, I must tell you that what I heard today was impressive."

"Wow, thanks! I'm proud of my team. They're the ones who deserve all the credit."

I smiled, knowing that nothing would have happened without his leadership. "If I may," I said, "I'd like to ask you about some things I've struggled with over the years, to see how the Market Organization might help."

"Sure," Carlton said, smiling. "What's first on your list?"

Scalability

"Scalability," I said. "As my companies have grown, it seems they periodically hit thresholds where a major rethink of the operating model was required. That's always quite disruptive. Is it possible to design an organization that can scale by orders of magnitude without the need for major organizational changes?"

"I think so," Carlton replied. "First, I believe that our principles — of structure, internal economy, culture, and metrics — apply to small organizations as well as very large ones."

I thought for a moment, and said, "Yes, I believe you're right. But take structure, for example. It's hard to imagine a small company's org chart remaining viable after it grows to 10 or 100 times its size."

It was Carlton's turn to ponder for a moment before he replied, "I think organizations have to continually adapt as they grow and as things change. So, the goal is not a static organization. It's an organization

that can adapt to changes without the need for any major shift in its
paradigm or operating model."

"I grant you that," I affirmed.

Scalability means that an organization can grow and adapt
without the need for any major shift in its paradigm or operating model.

"I'll go one step further," Carlton continued. "Beyond being adaptive,
the goal is to design an entrepreneurial organization that *drives* that
growth, and sees changes as opportunities."

"That's the holy grail," I said. "But specifically, what has had to change
in your structure or processes as you grew?"

"Nothing material," Carlton said. "We've been able to fill some spots
on the org chart with some missing talent, once we could afford them.

"Also, many lines of business have grown to the point of splitting into
two groups — either by creating another management position alongside
the existing one, or by leaving the manager in place and establishing
sub-groups at the next level. That's allowed a higher degree of specialization.

"And on occasion, we've added a new group to cover a new challenge
— like emerging technologies, some new products and services, and
new markets. But it's always obvious where it fits in our structure."

"Say more about those new groups," I requested.

"Well, when we added new products, either they fit within the domains
of existing product managers, or we expanded a domain or added a new
product manager. Nothing else changed. Product managers have the
P&L on those new businesses, but they don't have other functions
reporting to them. What they have instead is access to all the capabili-

ties of the entire organization, which is just the sort of support you want for new business lines.

"When we offered new services," Carlton continued, "we expanded the domain of an existing Service Provider. The same thing applied to new technologies; we just expanded the domains of existing Engineering groups. As those new services and technologies took hold and revenues grew, we split some of them out into domains of their own.

"When we entered new geographies (like our expansion into Europe), there are only a few functions that are subdivided by geography — Sales, Field Technicians, maybe some Marketing. Those functions added new groups over there. That's that.

"When we entered new markets, like auto and agricultural-equipment dealers, we added Sales domains, as well as all of the above.

"But in every case," he said, "the overall structure didn't change. We knew exactly where each new domain fit. And walk-throughs automatically integrated those new groups into the fabric of the organization."

"How about your internal economy?" I asked.

"Sometimes," Carlton explained, "when we created new groups, we had to divide up the internal-economy checkbooks a little differently. But growth hasn't changed any of the governance processes.

"And growth hasn't forced any change in our cultural principles.

"Also," he added, "we're continually refining metrics as we better understand what we want from each line of business. But growth doesn't necessitate any significant change in our approach to metrics.

"So all in all," Carlton concluded, "we've grown quite a bit without any major shift in our organizational operating model."

I nodded. It made sense. Beyond that, it was elegant.

> *A stable organization that is dynamic by design* [131 More]
> *is best equipped to deal with a complex and volatile world.*

Small Organizations

"Now, we're still a relatively small firm," Carlton cautioned. "I don't know if our experience will be applicable to your company."

"No, no, I think it's very applicable to my company," I assured him. "In fact, I can see your whole operating model applying to any large company. But I wonder, can this work in very small organizations — say a few dozen people."

"I believe so. For example, we think of Human Resources as a support function. But within HR, there are all the types of businesses. They have Service Providers like the HR employee database, compensation and benefits administration, and recruiting. They have Engineers like job grading, and comp-and-benefits design. They have Coordinators like employment policies. And they have Sales, what they used to call 'HR generalists,' dedicated to business units.

"So, our HR group has all the challenges of the company as a whole. But it only has a couple dozen people in it. Nonetheless, they've applied all the principles just within their group."

"What kinds of considerations do you take into account in small organizations like that?" I asked.

"Well," Carlton replied, "they can't specialize to the same degree as larger organizations. We don't want to be 'one deep' — depending on just one person for critical functions. So, we had to combine some specialties and do some cross-training. But as per the principles, we combine domains *within* types of business, not across.

"And we have working managers in more cases, since there may not be enough headcount in a group to justify a full-time manager.

"Sometimes, we had to put a leader's name in more than one box. We've had cases where a leader takes on two side-by-side boxes, and where a leader also manages a group that reports to them.

"Other than that," Carlton concluded, "in my experience, the whole operating model applies quite well to organizations of any size."

"Are the transformation processes the same?" I asked.

"Basically, yes," Carlton replied. "But they're easier. In a large organization, you might work with the top tier, then engage the next tier, then roll it out to all staff. But in a small organization, you can engage all the leaders up front and avoid that cascade process, as we did. And in very small organizations like our HR group, we can engage *all* the staff in the design process and avoid the whole roll-out phase."

Once you get above about a dozen employees,
organizational processes matter as much as
people, technology, and products.

— Charlie Shalvoy, seasoned tech venture CEO

Startups

"Okay," I said, "how about ventures? They start out really tiny; and typically, they don't worry about organizational issues until they grow to the point of needing more organizational maturity."

"Unfortunately, that's true," Carlton said. "Most founders don't think about organizational strategy until way too late. But that doesn't have to be true. Let me tell you a story that I heard from the organizational coach...."

"He once worked with a startup — three or four founders and a handful of staff. Everybody was doing everything, at high speed. And things were getting done. But there was confusion about accountabilities, and some things were falling through the cracks.

"Perhaps even more damning," Carlton continued, "they didn't know who was accountable for thinking of all the things that they *weren't* doing. The founders all felt responsible for everything, and no one was 'living and breathing' each internal line of business."

I related to this story. Right after business school, I started a company with a few friends. I smiled thinking back on how we did get it going, and did sell it — but that was despite our confusion and only with herculean efforts and a lot of luck!

Not to know how to manage is the
single largest reason for the failure of new ventures.

— Peter F. Drucker *132 Ref*

Carlton continued, "So, what the organizational coach did was lead those founders through a structure process, as if they were a big company. The resulting org chart had lots of boxes on it, representing all the lines of business they'd need someday.

"Of course, there were more boxes than people. So, the founders sorted their three or four names into all those boxes. Each of them took on a few lines of business.

"And, of course, they all continued to work closely together, and do whatever it took to get their company going."

"Then what did that structure accomplish?" I asked.

"What this big-company org chart did for them was to clarify who's the prime on each initiative; and who owns each line of business and should be thinking about its entire scope, now and into the future.

"Over time, they grew into the structure. When they were ready to hire, they selected the box they most needed to fill at that stage of growth, and knew exactly what competencies to look for.

"And with the Market Organization, they were assured that even as they formalized their processes, they'd maintain their entrepreneurial spirit."

"Interesting," I said. "I'd add that for those who hope to sell the company someday, if the organization is a toxic mess, buyers will walk away. But few startups have time to work on their organizations."

"Few *take* the time," Carlton replied.

"Touché!"

The Founder Bottleneck

"Let's look at ventures that have matured a bit," I said, "the ones that have grown to 50 or more people. Recently, I played golf with a buddy who's a VC (venture capitalist). He described a classic problem, and I'm thinking the Market Organization might have some answers."

"Say more," Carlton said.

"What happens," I said, "is that a few really smart and motivated people start up a company. It starts to work, so they go for funding and grow it. Then, it hits a ceiling.

"The problem is the founders. They're still running the company like it's a few guys in a garage. Everything goes through them, and *they* become the constraint to growth.

"A lot of VCs push the founders aside and install a professional CEO," I continued. "But then, the company loses the vision, passion, and smarts that created it. And that so-called professional CEO installs a bunch of bureaucratic processes that kill the entrepreneurial spirit in the company.

"Wouldn't the Market Organization make sense here?" I suggested.

"Absolutely!" Carlton exclaimed. "The bottleneck is that the founders *are* the organization's coordinating mechanisms. Everything is channeling through them — priorities, teamwork, strategic initiatives...."

"The Market Organization moves coordinating mechanisms from the founders to the organizational ecosystem," Carlton continued. "The internal economy (Chapter 9) handles priorities. Walk-throughs (Chapter 8) handle teamwork. And structure (Chapter 7) empowers people as entrepreneurs whose jobs include thinking about their strategies.

"That breaks the bottleneck and allows founders to rise up to a more strategic level. And it does this," he said, "while *reinforcing* entrepreneurship, not stifling it."

"At least it decouples two distinct issues," I observed, "the lack of processes (the bottleneck problem), and the founders' capabilities. First, fix the processes. Then, either the founders mature into leaders, or my friend has to take action."

"And even if a new CEO is needed," Carlton suggested, "with a Market Organization up and running, there'd be no need for bureaucracy."

Multi-product, Multi-national

"Okay, let's go to the other end of the spectrum," I said. "Let's talk about multi-product, multi-national companies. Don't you have to split into multiple operating companies at some point?"

"I hope not!" Carlton replied. "How would you split? By region? By product line? No matter how you do it, you lose synergies."

"True. But the practicality of such a complicated set of companies — how can you manage that globally?" I asked.

"Well, first off, I don't have to. It's not my job to manage everything that's going on. Thank goodness, because there's no way I could."

"Right, right. We don't want to be cogs in the machine," I concurred.

"Exactly," Carlton continued. "But to your question, we're a fully integrated company. As you've heard, *everything* is a global shared service. So, as we just discussed, as we grow and diversify, we just add domains to our existing operating model."

"You're committed to 100 percent integration, no matter how big you get?" I asked.

"We are," Carlton asserted. "And hopefully we'll get 100 percent of the potential synergies."

"But the global coordination challenges!?" I objected.

"We're all set up for that. Walk-throughs drive teamwork globally. The internal economy aligns our resources, including people's time and priorities. We have coordinated planning processes. And our culture of internal entrepreneurship makes it work. With all that, and after our experience with Covid-19, we're confident we can work and manage globally."

As I reflected on the vision of a fully integrated multi-product, multi-national company, the potential synergies were astounding. The link between the Market Organization and shareholder value became all the more clear to me.

In this digital world, geography is just a psychological barrier.
— Sergio Paiz, CEO, PDC

Chapter 31:
Acquisitions Integration

Chapter summary (key take-aways): page 491

"Carlton, here's what I think is a related topic.... I've done quite a few acquisitions over the years," I said. "It's been a great source of growth. Does your organizational operating model help at all with that?"

"Absolutely," he replied. "And sometimes in surprising ways. In the midst of negotiating a recent acquisition, the founder got a better offer from a big conglomerate. But he chose to sell to us because he wants to see his baby — his lifework and his loyal staff — in good hands." *133 Ref*

"Really!?"

"That's what he told me, and told others," Carlton said.

Acquisitions Integration

"That's a nice surprise," I said. "But I want to talk about the integration issues.... In any acquisition, you're going to have to pay for some good-will over book value. That's only worth it if you can get synergies out of the acquisition, right?"

"Right," Carlton concurred.

"If you're just a holding company," I said, "you'd get some financial synergies. But that isn't nearly enough, at least in my experience."

Again, Carlton agreed.

"And I don't want to settle for just brand synergies," I continued, "you know, keeping the acquired company independent but bringing them under our brand marketing. That doesn't get us much. We want to leverage *all* the capabilities of the firm to help acquired brands succeed."

"Exactly," Carlton said. "And vice versa. If the acquisition has any competencies that the rest of the company can use, we want those available to everybody too."

"Right!" I said. "So, the value of the acquisition depends on quick, comprehensive integration. Does your organizational operating model facilitate that integration process?" *134 More*

"It sure does," Carlton confirmed. "I'll tell you, that was really put to the test when we did an acquisition in Europe. It might seem small to you, but it was big for us."

"Tell me how it played out," I said.

"Well," Carlton said, "given the distance, some folks thought we'd have to run it as an independent business unit. But, of course, that wouldn't give us the synergies we were looking for.

"The good news was, we were acquisition ready. We had a number of things going for us that facilitated acquisition integration:

- "Our lines of business are so clear that we were able to precisely map each group in the acquired company to a domain in our structure.

- "Our strength in teamwork helped us work together across geographies and functions.

- "Our resource-governance processes easily (and explicitly) accommodated additional resources, lines of business (cost centers), and commitments.

- "We had a clearly defined culture that our new colleagues quickly understood. (And most loved it!)

- "And as I said, we're really good at working together without being physically together, and managing remote staff.

"So, we 'went for the gold' — full integration," he said. "As a result, our new European business got the support of the entire organization. And our American markets got the benefit of Europe's capabilities."

"Of course," Carlton added, "we have product managers for the acquired brands. They still live in Europe; but they have global domains and utilize all our global support functions. Everything else in the acquired company folded into existing shared-services groups."

Acquisitions without integration would have made us bigger, but would not have improved returns on capital. And we have to cover the good-will through synergies, or we'd destroy value. I credit our success at acquisitions integration to our structure.

— Sergio Paiz, CEO, PDC

"Did you leave a general manager in place in Europe?"

"There's no need for a general manager. Every team over there is part of the appropriate global domain. But since we had numerous people in Europe, all reporting to the right groups (mostly here), we did dedicate a person to the role of 'Site Coordinator' (Chapter 19).

Acquisition Integration Process

"How did you go about that integration process?" I asked.

"We take it in three steps: C-I-O," Carlton replied. "That stands for Consolidate, Integrate, Optimize."

C-I-O is a catchy mnemonic, I mused. Carlton explained its meaning:

Consolidate: "We let the acquired company run independently for a little while, to calm everybody down and give them time to learn our operating model.

"During that time, we train them in our culture, structure, walk-throughs, and our internal economy.

"And we communicate, communicate, communicate! We explain the strategic rationale, and answer all their questions honestly (most of which are about what's going to happen to them)."

Integrate: "Then," Carlton said, "we engage their leadership team in an analysis of where the various lines of business are in their org chart — the Rainbow Analysis (Chapter 27). That gives us the map to fit their groups into the right places in our structure."

"You make it sound easy," I quipped.

"Actually, for the most part, it is," Carlton replied. "At least it's fact-based and fair, not emotional."

"How do you handle redundant leaders?" I asked.

"In some cases, that isn't an issue when an acquisition has groups doing things that we weren't doing. Specifically in the case of Europe, they had some technologies and services that we didn't offer. So, those leaders stayed in place (under new bosses), even as we globalized their domains.

"But there were many overlaps," Carlton said. "We always want to pick the best-qualified person for each job. And the acquisition did bring us some great talent. So, when one of their groups mapped to one of our groups, we looked at both leaders and chose based on competencies (not which side they came from)."

"What happened to the leaders who didn't get the top job?" I asked.

"We didn't reduce their compensation, but they did have to move down under the selected manager. As you'd expect, some left, mostly from the acquired company.

"I'm sure many more looked around for other opportunities," Carlton continued. "But the acquired leaders saw the up-side of a fully integrated company. The majority put their egos aside and stayed.

"As for our original leaders, they knew that this is really a great place to work. I think most realized they wouldn't be as happy anywhere else. So, our retention numbers were really good."

"That's interesting," I said. "Now, what's the Optimize step?"

Optimize: "All our leaders are continually optimizing their businesses. So, that step goes on forever.

"But in the context of an acquisition, within each group, they share best practices from both sides, merge their processes, rationalize their assets, and look for ways to further specialize now that they're a larger group.

"By the way," Carlton observed, "note that we really don't get the synergies until the Optimize step. If we tried to pull costs out any sooner, all we'd do is reduce levels of service and potentially damage operational processes and important initiatives."

"I get it," I sighed. I knew that many CEOs and Boards are impatient, and undermine long-term value in the rush to get acquisitions to pay off. In contrast, C-I-O seemed eminently practical.

Our organizational operating model is one of complete integration; everything is a shared service, to maximize specialization, economies of scale, and synergies.

Recently, we acquired a company in Peru. Due to the distance, some thought we'd have to set it up as an independent business unit, replicating many of our operations and support functions.

However, it's been impressive to see how all the functions in Peru integrated seamlessly with their centralized counterparts, and we're gaining all the synergies I'd hoped for when I bought that company.

— Sergio Paiz, CEO, PDC

Chapter 32:
Innovation Everywhere (No Skunk-works)

Chapter summary (key take-aways): page 492

"Okay, on to the next topic," I said. "Let's talk about innovation — not just extending current product lines, not even just new generations of products, but *disruptive* innovation."

"Great topic!" Carlton exclaimed.

The Innovator's Dilemma

I explained my concern: "You may have read Clay Christensen's widely discussed *Innovator's Dilemma*." [135 Ref]

Christensen talks about how startup companies with innovative products that appeal to niche markets decimate well-managed, established companies — like the progression from IBM to Digital Equipment Corp., and then to Microsoft and Apple.

These niche players may not add much functionality to existing product lines; but customers generally don't use all the functionality that's already there anyhow. What these innovators do is bring new levels of convenience or integration, innovative capabilities, or lower costs.

These are things that niche markets really want. But traditional customers value them as well, perhaps more than yet-more extensions to existing products. Eventually, these startups grow beyond the niche and take over the mainstream market.

Christensen points out that good management practices for extending existing products (like focusing on existing customers' values, margins, and revenue growth rates) are exactly what kill disruptive innovations that open new markets (with different customers' values, low margins at first, and tiny revenues until they outgrow their niche).

Based on this, Christensen concludes that you need to set up a separate organization to pursue disruptive technologies — a separate company, or at least a separate group (like an "incubator" or a "skunk works") that's exempt from those management "best practices." *136 More*

The Costs of a Separate Innovation Group

"You don't buy Christensen's logic?" I asked.

"Well, I'm no Harvard professor," Carlton replied, "but I humbly disagree with Dr. Christensen's conclusion that you need a separate group for disruptive innovation."

"Why is that?"

"Look," Carlton said, "both types of innovation, sustaining and disruptive, require mostly the same kinds of capabilities — the same professional knowledge, skills, tools, even design and production methods.

"If we split a given specialty into two groups — one for the current business and one for innovation — we've just reduced our depth of specialization. That impacts everybody's performance (Principle 2 of structure).

"On the other hand," Carlton continued, "we want our innovation ventures to have access to all the depth of talent the firm can muster, wherever it reports. We don't want one little group trying to go it alone.

"Furthermore," he said, "we don't want to set up one group that deprives other groups of the fun, future-oriented part of their jobs. To us, that feels unethical. And it wastes a lot of bright minds who could be very creative if given the chance.

"Similarly, we don't want one group whose job is to put another group out of business. That would kill collaboration, and it's counter to the Golden Rule.

"But what's worse," Carlton asserted, "a separate innovation group creates two classes of citizenship — one group that gets to do all the politically visible, fun, strategic initiatives; and the 'drudges' who just keep today's business running. That's against our ethics. And it's pretty darn demoralizing for everybody outside the incubator.

"When the rest of the staff have reasons to resent the innovation group, and the innovation group has reasons to be defensive about its privileged position, relationships are strained and cooperation breaks down. The innovation group loses access to all the talent and institutional knowledge of legacy groups. And the transition of an innovation into production becomes more difficult.

"And meanwhile," Carlton added, "that separate group can't contain the same depth of expertise as the collection of all the specialists throughout the rest of the company put together. So, it can't keep up with the literature in all those fields of study. Over time, it becomes a bottleneck for innovation."

"There's another problem I've worried about," I added. "Resources. How would I determine the appropriate headcount for an innovation group?"

"That's right," Carlton said. "There's no fixed answer. Some require a lot of resources and others do not. And at some times during an innovation venture, we need major projects that engage lots of different competencies; while at other times, a small team may suffice. There's no way a fixed group of people would represent the right investment level all the time."

Carlton continued his indictment. "Thinking onward, what happens when that innovation group comes up with something that goes into production? Does the innovation group go on supporting and extending that technology? If they do, they're no longer in the disruption business. They become a whole separate business unit with its own infrastructure.

That would be the opposite of our fully integrated, maximum-synergies organizational strategy.

"This is a slippery slope. Do we end up becoming just a holding company with a bunch of little companies operating independently — no synergies? We can do better than that!" Carlton asserted.

I countered, "Couldn't you transfer the breakthrough innovations back into your mainstream organization once the concept is proven?"

"You could," he replied, "but that has problems too....

"The other groups have to climb the learning curve, studying what the innovation group already knows, which can be costly and time consuming. And sometimes, the 'not invented here' syndrome slows things down.

"But what concerns me more is this," Carlton said. "If that innovation group doesn't have operational responsibilities, then they don't have a strong incentive to design future products for manufacturability and supportability.

"They don't even have a strong incentive for first-time quality. They might say, 'Get it out, get the glory, and let those poor saps in the rest of the company deal with defects and production difficulties.'

"And worse still," he said, "we've violated the Golden Rule. One group decides another group's future. How could we hold our operational groups accountable for their businesses when they can't control their future products!?"

"Wow," I remarked, "what might seem logical on the surface has unintended consequences!"

"It sure does!" Carlton exclaimed.

Figure 39: Dysfunctions of Separate Innovation Groups   *137 Ref*

- Reduces specialization (hence, performance) by splitting professions across two groups
- Makes it difficult for the innovation initiative to access all the depth of talent and institutional knowledge throughout the organization
- Deprives other groups of the fun, future-oriented part of their jobs; demotivational, and wastes so many bright minds
- Puts one group in the business of putting another group out of business; undermines collaboration
- Creates two classes of citizenship: strategic group versus "obsolete products" groups; demoralizes staff; causes resentment and defensiveness; strains relations, and undermines cooperation
- Creates a bottleneck for innovation since one small group of relative generalists can't keep up with many professions or industries
- Inflexible in its level of investment in innovation over time
- If it operationalizes its innovation as a separate business unit:
  - Replicates lines of business (costly, reduced specialization, lost synergies)
  - Takes the innovation group out of the innovation business
- If the rest of the organization operationalizes innovations:
  - Requires knowledge transfer, redundant learning curves
  - Provides little incentive for designing for manufacturability and supportability, or for first-time quality
  - Violates the Golden Rule: one group decides another group's future; operational groups can't be held accountable

Innovation In Every Group

"So, what's the alternative?" I asked.

"We took to heart Christensen's concerns about management practices that kill innovation," Carlton replied. "But we came to a different conclusion about the root causes and the solutions.

"We used the framework of organizational systems (Figure 32) to get to what we believe are the real root causes....

Carlton explained, "We don't think the root cause of the Innovator's Dilemma is structure — that is, the need for a separate box on the org chart. We do innovation ventures *within our existing structure.* We want *all* our internal entrepreneurs innovating, including disrupting their own product lines."

Someone is going to make your product obsolete.
Make sure it's you.

— Edwin H. Land

"We addressed everybody's lack of time and money in our *internal economy,* especially our budget process. Everybody has time and resources for ongoing, sustaining innovation. It's built into their rates.

"And we have explicit funding for ventures — major innovation initiatives. Ventures are line items in our budgets. In addition, I have an innovation fund. All our entrepreneurial leaders can propose ideas. With the help of our Research and Innovation Coordinator (Chapter 22), I award grants (seed money) to get an idea to the point of a venture proposal that'll go into our budget.

"To Christensen's point," Carlton continued, "we don't require market analyses and ROI when we look at those proposals. We use the 'expected value' statistical concept: Odds times Stakes. The odds of a real market disrupter might be slim; but the stakes of being the first mover, or of going out of business if we don't get there first, are huge!"

"Doesn't investing in ventures bring down everybody's margins?" I asked.

"It does, in the short term. But so would funding a separate innovation group. I don't have a problem convincing the Board to invest when a long-shot opportunity looks like it could pay off well, or even save the company by disrupting our own market before someone else does."

"I think every Board understands that," I agreed. "And that pipeline of future inventions should bring *up* your stock evaluation."

"I wouldn't know about that," Carlton said humbly.

I pressed further. "So, you fund ventures. What about Christensen's other concerns, like the wrong metrics and planning processes?"

"We reflect the need for different metrics in both our internal economy (making those funding decisions) and in our *performance metrics.*

"As to getting everybody to think outside the box, we've put a lot of work into our *culture,* including entrepreneurship and judicious risk-taking."

"And, we've refined our strategic planning process (*methods*). In our strengths-weaknesses-opportunities-threats (SWOT) analysis, we proactively look for our vulnerabilities to disruption, and design strategies to be the first to disrupt our own markets."

"Is your approach to innovation working?" I asked.

"Right now, we have a number of promising innovation ventures going on. I can't point to one that has disrupted an industry. But this sort of thing requires the patience of a long-term investor in a portfolio of ideas." Carlton laughed. "I guess I'm a VC!

"I know Dr. Christensen would say that this isn't the way disruption has happened in the past," he concluded. "But that doesn't mean we can't do it! I think our organizational operating model *is* our most fundamental disruptive technology."

The Market Organization is a toolkit
that unlocks entrepreneurship at every level.

— Victor Jerez

Chapter 33:
Digital Business and the
Strategic Value of Technology

Chapter summary (key take-aways): page 492

"Carlton, if we may, I'd like to explore a particular kind of innovation — what people are calling 'digital business' or 'digital enterprise.'"

What is "Digital Business"?

"Sure," Carlton said. "Shall we start by defining what we mean by that?"

"Good idea! Tell me how you see it," I requested.

"I start," Carlton replied, "by looking at the various levels of benefits coming from digital technologies (Figure 40)."

Figure 40: Staircase of Strategic Value from Technology

6. Enhance product value (imbedded in product, IoT)
5. Improve customer relationships, loyalty, engagement
4. Improve human effectiveness (thinking, collaboration)
3. Reduce customers' costs (productivity)
2. Reduce IT's costs (internal efficiencies)
1. Keep the business running (deliver existing services)

"Levels 1 through 3 are just traditional operational benefits and efficiencies," Carlton pointed out.

"Levels 4 through 6 are *value-added* benefits — the strategic value of technologies.

"Originally," Carlton continued, "'digital business' meant just Level 5 — using IT to enhance relationships with customers.

"But now, some people use the term to mean Levels 4, 5, and 6 — all the value-added benefits of technologies.

"As it turns out, what it takes to deliver Level 5 is pretty much the same as what it takes to deliver Levels 4 and 6. So, when we talk about gearing up for digital business, we may as well be talking about how to deliver *all* those top-three levels of strategic value."

"That's interesting," I said. "I certainly want all of them."

Digital Business is Not a Technology

"Now here's one key observation," Carlton said. "'Digital business' is not a technology.

"Originally, 'digital business' meant things like smart-phone applications for customers, social media, technology-enabled marketing such as customer-tailored coupons and loyalty rewards, and a company's externally facing website.

"But now, we know that customer relationships can be enhanced by so many things. Digital business is really about the *entire customer experience*. That includes the way customers interact with our products, our staff, our marketing, our support — everything.

"And when you look at it that way," he said, "digital business isn't a subset of our technologies. It utilizes the entire range of technologies, as needed, to improve customers' experiences."

"That's a good way to look at it," I agreed. "It's a type of strategic value that can come from any IT products and services."

A Continual Process (Not a Project)

"Here's another observation," Carlton said. "I think you and I are both after a continual stream of initiatives that deliver on that promise of digital business, not just a project or two."

"Absolutely."

"Okay," Carlton continued. "So, it's not a matter of one bright guy or small group somewhere in our company who comes up with all the digital-business ideas. It has to be built into the way the whole organization operates."

"So," I asked the pivotal question, "how do you get an entire organization focused on digital-business opportunities?"

Requisite Components

"Let's look at all the functions that might be involved in a digital-business initiative," Carlton replied.

"First, we have people who are focused on creating value for customers — our externally facing product managers.

"Those product managers are continually looking for ways to grow their market share, insulate themselves against competitors, and improve margins. That's part of our entrepreneurial *culture.*

"They buy help from lots of different internal services — Sales, Marketing, Engineering, and so on. And all those support functions are hungry for help from technology, too.

"IT (in this case, our entire company) is eager to help all of them.

"To find digital-business opportunities," Carlton continued, "all our lines of business need help from people who specialize in understanding the linkage between technologies and their businesses. That's the role of

Sales (Account Reps; or in internal IT groups, Business Relationship Managers). That's a matter of *structure.*

"We expect those Account Reps to help customers discover technology-enabled business strategies (a capability, or *method*). That's a powerful contribution to their strategies even before we deliver any technologies.

"Then, Sales staff need a *method of strategic opportunity discovery* (Appendix 6) to identify specific digital-business opportunities.

"As a result of our culture, structure, and methods, we have a continual stream of digital-business ideas. But those projects need funding," Carlton noted.

"So, you need something in the internal economy," I surmised.

"Right!" Carlton said. "A few things, actually. We need *investment-based budgeting* to designate funding for digital-business initiatives. And the budget has to provide for continual product development, because we need diverse and up-to-date products in every line of business to tap emerging opportunities and stay a step ahead of our competitors.

"Also, we need a *demand-management process* that puts strategic opportunities at the top of the priority stack, ahead of more mundane projects and services that could easily chew up all our resources.

"And to lubricate that process, we need a value-added *benefits-estimation method* to justify those strategic investments. That's something Sales is trained to facilitate.

"And finally, we need to adjust our *metrics* to encourage judicious high-risk, high-payoff innovation investments."

Carlton had just defined exactly how the organizational systems need to be aligned for a sustainable digital-business strategy (Figure 41).

Figure 41: Aligning Organizational Systems for Digital Business and Strategic Value

- **Culture:** entrepreneurship, everybody continually looking to improve
- **Structure:** a Business Relationship Management group in IT, and perhaps a Function Sales consultant dedicated to digital business
- **Methods:** conceive technology-enabled business strategies
- **Methods:** strategic opportunity discovery
- **Internal Economy:** investment-based budgeting to provide funding for strategic initiatives and for continual product development
- **Internal Economy:** demand-management process so that strategic opportunities rise to the top of the priority stack
- **Methods:** value-added benefits estimation for business cases
- **Metrics:** encourage judicious investments in high-risk, high-payoff innovations

Role of a "Chief Digital Officer"

"So, Carlton, help me understand the role of a Chief Digital Officer....

"Some CEOs set up a whole separate IT group," I said. I told him about a past company where the Chief Digital Officer sat alongside the CIO. There was constant tension, primarily due to all the overlaps as the CDO built his empire in his desire to be independent of the CIO.

"Some CEOs," I continued, "position the CDO as doing a piece of Marketing's mission, which creates a lot of politics with Marketing. How do you see that role, if there even is one?"

"Sure," Carlton replied. "This role is important. But before I define it, let me tell you what it's *not*....

"A Chief Digital Officer isn't a Marketing function. Marketing helps product managers to communicate their messages. They're one *customer* of the digital-business concept, eager for technologies that help them communicate and engage customers better. But there's a lot more to digital business than that.

"It's not a separate IT group," Carlton continued. "As we've said, digital business needs access to all IT's lines of business and talents."

"Not only that," I added. "We certainly don't want to see a new 'Chief' and another IT department for every hot new technology-enabled opportunity that comes along! That's not scalable."

"Exactly," Carlton agreed. "Furthermore, digital business not a new business unit. It's a strategy for every business unit.

"So, what is it?" Carlton asked rhetorically. "A Chief Digital Officer is a Function Sales role. In most companies, the role should report to IT alongside the BRMs. In our case, she reports to Julio (Sales).

"She's a specialist in how businesses utilize technologies to enhance customer experiences. She links customer-experience strategies in any company or business unit to the appropriate IT products and services."

"I like the way you've positioned it," I said. "What exactly does she do day-by-day?"

"For one, she's an evangelist who lifts our understanding of what's possible, and gets us all thinking about digital-business opportunities.

"She also participates in our enterprise strategic planning process to help us envision business strategies which are enabled by technologies, and which enhance customers' engagement and loyalty.

"And, she participates in the opportunity-discovery process. When Account Reps (IT BRMs) discover a customer-experience opportunity, she joins the diagnostic process as a second-tier sales person.

"With her inspiration and analyses," Carlton concluded, "we've seen a lot of creative initiatives all over the company that have contributed to what I hope is considered an industry-leading customer experience."

Chapter 34:
Summary of Results Delivered by a Market Organization

Chapter summary (key take-aways): page 493

"Carlton, I've heard a lot of great stuff. It all makes sense to me, but it's all swimming around in my head. I'd like to step back and get a perspective on the benefits of operating this way."

"Sure. Where shall we begin?"

"Let's start from your customers' perspective," I suggested.

Benefits: Customers (Supplier of Choice)

"The benefits to customers? Let's see...." Carlton thought for a moment. "As you know, we have both external customers and internal customers. But I think they're both seeing the same things....

"The first thing I think they noticed was their Account Representatives. They love that default point of contact, our laser focus on their business challenges, and our consultative approach. That alone won us lots of friends.

"That's especially true internally. Our senior executives appreciate that Julio's team works with them to generate great technology-enabled business opportunities like our own digital-business strategies.

"I think customers also appreciate that we're delivering far more reliably on our commitments. Perhaps more important, we're delivering more relevant results. We have all the elements in place to deliver strategic value (Figure 41).

"Internal customers like being in control of support groups' priorities. And because they are, the whole company is aligned with our critical business needs and strategic initiatives.

"Also, I think we've proven that our prices — internally, we'd call them our rates (unit costs) — are fair, if not *very* competitive.

"Our products are innovative and diverse, so we're positioned to add more value to our customers' businesses.

"And in general, I think customers like the way we treat them — our culture of customer focus.

"At this point," Carlton concluded, "I think we're nearly there in terms of earning the position of *supplier of choice* to our external customers. And I'm certain that internal service providers are now considered the suppliers of choice within the company."

Proof of Success

"That's great," I said sincerely. "Do you have any hard evidence of customer satisfaction?"

"Well, you heard about our success with external customers. I think our 40 percent growth rate speaks to that."

"And how do you measure groups whose customers are internal?"

"Customer satisfaction and value delivered," Carlton replied.

Impacts on Reputation

"Do you feel you're getting recognized beyond your immediate customers?" I asked.

"Well, you're here," Carlton said with a laugh.

"That's true." I grinned.

"I do think we're being viewed as a well-run company," Carlton said. "That pays off in many ways — attracting customers, talent, acquisitions, even capital."

"Capital?"

"Yes," Carlton said. "I had an interesting conversation with our banker. He said he can make an argument to give us better terms because the bank knows we're well managed and a reliable partner." *138 Ref*

"That's very interesting," I said. "Reputation in the community can pay off in tangible ways."

Benefits: Staff (Employer of Choice)

"Okay," I pressed on, "let's talk about the benefits to your staff."

"Hmm, I think the most important benefit to staff is that demands are in line with resources. They don't have to put in long days, every day, and then go home feeling that they're still failing to meet expectations.

"Clear boundaries have helped, too. There's a lot less confusion about who's accountable for what, friction due to internal competition, and panic when we realized that no one was covering a needed capability.

"Another big benefit to staff is specialization," Carlton continued. "There was a little bit of resistance to that at first. People said they liked variety. But at the same time, they knew they weren't really good at many of the things they were doing, and that added to stress levels.

"Now, they can focus and get really good at one thing. That gives them a sense of confidence and pride in their expertise. So, jobs are more satisfying. And they know that specialists are more valued in the labor market than generalists, so it's been good for their careers.

"Meanwhile," Carlton noted, "I think they've discovered that they still get variety in their work. They're entrepreneurs, so they do everything for one line of business (rather than just a few tasks for many lines of business, none of which they owned).

"Of course, with specialization, we had to get really good at teamwork. I think people really like working together, rather than isolated in silos.

"And empowerment is really important to them. We never set people up to fail, with accountabilities beyond their authorities. They know we treat them fairly, and we have their backs.

"The bottom line is, our employee engagement scores are through the roof!" Carlton said with pride.

A Healthy Organization Attracts Talent

"By the way," Carlton added, "the transformation has helped us attract top talent without having to pay top dollar."

"How so?" I asked.

"We have a tough time recruiting in the tech industry," he explained. "It's a tight labor market. And with everyone's increased ability to support work-from-home, we're competing for talent globally. Plus, you know there's no way we can match companies like Amazon and Google on compensation and perquisites like free food and game rooms.

"Even if we could pay top dollar, we'd have people who show up for the money, not because they love working here. Those people aren't committed to our mission. They're always open to a better deal.

"The only way we can attract, inspire, and retain top talent," Carlton said, "is to be the place people would rather work — an *employer of choice.*"

"Employer of choice," I reflected. Another great term; and a great goal.

"You know," Carlton continued, "people want more than just good pay. They want a work environment that's empowering, creative, and social. They don't want to be routinely overworked; they want to be able to win at their jobs. They want respect. And they want to be valued. *139 Ref*

"That's what our organization gives them," Carlton asserted.

You're not going to be admired on the outside
unless you're admired on the inside.

— Bob Iger, CEO, Disney

Purpose

Carlton stared out the window for a moment, and then continued. "I'd go beyond all that.... A healthy organization *inspires* talent.

"People need *purpose,* he said, "something that makes their work fulfilling, a reason to get out of bed every morning, a reason to come to work energized. I think the Market Organization gives them that."

"Say more about that word 'purpose,'" I requested.

"Yes. I've thought a lot about that word," Carlton replied. "Here's what I came to: Purpose is doing something hard (a challenge you can be proud of accomplishing), something that requires your unique talents, and something that has value to others (Figure 42)."

Figure 42: Purpose

```
      SOMETHING HARD
  +   USES ONE'S TALENTS
  +   VALUE TO OTHERS
  ─────────────────────────
  =   PURPOSE
```

I took a moment to jot that down, and Carlton paused while I thought about *purpose.* Isn't that exactly what I was looking for in my next job?

I'd just spoken to a friend who had recently retired. He said he was getting bored having fun, and we'd both laughed. But really, he wasn't joking. Isn't *purpose* what he missed, and now craved?

My daughter had just quit a great job in investment banking; it was challenging and paid very well. She told me why she left and what she was looking for: some way to really contribute to society. She was yearning for *purpose*.

I looked at what I was doing and realized
I was just... making money and spending money.
But I wasn't doing anything for the world.

— Claudia Salvischiani [140 Ref]

"That's a great definition," I said. "And I see where you're going. The Market Organization gives people that sense of purpose."

"It does! They all have the challenge of running a business — one that matches up with their talents. And they know that their customers (external and internal) appreciate the value they deliver."

I nodded and said, "I guess those millennials don't have to go off and start their own freelance businesses when they can be empowered entre-preneurs with purpose inside a bigger business."

"Exactly!" Carlton exclaimed. "And it's not just millennials. We all want that."

"This discussion of purpose reminds me of Conscious Capitalism," I said. [141 Ref] "I think the Market Organization is well aligned with its tenets."

"It's more than just aligned," Carlton replied. "I see the Market Organi-zation as the mechanics by which we've implemented Conscious Capitalism." [142 More]

"I can see that. So, Carlton, what's *your* purpose?" I asked.

"To create amazing organizations! It's not only worthwhile and brings me a real sense of satisfaction. I've got to say, when you're pursuing your purpose, it's just plain fun!"

Spirituality... expresses our desire to find meaning in,
and to treat as an offering, what we do.

— Peter Block [143 Ref]

Bottom Line: The "Excellence Dividend"

"It seems the transformation paid off in many ways," I said.

"In every way!" Carlton replied. "Honestly, Tom Peters said it better than I ever could." He pulled out his dog-eared copy of *The Excellence Dividend* and showed me this paragraph: [144 Ref]

> *... businesses that are committed to excellence in every aspect of their internal and external dealings ... are better and more spirited places to work. Their employees are engaged and growing and preparing for tomorrow. Their customers are happier and inclined to spread tales of their excellence far and wide. Their communities welcome them as good neighbors. Their vendors welcome them as reliable partners. That in turn translates directly into bottom-line results and growth.*

"That's my goal," Carlton said, "and I think we're getting there."

Chapter 35:
Close of My Tour: A Leader Who Leaves a Legacy

Chapter summary (key take-aways): page 494

As the day came to its end, I was truly excited about the vision and the possibility of creating such a great organization. Now, I had just a few remaining questions for Carlton about his transformational leadership.

Talent Alone Isn't Enough

First, I had to challenge Carlton a bit. He credited all these benefits to the organizational operating model. But what about people?

"You know, Carlton, a lot of leaders and consultants believe it's all about talent. How much of your success, would you say, was because you hired great people?"

"Well, that's certainly part of it," he replied. "We do have some great people, at *all* levels. And they think like entrepreneurs, which you can't say about people in most companies, or even about most of our people six years ago.

"But great talent alone wouldn't have been enough," Carlton asserted. "You know, you might get the best people by paying the most. But you won't get the best from them if the organization isn't working well."

You might get the best people by paying the most.
But you won't get the best from them if the organization isn't working well.

"I agree," I said. "But to be sure I understand your point, can you give me some examples?"

Carlton described five examples of why great talent isn't enough:

- **Overlapping domains:** Managers with overlapping territories are set up to compete with one another. The stronger the talent, the more intense the in-fighting.

- **Impossible jobs:** Even high-performers can't be excellent at many different professions. They may do better than most, but they'll never do as well as teams of specialists.

- **Conflicts of interests:** Stronger talent doesn't solve conflicts of interests. For example, managers whose jobs are to keep things running and also to innovate are paid to go in two opposing directions. They gravitate to one or the other; and stronger talent just amplifies the imbalance.

- **Jumbled priorities:** If priorities aren't aligned, strong talent better delivers the wrong things.

- **Disempowerment:** What if Ann's job is to oversee Bob, and decide how Bob's group does its work? Stronger talent in Ann's job will disempower Bob more; and stronger talent in Bob's job will fight back and undermine Ann more effectively.

When placed in the same system,
people, however different, tend to produce similar results.

— Peter M. Senge [145 Ref]

"The reality is," Carlton continued, "we'll always have a bell-curve of talents. We can't depend on everybody being a super-achiever. We need an organization in which normal people can succeed, and super-achievers can super-succeed."

I liked that turn of phrase.

> *In well-designed organizations,*
> *normal people can succeed,*
> *and super-achievers can super-succeed.*

"Furthermore," Carlton added, "we often have to work with the cards we're dealt. It's rarely wise to come into a new job and fire your entire leadership team! It'll be tough to attract talent if you have a reputation for being cut-throat. And it's not fair; good people may be failing because of a bad organization."

Carlton continued, "My goal, of course, is to have both great people *and* a great organizational operating model that helps them succeed."

"That makes a lot of sense," I agreed.

"Beyond that," Carlton said, "I share your aspirations. I want to do more than just do a good job while I'm here. As you said so aptly this morning, I want to leave a lasting legacy of an organization that performs really well long after I'm gone.

"You know, great people come and go over time," he observed. "The only way to have a *lasting* impact is to focus on organizational systems — to drive a real *systemic* transformation."

> *...a great manager is essentially an organizational engineer....*
> *They see their organizations as machines and*
> *work assiduously to maintain and improve them.*
>
> — Ray Dalio [146 Ref]

Impacts on the Role of an Executive

"Carlton, how has the transformation affected *your* job?"

"A lot!" he replied. "This is a great place for me to work, too."

"You have my attention! What's changed for you?" I asked.

"I no longer spend much time on operational issues — priority debates, project delivery issues, resolving conflicts, and so on."

> *I stopped playing chess, and I became a gardener.*
> *...I needed to shift my focus from moving pieces on the board*
> *to shaping the ecosystem.*
>
> — General Stanley McChrystal, Commander,
> Joint Special Operations Task Force in Iraq [147 Ref]

"Now," Carlton said, "I have the luxury of looking at the big picture — shifts in our company's industries, trends in technologies, our competitive landscape, major threats, strategic directions.... I'm spending more time with my leadership team thinking about the future of the company.

"It's like back when I was a CIO," he related. "I remember being able to spend more time with my peers, in my corporate-officer hat, thinking about enterprise strategies.

"Also," Carlton added, "I've got more time to spend with my staff — mentoring people, coming together on a shared truth, [148 More] challenging them, helping them grapple with mental models that get in the way, and hopefully inspiring them a little bit.

"And my stress level is *much* lower. I don't have to pretend to have all the answers, and I'm not the sole source of strategic thinking and innovation. I'm surrounded by smart people who can deliver results.

"I love designing the organizational ecosystem, cultivating talent, and then watching all the great things our people accomplish! I have to say that the transformation has made my job one heck of a lot more fun!"

I thought back on why I'd quit my last job. Carlton had hit the nail on the head. This was exactly where I wanted to be.

---

*Those who practice [leadership as organizational design] find
deep satisfaction in being part of an organization
capable of producing results that people truly care about.*

— Peter M. Senge [149 Ref]

Why Do So Few Leaders Do This?

"Carlton, this is an impressive organization, and you're an exceptional leader. Tell me, why do you think so few leaders do this?"

He smiled modestly. "I agree with you; few leaders think this way, and fewer still actually drive real transformations."

Carlton thought for a moment, then said, "I think there are four types of leaders in the world (Figure 43)."

Figure 43: Four Types of Leaders

1. **Cost Cutter:**   slash-and-burn, cut costs, then move on
2. **Maintainer:**   keep what they inherit running, with small, incremental improvements
3. **Project Manager:**   lead a major project (like an acquisition or a strategic initiative)
4. **Transformer:**   build an organization that can succeed long after they've moved on

"What I think we're both saying is, that fourth type of leader is really scarce," Carlton noted.

"Maybe it's because leaders don't know what's possible," he speculated, "or because they don't know how to do it. *150 More* Maybe they love power and control. In my more cynical moments, I wonder if it's because they're risk averse, or just tired."

In a "leaders as heroes" organizational culture...
those who aspire to lead out of a desire to control, to gain fame,
or simply to be at the center of the action
will find little to attract them to the quiet design work of leadership.

— Peter M. Senge *151 Ref*

"You know, transformation is hard," Carlton continued. "It takes a vision. It takes determination. It takes humility. It takes patience and stamina. It's a lot of work. Fun work, but a lot of work.

"I don't know how many leaders are willing to take the risks and put in the effort," he said, "even though there are tremendous rewards in doing something so meaningful. What do you think?"

"Sadly, I have to agree," I replied. "It's hard enough to find leaders who know their functional areas, have a sense of the business, and can manage people. It's really rare to come across one who's all that *and* a type-four transformational leader."

Whenever anything is being accomplished,
it is being done... by a monomaniac with a mission.

— Peter F. Drucker *152 More*

What's Next?

"I'm just curious, Carlton. In your career, where do you go from here? CEO of a bigger tech company? Beyond tech?"

"Either might be fun. But remember, I'm a type-four leader. When the time comes, I'll be looking for an opportunity to do this again — to drive another transformation. That's what turns me on.

"But," he said, "I'm not really thinking about that yet. I've got more to do here. I don't intend to leave until this new way of working is self-sustaining — until it's institutionalized to the point where my successor would never want to take it apart."

There are two kinds of people:
those who finish what they start, and so on.

— Robert Byrne, international chess champion

Bottom Line Lessons

"Carlton, I'm afraid I've got a plane to catch. I want to sincerely thank you for inviting me in today."

"We were honored to have you. Was the day worthwhile for you?"

"Absolutely!" I exclaimed unreservedly. "I learned something useful in every meeting, things I can apply in my company. Beyond that, I've come to understand what real transformation is all about....

"I understand that transformation is not a strategic goal, like acquisitions or digital business. I know that strategies have to be dynamic in a volatile world.

"And," I continued, "I've learned not to use the word 'transformation' to mean just any big project, like outsourcing (e.g., cloud computing) or implementing a new manufacturing process.

"Sure, those are important challenges," I said. "But I know that the word 'transformation' should be reserved for something much bigger. If I use the word for something small, or use it more than once, then like crying wolf, it loses meaning.

"You've confirmed in my mind what transformation is really about. It transcends today's strategies and projects. Real transformation builds an organization that gets those strategies and projects right, all the time."

The word 'transformation' should be reserved for something much bigger than today's strategies and projects.
Real transformation is building an organization that gets those strategies and projects right, all the time.

Carlton nodded and smiled with approval.

"Carlton, what you've done is really break-through," I continued. "It's a game changer. Your success has given me the confidence, and the tools, to be a type-four transformational leader."

"Is that a promise?" Carlton grinned.

"It is," I said emphatically. And I meant it.

"Well then," Carlton quipped, "I'll be visiting your company someday."

"You'll always be welcome!" I said sincerely. "Carlton, thank you so very much."

~ APPENDIXES ~

**content that's of value to
implementors and practitioners
of the Market Organization**

Appendix 1:
What Internal Entrepreneurs Do Proactively

Operating as a business within a business does *not* mean being a passive order-taker. There are many things that internal entrepreneurs do proactively, without customers' permission, and which don't dis-empower customers or diminish customer focus. Here's a sampling:

- **Product/service innovation**: Internal entrepreneurs can, and must, innovate to keep their competencies and their product lines up-to-date. They don't wait for customers to tell them to innovate.

  For off-the-shelf products and services, they proactively put new products "on the store shelf" (making them available to customers), but only take them off the shelf (actually deploying them) when customers agree to buy them.

  For custom products, they proactively develop their skills and methods so that they're prepared to offer innovative approaches to customers' unique requirements.

- **Infrastructure**: Internal entrepreneurs proactively maintain and evolve their infrastructure (the assets they own for the purpose of providing services to customers). They decide what assets to buy, justifying those investment decisions based on *market* needs (input from the customer community as a whole, not any one customer).

- **Marketing**: Internal entrepreneurs market the strategic value of their products and services. This is not meant to be self-serving; the goal is to lift customers' awareness of the possibilities so as to engender more creative use of their products and services.

  With marketing, customers can choose whether to spend time consuming (reading/viewing) the materials. It's not using customers' time to push your agenda in a sales call, which would not be customer focused.

- **Sales**: Account Representatives proactively talk to customers about their business challenges. The goal is not to push products, but to help customers solve their problems and achieve their goals. They discover high-payoff opportunities to use the organization's products and services by listening well, and by bringing new insights to customers (Appendix 6).

  Beyond that, every entrepreneur "sells" *when invited* by customers to explain their products and services and their value.

- **Offer proposals**: In response to expressed needs (the What), engineers offer to develop proposals (solution alternatives studies). With the customer's permission, they define alternative solutions (the How) at different price-points, like "good/better/best," to inform customers of their options.

- **Help customers be smart buyers**: Entrepreneurs help customers analyze those alternatives in the context of *their* values (not the supplier's). This isn't making a recommendation (as if "we know what's best for you"). Rather, it's a consultative process that explores the customer's values; for example: "If speed is most important to you, pick alternative A; but if life-cycle costs are more important, select B."

- **Coordinate enterprise decisions**: For decisions which are to be made by the community of relevant stakeholders (such as policies and standards), Coordinators proactively put forward questions and coordinate the appropriate stakeholders as they decide.

Appendix 2:
Outsourcing and Supplier Integration

This Appendix is a conversation with Carlton on how to best utilize vendors. *153 Ref*

When Outsourcing Is Appropriate

"If all your leaders are internal suppliers," I asked, "what about vendors outside the company? Carlton, what's your take on outsourcing?"

"We do use vendors," he replied. "But we're not interested in a big one-time, top-down outsourcing study like some consultants sell. The decision-making process here is much more dynamic.

"We understand that, in general, outsourcing is more expensive than doing it ourselves. After all, we're paying other shareholders a profit. But there are specific situations where it's better to use vendors.

"One situation," Carlton said, "is when we need only a small portion of an expensive asset, like a high-performance super-computer. Our tele-communications lines are another example of that. So, through out-sourcing, we share expensive assets with other corporations.

"The same goes for people. When we can't afford a specialist on staff full-time, we use consultants and contractors.

"Another situation," Carlton continued, "is when we can't get the capital internally, even through capital leases. So then, we're willing to pay a bit more for a vendor's service in order to use its capital.

Describing the next situation, Carlton said, "Sometimes we have to outsource to gain access to vendors' proprietary technologies and intellectual property.

"But the most common reason we outsource," he said, "is to turn fixed costs into variable costs. With cloud computing, for example, we can scale volumes up and down quickly. The same goes for contractors. It's worth paying more per unit when we need that flexibility — when volumes vary widely. Our ideal strategy is to own resources to satisfy the valleys if that's less expensive, and then outsource the peaks."

Figure 44: When Outsourcing Is (and Isn't) Appropriate

Outsourcing should be used to...

- Access a portion of an expensive asset or specialist.
- Use vendor's capital.
- Gain access to vendor's proprietary intellectual property.
- Convert fixed costs into variable costs.

Outsourcing should NOT be used to...

o "Stick to your knitting" — you'll have no more people "knitting" after outsourcing a support function.

o Reduce management distraction — managing vendors via contracts, procurement staff, and lawyers can be more distracting than managing a leader of an internal support function.

o Increase control — paying vendors (who are customer focused and responsive) only avoids fixing internal functions which are not as easy to do business with as they should be. [154 More]

o Improve internal customer's treatment and their control over what they buy — a Market Organization does that.

o Get around an unsatisfactory support group — letting a function fail (rather than addressing root causes) risks permanently losing an important organizational competency. [155 More]

o Downsize and make somebody else lay off your staff or get rid of a bad leader — an expensive way to shirk your leadership duties.

o Sell off assets to gain immediate cash flow — a drastic way to save a sinking enterprise, with costly long-term consequences.

o Window dressing in preparation for selling the business (being acquired, or a stock offering) — due-diligence will see through this, and see increased operating costs.

"But," Carlton continued, "the economics are constantly changing. So instead of a one-time outsourcing study, all my leaders stay aware of what's out there. (They have to anyway, to stay ahead of their competition.) Then, they evaluate make-versus-buy in the context of the current economics and our needs."

"That makes a lot of sense," I said. "I've participated in quite a few, often heated, outsourcing debates. This decision framework and your dynamic approach will be very helpful."

Vendors are Extensions to Our Staff

Carlton smiled, and added, "I want to make one thing clear: When we use vendors, our staff are VARs (value-added resellers), not brokers. *Internal suppliers* sell the service to internal and external customers; and it's up to them to figure out how to deliver it, including managing any vendors. We treat vendors as extensions of our staff."

We're VARs (value-added resellers), not brokers.
We treat vendors as extensions to our staff.

"Why are you in the middle?" I asked.

"For one, we're entrepreneurs. We want to build the habit of buying *through* us, not around us.

"But as for the benefits to the enterprise, our staff add value in a number of ways: They make and uphold commitments to internal customers. They decide the mix of make-versus-buy. They're best qualified to select and manage vendors in their fields. They support what they and the vendor build. And they integrate vendors' services into ours.

"Essentially, our staff make sure vendors work for *our* shareholders as well as their own."

Appendix 3: Lines of Business in
Various Industries and Functions

This Appendix offers examples of the framework of types of businesses (Figure 9) applied to a variety of different industries and internal support functions:

Of course, every organization is different. The precise list of lines of business will be unique. These examples are *only intended as thought-starters*.

It's also important to understand that these examples are *not intended to be recommended organization charts*. The structure that each organization develops should be based on its unique needs.

In combination with the principles of structure (Figure 4), this list of lines of business provides a common language and a starting point for the design of an organization chart built of internal entrepreneurships and tailored to your needs.

NAVIGATION AID: Chapter 27 describes the process of designing organization charts around lines of business.

Holding Company (business is owning companies)

Sales and Marketing
> Direct Investors
> Brokers, Fund Managers
> Corporate Communications, Community Relations
> Investor Relations
> Government Relations (lobbying)

Engineers
> Applications: Business Development (acquisitions, divestitures)
> Base: Business Consulting (due diligence, assistance to companies)

Service Providers
> Asset: Operating Companies
> People-based
>> Product Support
>> Business Office (for headquarters, and optionally services to companies)
>>> Finance, Treasury, Credit, Collections
>>> Information Technology
>>> Human Resources, Employee Education, Personal Services (including medical)
>>> Legal Counsel
>>> Procurement, Supplier Management
>>> Asset Management
>>> Facilities, Property Management
>>> Administration, Events
>>> Travel, Fleet, Corporate Airline

Coordinators (for headquarters, and optionally services to companies)
> Business Planning (strategic and operational), Economist, Research Portfolio Coordination
> Business Development (acquisitions, divestitures)
> Organizational Effectiveness (including acquisition integration, employee communications, diversity, safety, quality)
> Standards, Design (product commonality and integration)
> Business Continuity
> Risk, Security
> Regulatory Compliance

Audit (including compliance)

Operating Company (business is selling products and services)

Sales and Marketing
    Sales
        Account
            Geographic Territories
            Major Accounts
            Resellers and Brokers
            Government Relations (lobbying)
        Function
            Vertical Markets
        Retail
            eCommerce, Catalog Sales, Telemarketing
            Stores by Type, Geography
        Sales Support
    Marketing
        Branding, Strategy
        Merchandising
        Communications, Advertising, Collateral
        Corporate Communications, Community Relations
        Investor Relations
        Market Research, Pricing Analysis
Engineers
    Applications: Design Engineering (products)
    Base
        Industrial Design, Packaging
        Design Engineering (common components), Analytics
        Manufacturing Engineering
        Writing, Educational Materials Design
Service Providers
    Asset-based: Operations
        Manufacturing
        Production Planning (across plants)
        Logistics, Distribution, Transportation
        Warehousing
        Inventory Management, Replenishment

People-based
- Product Support
  - Customer Service
  - Field Technicians
  - Customer Education
- Business Office (unless functions related to product production)
  - Finance, Treasury, Credit, Collections
  - Information Technology
  - Human Resources, Employee Education, Personal Services (including medical)
  - Legal Counsel
  - Procurement, Supplier Management
  - Asset Management
  - Facilities, Property Management, Food Services
  - Administration, Events
  - Travel, Fleet, Corporate Airline

Coordinators: Enterprise Policy and Planning
- Business Planning (strategic and operational), Economist, Research Portfolio Coordination
- Business Development (acquisitions, divestitures)
- Organizational Effectiveness (including acquisition integration, employee communications, diversity, safety, quality)
- Standards, Design (product commonality and integration)
- Business Continuity
- Risk, Security
- Regulatory Compliance

Audit (including compliance)

Health Care Provider

Sales and Marketing
    Sales
        Account
            Payers (Insurance Companies, HMOs)
            Research Funding Sources
            Partners
            Government Relations (lobbying)
        Function
            Cost, Outcomes Analysis
        Retail
            Private Practitioner Relations
        Sales Support
    Marketing
        Branding, Strategy
        Communications, Advertising, Collateral
        Corporate Communications, Community Relations
        Investor Relations
        Fund Raising
        Market Research
Engineers: Chief Medical Officer
    Applications:
        Primary Care Physicians
    Base
        Clinical Practices
        Medical Practices (safety, re-admissions analysis, infection control)
        Nursing Services
Service Providers
    Asset-based: Operations
        Clinics by geography
        Hospitals
            Beds
            ICU
            ER
            OR
            Respiratory, etc.
        Medical Support Services (labs)
        Pharmacies
        Living Facilities (assisted living, retirement)
        Facilities, Property Management, Laundry
        Food services

People-based
> Product Support
>> Admissions
>> Patient Advocates, Customer Service
>> Employee Health (immunization, contamination treatments)
>> Non-clinical Patient Care (child care, pastors)
> Business Office
>> Medical Records
>> Finance, Treasury, Credit, Collections, Reimbursements
>> Information Technology
>> Human Resources, Employee Education, Personal Services (including medical)
>> Legal Counsel
>> Procurement, Supplier Management
>> Logistics, Storage, Warehouse
>> Asset Management
>> Administration, Events
>> Travel, Fleet

Coordinators: Enterprise Policy and Planning
> Business Planning (strategic and operational), Economist, Research Portfolio Coordination
> Business Development (acquisitions, divestitures)
> Organizational Effectiveness (including acquisition integration, employee communications, diversity, safety, quality)
> Business Continuity
> Risk, Security
> Regulatory Compliance (regulations, accreditation)
> Delivery Policy Standards, Design (medical policy, service commonality and integration)

Audit
> Financial Audit
> Corporate Compliance
> Utilization/Outcomes Reviews

Insurance Company

Sales and Marketing
    Sales
        Account
            Company Agents by Geographic Territories
            Major Accounts
            Brokers
            Government Relations (lobbying)
        Function
            Financial Planning Advisors
            Risk Management Advisors
            Vertical Markets
        Retail
            eCommerce, Telemarketing
            Company Agencies by Geography
        Sales Support
    Marketing
        Branding, Strategy
        Communications, Advertising, Collateral
        Corporate Communications, Community Relations
        Investor Relations
        Market Research
Engineers
    Applications
        Life
        Property and Casualty
        Health and Safety
        Disability, Workman's Compensation
    Base
        Actuary
Service Providers
    Asset-based: Operations
        Underwriting
        Enrollment
        Claims
        Asset Management

People-based
    Product Support
        Policy-holder Services (customer service)
        Policy-holder Risk Management (client education and consulting)
        Agent/Broker Education
    Business Office
        Finance, Treasury, Credit, Collections
        Information Technology
        Human Resources, Employee Education, Personal Services (including medical)
        Legal Counsel
        Procurement, Supplier Management
        Asset Management
        Facilities, Property Management, Food Services
        Administration, Events
        Travel, Fleet, Corporate Airline
Coordinators: Enterprise Policy and Planning
    Business Planning (strategic and operational), Economist, Research Portfolio Coordination
    Business Development (acquisitions, divestitures)
    Organizational Effectiveness (including acquisition integration, employee communications, diversity, safety, quality)
    Product Planning
    Business Continuity
    Risk, Security
    Regulatory Compliance
Audit (including compliance)

Higher Education (University)

Sales and Marketing
    Sales
        Account
            Admissions (recruiting)
            Grants
            Outreach
            Alumni Relations
            Government Relations (lobbying)
        Function
            Vertical Markets
        Sales Support
    Marketing
        Branding, Strategy
        Communications, Advertising, Collateral
        Corporate Communications, Community Relations
        Investor Relations (if for-profit)
        Market Research
Engineers
    Applications
        Schools
    Base
        Curriculum and instructional design
Service Providers
    Asset-based: Operations
        Classrooms, Labs
        Distance education technologies
        Residence halls
        Library
    People-based
        Product Support
            Registrar
            Admissions processing
            Student counseling

Business Office

Finance, Treasury, Credit, Collections

Information Technology (including instructional technologies)

Human Resources, Employee Education, Personal Services (including medical)

Legal Counsel

Procurement, Supplier Management

Asset Management

Facilities, Property Management, Food Services

Administration, Events

Travel, Fleet, Corporate Airline

Coordinators: Enterprise Policy and Planning

Student success, student experience, retention

Audit response (including accreditation)

Business Planning (strategic and operational), Economist, Research Portfolio Coordination

Business Development (acquisitions, divestitures)

Organizational Effectiveness (including acquisition integration, employee communications, diversity, safety, quality)

Product Planning

Business Continuity

Risk, Security

Regulatory Compliance

Audit (including compliance)

Information Technologies (IT) Department

Sales and Marketing
 Sales
   Account: Business Relationship Managers
   Function (specialists in uses of IT, such as digital enterprise, data, supply chain)
   Retail: Contact Center, eCommerce website
   Support: Business Analysts
 Marketing
   Client Communications (IT catalog, website, brochures, newsletters, events, tours)
   Market Research (customer satisfaction surveys; emerging technologies demand assessments)
Engineers
 Applications Engineering
 Base Engineering
   Platform Engineering (servers, PCs, DBMS, middleware, networks)
   End-user Computing (tools for thinking, across all platforms)
   Methods and Tools (development tools and methods, languages and compilers, basic computer science)
   Ontology, information engineering, logical data modeling, meta-data repository
   Information Modeling (artificial intelligence, operations research, statistics, mathematics)
Service Providers
 Asset-based: Infrastructure Services (operations)
   Data Center
   Computing Services
   Storage Services
   Input/Output Services (shared printers, scanners)
   DBMS Services
   Applications Hosting
   Software as a Service (end-user computing services such as email, shared-use applications such as service management)
   Enterprise Data Warehouse, Business Intelligence
   Device Rental (PCs, projectors, phones for temporary use)
   Telephone Services, Teleconferencing
   Network Services
   Archival Services

People-based
  Product Support
      Customer Service (service desk, help desk, incident management)
      Field Technicians
      Testing Services
      Access Administration
      Customer Education
      Ad Hoc Reporting, Data Science
      Telephone Directory Assistance
  Business Office (unless functions related to product production)
      Project Management Office
      Finance
      Procurement, Supplier Management and Integration
      Asset Management
      Facilities, Asset Management
      Administration, Events
      Data Repository Administration
Coordinators
  IT Business Planning (strategic and operational), Research Portfolio Coordination
  IT Organizational Effectiveness (including ITIL, Lean/Six-Sigma, change management)
  IT Audit Response
  IT Business Continuity
  Enterprise Information Security (CISO), Risk
  IT Regulatory Compliance
  IT Standards, Design (Enterprise Architecture)
  Enterprise Information Policy

Human Resources (HR) Department

Sales and Marketing
    Sales
        Account: HR "Generalists" by client organization
        Function: Acquisitions, Divestitures, Consolidations, Restructuring
        Retail: Employee Relations (contact center), eCommerce website
    Marketing: Employee Communications, Employee Surveys (including engagement)
Engineers
    Applications: Organization
        Job Design and Evaluation
        Performance Management Methods
        Compensation and Benefits Design
        Labor Relations
    Base: Employee
        Organizational Development (leadership, teamwork)
        Career Development Planning
        Talent Management, Succession Planning
        Employee Training, Development and Coaching
        Severance and Retirement
        Health and Safety
        Employee Assistance Programs
Service Providers
    Asset-based
        Employee Data Administration
        Compensation and Benefits Administration
        Enterprise (internal) University
        Personal Services (including medical)
        Search (job postings, screening, recruiting, new-hire administration)
        Temporary Employees
        Relocation
        Appraisal Processing (360-degree data analysis)
        Awards Administration
        Grievance Administration
    People-based
        Employee Support (call center)
        HR Finance
        HR Administration, Events
Coordinators
    Enterprise Employment Policy
    HR Business Planning (strategic and operational), Research Portfolio

Finance Department

Sales and Marketing
> Sales
>> Account: Business Unit Liaisons
>> Function: Mergers/acquisitions/divestitures, consolidations, restructuring
> Marketing: Client Communications

Engineers
> Applications
>> Vendor Viability Analysis
>> Acquisitions Analysis
> Base
>> Financial Analysis
>> Risk Analysis
>> Tax, Transfer Pricing
>> Capital Acquisition (subset of Treasury)
>> Economic Analysis and Forecasting

Service Providers
> Asset-based: Operations
>> Accounting (financial reporting)
>>> Transactions Processing
>>> Reporting
>>> Budget Variance Tracking
>>> Accounts Payable
>>> Billing and Receivables (if internal, for chargebacks)
>> Tax Filings, Submissions
>> Asset Tracking
>> Cash Management (subset of Treasury)
>> Foreign exchange, hedging
>> Insurance, risk management
> People-based: Customer Service

Coordinators
> Finance Business Planning (strategic and operational), Research Portfolio Coordination
> Finance Organizational Effectiveness
> Enterprise Financial Policy
> Finance Business Continuity
> Finance Risk, Security
> Finance Regulatory Compliance

Audit (if not covered by enterprise audit)
> Budget Allocation Decisions
> Financial Audit

Training / Education Department

Sales and Marketing
>   Sales
>   >   Account: Client Liaisons
>   >   Function: Career Development Planning
>   >   Retail: Student Services, Registration, eCommerce website
>   Marketing
>   >   Employee Communications
>   >   Employee Surveys

Engineers: Curriculum Design
>   Applications: Course product managers (substructured by course content, e.g., user skills, business skills, technologies)
>   Base: Learning Theory/Pedagogy, Curriculum Design, Computer-aided Instruction Courseware

Service Providers
>   Asset-based
>   >   Classroom Facilities and Catering
>   >   Online Learning Platform (LMS)
>   People-based
>   >   Product Support
>   >   >   Customer Service
>   >   >   Education Administration (student registration, tracking, course administration)
>   >   >   Teachers (generic)
>   >   Business Office
>   >   >   Training Finance
>   >   >   Training Procurement, Supplier Management
>   >   >   Training Administration, Events

Coordinators
>   Training Business Planning (strategic and operational), Research Portfolio Coordination
>   Training Organizational Effectiveness
>   Enterprise Education Policy

Public Relations / Corporate Communications Department

Sales and Marketing
    Sales
        Account: Liaisons by channels
        Retail
            Receptionist
            Liaison to internal clients
    Marketing: Enterprise Web Home Page, Brochures
Engineers: Communications Specialists
    Applications: Program managers
    Base
        Advertising
        Speaking and Protocol
        Audience Research
Service Providers
    Asset-based: Communications Services
        Materials (inventory, equipment)
        Media Management, Tracking
        Printing and Production
        Lists and Dissemination
        Meeting and Events Management
        Speakers Bureau
        Tours
    People-based
        Product Support
            Professional Writing (drafting, editing)
            Multi-media (video, photography, audiovisual, graphics arts)
            Language Translation, Localization
            Editorial
        Business Office
            Finance
            Administration, Events
Coordinators: Enterprise Policy and Planning
    PR Business Planning (strategic and operational), Research Portfolio Coordination
    PR Organizational Effectiveness (including acquisition integration, employee communications, diversity, safety, quality)
    Enterprise Communications Policy (message commonality and integration)
    PR Business Continuity
    PR Risk, Security
    PR Regulatory Compliance

Appendix 4:
Culture: Examples of Behavioral Principles

Culture is best defined by a set of actionable behavioral principles. Here are *just a few examples* of behavioral principles, under each of the 13 Themes, to illustrate the concept. They're drawn from a comprehensive compendium of "best practices" behavioral principles. [156 Ref]

Note that principles are often followed by corollaries that explain them in more detail or describe what to do in specific circumstances.

Please remember, these are only examples.

NAVIGATION AID: See Chapter 12 for a definition of culture and the behavioral approach, and Chapter 29 for an overview of the implementation process.

Ethics (right versus wrong)

- We do not permit personal conflicts of interests. We do not personally materially profit directly from our business activities, i.e., from doing our jobs or from things we do because of our position in the company (e.g., taking material gifts from vendors).

- We do not sexually harass anyone or link career success to personal favors or to relationships of any kind. Sexual harassment means unwelcome sexual advances, or language that creates an uncomfortable or hostile work environment.

- We do not discriminate against people on the basis of race, national origin, religion, gender, physical abilities, age, sexual orientation, marital status, political beliefs, or any other factor not related to job performance.

Integrity (earning trust)

- We meet all our commitments.

    o   We don't make commitments we cannot meet.

    o   When someone requests (or demands) something we cannot do, we explain that we cannot do it and offer feasible options (the "graceful no") rather than say yes and then fail.

Interpersonal Relations (how we work with others)

- We make every effort to understand another's point before we respond to it.

- We treat everyone with courtesy, respect, and dignity; and we listen to their views, regardless of their position, grade level, or seniority.

- We do not let disagreements fester, but resolve them quickly through honest discussions (within the bounds of human-resources policies and labor contracts).

Meetings (scheduled business events) *157 More*

- We ensure that our meetings are well managed and effective by contributing to the meeting process as well as content.

    o   We call for a decision as soon as further discussion seems unproductive.

    o   When a topic is not yet resolved and a new topic is raised, we consciously "park" one issue until the other is brought to closure or postponed (rather than talking about two issues at once, or letting one go unresolved).

Cooperation (one organization)

- We freely pass leads, referrals, and other valuable information to our peers.

- Once the appropriate stakeholders make a decision, we support their decision (even if we don't agree with it) through our attitudes, communications, and actions. *158 Ref*

Teamwork (project teams)

- When contracting with customers, we commit only our own groups. We don't make commitments for other groups.

  o We determine only our own prices and time-frames. If subcontracts are required, we ask our internal suppliers for their prices and time-frames before we finalize ours.

Empowerment (matching authority to accountability)

- When we ask things of others:

  o We ask people for and measure deliverables (results), not tasks, processes, and effort.

    » We base the magnitude and complexity of the deliverable on the degree of confidence people have earned. I.e., if we lack confidence in people's ability to do big projects, we empower them in smaller chunks rather than micromanage them.

  o We provide all the resources, information, and decision authorities needed to deliver the agreed results.

Customer Focus (how to treat customers)

- We serve our customers; we do not control them.

  o We do not presume to know our customers' businesses better than they do. We do not do what we think is "best for the company" or "best for our customer's customers" (second-guessing and disempowering our customers).

Entrepreneurship (remaining competitive)

- We do whatever it takes to manage our business within a business, rather than just doing assigned tasks or keeping current resources busy.

- We continually improve our value to customers.

  o We choose the most economic means to deliver our products, whether it's "make" or "buy."

Contracts (making commitments)

- We form clear contracts with our customers and suppliers before we begin projects. Contracts define mutual accountabilities; they're not bureaucratic hurdles or legalistic protections.

Quality (how we fulfill commitments)

- We produce quality products, where "quality" is a measure of the goodness of design/delivery within customers' requirements (professional excellence), not price point (level of service or functionality).

  o In addition to all agreed deliverables, we proactively include qualities that must be present to make the intended uses of our products (i.e., "batteries *are* included").

Risk (who takes risks, how they're evaluated)

- We make informed decisions about risks, and do not shy away from taking judicious risks where the possibility of the potential benefits outweighs the possibility of the potential losses (i.e., positive expected value, adjusted for risk profile).

    o   When making investment decisions, we evaluate all future outcomes (costs and benefits), but ignore past investments. (I.e., sunk costs are irrelevant.)

- We identify risks at the beginning of a project, and plan to mitigate both the odds of failures and the consequences of failures (risk planning).

- We evaluate people's decisions, not the outcomes. When people take judicious risks and do everything in their power to succeed, yet fail due to factors beyond their control (i.e., when good decisions result in bad outcomes), we do not treat the lack of results as a performance deficiency.

Feedback (measuring results, consequences)

- We provide feedback to one another (including to peers, subordinates, and supervisors) in a timely, constructive manner.

    o   We don't let a single failure overshadow successes; i.e., let one failure affect the assessment of performance at other deliverables. (No "branding.")

Appendix 5:
Appropriate Roles of Committees

Many companies are rife with committees, often lacking clear charters.

At best, poorly chartered committees waste time and slow organizations down with unnecessary bureaucratic hurdles. At worst, they disempower those accountable for getting work done, blunt staff's entrepreneurial spirit, and create obstacles to innovation whereby everybody has to agree before anything gets done.

Rules on the Use of Committees

Why do we need so many committees? One oft-cited reason is to provide a forum to keep leaders informed. But, of course, you don't need committees (or even meetings) to disseminate information. It's far more efficient to simply send information out to affected parties whenever appropriate.

That suggests rule #1: Meetings should only be used for two-way communications, such as sharing and discussing information, or collaborating on shared decisions. And regularly scheduled meetings (as with committees) should only be used for two-way exchanges that must happen regularly.

Rule #2 is founded on the Golden Rule: Committees should never be given authorities. Members of a committee may pool their respective authorities over shared decisions. But vesting any authorities in a committee (other than the sum of its members' authorities) inevitably disempowers somebody. And committees should never make decisions that are within the authorities of individual leaders.

Rule #3 is closely related: Committees should not have "oversight" responsibilities. If a committee has oversight authority over a group, it disempowers that manager's manager. Controls should be exercised via the legitimate authority of the management reporting hierarchy, not via a committee of peers usurping the authorities of a boss or creating unnecessary hurdles to getting work done. (See Stakeholders below for a different definition of oversight.)

Rule #4 is the most obvious and yet it's often ignored: Every committee should have a specific, well-defined and documented purpose. There should be no "steering committees" with vague charters that let them meddle in leaders' operational decisions.

When the same executives participate in multiple committees, it's all the more critical to precisely define the purpose of each. Conflicts of interests can arise. For example, for an internal service provider, an Advisory Board is supposed to help the organization succeed, while a Purser is a demanding customer. Even if the same people are on both committees, the committees' purposes (and their agendas) should never be mixed.

Figure 45: Four Rules on the Use of Committees

1. Use committees only for regular two-way communications (e.g., collaboration or shared decisions).
2. Vest no authority in committees (other than the pooled authorities of its members).
3. Don't use committees for oversight (disempowering the boss).
4. Define and document a specific purpose for every committee.

Types of Committees

In a Market Organization, there are a limited number of appropriate purposes for committees (Figure 46). (Some are only relevant to internal service providers, marked "[Internal]".) Following is more detail on each type of committee.

Figure 46: Appropriate Roles for Committees

- **Advisory Board:** An internal "board of directors" that helps a business within a business succeed, with advice at the strategic (not operational) level.

- **Stakeholders:** A set of people who are impacted by a class of decisions, and hence share authority over those decisions.

- **Purser:** A committee that owns a "checkbook," represents internal customers, and decides priorities for an internal service provider.

- **Consortium:** A specific set of internal customers who together purchase and share a specific product or service.

- **User Group:** An association of people who share with one another their experiences using a specific product or service.

- **Focus Group:** People representing customers who share with the organization their values, opinions, decisions, and ideas.

- **Professional Community:** If a function is decentralized, the members of a common profession (regardless of where in the enterprise they report) who share experiences and advance the profession.

Advisory Board [Internal]

An internal "board of directors" helps a business within a business succeed.

Like any good corporate Board, they do not micro-manage the executive or engage in discussions of operational issues. Instead, they add value by coaching the executive on key strategic and leadership issues.

Unlike a corporate Board, this type of committee must not usurp the authority of the organization's supervisor (one up from the organization's executive). In an empowered organization, bosses (and no one else) have the job of managing subordinate leaders. Nobody needs two bosses! This type of committee has no "oversight" authorities over the organization it serves.

Similarly, an Advisory Board has no decision authorities.

An internal Advisory Board should include people who can add value to the executive's thinking. It may include outside parties such as major customers, vendors, and trusted consultants. It does not need to represent all the internal service provider's customers.

Again unlike a corporate Board, it's there to serve (not manage) the executive. So, its composition and agenda should be controlled by the executive.

Stakeholders

The set of people who are impacted by a class of decisions, and hence share authority over those decisions (per the Golden Rule).

For example, a policy or standard may impinge on many people's work. That policy should be designed by the stakeholders; or at a minimum, they should have the authority to approve any such a policy. This ensures that one group cannot unilaterally issue edicts that constrain others' ability to do their jobs.

Another example of shared interests is where decisions about one product impact other products in a brand. Examples include product designs (where a "family resemblance" helps build the brand), pricing, marketing strategy, and advertising messages. In these situations, a product manager should be required to gain the consensus of all affected product managers before making such decisions.

We had a committee that decided policies, and
variances from policies, in product pricing.
We didn't want one product manager tipping the market
and forcing price reductions in other product lines.

— Sergio Paiz, CEO, PDC

In operational functions, another example is "change control." Before anything new is introduced into a production environment, all those who could potentially be harmed by the change should share the authority to approve it.

When the organization sells a system of interconnected solutions, another example is interoperability. One business unit may wish to buy a solution (or make a change to an existing solution) that will harm others — in IT, for example, by fragmenting data or business processes, precluding others' access to needed data, costing others more (e.g., the increased costs of integrations due to standards variances), or actually causing other systems to fail (the "ripple" effect). Those other affected business units should have a say in that decision.

In each of these examples, one person's decision can have unintended consequences for others. Where such interdependencies are recurring, a Stakeholder committee represents those who might be affected; it gives them authorities over a specific class of decisions to protect themselves.

Stakeholder committees may not need to meet regularly. They may be convened on an as-needed basis.

When the selection of people varies based on the specific decision being discussed, a committee should not be formed. Instead, a Coordinator should be identified who then brings together the right people as needed. Product design standards (Chapter 23) are an example of this.

Purser [Internal]

In a Market Organization, an internal support function's budget is treated as prepaid revenues — a "checkbook" to buy the department's products and services in the year ahead. (See Chapter 11.)

A Purser committee owns all or part of that checkbook, and decides what checks to write. In other words, it sets priorities among the many competing requests coming from the customers it represents, and decides what to "buy" from the organization within the bounds of its checkbook.

A Purser committee's only job is to manage a specific checkbook. It does not have the power to control other "sales," e.g., when a business unit uses its own budget to buy additional things from the internal support department.

Any committees which do not own a checkbook may advise the Purser, and may filter requests before they're submitted to the Purser for approval, i.e., they can say no to projects. But lacking a checkbook, these other committees cannot approve projects (they cannot say yes). They are Stakeholders, not Pursers.

A Purser committee should fairly represent the people who benefit from its checkbook. The highest-level Purser should represent the enterprise as a whole — all the business units. If they divide the checkbook into sub-checkbooks (Figure 15), each checkbook needs its own Purser committee representing specific subsets of the client community.

The internal supplier itself should not be a voting member because, in the spirit of building great relations with its customers, it should not judge customers' requests or become an obstacle to them.

Consortium [Internal]

Sometimes, multiple business units share an asset or service by forming a Consortium that acts as a single customer to an internal service provider. (In IT, for example, a number of business units share ownership of the ERP system.)

Since the members of a Consortium share a single thing (an asset or a service), they must speak with one voice as a single customer. They share decision making, costs, and ownership of the results.

A Consortium is distinct from the market as a whole. "Off-the-shelf" products and services are made available to any and all who wish to buy them. They're not customized to satisfy requirements defined by specific customers or Consortia. Instead, they're designed to satisfy the bulk of the market as a whole (Chapter 17). The market as a whole is not a Consortium; each customer buys independently.

Again using IT as a familiar example, the entire company buys the email service; but they don't all have to agree on what they buy. IT decides what to offer (hopefully with input from customers); then, customers independently subscribe to the service. This is not a consortium situation.

A Consortium is a customer to an internal service provider. That supplier is not a member of the Consortium committee (although it may facilitate it).

User Group

User Groups comprise people who use specific products or services.

A User Group is distinct from a Consortium in that each member of the user group can (or, more likely, did) purchase the products or services independently. They do not share a single contract with the supplier organization (as does a Consortium).

User Groups meet to exchange information that will help them get value from the organization's products or services. Membership is generally voluntary and open to all who are interested.

The internal supplier organization is not a member of its User Group; it just facilitates it (a marketing service).

User Groups have no authority over the supplier.

User Groups may also serve as Focus Groups (below), giving the organization feedback.

Focus Group

A Focus Group (a.k.a., advisory panel) represents an internal service provider's market (current and potential customers), and shares with the organization its values, opinions, decisions, and ideas, for example, to guide research and product-development activities.

Focus Groups meet at the request of the organization, not necessarily regularly, and answer questions provided by the organization. They do not make decisions, and have no authority over the organization.

Technically, a Focus Group is not a committee since it should be constituted only when needed, and just the right people should be invited based on the questions at hand. It's mentioned here because some organizations use committees in this way.

Facilitation of Focus Groups is a market research service.

Professional Community

A Professional Community includes the members of a common profession, regardless of where in the enterprise they report. They meet regularly to exchange their experiences, share research findings, agree on standards and policies, and further the interests of their profession.

If a function is decentralized, connecting the members of a Professional Community is particularly important since their opportunities for collaboration may otherwise be limited. This is a weak patch for one of the many costs of decentralization.

Membership is generally voluntary and open to all who are interested.

Appendix 6: Sales Opportunity Discovery Method

This Appendix expands on Chapter 15 with the details of the Sales opportunity discovery method. [159 Ref]

This Appendix is not a tutorial on selling. Rather, it describes a business-driven *method* to help customers discover high-payoff opportunities for use of your products and services, a method which exemplifies the educational, counselor, or "challenger" sale. [160 Ref]

This method is used to define a project (a sale) — i.e., requirements which are directly linked to a customer's business imperatives. It's used with specific customers (individuals). Its purpose is to discover a specific high-payoff opportunity for the organization's products and services.

It can be used by both external-facing sales forces and Business Relationship Managers within internal support functions such as IT. Indeed, it epitomizes the value of a Sales function within internal service providers.

This method is applicable to organizations which offer multiple or custom products/services, and which interact with customers during the sales process. (Vendors of off-the-shelf products/services that are sold via channels such as the internet benefit from relationship selling, i.e., finding ways to enhance customer loyalty. But they typically don't have the opportunity to use counselor-selling methods such as this.)

In this Appendix, we continue the dialog in Chapter 15 with Julio, the head of Sales. Julio uses *IT as an example,* although the method is equally applicable to any internal service provider as well as any companies that sell multiple products and services or custom solutions to external customers.

Start with Business

Speaking about IT:

> "Julio, what does an IT opportunity look like?" I asked. "Are you looking for business processes to automate?"
>
> "IT can do a lot more than just automate routine business processes," he replied. "We're not going to go in and start mapping processes, not until we know that is what's most relevant."

"So, what's the starting point?" I asked. "Does the sales process begin with the customer requesting a particular product?"

Julio laughed. "Sometimes customers have a specific product in mind. And if they insist, we give them what they want without further discussion.

"But we always try to get them to start with their business needs, so that we have a chance to discover which products will add the most value to their businesses. We say something like, 'Of course we can give you that. But we'll do a much better job of serving you if we understand how that solution will contribute to your business.' We try to seduce them into our opportunity-discovery process."

Not a Matter of Analysis

"Okay," I said, "then let's talk about your opportunity discovery process. Do you gather data and analyze customers' needs?"

"No, it's not an analysis process. It is a collaborative exploration. They know their businesses; and we know our products and services, and how they can contribute to customers' businesses. Discoveries come from combining our two different perspectives."

"Do you just sit and brainstorm?" I asked.

"Oh, no," Julio exclaimed. "We've studied a *method* of opportunity discovery. It's a semi-structured interview technique."

Customer's Deliverables

"Okay, walk me through a typical customer interview," I requested.

"Sure." Julio said. "We start by ensuring that we understand what they do. Usually, this confirms what we already know. But sometimes, there are surprises.

"Then, we ask them, 'What do you owe your boss this year?'

"They'll say, 'A, B, and C.' Then we'll ask, 'If you deliver A, B, and C, and nothing else, would you call it a successful year?' We keep probing until we fully understand everything significant that's on their plate — their *deliverables.*"

"People love to talk about themselves," I observed. "This sounds like a good way to start."

"You're right," Julio said, "it engages them. And sometimes just talking to us gives them a perspective on their priorities."

"So, what do you do with their list of deliverables?" I asked.

"We ask them which one of those challenges they want to talk about today. Which is most urgent? Which is most strategic? Which is at the top of their boss' priority list?"

"That makes sense," I said. "If you can help them with that, you've got their attention!"

"Correct." Julio agreed. "What we're looking for is a concept that our customer is willing to fight for — something critical to their success."

Drilling Down to Critical Success Factors

"Okay, what's next?" I asked.

"Next, we drill down on that one deliverable. For just that one, we ask them what the key challenges are. We're listening for their *critical success factors* (CSFs) — their hurdles, and the few things they need to accomplish to succeed at that deliverable." [161 Ref]

"I imagine they get some value out of that, too," I noted.

"Often they do. It helps them focus on their most important issues."

Julio went on describing the interview process. "Then, we ask them to pick just one of those critical success factors, the one that they'd most like help with. We ask them which one is really keeping them up at night. And we drill down on just that one."

Drilling Down to Critical Capabilities

"At this point," I summarized, "we're looking at just one of their most strategic deliverables; and within that, the one hurdle that concerns them the most. So far, you haven't talked about any solutions, right?"

"That's absolutely right!" Julio confirmed. "But we're halfway there."

"I'm waiting to see how long an IT guy can hold on before bringing technology into the discussion," I joked.

Julio laughed with me, then continued. "The next step is to drill down on that one CSF they picked, to the *critical capabilities* they need. These are things they need to be good at, hopefully related to our products and services — in IT, we call them information success factors (ISFs). [162 Ref]

"We ask them, 'What's so tough about that? What do you have to be good at to achieve that critical success factor?'

"We'll hear things like generating creative ideas. Or analyzing alternatives and making decisions in the face of uncertainty. Or teams collaborating across geographies. Or getting diverse people to come to agreement. Or selling others. Or winning negotiations. Or designing complex solutions. You get the idea?"

"I do," I said. "Critical capabilities are the things that customers need to be good at which your products can help with. And I bet you're going to tell me that you pick just one of those and drill down again."

Brainstorming Opportunities

"You've got it!" Julio exclaimed. "Now, finally, we'll bring our products and services into the discussion. Looking at just one critical capability, we brainstorm solutions that might help.

"For example, if their critical capability is team collaboration, we might envision telepresence and collaborative tools. Or if they're having trouble agreeing, maybe access to common data will bring them to the same conclusion. Or maybe some sort of shared decision model.

"If the issue is the efficiency or reliability of routine business processes, *only then* do we get into business-process and value-stream mapping."

Results

"What we end up with," Julio summarized, "is a clear logical path from their business deliverable,
    to one of their critical success factors,
        to a critical capability,
            to the definition of a specific solution."

"At that point," I said, "you've got the sale!"

"And," Julio said, "we know we're adding the most value to their business."

Appendix 7:
The Business of Information Security

Many executives consider information security a *control* function. This Appendix shows how it can be far more effective when reconstrued as a *service* function. This concept can be applied to any compliance function (e.g., regulatory compliance and policy compliance).

The traditional approach to information security is to appoint a Chief Information Security Officer (CISO) *with accountability for the organization's security.*

As per the Golden Rule, such a traditional CISO must demand the authorities needed to fulfill that accountability. The function must have the power to issue edicts, decide controls, and audit compliance.

The alternative suggested here is to hold *everybody* accountable for their own behaviors — including their information security.

Everybody should be held accountable for their own behaviors, including their information security.

This alternative approach changes the role of Information Security from a control function to a *services* business that helps others with their accountabilities.

This Appendix is an elaboration of Chapter 21, a discussion with Johan, the Chief Information Security Officer (CISO). He describes the catalog of services of an Information Security function, and why focusing on services works better than a traditional control-oriented approach: [163 Ref]

Johan explained his service catalog as follows:

Strategy: "We coordinate the security strategy, in collaboration with all the stakeholders. In it, we look at all our assets, their vulnerabilities, and the threats we're facing. This gives us a big-picture view of our risks. Based on that, we propose risk-mitigating initiatives."

Why the services approach is more effective: "Now, when we facilitate an update of our security strategy, everyone participates. And when I take our plans to the Board, my peers know I'm trying to get support for *their* initiatives, not mine — to help them achieve their objectives. So, we come up with much better plans."

Funding: "I present the strategy to executives and the Board. But this isn't a sales pitch for my benefit. It's an advisory service to help the Board make their security investment decisions.

"We help them determine their risk tolerance (how much risk they're willing to accept) and their risk acceptance (how much of that target they can afford at this time, given the costs of security initiatives). We help the Board manage the security portfolio, directing investments to the most significant risks. This gets us funding for the initiatives that are in the strategy."

Why the services approach is more effective: "Now, we're getting real traction on defining the Board's target risk level. Helping them decide (rather than me making the decisions and then pitching the Board) resulted in a big increase in funding for security initiatives.

"But there's never enough money for everything, so sometimes they accept some risks because they can't spend more on security initiatives. At least they're talking to us in concrete terms, not leaving it vague and then later pinning the blame on Carlton and me when things go wrong."

Policies: "We coordinate the development of security policies, and we build awareness to encourage compliance. Some people call this 'governance, risk, and compliance' (GRC); but remember, we're not in the business of governing or policing compliance."

Why the services approach is more effective: "Now, when we need new policies, we don't issue edicts. We engage stakeholders and drive for consensus. Since my peers are involved in deciding the policies, the policies are better written and people understand them far better. And because they were involved, stakeholders are more willing to comply.

"Of course, once a policy is established, we're in the business of building awareness and helping people comply, so that helps too."

Monitoring: "We sell a monitoring service to identify potential incursions. That's our Security Operations Center. It's a service we provide to Operations, which is accountable for delivering safe services. We analyze their log data and notify them of potential incursions."

Why the services approach is more effective: "Understanding that Operations is our customer has greatly improved our working relationship. There's no confusion about accountabilities or boundaries — what they monitor versus what we monitor. And we even share some tools that help us both."

Incident-containment coordination: "When there's an incident, we coordinate containment — like taking a specific server off-line. Really, that's Operations' decision, since they're accountable for service delivery. But they've preauthorized us to act quickly on their behalf if there's any chance of material damages."

Why the services approach is more effective: "When there's an incident, it's not my group alone trying to contain it. It's everybody's top priority. So, we're much quicker at containing threats, which reduces damages."

Recovery analysis: "After an incident is contained, we contribute to the recovery process."

Why the services approach is more effective: "After containment, in the recovery process, accountabilities are clear. The Business Continuity Coordinator coordinates the recovery. Operations and Engineering know how to get the infrastructure back on-line, restore data, and so forth. Information Security provides the identification of the malware and analysis of the damages it caused (including data losses).

"It's a comprehensive and coordinated effort. We're not missing anything or stepping on one another's toes."

Preventative-actions identification: "Once we've recovered, we help asset owners (like Operations which owns infrastructure and customers who own solutions) to define initiatives that will protect them from that kind of threat in the future."

Why the services approach is more effective: "When we recommend preventative actions, we get lots of cooperation now (where we used to be a low priority). Everyone knows we're just trying to help them stay safe. Our recommendations are much more likely to be implemented."

Vulnerability assessments: "We sell vulnerability assessments, both at the enterprisewide level and of specific assets (like applications), so that asset owners know their risks. One form of that is penetration testing (including ethical hacking).

"These assessments generate ideas for projects to harden us against threats. Sometimes it's as simple as applying a patch or making a config-uration change. But in some cases, it requires more; and the assess-ments help to justify those investments.

"Oh, and we also assess requests for data and system access rights. The final decision is up to the asset owners; and they're fully accountable for their decisions about the use of their assets. But we inform them of potential trouble, like giving an employee who already can issue checks the right to register new vendors."

Why the services approach is more effective: "Now, when we do vulner-ability assessments, people are supportive. They know we're not out to get in their way or get them in trouble; we turn the findings over to them so that they can implement risk-mitigation technologies and processes.

"So, with their cooperation, we're better at finding our vulnerabilities. And since the asset owners are accountable for the mitigation projects, things get done. We just help by coordinating the security initiatives in the enterprise risk registry."

Vendor assessments: "We help others assess proposed vendors and vendor contracts for risks."

Why the services approach is more effective: "People voluntarily reach out to us for help assessing their vendors' products and contracts. And they engage us much earlier in the design cycle. Nowadays, we don't have to force our way in at the last minute and then get blamed for holding up projects."

Design advice: "We help engineers design security into their products, including recommendations for defenses and controls."

Why the services approach is more effective: "Engineers voluntarily bring us into their projects early on. We're a subcontractor to them. They see us as helping them produce quality solutions, not a hurdle that slows them down."

Threat alerts: "Our job is to stay up-to-the-minute on new threats, and to keep the relevant people informed about emerging threats and what they can do to protect themselves."

Why the services approach is more effective: "It's not me alone trying to defend the company. Now, my peers appreciate our notifications and they're much more likely to take action."

Awareness: "More broadly, we keep company executives and the Board informed of material threats, the status of our defenses and readiness, and security strategies."

Why the services approach is more effective: "Now, when we inform executives and the Board about the status of our security posture, it's not like I'm tattling on my peers. We're helping decision-makers assess their own performance and the state of their investments. It's a more constructive dialog."

Training: "We offer training (including ethical phishing), notifications of urgent needs, and various awareness-building initiatives."

Why the services approach is more effective: "Now that they know they're accountable, people take our training and communications more seriously, and they're more careful.

"I remember one time, before the transformation, we sent a phishing email to everybody in the company, and if they clicked on the link, it took them to a page we'd set up that scolded them (and logged the response). Well, more than half the IT staff fell for it! And even more on the business side. What a disaster, and an embarrassment for IT! Now, very few people click the link. We're much safer."

Audit coordination: "When external auditors come in to judge our security posture, like for PCI DSS compliance, we're the point of contact. And we coordinate the whole company's response to the auditors."

Why the services approach is more effective: "Everybody knows that they're accountable (not me) for answering auditors' questions about their domains. We're just a coordination service. So, they're not defensive around us. I think they appreciate our help coordinating the process and our advice on their responses."

ENDNOTES

1. *[page xii]* Five organizational systems define the ecosystem within which we work, and determine the character and performance of organizations. See Figure 32.

2. *[page xiii]* See Chapter 7 for principles of structure.

3. *[page xiv]* See Chapter 10 on investment-based budgeting.

4. *[page xv]* See Chapter 11 on demand management (priority setting).

5. *[page xvi]* See Chapter 27 on how to implement a principle-based organizational structure.

6. *[page 6]* Sinek, Simon. *Start With Why: how great leaders inspire everyone to take action.* New York, NY: Penguin Group. 2009.

7. *[page 8]* www.warhistoryonline.com/napoleon/jena-auerstadt-greatest-defeat-prussian-military-history-courtesy-napoleon.html
Also: en.m.wikipedia.org/wiki/
Battle_of_Jena%E2%80%93Auerstedt

8. *[page 9]* Drucker, Peter F. *The New Realities.* New York, NY: Harper & Row. 1989. Page 227.
Full quote: "Not to innovate is the single largest reason for the decline of existing organizations. Not to know how to manage is the single largest reason for the failure of new ventures."

9. *[page 12]* Covey, Stephen R. *The 7 Habits of Highly Effective People.* New York, NY: Fireside. 1990. Page 95.

10. *[page 13]* Forrester, Jay W. "A New Corporate Design." *Industrial Management Review.* Boston, MA: MIT Sloan School of Management. Volume 7, number 1. Fall, 1965. Page 5.

11. *[page 14]* Block, Peter. *The Empowered Manager: positive political skills at work.* San Francisco, CA: Jossey-Bass. 1987. Page 107.

12. *[page 16]* The organizational challenges of an IT department are much the same as those of companies as a whole. In fact, IT is as complex as many entire companies. IT produces custom products, commodities, and ongoing services. IT has to contend with

competition (decentralization and outsourcing). IT organizations include:

- Sales (albeit internal) and Marketing (an education mission)
- Many layers of Engineering, with complex architectural issues
- Manufacturing, with plants and equipment
- Customer service
- All the usual business support functions

13. *[page 24]* This case example came from Derek Weber, President, goBRANDgo!.

14. *[page 28]* The misguided maxim, "structure follows strategy," was most clearly stated by: Chandler, Alfred D. *Strategy and Structure*. Cambridge, MA: The MIT Press. 1962.

15. *[page 28]* The acronym "VUCA" was coined by: Thurman, Maxwell P. "Strategic Leadership." Presentation to the Strategic Leadership Conference, US Army War College, Carlisle Barracks, PA. February 11, 1991.

16. *[page 29]* Teece, David J.; Gary Pisano; and Amy Shuen. "Dynamic capabilities and strategic management." *Strategic Management Journal*. Volume 18, Number 7. August, 1997. Pages 509-533.

17. *[page 32]* Sergio Paiz, CEO of PDC (a Guatemala-based multi-national company) has implemented much of this vision.
Source: Meyer, N. Dean. *Principle-based Organizational Structure: a handbook to help you engineer entrepreneurial thinking and teamwork into organizations of any size*. Danbury, CT: NDMA Publishing. 2017. Page xiii.

18. *[page 34]* Meyer, N. Dean. *An Introduction to the Business-Within-a-Business Paradigm*. Danbury, CT: NDMA Publishing. 2002.
Prior thought leadership envisioned groups as for-profit businesses:
von Mises, Ludwig Heinrich Edler. *Bureaucracy*. New Haven, CT: Yale University Press. 1944. Page 33.
Forrester, Jay W. "A New Corporate Design." *Industrial Management Review*. Boston, MA: Sloan School of Management, MIT. Volume 7, number 1. Fall, 1965. Page 5.
Pinchot, Gifford. *Intrapreneuring*. New York, NY: Harper & Row. 1985.
Halal, William E.; and Ali Geranmayeh; John Pourdehnad.

Internal Markets: bringing the power of free enterprise inside your organization. John Wiley & Sons, Inc. 1993.

19. *[page 35]*   Dylan, Bob. "Gotta Serve Somebody." From *Slow Train Coming.* Columbia. 1979.

20. *[page 36]*   von Mises, Ludwig Heinrich Edler. *Bureaucracy.* New Haven, CT: Yale University Press. 1944. Page 36.

21. *[page 38]*   Peters, Thomas J. *The Excellence Dividend.* New York, NY: Vintage Books. 2018. Page 298.

22. *[page 39]*   Peters, Thomas J. *Thriving on Chaos.* New York, NY: Alfred A. Knopf, Inc. 1987. Page 286.

23. *[page 41]*   Jaques, Elliott. *Requisite Organization.* Arlington, VA: Cason Hall & Co. 1998.

24. *[page 42]*   Senge, Peter M. "The Leader's New Work: Building Learning Organizations." *Sloan Management Review.* Boston, MA: MIT Sloan School of Management. Fall, 1990. Page 7.

25. *[page 43]*   Drucker, Peter F. *Innovation and Entrepreneurship.* New York, NY: Harper & Row. 1985.

26. *[page 44]*   Kanter, Rosabeth Moss. *When Giants Learn to Dance.* New York, NY: Touchstone. 1989. Page 52.

27. *[page 45]*   Canetti, Elias. *Auto-da-Fé.* New York, NY: Farrar, Straus and Giroux. 1935, 1946 in English. Part III, Chapter 2.

28. *[page 46]*   The limitations of top-down command-and-control are very well articulated in: McChrystal, Stanley. *Team of Teams.* New York, NY: Penguin Publishing Group. 2015. Part 1.

29. *[page 47]*   Stanley McChrystal illustrates the importance of empowerment with a description of how British Admiral Horatio Nelson defeated Napoleon's superior Franco-Spanish fleet in 1805.

Traditionally, naval battles were fought with the opposing forces in two straight lines, ships positioned sideways to permit cannon fire. Ship captains weren't told the overall plan, and were instructed to await and follow orders. Commands were communicated via flags from ship to ship, often difficult to see amidst the smoke of battle.

Nelson used a very different tactic. He sailed his warships directly at Napoleon's forces and decimated them as his ships punched through the line.

This tactic wasn't new. McChrystal explained, "...his unique innovation lay in his managerial style and the culture he had cultivated among his forces." Instead of top-down command-and-control, Nelson shared information (including the strategy) openly with his captains, and then empowered them to act on their own initiative.

McChrystal concluded, "At the heart of his success was patient, yet relentless, nurturing of competence and adaptability within his crews.... Nelson's real genius lay not in the clever maneuver for which he is remembered, but in the years of innovative management and leadership that preceded it."

Source: McChrystal, Stanley. *Team of Teams*. New York, NY: Penguin Publishing Group. 2015. Pages 28-31.

30. *[page 47]* Quote from speech at the 2016 Democratic Convention.

31. *[page 48]* King, Martin Luther. "Letter From a Birmingham Jail." April 16, 1963.

32. *[page 48]* DePree, Max. *Leadership Jazz*. New York, NY: Doubleday. 1992. Page 221.

33. *[page 49]* Stack, Jack; and Bo Burlingham. *The Great Game of Business: the only sensible way to run a company*. New York, NY: Crown Business. 2013. Page 3.

34. *[page 49]* Statement made before Normandy invasion, June, 1944.
    Source: Wallace, Brinton G. *Patton and his Third Army*. Harrisburg, PA: Military Service Publishing Co. 1946. Page 357.

35. *[page 52]* Ackoff, Russell L. *Ackoff's Fables: irreverent reflections on business and bureaucracy*. New York, NY: John Wiley & Sons. 1991. Page 131.

36. *[page 53]* Further explanation of the relationship of an empowered, entrepreneurial operating model, Covid-19, and work-from-home is in this quote from Sergio Paiz, CEO of PDC:

"When Covid-19 hit, getting into work-from-home was seamless. Everybody had a clear understanding of their accountabilities, and we were already managing by results (not tasks and effort).

"We don't measure hours of work, or the time when people decide to work (with obvious exceptions). We even stopped measuring vacation days (for the leadership team) a couple of years earlier. People are empowered to decide for themselves when to take a vacation and for how long. This really made our leaders feel that they are true entrepreneurs, owners of their time, and thus 100 percent responsible for their results.

"In many ways, work-from-home has been as effective as (or, I could even argue, more effective than) office work. Our business results and operational efficiencies are up. And people are working better as a team, independent of their locations. (Before, staff in our headquarters location had an advantage.)

"Frankly, I feel we have ridded ourselves of all geographical barriers to growth."

37. *[page 53]*   Sinek, Simon. *Start with Why*. New York, NY: Penguin Group. 2009. Page 7.

38. *[page 56]*   Two good sources of personal-effectiveness practices consistent with the Market Organization are:
Covey, Stephen R. *The 7 Habits of Highly Effective People*. New York, NY: Fireside. 1990.
Dalio, Ray. *Principles*. New York, NY: Simon & Schuster. 2017.

39. *[page 62]*   Meyer, N. Dean. *Principle-based Organizational Structure: a handbook to help you engineer entrepreneurial thinking and teamwork into organizations of any size*. Danbury, CT: NDMA Publishing. 2017.

40. *[page 63]*   In addition to structure, the internal economy must be designed to give every group an appropriate amount of time and money for innovation.

41. *[page 65]*   Smith, Adam. *An Inquiry into the Nature and Causes of the Wealth of Nations*. London: J. M. Dent & Sons Ltd. 1776.

42. *[page 65]*   The phrase "jack of all trades and master of none" is attributed to: Greene, Robert. "Greene's Groats-Worth of Witte, bought with a million of Repentance." 1592.
Ironically, Greene was disparaging actor-turned-playwright William Shakespeare, in this first published mention of Shakespeare.

43. *[page 72]* Porter, Michael E. *Competitive Advantage: creating and sustaining superior performance.* New York, NY: The Free Press. 1985. Page 17.

44. *[page 73]* Meyer, N. Dean. *Principle-based Organizational Structure: a handbook to help you engineer entrepreneurial thinking and teamwork into organizations of any size.* Danbury, CT: NDMA Publishing. 2017. Part 3.

45. *[page 73]* Gino Wickman's "EOS" (Entrepreneurial Operating System) teaches small firms ($2-20 million) basic business practices, like a rhythm of meetings. However, its "Accountability Matrix" approach to structure is not based on principles, and diverges from the Market Organization in some fundamental ways:

    - Jobs are defined by the "roles" they play (a mixture of functions and tasks), not as businesses.

    - Its simplistic framework of functions — only sales/marketing, operations, and finance — buries strategic functions like engineering under operations, and IT and HR under Finance.

    - It casts the top executive as the "Integrator" who is the sole owner of a P&L, since subordinates are not viewed as empowered entrepreneurs.

    - The top executive personally does cross-boundary linking in lieu of walk-throughs (not scalable) and in lieu of Coordinators (professions in their own right).

    - Vision comes from the "Owner," from the top down, rather than from everybody.

    The "E" in EOS means it's intended for entrepreneurs running very small businesses. But in many ways, it's the opposite of the "everybody is an entrepreneur" ethos of a Market Organization.

    Source: Wickman, Gino. *Traction: get a grip on your business.* Dallas, TX: BenBella Books. 2011. Chapter 4.

46. *[page 74]* Meyer, N. Dean. *Principle-based Organizational Structure: a handbook to help you engineer entrepreneurial thinking and teamwork into organizations of any size.* Danbury, CT: NDMA Publishing. 2017. Chapter 28.

47. *[page 74]* Stack, Jack; and Bo Burlingham. *The Great Game of Business: the only sensible way to run a company.* New York, NY: Crown Business. 2013. Page 43.

48. *[page 75]* Stack, Jack; and Bo Burlingham. *The Great Game of Business: the only sensible way to run a company.* New York, NY: Crown Business. 2013. Page 47.

49. *[page 76]* Peters, Thomas J. *The Excellence Dividend.* New York, NY: Vintage Books. 2018. Page 14.

50. *[page 79]* von Mises, Ludwig Heinrich Edler. *Human Action: a treatise on economics.* New Haven, CT: Yale University Press. 1949. Page 194.

51. *[page 79]* McChrystal, Stanley. *Team of Teams.* New York, NY: Penguin Publishing Group. 2015. Chapter 6.

McChrystal describes teams of specialists, each of which delivers component results, plus an overarching "team of teams" with a shared purpose: the mission. We would call it a 'team of groups,' where the groups are internal lines of business that provide their products and services to project teams, as laid out in walk-throughs.

McChrystal points out that prime contractors must do more than parcel out subcontracts. They also must create a shared sense of purpose, open sharing of information, and a team spirit that transcends specific deliverables — what McChrystal calls "shared consciousness." He offers great advice on how the prime contractor can pull together all the subcontractors into a cohesive team.

52. *[page 82]* Tapscott, Don; and Art Caston. *Paradigm Shift: the new promise of information technology.* New York, NY: McGraw-Hill. 1993. Page 33.

53. *[page 83]* Meyer, N. Dean. *Internal Market Economics: practical resource-governance processes based on principles we all believe in.* Danbury, CT: NDMA Publishing. 2013.
Original introduction to concepts: Meyer, N. Dean. *RoadMap: how to understand, diagnose, and fix your organization.* Danbury, CT: NDMA Publishing. 1997. Chapter 12.

54. *[page 83]* Samuelson, Paul A. *Economics.* New York, NY: McGraw-Hill Book Company. 1973. Page 3.

55. *[page 87]* The phrase "follow the money" was popularized by the 1976 docudrama, "All the President's Men." Screenwriter William Goldman attributed it to informant "Deep Throat" who helped

reveal Nixon's Watergate scandal. In this use, no corruption is implied.

56. *[page 90]* A cost model assigns all indirect costs to the appropriate products and services. There were significant inaccuracies in activity-based costing (ABC). And the objective in a Market Organization is to calculate the cost of deliverables, not activities. Furthermore, ABC didn't treat support functions as businesses, just as 'cost pools' (discouraging entrepreneurship).

A modern service-based costing model treats support functions as businesses that sell their services to other groups, or to the enterprise as a whole. One problem these internal sales create is that, in real life, there's massive circularity — A sells to B, who sells to C, who sells to A. In most organizations, there are hundreds of real-world circles. A modern cost-modeling tool manages that.

Source: Meyer, N. Dean. *Internal Market Economics: practical resource-governance processes based on principles we all believe in.* Danbury, CT: NDMA Publishing. 2013. Appendix 4.

57. *[page 91]* Rows in an investment-based budget can include pools of hours for repairs and ongoing enhancements to existing products, consistent with the SAFe-Agile notion of "product owners" (who are actually suppliers, not asset-owners) and resources dedicated to continually refining existing products. Investment-based budgeting empowers leaders to constrain these pools and redirect resources to more strategic, higher-return projects (other rows).

58. *[page 91]* With investment-based budgeting, CEOs and CFOs get much better insights into the benefits of budgets because internal customers defend the projects and services they want to buy. Shared-service suppliers just defend investments in their businesses, like infrastructure and innovation. With the people in the best position to know explaining the value, or explaining the business impacts of cuts, executives can make better budget decisions.

59. *[page 94]* The best kind of cost benchmarks are fully burdened rates (unit costs). They answer the question, "Like for like, can we buy it cheaper than it costs us to make it?"

Benchmarking of rates is far more accurate than high-level cost towers, or percentages of revenues. Consider this: What if your costs are higher than your peers in your industry? Is that because you're inefficient? Or is it because your strategy or the nature of your business forces you to pay more (such as higher telecommunications costs because you've chosen to globalize your workforce)? Or could it be because you're making more extensive use of a service to gain strategic advantages (such as those at the leading edge of digital business who spend more than peers on IT)?

With high-level industry comparisons of spending, there's no way to know whether spending more than peers is bad or good.

60. *[page 95]* Meyer, N. Dean. *Downsizing Without Destroying: how to trim what your organization does rather than destroy its ability to do anything at all.* Danbury, CT: NDMA Publishing. 2008.

61. *[page 96]* If you don't do cross-departmental chargebacks, the indirect costs of the services that groups receive from other departments, and of enterprise services and overhead, are in other departments' budgets (checkbooks/revenues). Hence, they're not in the receiving department's cost structure or rates (even if the receiving department has some control over them as a purser). For the purpose of benchmarking, to be fair, you have to include them.

These costs are visible in other departments' investment-based budgets. (Consider just indirect costs, not subcontracts which are direct and generally do not go into the prime's rates.) In another run of the cost model specifically to calculate rates for benchmarking, they're factored in as external costs (like vendors).

62. *[page 102]* More on the use of contractors when revenues over and above the budget are provided for additional deliverables:

By pricing at full cost, including management overhead (not just the marginal cost of contractors), incremental jobs don't take resources away from deliverables funded by the budget. The management overhead built into the rates can be used to hire some extra contractor-hours to off-load staff so that employees have time to manage the contractors.

Note that the contractors acquired with fee-for-service funding don't have to be used on that incremental project. It's good practice to use contractors to off-load employees of more routine work, so that employees can do the more innovative projects.

63. *[page 103]* Corporate-good services are sold to the enterprise as a whole (i.e., to the Board). They include things like enterprise policy facilitation, "consumer reports" type studies, and contributions to economic-commons like the enterprise's reputation and safety (such as many aspects of security).

The costs of corporate-good services should not be imbedded in the rates for other services. Doing so would make internal service providers inappropriately appear less competitive. And business units should not pay for corporate-good services other than via the profits they remit to the enterprise.

Corporate-good services are distinct from mass-market services which are sold to all (or many of) the business units. Mass-market services have commercial value to each customer. Examples include IT's network, and HR's compensation administration.

64. *[page 108]* Internal contracts are firm commitments made by specific customers and specific internal suppliers for specific deliverables. They document at least the following:

- The name of the customer.
- The name of the supplier.
- The title of the contract, such as the name of the project.
- The product or service to be delivered, drawn verbatim from the supplier's catalog.
- The start date (a solid commitment, not a "target" or "priority"). Prior to confirming this date, the document is a "proposal," not a "contract."
- An estimate of the elapsed time from the start date.
- The price, and the terms of payment (e.g., direct budget or fee-for-service), renewal, and termination.
- The customer's accountabilities (e.g., "We can only meet this commitment if the customer does this...").
- Any risks and assumptions about other dependencies outside of the control of the customer and the supplier (e.g., "We can only meet this commitment if the company does this...").
- A minimum of necessary administrative information.

65. *[page 112]* Meyer, N. Dean. *Meyer's Rules of Order: how to hold highly productive business meetings.* Danbury, CT: NDMA Publishing. 2001.

66. *[page 113]*   Schein, Edgar H. *Organizational Culture and Leader-ship*. San Francisco, CA: Jossey-Bass Publishers. 1986. Page 33.

The better-known saying, "Culture eats strategy for breakfast," came much later, from an unknown source. It was used (but not cited) by The Giga Information Group in March, 2000, and has been credited to Peter Drucker (without evidence).

67. *[page 114]*   Edgar Schein defined organizational culture as the "basic assumptions and beliefs that are shared by members of an organiza-tion." These, he said, drive both behaviors (artifacts) and values. Changing either values or behaviors impacts these underlying assumptions and beliefs, which explains why each drives the other.

Source: Schein, Edgar H. *Organizational Culture and Leadership*. San Francisco, CA: Jossey-Bass Publishers. 1986. Page 6.

68. *[page 116]*   Ben Horowitz points out that bushido, the code of the samurai who ruled Japan for 700 years, defined principles as "virtues" rather than "values." As he said, "...virtues are what you do, while values are merely what you believe."

Source: Horowitz, Ben. *What You Do Is Who You Are: how to create your business culture*. New York, NY: HarperCollins. 2019. Page 13.

69. *[page 118]*   This unexpected benefit of a behavior-based culture came from Jim Hatch, then CIO of Case Tractor.

70. *[page 120]*   These case examples of metrics that misfired came from Gerald Pogue.

71. *[page 121]*   Stack, Jack; and Bo Burlingham. *The Great Game of Business: the only sensible way to run a company*. New York, NY: Crown Business. 2013.

72. *[page 122]*   This case example of metrics that misfired came from Gerald Pogue.

73. *[page 123]*   Huang, Szu-chi; Stephanie C. Lin; and Ying Zhang. "When Individual Goal Pursuit Turns Competitive: how we sabotage and coast." American Psychological Association: *Journal of Personality and Social Psychology*. Volume 117, number 3. 2019. Pages 605-620.

74. *[page 123]* "Objectives and key results" (OKRs) was coined by Andy Grove at Intel, based on management by objectives (MBO) proposed by Peter Drucker and later popularized by John Doerr.

Source: Grove, Andrew S. *High Output Management.* New York, NY: Random House. 1983. Pages 110-114.

Source: Drucker, Peter F. *The Practice of Management.* New York, NY: Harper & Row. 1954. Chapter 11.

75. *[page 129]* Senge, Peter M. *The Fifth Discipline.* New York, NY: Doubleday. 2006. Page 269.

76. *[page 130]* Clear, James. *Atomic Habits.* New York, NY: Avery. 2018. Page 24.

77. *[page 141]* Sayles, Leonard R. "Matrix Management: The Structure with a Future." *Organizational Dynamics,* Autumn, 1976. Pages 2-17.

78. *[page 145]* This reflects the way any innovation penetrates a market.

Source: Rogers, Everett M. *Diffusion of Innovations.* New York, NY: The Free Press. 1962.

79. *[page 145]* "Rien ne réussit comme le succês...."
Janin, M. Jules. "Le Chemin De Traverse." 1836.

Accredited to Janin in a review by Auguste Bussiére in: *Revue des Deux Mondes.* January, 1837. Page 116.

Later popularized by: Dumas, Alexander. *AngePitou* (also known as *Storming the Bastille* or *Six Years Later*). 1854.

80. *[page 147]* A Chief Data Officer (CDO) is primarily a Function Sales consultant (Chapter 15). This is not a technology-related job. It's expertise (bottom of the T) is *data science* — extracting meaning from data based on in-depth expertise in the linkage between business questions/decisions and data.

The Chief Data Officer role includes:

- Helping Account Representatives (Business Relationship Managers) with opportunity discovery, translating business questions into data requirements.
- Helping extract meaning from data by analyzing data to answer customers' questions or guide decisions. This includes data harmonization which melds data from different sources to provide deeper insights.

■   Helping the Data Warehouse Operations leader with their business strategies, include market requirements for data.

■   Advising applications developers and ad-hoc reporting service providers on report design.

Other lines of business essential to utilizing data as a strategic asset, but distinct from the profession of data science, include:

■   Data warehouse: an Asset-based Service Provider (Operations) function (Chapter 17).

■   Analytics tools: data query, reporting, and analysis tools; a Base Engineering (end-user computing) function (Chapter 16).

■   Information modeling: includes artificial intelligence, statistics, and other analytics methods and models; a Base Engineering function (Chapter 16).

■   Ontology, information engineering: includes the meta-data repository (standard vocabulary), logical data modeling, and technical architecture of data; a Base Engineering function (Chapter 16).

■   Data cleansing: fixing data based on algorithms (not on an understanding of truth); a People-based Service Provider (Chapter 18).

■   Reporting services: ad hoc reports, data cubes; a People-based Service Provider function (Chapter 18).

Optimally, these other functions report to the appropriate leaders of their lines of business. This maximizes professional synergies (Chapter 7), while still producing a coherent data strategy through teamwork.

However, in the absence of excellence in teamwork, some or all of those other functions may report to a Chief Data Officer. While this sacrifices synergies, it encourages a coherent data strategy with less dependence on cross-boundary teamwork.

81. *[page 149]*   In the 1970s, Agile way-finding was called "heuristic design," and later "adaptive development," "evolutionary development," and "middle-out design."
Source: Markus, M. Lynne. *Systems in Organizations*. Marshfield, MA: Pitman. 1984. Page 105.

82. *[page 149]* In a consortium agreement, the members decide how they'll share the costs, how they'll make decisions, rules of entry if others later want to use the asset, rules of departure if a member later wants to drop out, etc.

83. *[page 150]* In IT, if customers don't agree to form a consortium to address similar needs, engineers can still deliver some synergies by proactively reusing code, using standard interfaces for future interoperability, commonizing data structures, and at a minimum, reusing competencies. But this only occurs if Applications Engineering is substructured by data objects, not business units.

84. *[page 151]* Meyer, N. Dean; and Mary E. Boone. *The Information Edge*. Danbury, CT: NDMA Publishing. 1987, 1995. Chapter 14.

85. *[page 153]* Taylor, James C.; and David F. Felton. *Performance By Design: sociotechnical systems in North America*. Upper Saddle River, NJ: Prentice-Hall. 1992.

86. *[page 161]* In IT, purpose-specific applications are solutions that manage information about specific topics — "data objects" like customers, money, and employees — or that present information to specific professions or business processes. The scope includes websites, smart phones apps, and real-time operational technologies.

87. *[page 162]* In IT, Base Engineering includes:

- "Platforms" includes hardware, and environmental software whose primary intent is managing the hardware (operating systems, systems-level utilities). It has two customers:
  - o It sells to IT Operations (infrastructure services) the assets they use to produce services, e.g., computer servers, storage, networks.
  - o It sells to customers individual-use devices, e.g., PCs, tablets, and smart phones (unless those are managed as a fleet and rented to users by IT Operations).

- Middleware includes tools for managing the infrastructure, such as the monitoring tools in the data center. It also includes database management systems (DBMS, CMS, web portals), inter-application integration engines (messaging, data transfers), and other services to applications.

- End-user computing (EUC) includes the wide range of *tools for thinking and collaboration* which aren't data-object specific.

  End-user computing does not mean PCs. (A PC is a computing platform that can run applications, EUC, and operational controls.) EUC tools run on any platform.

  EUC includes:
  - o Text editing tools like Microsoft Word,[R] Google Docs,[R] electronic publishing, and PDF tools.
  - o Number-oriented tools like Microsoft Excel,[R] Google Sheets,[R] all the way up to data modeling and big-data analysis tools.
  - o Graphics tools, including raster (photos) and vector (charts, computer-aided design).
  - o Calendars, time management, reminder tools.
  - o Query tools, from browsers to data reporting tools.
  - o Collaborative tools like messaging, team support, social media, and all forms of teleconferencing.

- Methods and tools for use by the organization itself include programming languages and compilers, testing platforms, and DevOps tools. Examples of methods include Agile, testing and validation, and basic computer science.

- Data modeling disciplines include ontology (the meaning of words, including the meta-data repository), logical data modeling, and data architecture (e.g., in a data warehouse).

- Information modeling disciplines include artificial intelligence, operations research and management science, and mathematics.

Base Engineering's customers include other engineers, Operations (infrastructure services), and business customers.

88. *[page 163]* Examples of the subcontractors on IT applications-development teams include:
- Base Engineering can provide a logical data model, advice on computer platforms, and integrations (data links to other applications) from middleware experts.
- The PMO (Project Management Office) can help with project planning and then ongoing project facilitation.

- Input on design constraints comes from the Standards and Design Patterns Coordinator (enterprise architect).

- The Information Security team provides evaluations of vendor products and internal designs, and helps engineers design controls into solutions.

- Operations (Asset-based Service Providers) provides development environments and installs the application in their production environment, often with help from Base Engineering.

- In some cases, Field Technicians are needed to do installations in remote locations.

89. *[page 165]* More on the choice of IT development methods:

For some projects, the "Waterfall" method is appropriate. Engineers work sequentially down from requirements to high-level designs, detailed designs, specifications, and then the final product. It's the most efficient and thorough design method, especially for large projects, when requirements are fully defined.

But in other cases, customers can only describe the requirements in an approximate way. They need to see an example before they can describe the details of what they want.

Using an iterative approach ("way-finding"), IT quickly designs and builds a "minimum viable product." Customers evaluate and learn from it, refining requirements through a series of iterations. This is the essence of the "Agile" method.

Agile is often used when trying to invent something that hasn't been done before. Common examples include applications for external customers' smart phones and externally facing websites.

With Agile, it's important to never lose sight of the business opportunity ("problem framing") and business requirements (including user stories and use cases). Agile is not an excuse for dedicating a team of developers to a customer or product, and then unendingly building and enhancing solutions based on that customer's requests, without concern for business value or priorities.

The Market Organization is a scalable framework around Agile, an alternative to other frameworks that are not based on organizational design principles. Key differences: Their notion of long-lived teams dedicated to products is counter to flexible teaming through walk-throughs (just the right people at just the right time for each project, Chapter 8). And dynamic priorities are decided by pursers through internal market economics (not assuming that enhancements to existing products are always a top priority, Chapter 11).

90. *[page 169]*   This case example came from Randy Prueitt, then at Aurora Health Care.

91. *[page 170]*   Aesop. *Aesop's Fables: The Hare and the Tortoise.* Greece. 620-564 BCE.

92. *[page 173]*   In IT, early in the implementation phase, Engineers work with Service Providers to help them plan needed infrastructure and to broker service-level agreements needed to operate and support the solution once it's in production.

93. *[page 173]*   In IT, when a solution involves vendor services (such as software-as-a-service, or cloud computing), Engineers provide the technical requirements within the vendor contract (leaving business terms to the customer). They also contribute their expertise to the vendor contracting process, and configure and integrate vendor services.

94. *[page 173]*   Quality is not about adding functionality. That's a matter of price-point. Quality means professionalism at any price-point.

Part of quality is including all the attributes (not functions) that the customer will need to make the intended uses of the solution. Examples in IT include required documentation, parameters and metrics ("knobs and dials") that will be needed for ongoing operations, install/uninstall utilities, back-up utilities, error diagnostics, and appropriate security features.

95. *[page 174]*   In many cases, there's a trade-off between ease of learning and ease of use.

For example, a Ferrari is not easy to learn; but it's easy for a trained driver to operate at very high levels of performance. An economy car, on the other hand, is easy to learn; but it's very difficult to drive on a race track.

Engineers do their best to make things as easy as possible to learn at the required level of performance. But that just moves the curve out; it doesn't eliminate the trade-off. At some point, the customer must decide the balance between ease of learning and ease of use.

96. *[page 175]* Crosby, Philip B. *Quality Is Free: the art of making quality certain: how to manage quality so that it becomes a source of profit for your business.* New York, NY: McGraw-Hill. 1979.

97. *[page 177]* This case example came from Randy Prueitt, then at Abbott Laboratories.

98. *[page 177]* Some organizations inappropriately split Engineering into groups for new solutions, and separate groups for maintaining existing solutions. This has costs and risks:

- Both development and maintenance require the same specialists — the same professional knowledge, skills, and tools. Splitting those specialists into two groups reduces specialization, impacting everybody's performance (Principle 2 of structure).

- There are reduced incentives for first-time quality, since developers can get credit for finishing a project and leave it to the maintainers to fix the defects. Also, developers get less feedback on the quality of their work when they're not involved in repairs.

- There's an added cost of knowledge transfer from developers to maintainers, an extra learning curve.

- Maintainers who are unaware of the developers' design architecture may inadvertently install repairs and enhancements (design changes) that damage the integrity of the solution.

- Resource flexibility is reduced, in that when there aren't repairs to be done, it's difficult to shift maintenance staff to development projects (and vice versa).

- It creates two classes of citizenship, with developers seen as having greater talents and career potential. That's of questionable ethics, and is demotivational for maintainers.

This split is often the result of a mistaken root-cause analysis, attempting to reserve time for development and for maintenance (an internal economy challenge) by compromising the structure.

More: Meyer, N. Dean. *Principle-based Organizational Structure: a handbook to help you engineer entrepreneurial thinking and teamwork into organizations of any size.* Danbury, CT: NDMA Publishing. 2017. Chapter 24.

99. *[page 181]*   This case example came from Joe Phillips, then CIO at Blockbuster.

100. *[page 183]*   In IT, the stewardship (hosting) service includes:

- During a solution alternatives study, coordinating the various infrastructure service providers in providing estimates of ongoing operational costs for each alternative.

- As the prime contractor, subcontracting for requisite infrastructure services and other operational services such as access administration and cybersecurity monitoring.

- Ongoing tasks required to keep the solution operational.

- Usage monitoring and license utilization tracking (comparing actual utilization with licenses purchased). Supplier Management (a People-based Service Provider) can be subcontracted to help track available licenses as per vendor contracts.

- Performance monitoring (of customer-owned assets, not underlying infrastructure services), and responding to customers' complaints about performance; subcontracts to: other Asset-based Service Providers to acquire adequate capacity; and other Asset-based Service Providers and Applications Engineers to diagnose application-level performance constraints and performance-improvement opportunities.

- With regard to vendors who provide services to the solution-owner, monitoring vendor performance and (to the extent empowered by the solution-owner) representing the solution-owner in negotiations with vendors.

- Problem management assistance, identifying patterns in incidents, diagnosing root causes, and recommending investments to applications owners and infrastructure-service providers.

- Application-level release management (coordinating installation time-windows).

- Notifications and reminders of asset owners' accountabilities.

- Notifications to the asset owner's customers (users) of operational events such as planned outages.

- Coordination of disaster recovery of this asset (with subcontracts to engineers). (Coordination of recovery of subcontracted services is left to the subcontractors.)

- Optionally, notification of variances on defined metrics.

- Optionally, ordering and overseeing preauthorized supplies purchases, repairs, and upgrades (a type of enhancements).

101. *[page 187]* In IT, one pillar of DevOps is streamlining the flow from development to operations by breaking down barriers between developers and operators. That doesn't mean that those two lines of business should be combined into one group. Nor does it have to mean shared accountabilities, which undermines individual accountabilities. Seamless teamwork can be accomplished through walk-throughs and well-designed processes.

102. *[page 191]* More on the IT Access Administration function:

Access Administration (a People-based Service Provider) does not decide who has the right to access services. That authority resides with asset owners, who get advice on risks from the Information Security function.

E.g., Operations (Asset-based Service Provider) is accountable for selling its services. So, only it has the authority to make commitments to provide those services to subscribers, i.e., to grant access rights to its services. Operations remains accountable for the safety of its services, including for its access-rights decisions.

Similarly, most IT applications are owned by business customers. They have the authority to decide who gets to use their assets, and full accountability for their decisions.

Access Administration helps asset owners by facilitating the approval process and administering a repository of access rights.

While administrative, it's value goes beyond just saving others time. For example, new employees need access to the network, collaboration tools like email, various applications, and so on. Access Administration provides a single point of contact and coordination for granting access to all those distinct services.

It also improves security by ensuring that all new requests have the necessary approvals. And when an employee leaves the company, it can shut down all their access rights quickly.

As a common repository of access rights evolves, it enables other improvements like single-sign-on.

The concept of Access Administration may apply enterprisewide (outside IT), to coalesce the various customer interface-points,

especially as an enterprise increasingly depends on online relationships and delivers various online services.

103. *[page 207]*   www.bbc.com/news/technology-50744333

104. *[page 218]*   www.pmi.org

105. *[page 236]*   There are misconceptions about strategic planning for
internal service providers like IT:

Contrary to what some consultants sell, internal service providers'
strategies are *not* driven by the company's business strategies.
Internal service providers' *projects* (not strategies) are driven by
business strategies. Sales (not planning) helps customers look at
business strategies and discover opportunities. This is a continual
process, not done once a year in an annual plan.

Internal service providers' strategies are not a list of strategic
projects, any more than a company's strategic plan is a list of the
sales it hopes to make in the coming year. Just as for companies,
strategy is at a higher level. It answers the questions: *What
businesses do we want to be in the future; and how do we plan to
get from here to there?*

The company's current business strategies are one input. Beyond
that, industry trends, technology trends, regulatory and economic
forecasts, and competitive threats (including disruption) are
relevant. SWOT analysis (strengths, weaknesses, opportunities,
and threats) is helpful. The resulting plan includes technology
directions, new products and services, major internal process-
improvement initiatives, and innovation initiatives.

106. *[page 239]*   An IT Business Continuity function does more than
coordinate IT's business-continuity plans. It also helps asset
owners (like customers who own applications) develop the
technology-impacted portions of their business continuity plans.

Additionally, it helps customers analyze the business-continuity
capabilities needed in proposed investments (e.g., new applications)
and vendor relationships.

107. *[page 240]*   IT can facilitate enterprise information and data governance policies, which address who owns data (typically the group
that generates it); information sharing (e.g., open sharing unless

there's reason not to, versus need-to-know); the appropriate use of enterprise information and technology assets, including what people can and cannot say in public (such as in social media; e.g., staff must not make recommendations for use of the company's products if those products weren't intended for that purpose).

108. *[page 241]* Internal service providers (like IT) may have their own Regulatory Compliance functions. In collaboration with Corporate Regulatory Compliance groups, they serve the department itself with the full range of compliance services.

In addition, they work enterprisewide on compliance issues specific to the function. For example, IT helps business units understand information- and technology-related regulations (such as how they handle sensitive customer data).

109. *[page 241]* A risk registry documents sources of risks, and their probabilities, potential business impacts, and remediation status. An enterprise risk registry includes information security and other risks, such as business continuity, employee safety, product safety, and reputational risks. Ideally, they're integrated in a single registry, even if different groups coordinate remediation. However, in many companies, IT maintains the information-security risk registry, and a corporate risk management group maintains a separate registry for the rest.

110. *[page 244]* Some define IT architecture as a framework for mapping business functions and designing comprehensive solutions that automate them. This is a limited view of the role of IT, an inflexible approach to strategic alignment, and an unconstructive definition of "architecture."
Example: Zachman, John A. "A Framework for Information Systems Architecture." *IBM Systems Journal.* Volume 26, number 3. 1987.

111. *[page 245]* More on standards within IT: Standards are not preferred products and models, like the currently recommended brand and model of PC. That's up to the individual entrepreneurs, in this example the PC group. In IT, standards are best defined by APIs and protocols — the way that various technology components plug together — for example, interfaces like the Windows API, or data-interchange protocols.

112. *[page 248]*   In IT, "micro-services architecture" (a.k.a., "service-oriented architecture") designs systems with well-defined interfaces (like doorways), and other systems that want to interact with that system and its data come in through those doorways.

113. *[page 256]*   This case example describes a former CIO of a global pharmaceutical company based in Switzerland.

114. *[page 260]*   Profits from external sales belong to the enterprise, not the selling group. For the rationale, see Chapter 11.

115. *[page 266]*   Sinek, Simon. *Start with Why.* New York, NY: Penguin Group. 2009. Page 228.

116. *[page 267]*   Senge, Peter M. *The Fifth Discipline.* New York, NY: Doubleday. 2006. Page 192.

117. *[page 268]*   "Bill Gates: The Importance of Making Mistakes." *USAir Magazine.* July, 1995. Page 48.

118. *[page 269]*   Dalio views organizations as "machines," supporting the view in this book (Part 3) that organizations are ecosystems made of five systems that leaders can deliberately design. On page 483, Dalio said: "The most common mistake I see people make is dealing with their problems as one-offs rather than using them to diagnose how their machine is working so that they can improve it."
Source: Dalio, Ray. *Principles.* New York, NY: Simon & Schuster. 2017. Pages 452-453.

119. *[page 269]*   An unnamed manager (interviewee) quoted in: Huising, Ruthanne. "Can You Know Too Much About Your Organization?" *Harvard Business Review.* December 4, 2019.

120. *[page 270]*   Beer, Stafford. *The Heart of Enterprise.* Chichester, England: John Wiley & Sons Ltd. 1979.

121. *[page 271]*   Meyer, N. Dean. *RoadMap: how to understand, diagnose, and fix your organization.* Danbury, CT: NDMA Publishing. 1998.

122. *[page 272]*   Dalio said: "You or some other capable mechanic needs to identify those problems and look under the hood of the machine to diagnose their root causes. You or whoever is diagnosing those problems has to understand what the parts of the machine — the

designs and the people — are like and how they work together to produce the outcomes."
Source: Dalio, Ray. *Principles*. New York, NY: Simon & Schuster. 2017. Page 449.

123. *[page 273]* Clear, James. *Atomic Habits*. New York, NY: Avery. 2018. Page 25.

124. *[page 276]* This anecdote came from Noel Thomas, then Vice President of R&D, Dofasco Steel.

125. *[page 285]* Meyer, N. Dean. *Principle-based Organizational Structure: a handbook to help you engineer entrepreneurial thinking and teamwork into organizations of any size.* Danbury, CT: NDMA Publishing. 2017. Chapter 45.

126. *[page 292]* Bridges, William. *Managing Transitions: Making the Most Out of Change.* Boston, MA: Nicholas Brealey Publishing. 1995.

127. *[page 294]* Meyer, N. Dean. *Principle-based Organizational Structure: a handbook to help you engineer entrepreneurial thinking and teamwork into organizations of any size.* Danbury, CT: NDMA Publishing. 2017. Page xxii.

128. *[page 296]* www.FullCost.com

129. *[page 306]* Ben Horowitz defined culture as "a system of behaviors that you hope most people will follow, most of the time."
Source: Horowitz, Ben. *What You Do Is Who You Are: how to create your business culture.* New York, NY: HarperCollins. 2019. Page 17.

130. *[page 307]* This case example came from Jim Hatch, then CIO of Case Tractor.

131. *[page 314]* David Teece, Gary Pisano, and Amy Shuen define an organization's "dynamic capabilities" as "the firm's ability to integrate, build, and reconfigure internal and external competences to address rapidly changing environments." They suggest that competitive advantage rests on "distinctive processes (ways of coordinating and combining)...." They say this "depends in large measure on honing internal technological, organizational, and managerial processes." In a Market Organization, these processes include

walk-throughs (Chapter 8), demand-management (Chapter 11), and treating vendors as part of every group's staff (Appendix 2).

Source: Teece, David J.; Gary Pisano; and Amy Shuen. "Dynamic capabilities and strategic management." *Strategic Management Journal*. Volume 18, Number 7. August, 1997. Pages 509-533.

132. *[page 316]* Drucker, Peter F. *The New Realities*. New York, NY: Harper & Row. 1989. Page 227.

Full quote: "Not to innovate is the single largest reason for the decline of existing organizations. Not to know how to manage is the single largest reason for the failure of new ventures."

133. *[page 320]* This actual experience with an acquisition came from Sergio Paiz, CEO of PDC.

134. *[page 321]* There are three ways a company can utilize a principle-based approach to structure (Chapter 7) to facilitate acquisition integration:

- **Acquisition ready:** By applying the principles to a company, it's ready for future acquisitions with easy mapping of every function in the acquired company.

- **Tuck-in:** To merge an acquisition into the company's existing structure, the Rainbow Analysis identifies lines of business in the acquisition (and in the company if it isn't yet structured by lines of business). Then, the mapping is straightforward and fact-based.

- **Design a new structure together:** If a company has not yet structured by lines of business and an acquisition is large, the structure process (Chapter 27) is an ideal way to merge the two entities — as per the old saying, "When a couple gets married, they shouldn't move into his house or hers; they should build a new home together."

135. *[page 325]* Christensen, Clayton M. *The Innovator's Dilemma: when new technologies cause great firms to fail*. Boston, MA: Harvard Business Review Press. 1997.

136. *[page 326]* O'Reilly and Tushman labeled a separate group for breakthrough innovations, linked to the rest of the organization through senior management, an "ambidextrous organization."

Their research correlated success at both innovation and ongoing business operations with this structural form; that is, it does better than traditional functional organizations (which haven't addressed their root causes), cross-functional teams that may not be funded, and "skunk-works" completely disconnected from the mainstream organization. But, of course, they had no way to compare performance with a Market Organization that has built its structure on principles, its resource-governance processes on market economics, and its culture on entrepreneurship.

Source: O'Reilly II, Charles A.; and Michael L. Tushman. "The Ambidextrous Organization." *Harvard Business Review*. April, 2004.

137. *[page 329]* Drawn from a case study that documents the dysfunctions of a separate innovation group in: Meyer, N. Dean. *Principle-based Organizational Structure: a handbook to help you engineer entrepreneurial thinking and teamwork into organizations of any size.* Danbury, CT: NDMA Publishing. 2017. Chapter 24.

138. *[page 340]* This actual experience with a bank came from Sergio Paiz, CEO of PDC. He said, "Our banks now view us as a model of excellence in leadership. As a result, we're getting better rates and lesser guarantees."

139. *[page 341]* McCormack, Ade G. *Beyond Nine to Five: your career guide for the digital age.* Buckinghamshire, UK: Auridian Press. 2015.

140. *[page 343]* Hawk, Steve. "We Bring Stanford to You." *Stanford Business.* Stanford, CA: Stanford Graduate School of Business. Spring, 2021. Page 38.

141. *[page 343]* Mackey, John; and Rajendra Sisodia. *Conscious Capitalism: liberating the heroic spirit of business.* Boston, MA: Harvard Business Review Press. 2014.

142. *[page 343]* Conscious Capitalism (a.k.a., stakeholder capitalism) has four fundamental tenets:

- **Higher purpose** than just profits. The purpose of an enterprise — its *raison d'être,* and its corporate social responsibility — don't come directly from the Market Organization. What the Market Organization provides is the machine that can achieve that purpose and afford those contributions to the community.

Beyond that, the business-within-a-business paradigm gives everybody an individual higher purpose.

- **Stakeholder orientation** tasks a firm with satisfying the needs of all its stakeholders, including shareholders, employees, customers, suppliers, and the community. This is rooted in the renown Johnson & Johnson "Credo" authored by the company's co-founder, Robert Wood Johnson, in 1943.

  The Market Organization makes an organization a supplier of choice to its customers, and employer of choice to its staff. It treats vendors as part of its team (Appendix 2). And it builds value for shareholders.

- **Conscious leadership** builds a focus on purpose and stake-holders throughout the organization.

  The Market Organization gives Conscious Leaders the mechanics to align everybody with the company's value-creating goals, e.g., walk-throughs, the internal economy, and Coordinator functions.

- **Conscious culture** builds into the organization the practices that support purpose and stakeholders. Culture (Chapter 12) is one of the five organizational systems that are deliberately designed. Ethics, integrity (trust), empowerment, teamwork, cooperation, customer focus, interpersonal relations are all Themes within culture.

  Of course, the Market Organization addresses all five organizational systems (Figure 32), not just culture.

Conscious Capitalism is a philosophy and a goal. The Market Organization provides pragmatic tools to implement it.

143. *[page 344]* Block, Peter. *Stewardship: choosing service over self-interest.* San Francisco, CA: Berrett-Koehler Publishers. 1993. Page 48.

144. *[page 344]* Peters, Thomas J. *The Excellence Dividend.* New York, NY: Vintage Books. 2018. Pages xvi-xvii.

145. *[page 346]* Senge, Peter M. *The Fifth Discipline.* New York, NY: Doubleday. 2006. Page 42.

146. *[page 347]* Dalio, Ray. *Principles.* New York, NY: Simon & Schuster. 2017. Page 451.

147. *[page 348]*   McChrystal, Stanley. *Team of Teams*. New York, NY: Penguin Publishing Group. 2015. Page 226.

148. *[page 348]*   Dalio stressed the importance of spending time with one's staff: "The greatest influence you can have over intelligent people — and the greatest influence they will have on you — comes from constantly getting in sync about what is true and what is best so that you all want the same things."
Source: Dalio, Ray. *Principles*. New York, NY: Simon & Schuster. 2017. Page 466.

149. *[page 349]*   Senge, Peter M. *The Fifth Discipline*. New York: Doubleday. 2006. Page 328.

150. *[page 350]*   Peter Senge said: "In a learning organization, leaders... require new skills: the ability to build shared vision, to bring to the surface and challenge prevailing mental models, and to foster more systemic patterns of thinking."
Source: Senge, Peter M. "The Leader's New Work: Building Learning Organizations." *Sloan Management Review*. Boston, MA: MIT Sloan School of Management. Fall, 1990. Pages 7-23.

151. *[page 350]*   Senge, Peter M. *The Fifth Discipline*. New York, NY: Doubleday. 2006. Page 328.

152. *[page 350]*   More of this famous quote from Peter Drucker:

"Bucky Fuller and Marshall McLuhan exemplify to me the importance of being single-minded. The single-minded ones, the monomaniacs, are the only true achievers. The rest, the ones like me, may have more fun; but they fritter themselves away. The Fullers and the McLuhans carry out a 'mission', the rest of us have 'interests'. Whenever anything is being accomplished, it is being done, I have learned, by a monomaniac with a mission.

"The monomaniac is unlikely to succeed. Most leave only their bleached bones in the roadless dessert. But the rest of us, with multiple interests instead of one single mission, are certain to fail and to have no impact at all."

Source: Drucker, Peter F. *Adventures of a Bystander*. New York, NY: Harper Row. 1978. Page 255.

153. *[page 357]*   Meyer, N. Dean. *Outsourcing: how to make vendors work for your shareholders.* Danbury, CT: NDMA Publishing. 1999.

154. *[page 358]*   Economist Ronald Coase hypothesized that entrepreneurs form organizations to reduce the transactions costs inherent in outsourcing (procurement, legal contracting, taxes on transactions, government interventions such as quotas and rationing, and the difficulty of specifying deliverables in long-term, non-commodity contracts).

Nonetheless, some people prefer vendors over internal support staff, even if they're more expensive, because they're more customer focused and responsive. The easier it is to do business with internal support staff, the lower the internal transactions costs and the less the incentives for outsourcing.

Source: Coase, Ronald H. "The Nature of the Firm." Blackwell Publishing: *Economica.* Volume 4, number 16. November, 1937. Pages 386-405.

155. *[page 358]*   A Market Organization makes internal service providers easy to do business with. As economist Oliver Williamson describes, reduced internal transactions costs make outsourcing less cost-effective.

Source: Williamson, Oliver E. *Markets and Hierarchies: analysis and antitrust implications.* New York, NY: Free Press. 1975.

156. *[page 376]*   Meyer, N. Dean. <u>*Culture In Action* Reference Library</u>. Available under license from N. Dean Meyer and Associates Inc. See: www.ndma.com/culture

157. *[page 377]*   The full set of meeting behaviors can be found in: Meyer N. Dean. *Meyer's Rules of Order: how to hold highly productive business meetings.* Danbury, CT: NDMA Publishing. 2001.

158. *[page 378]*   George S. Patton is widely attributed as saying, "Lead me, follow me, or get out of my way."

Later, Scott McNealy said, "Agree and commit, disagree and commit, or get out of the way."

Source: Southwick, Karen. *High Noon: the inside story of Scott*

McNealy and the rise of Sun Microsystems. John Wiley & Sons, Inc. 1999. Page 39.

This quote is also attributed to Thomas Paine, without evidence. It may, in fact, have originated in an early motorcycle magazine cartoon: "PUSH! If you can't push, PULL — if you [can't] pull, please get out of the way."

Source: *Motorcycle Illustrated.* Volume 4, number 17. June, 1909. (Attribution by: *Dictionary of Modern Proverbs.* New Haven, CT: Yale University Press. 2012. Page 273.)

159. *[page 389]* Meyer, N. Dean and Mary E. Boone. *The Information Edge.* Danbury, CT: NDMA Publishing. 1987, 1995. Chapter 13.

160. *[page 389]* Dixon, Matthew; and Brent Adamson. *The Challenger Sale: taking control of the customer conversation.* New York, NY: Portfolio, Penguin Group. 2011.

161. *[page 392]* The term "critical success factors" was coined by: Rockart, John F. "Chief executives define their own data needs." *Harvard Business Review.* March, 1979. Pages 81-93.

162. *[page 392]* Meyer, N. Dean and Mary E. Boone. *The Information Edge.* Danbury, CT: NDMA Publishing. 1987, 1995. Page 316.

163. *[page 394]* I'm grateful to Jonathan Maurer for his help with Chapter 21 and Appendix 7.

ACKNOWLEDGEMENTS

My thanks to the many leaders who, over past decades, worked with me to test and refine the vision and processes presented in this book.

A special thanks to my friend and colleague, Preston Simons, for the Foreword — the story of his experiences implementing a Market Organization. Also, special thanks to another friend and colleague, Sergio Paiz, for his many quotes and case examples. I've learned a lot from both of them.

Also, my sincere thanks to those who gave me input to, and feedback on, the manuscript, especially:

Faruq Ahmad, a venture capitalist with lots of heart

Luke Anderson, who treats internal Finance as a business

Janma Bardi, founder of a successful tech venture

Mary Boone, guru in tech-enabled human communications

Kirk Botula, venture CEO and organization builder

Romero Castillo, spanning business and organizational strategies

August Ceradini, entrepreneur and small-business roundtable facilitator

Wes Clelland, socially conscious real-estate investor

Leo De La Fuente, transformational operating executive

Fred Dewey, humanistic startup and turnaround CEO

Troy DuMoulin, preeminent service-management (ITIL) guru

Paul Edmisten, CIO with a passion for operational excellence

Mark Eustis, health care CEO with a vision

Remy Evard, brilliant tech leader in the scientific community

Yomi Famurewa, astute IT industry observer and coach to CIOs

Mike Fulton, a true believer in systemic innovation

Lee Gerney, a humble leader who sincerely seeks excellence

Rick Hartnack, seasoned financial-services Board chairman

Barbara Healy, masterful and graceful executive coach

Jack Healy, wise and caring non-profit CEO

Max Henry, experienced and kind coach to entrepreneurs

Victor Jerez, master of strategy and acquisitions

Peter G. W. Keen, one of the best professors I've known

Javier Livas, practical cybernetician and systems thinker

Huron Low, young entrepreneur and already an organizational builder

Lee Marder, a source of love and inspiration my entire life

Don Martin, CIO, former NASA engineer, and entrepreneurial spirit

Jonathan Maurer, enlightened and trusted CISO

Stanley McChrystal, insightful, reflective, and brave leader

Ade McCormack, guru on what people want from work

Steve Monaghan, entrepreneurial leader in government

Sam Prochazka, a successful CEO who models life-long learning

Susan Rho, my other half who made writing this book possible

Gary Rietz, transformational mid-cap CIO

Geoff Routledge, a bridge between business and technology

Jess Rovello, a very successful, culture-conscious tech CEO

Mark Schultze, from internal IT to technology entrepreneur

Charlie Shalvoy, serial entrepreneur and tech-ventures CEO

Dave Shepherd, both an entrepreneur and an organizational leader

Maxwell H. Sims, brain scientist and entrepreneur

Don Tapscott, insightful futurist, author, and blockchain guru

Stuart Ward, Agile guru who lives the Market Organization

Derek Weber, high-energy entrepreneur and inquisitive mind

Carman Wenkoff, a caring, transformational CIO

Nick Wilczek, aspirational and enthusiastic government leader

Stu Winby, organizational performance guru to CEOs

Ron Yarwood, ITIL and service-management practitioner

Roger Young, high-energy leadership development and transitions expert

Juan Pablo Zelaya, professor and innovative wellness entrepreneur

Julio Zelaya, respected LatAm organizational consultant

INDEX OF REFERENCES
(People I Cite)

INDEX OF TOPICS

BOOK SUMMARY

NAVIGATION AID: If you're interested in better understanding any point, you'll see page references back into the book.

PART 1: My Next Career Adventure

1: My Next Adventure: Build a Legacy

Even C-level executives can get worn down by the day-to-day grind of the job. *[page 6]* The problem is, they become "cogs in the machine" and bottlenecks in the organization. *[page 7]*

A clue to the way out of this trap comes from Frederick the Great. He was a great military (read "business") strategist, but he didn't leave behind an army that could succeed without him at the helm. *[page 8]*

Truly great leaders leave a lasting legacy of organizations that can succeed long after they've moved on. A focus on *organizational transformation* can lift executives out of the grind, dramatically improve organizational performance, and provide a fascinating career adventure. *[page 9]*

2: If You Don't Know Where You're Going...

...any road will do. Transformations are founded on a clear definition of the end-state — a blueprint of the future organization you intend to build. *[page 12]*

This kind of vision is not a business goal (like revenue growth), or a strategy (like acquisitions or digital business). It describes an organization that can invent and deliver a continual stream of strategies to meet ever-evolving goals. *[page 13]*

To inspire, a vision must be something ambitious — a real "stretch assignment." It should be compelling and of extraordinary value. It's not about "best practices"; it's about *ideal* practices. *[page 13]*

To serve as a blueprint, a vision must be clear and comprehensive. It's more than a slogan or vague promise. It's a detailed description of how the end-state organization will work. *[page 13, see also 264]*

This book imagines a visionary organization. *[page 14]* Studying this vision can help you craft and communicate your own vision, the first step in a transformation journey. *[page 16]*

PART 2: Foundations

3: The Lay of the Land at this Company

Some businesses sell off-the-shelf products and services, and others sell custom solutions (like engineering and professional-services businesses). The fictitious company described in this book does both. *[page 20]*

Multi-product and multi-geography companies (like the one in this book) have tremendous opportunities for synergies, but only if they are fully integrated (not self-sufficient business units for each product or country). *[page 22, see also 318]*

When companies consume their own products, full integration means that the same groups that serve external customers also serve internal customers. There are many benefits to "eating your own dog food" (listed). *[page 23]*

4: The Decision to Invest in Transformation

Does your organization really need a transformation? If you have any doubts, common symptoms which indicate the need are listed. *[page 25]*

Piecemeal, evolutionary changes are not the best way to solve myriad symptoms rooted in systemic problems. To really move the needle, you need a comprehensive vision and plan (which is then implemented step by step). *[page 26]*

Organizational transformations should *not* be driven by current business strategies. In a volatile world, organizations must rapidly reconfigure themselves to execute ever-changing strategies. Beyond that, organizations must be designed to *discover* tomorrow's strategies. *Organizational* strategy comes before business strategy. *[page 28]*

5: Coherence Coming from an Underlying Paradigm: Every Group is a Business Within a Business

The many detailed statements that make up a comprehensive vision must all work together as a coherent system. Thus, before laying out a vision, you need an underlying paradigm that serves as your well-spring, the foundation on which all the pieces of your vision are based. The business-within-a-business paradigm can be that well-spring. *[page 33]*

To be clear, the business-within-a-business paradigm is *not* outsourcing, chargebacks, profit centers, free reign, or passive order-takers. *[page 34]* It simply means that everyone thinks and acts like an entrepreneur running a small business. Staff don't expect to take home the profits, but they know they're there to serve customers, external and internal. *The organization is a network of entrepreneurs — a "Market Organization."* *[page 35]*

Objection 1: Skeptics fear that a Market Organization distances support staff from their internal customers. They advocate the opposite — declaring everybody "partners in the business." But in practice, this confuses authorities and accountabilities, ultimately undermines good partnerships, and discourages initiative. *[page 36]*

Objection 2: Some view only externally facing functions as businesses. In a Market Organization, *every* business within a business is valued. Some serve external customers; some internal; many serve both. But all are important. There are no "second-class citizens." *[page 38]*

Objection 3: Not everybody is a natural entrepreneur. But through a transformation process, most people can learn to think and act like internal entrepreneurs. *[page 38]*

Since everybody runs a business within a business, *everybody* is a "product manager" for their own products and services. *[page 40]* Product managers are responsible for lines of business (not just marketing a product). They sell products and services, and buy all the help they need from throughout the enterprise. All the same behaviors of customer focus, entrepreneurship, teamwork, and accountability for results apply equally to all, regardless of whether their customers are external or internal. *[page 40]*

In a Market Organization, strategic thinking is not limited to senior executives. Everyone is responsible for the future of their business. Everyone develops their strategies for their business, in coordination with their peers throughout the organization. They convert those strategies to tactics, and drive those initiatives. *[pages 41, 355]*

There are many benefits of the business-within-a-business paradigm, including: customer focus, accountability for results, quality, efficiency and cost control, flexibility and agility, innovation, teamwork, appropriate use of vendors, safety, judicious risk-taking, strategic alignment, and empowerment. *[page 42]*

The business-within-a-business paradigm can be your North Star to help you sift the good management ideas from the bad, and to guide you in crafting your vision. *[page 44]*

6: The Golden Rule: Empowerment, and What it Really Means

A core principle driving every aspect of the vision in this book is *empowerment.* *[page 46]* Its definition is straightforward: Authorities and accountabilities match. *[page 47]*

Critical to empowerment is how you ask people for things (down, up, or sideways): Ask for results, not tasks. Additionally, the requestor must ensure that the supplier has all the resources, information, and decision authorities needed to do the job. *[pages 49, 50]* Leaders can still offer coaching without disempowering their staff. *[page 51]*

Can you empower less capable people? Yes. Just empower them in smaller chunks. *[page 52]*

Work-from-home programs provide access to qualified staff, and can be very productive work environments. In an empowered organization, people are managed by their results. That makes work-from-home easier to manage. Freelance workers are also easier to manage. *[page 52]*

Empowerment doesn't mean that staff can choose to work on any project that interests them. Leaders need to be able to align resources with strategies. Staff are empowered to *serve their customers* as they see fit (no different from the empowerment of small-business owners). What people really want is respect, an energized and high-performing culture, control over their destiny, and the knowledge that they're making a difference in the world. *[page 54]*

In an empowered organization, performance management focuses on metrics of results, not effort (on outputs, not inputs). *[page 54]*

Empowerment is not about discarding the organizational hierarchy. Hierarchy is a good way to lay out domains. And bosses are good for communicating and coordinating with peers, making hiring decisions, developing and inspiring staff, performance management, coordinating shared decisions within a group, and keeping upper management informed. *[page 55]* But in an empowered organization, managers don't "command and control." Managers' duties are listed. *[page 55, see also 348]*

PART 3: Organizational Operating Model

7: Organization Chart

Organizational structure is the root cause of many common symptoms, including: confused accountabilities, redundant efforts, people set up to fail doing too many things at once, poor cross-boundary teamwork, lack of customer focus, slow pace of innovation, lack of entrepreneurial initiative, and low morale. *[page 61]*

Organizational structure is an engineering science, with firm principles and clear frameworks. *[page 62]* Seven principles of structure are listed. *[page 62]*

The Golden Rule (empowerment) is the first Principle. No group is chartered to disempower another group. *[page 63, see also 47]*

Specialization (the first half of Principle 2) improves performance in many ways (listed). Specialists are T-shaped people; they know a little about many things so as to be able to team; and they bring real depth to one field of study (their bottom-of-the-T). *[page 64]*

Specialization requires great cross-boundary teamwork (the second half of Principle 2). Without teamwork, groups revert into self-sufficient "silos" of generalists, regardless of the organization chart. *[page 66]*

It takes more than a few words in a box to define clear boundaries, and ensure there are no gaps (missing lines of business) or overlaps (internal competition). Per Principle 3, "domains" are precisely worded boundaries defining what each group sells. *[page 67]*

As lines of business are subdivided at the next level of the organization chart, the basis for substructure should exactly match what that line of business is supposed to be good at (Principle 4). For example, Sales is supposed to be expert at knowing customers; so the appropriate substructure is by client (market segment), not product line. *[page 67]*

Lines of business are not combined in ways that create conflicts of interests (Principle 5). (Five conflicts of interests are listed.) *[page 69]*

Per Principle 6, similar lines of business are clustered under a common boss to gain professional synergies (listed). *[pages 71, 72]*

Principle 7 is key. In a Market Organization, every group is defined as a business within a business. *[page 71]* (A framework of all the types of businesses within organizations is provided. *[page 73]*)

These principles make an open, participative restructuring process safe by providing a basis for fact-based discussions (rather than opinions, politics, and emotions). *[page 73]*

8: Cross-boundary Teamwork: Walk-throughs

Specialization requires cross-boundary teamwork. *[page 77]* "High-performance teamwork" is when each project team includes just the right specialists (from anywhere in the organization); at just the right time (as contributions are needed, not fixed teams for the whole project); with a common purpose, but also with clear individual accountabilities; and a clear chain of command within each team (one person who's accountable for the whole project, and who leads and coordinates the team and resolves any disputes). *[page 76]*

High-performance teamwork is built on a process called *walk-throughs*. Teams form by identifying the "prime contractor" for a project; then, that group requests the subcontracts (deliverables) needed from other groups. *[page 78, see also 163]*

Walk-throughs are done for every project and service. They're facilitated by the Organizational Effectiveness group, and then given to the PMO to turn into detailed project plans. *[page 81]*

A Market Organization is both stable and dynamic. A hierarchical organization chart ensures that all the needed specialists are available, and gives everybody a home where they can cultivate their specialized competencies. Then, with walk-throughs, teamwork flows freely across that hierarchy as specialists are dynamically combined on teams as needs warrant. *[page 81]*

9: Resource Governance: Internal Market Economics

Teamwork depends on aligned priorities. If one group's highest priority is another's lowest, teamwork isn't going to work. *[page 83]*

The "internal economy" comprise all the resource-governance processes which manage time, money, and assets. Designing them around principles of *market economics* improves their effectiveness, and eliminates unnecessary bureaucracy. *[page 83]*

Objectives of the internal economy include: link funding (budgets) to business needs and investment opportunities; align priorities with enterprise strategies; permit reinvestment in the sustainability of every internal business; fund infrastructure and innovation investments; and benchmark costs against the market. *[page 85]*

An internal economy comprises three subsystems: planning and budgeting, demand management (priority setting), and accounting. *[page 86]*

10: Investment-based Budgeting

Since organizations are viewed as businesses within a business, budgets are provided *not* to cover costs, but rather as money put on deposit with a supplier to buy its products (projects) and services in the coming year (pre-paid revenues). *[page 88]*

"Investment-based budgets" forecast the costs of the products and services each group plans to deliver in the coming year (not just what it plans to spend). *[page 89, see also 235, 295]* In it, there's a cost model that assigns all costs (including indirect) to the products and services each group sells. It's like activity-based costing, but more advanced. *[page 89]*

An investment-based budget sorts deliverables into categories like keep-the-lights-on services, maintenance of current assets, deferred mainte-nance, growth, safety and security, strategic projects, innovation projects, etc. During budget negotiations, you can drill down into any category and see decisionable projects and services. *[page 90]*

Investment-based budgeting ensures that projects are fully funded, including the costs of all the groups in the organization that will be involved (the prime contractor and all the subcontractors). This way, there are no impediments to teamwork or strategy execution. *[page 91]*

Innovation is funded in two ways. Ongoing innovation is built into rates and managed within each group. Major initiatives are funded as line-items in an investment-based budget. *[page 91]*

Note that budget pressures ("do more with less") are not an appropriate way to seek cost efficiencies. That just forces executives to make promises they can't keep. *[page 93]* In a Market Organization, leaders pursue efficiencies all the time, not just once a year during budget negotiations (reasons described). *[page 93]*

If a spending cut (downsizing) is needed, leaders start by deciding which deliverables to cut (lower-payoff projects and services, or initiatives the company can no longer afford — rows in an investment-based budget). Then, costs for just those deliverables are cut. This is far more effective than across-the-board cuts which cripple an organization's ability to produce anything, even the important deliverables. *[page 94]*

The cost model imbedded in an investment-based budget also calculates cost-based rates (unit costs), useful for pricing new projects during the year, and for benchmarking costs against vendors (a metric). *[page 95]*

11: Demand Management (Priority Setting)

Once budgets are set, strategies inevitably change as new problems and opportunities arise. A process is needed to adjust priorities dynamically, while still limiting demand to available resources. *[page 97]*

Assigning support groups to internal customers (as in a matrix or decentralization) allows internal customers to control the priorities of internal service providers. But using structure to address internal-economy challenges causes many other problems (described). *[page 98, see also 141]*

A better approach is to assign "checkbooks" (created by an organization's budget) to internal customers. Internal customers decide what checks to write (which projects and services to fund). This is not just a steering committee that prioritizes major projects. It manages an investment portfolio. *[page 99]*

Empowering internal customers to decide support groups' priorities improves returns on investments, aligns staff with enterprise strategies, and balances supply and demand (manages expectations). *[page 100]* It delivers virtually all the benefits of internal chargebacks, without the risks and administrative costs. *[page 100]*

Projects can be funded either by asking a purser to approve it (and de-prioritize something else). Or, customers can transfer money from their own budgets to an internal supplier, who can use it to expand capacity via contractors and vendors. Sometimes, major initiatives are given incremental enterprise funding. *[page 101]*

Checkbooks which represent internal support groups' budgets are assigned to individual business units, and to consortia for shared needs. Another checkbook funds enterprise initiatives and corporate-good services. And the checkbook for investments in infrastructure and innovation are managed by each group. *[page 103, see also 409 (endnote 63)]*

Investment-based budgets determine how much to put in each checkbook and what things cost. That's why it's prerequisite to setting up this demand-management process. *[page 103]*

Often, myriad committees think they can approve projects, even though they don't have any spending authorities. In a Market Organization, some are "pursers" with checkbooks and the power to approve projects. The rest simply make recommendations; they can say no to projects, but they can't say yes because they don't have a checkbook with which to fund projects. *[page 103]*

Internal entrepreneurs are managed to break-even P&Ls, not budget variances. Thus, if their customers want to spend more on a high-value product or service (and provide the money to cover its full cost), the supplier's revenues increase so there's no "negative variance" to be explained. *[page 105]*

Costs of capital are controlled by assessing every P&L with an interest charge for capital employed. Requests for capital are evaluated as a bank would, based on risks and returns. *[page 106]*

CFO impacts: A market-based internal economy focuses the CFO on working with business leaders to optimize returns, rather than simply demanding spending limits that cause others to fail. *[page 108]* Cost accounting measures actual consumption, rather than allocations based on high-level formulas. *[page 109]*

The profits from external sales belong to the enterprise, not the product managers. This way, profits can be reinvested where they're most needed, not necessarily in the group that generated them. And this way, there's no advantage to selling externally (at a profit) and ignoring one's internal customers (where sales are at break-even). *[page 110]*

12: Culture

You can't expect staff to behave well if you haven't defined what "well" means. Culture change addresses the problems of both dysfunctional behaviors and missing behaviors. (Examples are given.) *[page 112]*

Culture is defined as "the way we all work around here." It encompasses both (1) values/attitudes/feelings, and (2) behaviors. They're interlinked; a change in either drives change in the other. *[page 114]* It's easier and faster to implement changes in behaviors than in values (consistent with modern learning theory). A major culture change can be accomplished in less than a year with a behavioral approach. *[page 115]*

To define a culture, there are 13 Themes (listed). Under each are a page or two of specific, actionable behavioral principles. *[pages 116, 376]*

The results of a culture transformation are far-reaching (described). *[page 117]* A clearly defined culture can even help attract top talent. *[page 118]*

13: Metrics

Metrics address two problems: (1) If people are failing and don't know it, performance metrics give them the incentive to improve. (2) Dashboards provide the real-time data people need to perform. *[page 119]*

Common pitfalls in metrics: While people should be given feedback continually, performance appraisals should be annual so that people are willing to take on longer-term projects. Staff should never be graded on a curve, forcing managers to rate some people low even if they are high performers; that undermines mutual support. And performance metrics should focus only on results, not tasks. *[page 119]*

Only measure people on what they can control. Shared metrics can have unintended consequences (described). In an aligned organization, there should be no need for shared metrics since one's personal success is tied to serving customers (internal and external), and hence to teamwork and contributions to the enterprise. *[page 121]*

It's more important that performance metrics are comprehensive than precise, so that people don't suboptimize a subset of their goals. For example, a few OKRs would not suffice. Similarly, metrics should include long-term value as well as short-term results. To be comprehensive, metrics may be qualitative as well as quantitative. *[page 123]* Examples of entrepreneurial metrics are listed. *[page 124]*

Dashboards help people achieve results. And while performance metrics should focus on results, for dashboards, it's fine to measure processes and tasks (in advance of results) if that's helpful to people. *[page 125]*

14: Reflections on Systemic Governance

"Governance" means *all* the processes by which we coordinate and control our resources and actions (not just oversight). *[page 127]*

Governance takes on a different form in a Market Organization. Instead of oversight through committees and support functions, controls are imbedded in the organizational ecosystem. *[page 127]* Systemic controls are less expensive and more effective than human oversight. *[page 128]*

Committees often create unnecessary bureaucracy under the guise of governance. In the Market Organization, there are a limited number of legitimate roles for committees (described). *[pages 129, 381]*

Coordination is not achieved by top-down command-and-control, or by executives rolling out strategies, setting objectives, and controlling budgets. These methods are not very effective at aligning large organizations, particularly when success demands agility. *[page 130]* Instead, like the national economy as a whole, internal market economics coordinates independent businesses with common goals and strategies. *[page 131]*

PART 4: Internal Lines of Business, and How They Work

15: Sales and Marketing: Both External and Internal

Obviously, most businesses need Sales functions in some form. But so do internal service providers like IT. A Business Relationship Management (BRM) function is, essentially, a sales force for a business within a business. *[page 134]* And whether internal or external, the job of Sales is much the same: It's to build highly effective relationships and deliver strategic value to customers. *[page 135]*

In internal service providers like IT, it's not appropriate to expect senior leaders of other functions to fulfill the Sales job. They don't have the time to maintain contacts with customers, invest in partnerships, study the methods of Sales, and proactively discover opportunities. *[page 137]*

Furthermore, to find high-payoff opportunities, Sales must be *business-driven and unbiased* with regard to their organization's products and services (not product-driven). Senior leaders who are dedicated to subsets of your product line cannot be unbiased. *[page 137]*

Business-driven selling helps customers diagnose their business needs, rather than pushing specific products (no "solution in search of a problem"). *[page 138]*

Sales staff have a unique expertise. They gain a deep understanding of customers and their businesses. And they study the *linkage* between an organization's products/services and customers' businesses (your value propositions). *[page 139]*

Sales staff are not accountable for project delivery — i.e., for delivering other groups' products and services. *[page 140]*

For standard (off-the-shelf) products and services, sales are based on value and relationships. But for multi-product and custom solutions, the key to selling is to maximize your value to the customer with just the right subset of your products and services. The best approach is counselor selling (which is really a form of consulting). *[page 142]*

To find strategic opportunities, Sales focuses on key customers and what's unique about them (not what everybody has in common), because everybody has a unique role in their enterprise's strategies. *[page 144]* Furthermore, to be strategic, Sales looks for well-focused opportunities to address a specific business challenge. (They don't try to identify everything that a customer might need.) *[page 145]*

An essential skill for both internal and external Sales is a method to discover strategic opportunities. The result is a clear logical path from a customer's most pressing business deliverable, to a critical success factor, to a needed capability, to the definition of a specific solution. *[pages 146, 389]*

This opportunity-discovery process may involve experts in clients' professions and processes, termed "Function Sales." Examples in IT include a Chief Digital Officer and Chief Data Officer. *[pages 147, 336, 411 (endnote 80)]* Once an opportunity is defined, business analysts may help develop requests for proposals or detailed requirements. *[page 148]*

For internal service providers, Sales facilitates cross-business-unit synergies by bringing customers with common needs together into consortia. *[page 149]*

The boundary between Sales and Engineering is straightforward: Sales does the What; Engineering does the How. As such, Sales staff (including business analysts) should not do high-level designs (an engineering task). *[page 150]*

Business cases (to help customers get funding for opportunities) are customers' responsibility.   Sales can help them quantify expected benefits (including so-called "intangible" strategic value). *[page 151]* A benefits estimation method creates a path of logic from the solution, to how it will change the business, to the value of that change. *[page 152]*

It's up to customers to make use of the solutions and realize their benefits.   Sales can help by defining the business changes customers need to make in order to gain value from the solution. *[page 152]*

Account Sales are assigned to key accounts (or in internal service providers, to business units and the key executives in them).   There's also a role for Retail Sales to serve all other customers; this includes on-demand inquiries (inside sales) and eCommerce. *[page 154]*

In the "hunters/farmers" sales distinction (where farmers are "customer success" coordinators), the farmers are considered a service to Account Sales.   That way, Account Representatives retain full accountability for (and control of) their accounts. *[page 154]*

Sales is a business within a business, with a catalog of services (listed). *[page 155]*

Marketing is also of value to customers.   It builds awareness of the potential benefits of your products and services.   Marketing is important for internal service providers as well as companies. *[page 156]*

Sales Support specializes in selling methods and tools.   It provides sales training, sales materials, CRM and other tools, lead generation, metrics and analyses, proposal writers, and requirements writers. *[pages 157, 158]*

Relationship- and counselor-selling require different metrics and compensation programs.   Commissions, which encourage a short-term focus on revenues, are just one part of the plan.   Incentives are also based on factors that lead to a long-term stream of revenues. *[page 158]*

16: Engineering: How Projects Are Delivered

Engineers sell custom solutions.   (Standard, off-the-shelf products and services are an Operations function.) *[page 160, see also 186]*

Engineering domains can be split between those which are purpose-specific, and generic components, disciplines, and infrastructure. *[page 161]*

> In IT, "purpose specific" means applications which are either data-object-specific or which present multi-object data to specific business professions or processes. *[page 413 (endnote 86)]*

Engineering focuses on innovation, quality in design, project delivery, integrating vendor products and services, and supporting what it sells. *[page 162]*

Teamwork among engineering domains is essential, because many different competencies are needed on project teams. Walk-throughs are done at the start of every project. *[page 163, see also 78]*

The key to good project estimates and fiscal control is "phase-gating." Once requirements are defined (by Sales), the next step is a "solution alternatives study" which analyzes one or more alternative approaches to fulfilling customers' requirements. After that's done, engineers can provide realistic estimates of the solution-implementation phase. *[page 165]*

> The solutions alternatives study is a critical step that cannot be skipped. It provides the information needed to make an informed decision (such as technical scope, costs, risks, pros and cons). *[page 168]* Some customers may be in a rush to start and want to skip this phase. They need to understand that doing so will ultimately slow delivery of the final results and cause more problems later. *[page 169]*

> Design alternatives which require new operational services or technologies must be approved by Operations. *[page 170]*

In the spirit of customer focus, engineers do not make recommendations. Instead, they help customers choose from among alternatives based on *customers'* values, not their own. *[page 172]*

Engineering quality means professionalism in design, not price point. (Attributes of product quality are listed.) *[page 173]* Quality includes "ripple chasing" when changes in one product cause problems in other products; fixing ripples is not a separate project. *[page 173, see also 248]*

The final step is a smooth transition into operations. This starts at the beginning of the implementation phase (not the end). *[page 175]*

Sometimes, customers want to buy from a competitor (internally, that means directly from a vendor) and then expect your engineers to support what they've bought. It's best to offer that support (no "sour grapes") but define very specific and clear support contracts. *[page 176]*

Beyond design and development projects, engineers are responsible for repairing what they've sold; they may use field technicians to leverage their time for routine repairs. Engineers also offer services such as production support, incident diagnosis, repairs, enhancements, capacity studies, configuration tuning, and product road-maps.
[page 177, see also 199, 212]

17: Operations: Ongoing Services and Off-the-Shelf Products

Operations functions produce a continuous flow of identical things, like water from the tap. *[page 179]*

It's dysfunctional to treat Operations as a dumping ground for whatever Engineering comes up with. If you do, you cannot hold them account-able for reliable operations. *[page 180]*

Operations is an entrepreneurial business, with three broad domains: (1) manufacturing and logistics; (2) services based on ownership of assets (infrastructure); and (3) product management for off-the-shelf products. *[page 182]*

> Operations can be a steward for products that customers bought from the organization, providing a single point of contact for all the operational services that support those customer-owned products. (In IT, this is "applications hosting.") *[page 183]*

Operations has a bias toward stability, but it can (and must) innovate. It's proactive in offering new services, but only when there's a sufficient market and the underlying technologies are reliable. *[page 184]*

Throughout Operations, service quality is measured by safety, availabil-ity, reliability, and agreed levels of performance. *[page 185]*

Contrary to conventional wisdom, Operations (not Marketing) is the best place to put product management of off-the-shelf products. *[page 186]*

Operations should be involved early in engineering projects so that it's ready when the product is ready for deployment. *[page 187]*

Capacity planning is done at the enterprise level, not project-by-project or product-by-product. *[page 188]*

Operations professionals are skilled in service management, and responsible for all that entails (listed). *[pages 189, 190]*

18: Customer Service: How Incidents are Managed

There are a variety of operational services produced by people rather than assets. Examples include customer service, field technicians, project facilitation (PMO), access administration, data administration, and repository administration. *[page 191]*

The primary product of Customer Service is "support": answers to questions about operating your products, and management of "incidents" such as product defects and service problems. *[page 192]*

Customer Service does not sell repairs (solution design changes to address defects); engineers do. Customer Service can resolve many incidents without repairs. If it cannot, it "brokers" repair contracts with the appropriate engineering group, and closes the ticket. (It does not track the backlog of engineering requests.) *[page 193]*

Asset owners are the real customers for support (not callers). They either use the asset themselves, like their PCs; or they use the asset to provide a service to *their* customers, in which case their service comes with support. Asset owners decide the level of service. *[page 196]*

First, Customer Service tries to resolve the incident based on instructions in its knowledge-base. If its knowledge-base is insufficient, it doesn't try to guess; it engages engineers to help. *[page 196]*

The knowledge-base is key. Engineers add to it with each new solution. Customer Service adds to it as they learn from incident resolutions. *[page 197]* The knowledge-base can also permit web-based self-help. *[page 198]*

If it cannot resolve the incident based on the knowledge-base, Customer Service doesn't "hand off" tickets. It owns tickets cradle-to-grave, and subcontracts for help from engineers as needed. *[page 198]*

If engineers are unresponsive, Customer Service should not establish a "second-level support" group of quasi-engineers. Instead, it should address the root causes of a lack of cooperation. *[page 199]*

Customer Service may have level-two customer support groups for a different reason. They are customer service professionals (not junior engineers) who specialize in certain types of problems (not products or technologies). *[page 202]*

For internal service providers, it may be a challenge to wean customers off calling their favorite engineer, and instead call Customer Service. A list of reasons why it's better for customers to call Customer Service first can be helpful (included). *[page 203]*

Another service is problem management data, used to identify patterns in incidents that suggest ways to reduce future incidents. *[page 204]*

Customer Service may also take orders (service requests) on behalf of the organization. They are not responsible for service delivery; this is just an order-processing function. *[page 205]*

Customer Service may also help customers update their account information. This requires excellence in authenticating callers. *[page 207]*

Customer Service staff should be evaluated by customer satisfaction, not productivity. *[page 207]* There are a number of workforce management practices that improve productivity (discussed). *[page 208]*

19: Field Technicians: How to Cover Remote Locations

For internal service providers, staff in remote locations should not be considered full-service suppliers of the organization's services. Doing so creates many problems (listed). *[page 210]*

Instead, headquarters experts are accountable for providing their products and services everywhere, and use remote staff as "eyes and hands in the field." *[page 212]* This delivers both local presence and all the expertise of headquarters specialists. It solves all the problems of "renegade" remote staff. *[page 214]* It also opens better career paths for remote staff. *[page 215]*

Large remote locations may include more than field technicians. Staff may report to different groups in headquarters, according to their specialties. Site Coordinators may be appointed to help the various headquarters bosses with local supervisory duties. *[page 216]*

20: Project Management Office: Roles Within Project Teams

A Project Management Office (PMO) is expert in project-management methods and tools. *[page 218]* As such, it cannot "manage" projects in the sense of being accountable for other groups' project deliverables. Instead, it sells project planning and support services to those who are accountable for the delivery of their own products and services. *[page 218]*

Many functions, not just engineering, manage projects and can utilize a PMO. *[page 219]*

A PMO owns and provides others access to project- and portfolio-management (PPM) software. It helps managers track and assign their resources. It also owns the request-management system, and facilitates project intake and purser committees. *[page 219]*

A PMO can also manage a project dashboard for the organization. To make that work, the executive must require project status reports from everybody. The PMO provides a communications channel; but everybody is accountable for their own data within the dashboard. *[page 220]*

21: Compliance: The Example of Information Security

Information security is a critical issue for every CIO, CEO, and Board. *[page 222]*

If you hold your Chief Information Security Officer (CISO) *accountable* for security, they will require the authorities necessary to enforce it — the ability to issue edicts, audit others, and enforce policies. *[page 223]*

> This command-and-control approach has three serious flaws: (1) Others don't feel accountable and won't put much effort into security. (2) Others have an incentive to circumvent security policies since their jobs are to produce products/services and security slows them down. (3) Others could ignore security concerns and let the CISO take the blame. *[page 224]*

> People won't challenge a CISO. But relationships can become strained, which ultimately reduces the effectiveness of the CISO. *[page 225]*

A more effective approach is to hold *everybody* accountable for their own behaviors, including security. Then, the CISO is positioned as a service to help them. *[pages 225, 394]*

With this approach, Information Security must define its catalog of services. (A sample catalog is included.) *[page 394]*

> For example, a CISO can offer "assessments" to those who are accountable, rather than "audits" to catch them when they do something wrong. *[page 394]* To the extent that audits are still needed, they should be done by Corporate Internal Audit, not the CISO, so as to avoid conflicts of interests and leave the security function in a helper relationship with its peers. *[page 228]*

This approach to information security is equally applicable to many other governance challenges, including regulatory compliance. *[page 231]*

22: Coordinators: Organization, Plans, and Policies

Shared decisions — things like plans, policies, and standards — should be made by a consensus of stakeholders (not any one group). Coordinators bring together the right stakeholders, and facilitating them to consensus on shared decisions. *[page 233]*

Organizational Effectiveness is a Coordinator function. It leads the transformation process, as well as ongoing facilitation of organizational processes and improvements. It also coordinates acquisition integrations, change control, staff communications, diversity, quality, and safety programs. *[page 233]*

Planning is another Coordinator function. Empowered entrepreneurs do their own plans; but coordination is required to get them all to come together into the organization's plan. *[page 235, see also 89, 295]*

A Research and Innovation Coordinator doesn't do research. Rather, this function helps everybody prepare funding proposals for innovation initiatives. And it helps the top executive manage the portfolio of innovation investments in the context of business strategies. *[page 237]*

Business Continuity Planning includes disaster recovery planning. In addition, it proactively anticipates disasters and plans ways to mitigate the risks and the damages. *[pages 238, 420 (endnote 106)]*

Regulatory Compliance is a Coordinator function that helps everybody fulfill their accountabilities for compliance. It also works with corporate lobbyists to proactively influence regulations. *[page 240]*

A Risk Coordinator helps others analyze and plan to mitigate risks, and maintains the enterprise risk registry. *[page 241]*

Audit Response Coordinators help everybody prepare for external audits, coordinate the organization's response to audits, and coordinate efforts to remediate findings. They help others by assessing readiness, but do not audit others. *[page 241]*

These Coordinator functions require a small group of very senior people who have the ability to lead discussions among experts, while staying neutral on outcomes and facilitating consensus. *[page 242]*

23: Architecture: Integrating Multiple Product Lines

Another Coordinator function addresses product-design standards. (In IT, this may be called an "Enterprise Architect.") *[page 243]* This is not an innovation group (everybody innovates). And it doesn't design anything (engineers do). *[page 243]*

Standards are deliberate constraints on the design of products so as to save money and facilitate the future integration of the product line. *[pages 244, 421 (endnote 111)]*

> There's typically one Engineering group that's the expert on a given standard. But other Engineering groups need to comply with it. And Service Providers need to support it. Thus, standards should be decided by a consensus of stakeholders. *[page 246]*

> Customers who might pay the future costs of integration should have the authority to decide variances (since they bear the consequences). *[page 247]*

Another product design challenge is "ripples" — where a change in one product impacts other products. Fixing those other affected products is not a separate project — it should be funded as part of the project which caused the ripples. *[page 248, see also 173]*

> Design Patterns Coordinators help engineers identify ripples. Proactively, they facilitate consensus on design patterns that minimize future ripples. And they identify opportunities for simplification of the product line and elimination of redundancies (in IT, an example is applications rationalization). *[page 249]*

24: Business Office: Support Services and Consolidation of Shared Services

A Business Office provides services which are not unique to an organization's industry or products, including: finance, IT (though not in this story), procurement, HR, legal, facilities, and administration. *[page 251]*

While these may be shared services, other departments may also include business support staff. A shared-services policy suggests that business units buy services from shared-services departments whenever possible, and only use local business-support staff for services which shared-services doesn't provide. *[page 252]*

When there are decentralized support groups, they should be the full-service suppliers (prime contractors) to their departments; but they should "outsource" as much as possible to corporate services. *[page 255]*

There are two ways to consolidate decentralized staff: Analysis of their work could determine which are to be transferred to shared services, but that risks taking people away from business units against their will. A safer approach is for shared services to earn the business over time as business units accept their proposals (voluntary consolidations). *[page 255]*

Consolidation means that shared-services departments promise the same or better services, and are paid for those services through the transfer of people and budgets. It's good for internal customers. It's also good for staff who enjoy working with their professional peers, and who have better career opportunities in a larger central group. *[page 258]*

To earn the business, a shared-services organization must be customer focused, build great relationships, fulfill every commitment, and be a good value. It also requires a Sales function to provide internal customers with a point of contact and to align support services with business-units' needs. *[page 258]*

PART 5: Feet on the Ground: Implementing the Vision

25: Planning the Transformation Road-map: The Foundation for Change

Transformation planning determines the sequence of systemic changes that will build your vision. It also establishes a solid foundation for change, with three essential elements: dissatisfaction with the status quo; vision of the end-state; and a clear path from here to there. *[page 262]*

Transformation planning begins with listening — up, down, and side-ways, to bosses, staff, customers, and key vendors. The goal is to make all stakeholders feel heard, and to gather data on both problems and aspirations. *[page 264]*

The next step is to establish a clear, detailed vision of the end-state. Vision is the antidote to simply reacting to today's problems. (Examples of vision statements are given.) *[page 264, see also 12]*

Next, respecting the feedback from the listening step, assess the gaps in your current organization against your vision (your "stretch assignment," beyond just today's immediate problems). *[page 267]*

Gaps are generally symptoms, not root causes. Nonetheless, some are so urgent as to require immediate attention. But this "triage" list should be kept short, since fixing these symptoms postpones getting to the systemic phase where root causes are addressed. *[page 269]*

Root causes are defects in the organizational ecosystem — the five organizational systems (structure, resource-governance processes, culture, processes and tools, and metrics and consequences) that are causing your good people to create the gaps. *[page 269]*

Once root causes are identified, specific transformation initiatives are then determined, and they're sequenced based on both urgency and their technical interdependencies. *[page 273]* That sequence of systemic initiatives becomes your *organizational strategy* (transformation road-map). *[page 274]*

Organizational strategy is foundational to business strategies. It's a plan for developing a high-performing organization (which should be stable) that continually develops business strategies (which, by their nature, must be dynamic) and is capable of delivering them. *[page 275, see also 28]*

A real transformation takes at least four years (with benefits all along the way, of course). *[page 275]*

At every milestone in a transformation process (including the completion of the vision and strategy), communication is essential. The more you communicate to staff and customers (within a few limits, listed), the more you capture hearts and minds, and the better the transformation will go. *[page 277]*

26: The Power of Participation

Transformations are best implemented through participative processes that engage the leadership team in the design and roll-out of each organizational system. This takes time — both leaders' time and elapsed time — but it's essential. Transformation is not just a new structure or financial processes; it's a change in the way people think and act. Time spent on a participative process pays off in speed of deployment and transformational impacts. *[page 279]*

Decisions are made by consensus. "Consensus" means that *all stake-holders understand the decision well enough to teach it, and (whether or not it's their first choice) are willing to support the decision.* This ensures that no one is victimized by decisions which affect them being made without their consent. *[page 282]*

27: Implementing Change: Structure

A participative restructuring process (addressing both the organization chart and teamwork processes) is done in a series of workshops of the leadership team. (Steps in the process are listed.) *[page 284]*

First, in the Rainbow Analysis, leaders color-code the current organization chart by types of businesses in each group. Four questions then reveal structural problems (listed). *[page 284]*

Then, leaders brainstorm all the lines of business that are needed, now and in the foreseeable future. Those lines of business are clustered based on synergies. The clusters represent tier-one jobs. Tier-one clusters are subdivided into tier-two/three clusters, defining all the boxes on the organization chart as lines of business. *[page 286]*

Next, leaders are assigned to the boxes, respecting their preferences. *[page 288]*

Leaders write "domains" which document each group's boundaries. They're written like business charters, defining what groups "sell" (not what they do), now and into the future. *[page 288]*

For each domain, leaders craft catalogs which define their products and services, at the level of granularity of the purchase decision. *[page 289]*

Specialization requires excellent cross-boundary teamwork. Thus, the next step — walk-throughs — is a critical part of a restructuring process. After enough practice, leaders develop a common understanding of exactly how real work will be done in the new structure. *[page 291]*

Finally, leaders assign all staff, contractors, assets, and vendor contracts to the new domains. And they prepare for the go-live all-staff meeting, a milestone event. *[page 292]*

After go-live, a careful migration process ensures that no commitments are missed. Everybody goes on doing what they'd been doing (perhaps under a new boss) until they document all their commitments and work out migration plans for the ones that no longer fit their domains. *[page 293]*

28: Implementing Change: Internal Economy

Within an internal economy, there are three subsystems: planning, demand management, and accounting. It's best to focus on one at a time. *[page 295]*

The best place to start is the annual business and budget planning process (investment-based budgeting). (The steps in the process are described.) *[page 295, see also 89]*

Demand-management (priority-setting) processes allow customers to set internal suppliers' priorities, within the bounds of available resources, dynamically throughout the year. (Essential processes are listed.) *[page 298, see also 99]*

Accounting systems are treated last. Historic data are for seasoning management judgments, not replacing them. *[page 300]* Time-tracking also comes late in the transformation road-map, after people understand the value of time tracking to their businesses. *[page 301]*

29: Implementing Change: Culture

Implementing culture change begins with the leadership team crafting actionable behavioral principles. *[page 303]*

The roll-out teaches staff the expected behaviors, Theme by Theme, over a period of months. And while teaching, leaders listen, then revise the behavioral principles as appropriate. *[page 304]*

By the end of one year, it's not uncommon to see 80 percent of the staff practicing 80 percent of the behaviors 80 percent of the time. *[page 306]*

This process can benefit from expert facilitation, a well-planned process, and a database of "best practices" behaviors that helps you craft your own behavioral principles. *[pages 306, 376]*

Once the change is implemented, leaders must continually reinforce it through performance metrics and "walking the talk." *[page 307]*

PART 6: Leadership Perspectives

30: Scalability, Startups, and Multi-nationals

Scalability means that an organization can adapt to changes without the need for a major shift in its operating model. New technologies, products and services, geographies, and markets create new domains which automatically mesh with the rest of the organization. There should be no need for another restructuring as an organization grows and evolves. *[page 311]*

Even startups and very small companies can benefit from formalizing an organization that can scale without loss of their entrepreneurial spirit. *[pages 314, 315]*

As ventures grow, their founders often become a bottleneck that constrains continued growth. That's because they *are* the coordinating mechanism, deciding priorities, teamwork, and strategic initiatives. The Market Organization moves those coordinating mechanisms to the organizational ecosystem, eliminating the "founder bottleneck" without losing the vision and passion embodied in those key people, and without stifling entrepreneurship. *[page 317]*

Multi-product, multi-national organizations can maximize synergies and economies of scale with a fully integrated structure where everything is a global shared service. *[page 318, see also 22]*

31: Acquisitions Integration

Acquisition integration is facilitated by clear lines of business, indicating where to place each acquired group in the organization's structure; and by an organizational operating model that allows the acquired product lines to access all the resources of the firm (and vice versa). *[page 320]*

Acquisitions integration has three steps: C-I-O — Consolidate, Integrate, Optimize. The Consolidate step gives the acquired company time to acclimate. Integrate folds acquired groups into existing groups in the structure by deconstructing their lines of business. Optimize is then done over time by the combined talent in each group. *[page 322]*

32: Innovation Everywhere (No Skunk-works)

Some say that disruptive innovation requires a structure (group) separate from the mainstream organization. *[page 325]*. This has significant costs, both to innovation efforts and to the rest of the organization. *[page 326]*

The Market Organization induces innovation in *every* group (including disruptive innovation). Every group strives to obsolete its own product line. This requires a funding channel (internal economy) and different metrics. *[page 329]*

33: Digital Business and the Strategic Value of Technology

"Digital business" refers to the use of technologies to enhance customers' experiences (although some use the term to mean any of three types of strategic value of technology, listed). *[page 332]*

Digital business is not a technology (such as applications for customers' smart phones or websites). It utilizes the entire range of technologies to contribute to great customer experiences. *[page 333]*

Furthermore, digital business is not a one-time project or program. It's a continual stream of projects that result from an entire organization focused on digital-business opportunities. *[page 334]*

A Market Organization aligns all the organizational systems to achieve the promise of digital business: structure (a Sales function in IT, a.k.a., Business Relationship Managers, and a Function Sales consultant dedicated to digital business); methods (strategic opportunity discovery, and value-added benefits estimation); internal economy (investment-based budgeting to provide funding, and demand management to prioritize strategic opportunities); and metrics (encourage judicious high-risk, high-payoff investments). *[page 334]*

Chief Digital Officers do not run a separate Marketing or IT group. They are Function Sales consultants — experts in how businesses utilize technologies to enhance customer experiences. CDOs are evangelists, participate in enterprise strategic planning, and serve as a part of the sales force within IT to help discover digital-business opportunities. *[page 336, see also 147]*

34: Summary of Results Delivered by a Market Organization

There are many benefits of implementing a Market Organization.

From the perspective of an organization's customers, they appreciate: an effective point of interface (account representatives); reliable delivery of commitments; being in control of internal suppliers' priorities; partnering to find strategic opportunities; competitive prices; and customer focus. A Market Organization makes you the "supplier of choice" to your customers. *[page 338]*

There are also many benefits to the organization's staff, including: expectations in line with resources; clear boundaries and accountabilities; increased specialization (which is good for their careers); the fulfillment that comes from doing everything to run a small business (rather than dabbling in many businesses and owning none); teamwork; and empowerment (staff aren't set up to fail with accountabilities beyond their authorities). *[page 340]*

Becoming an "employer of choice" attracts great people, even if you can't afford to pay top dollar. *[page 341]*

Perhaps the most profound benefit to staff is the sense of *purpose* they get being in business to serve customers who value their work. *[page 342]*

The Market Organization is consistent with all four tenets of Conscious Capitalism. In fact, it provides the mechanics to implement Conscious Capitalism. *[page 343]*

35: Close of My Tour: A Leader Who Leaves a Legacy

Some say all it takes for an organization to succeed is top talent. But talent is *not* enough. Great people cannot perform well if your organizational ecosystem is poorly designed (reasons listed). *[page 345]*

A transformation changes the executive's role into something far more strategic. With less time absorbed by operational issues, there's more time to look at the big picture, think about the future of the company, and mentor and inspire staff. *[page 348, see also 55]*

Why do so few leaders do this? There are four types of leaders: cost cutters, maintainers, project managers, and transformers. Very few leaders are transformers, willing to take the risks and put in the effort to leave the legacy of a great organization. *[page 349]*

If you want to drive meaningful change, reserve the word "transformation" for something big. It's not a strategic goal. It's not a project. Real transformation builds an organization that gets those strategies and projects right, all the time. *[page 351]*

Great leaders leave the legacy of organizations
that performs brilliantly long after they've moved on.

Other Books by N. Dean Meyer

Principle-based Organizational Structure: a handbook to help you engineer entrepreneurial thinking and teamwork into organizations of any size. 2017. (book)

Internal Market Economics: practical resource-governance processes based on principles we all believe in. 2013. (book)

An Introduction to the Business-Within-a-Business Paradigm. 2002. (monograph)

RoadMap: how to understand, diagnose, and fix your organization. 1998. (book)

Fast Track to Changing Corporate Culture. 2003. (monograph)

Meyer's Rules of Order: how to hold highly productive business meetings. 2001. (pocket book of behavioral principles)

Outsourcing: how to make vendors work for your shareholders. 1999. (book)

Decentralization: fantasies, failings, and fundamentals. 1998. (book)

Downsizing Without Destroying: how to trim what your organization does rather than destroy its ability to do anything at all. 2003, 2008. (monograph)

The New Lexicon of Leadership: dictionary of terms used in leadership and organizational design. 2012. (report)

The Information Edge with Mary E. Boone. 1987, 1995. (book)

About the Author

In the field of organizational design, Dean Meyer is both a visionary and a pragmatic engineer. His vision is based on the *businesses-within-a-business paradigm,* where every group is an entrepreneurship that produces products and services for customers inside and outside the firm (the Market Organization). He has implemented this vision in corporate, government, and non-profit organizations through  *principle-based design of an organization's ecosystem:* its structure, resource-governance processes, culture, and metrics.

Dean has written eight books, and numerous monographs and articles.

His book, *Principle-based Organizational Structure,* defined a new science of organization charts and cross-boundary teamwork processes.

His book, *Internal Market Economics,* applied principles of market economics inside companies to design non-bureaucratic, business-driven resource-governance processes.

And he developed a behavioral approach to corporate culture that leads to meaningful change in less than a year.

This book is the capstone of his career. In it, he presents a clear picture of how organizations should work, and explains how to implement that vision through participative change processes.

Dean coaches executives on organizational issues, and facilitates transformation processes. He is a native of San Francisco and resident of Connecticut. He received a BS from the University of California at Berkeley, and an MBA from Stanford University.
For more, see < www.ndma.com >.